Gaming Cultures and Place In Asia-Pacific

Routledge Studies in New Media and Cyberculture

Gaming Cultures and Place in Asia-Pacific

Edited by Larissa Hjorth
and Dean Chan

Routledge
Taylor & Francis Group
New York   London

First published 2009
by Routledge
2 Park Square, Milton Park, Abingdon, Oxon OX14 4RN
Simultaneously published in the USA and Canada by Routledge
711 Third Avenue, New York, NY 10017
Routledge is an imprint of the Taylor & Francis Group, an informa business

First issued in paperback 2012

© 2009 Taylor & Francis

Typeset in Sabon by IBT Global.

Library of Congress Cataloging in Publication Data

Gaming cultures and place in Asia-Pacific / edited by Larissa Hjorth and Dean Chan.
    p. cm. — (Routledge studies in new media and cyberculture ; 5)
    Includes index.
1. Computer games—Social aspects—Pacific Area.   I. Hjorth, Larissa.   II. Chan, Dean.
    GV1469.17.S63G36 2009
    306.4'87—dc22
    2008054181

ISBN13: 978-0-415-99627-3 (hbk)
ISBN13: 978-0-203-87595-7 (ebk)
ISBN13: 978-0-415-53589-2 (pbk)

Photograph by David Prater

Contents

Figures

Tables

Acknowledgments

Dean would like to acknowledge the School of Communications and Arts, and the Faculty of Education and Arts, Edith Cowan University, for offering him essential time out from teaching in the form of a Postdoctoral Research Fellowship between 2004 and 2007, which enabled him to get started on all things ludological.

Larissa would like to acknowledge the support of the RMIT University Games Programs, the CICC (Communication Interface and Culture Content) research group and the GRC (Games Research Centre) at Yonsei University for her fellowship in 2007. She would also like to thank the ARC Cultural Research Network and all the cosplayers and female gamers that opened up their hearts, computers and tactics of game play in the name of research.

The editors would like to thank all the authors as well as a special thanks to Emma-Kate Dowdell for providing invaluable editorial assistance.

1 Locating the Game
Gaming Cultures in/and the Asia-Pacific

Larissa Hjorth and Dean Chan

The Asia-Pacific region is a geo-political and economic construct. Spanning East and South East Asia as well as countries in the southern Pacific Ocean and Pacific Rim, including Australia and New Zealand, the collectivizing of such disparate nations and cultures perhaps only largely makes sense as a post-World War II political and economic imaginary, as opposed to a purely geographic cartography. Yet, at the same time, the magnitudes of thinking through what Jen Webb characterizes as "the Asia-Pacific effect" is essential. Although created "in language by . . . national and geopolitical entities . . . there is an effect of Asia-Pacific which allows us to talk about it as a Real thing."[1] Webb argues that the space for agency created by the Asia-Pacific effect enables regional cultural producers and organizations to represent themselves, both individually and collectively, "rather than be represented by old colonialist patterns and practices" and they can thereby "claim a legitimated voice . . . and challenge the hegemony of 'Euramerican' narratives, values and aesthetics."[2]

The Asia-Pacific effect provides a valid polemical and pedagogical framework to assess the production, circulation and consumption of gaming within the region. Specifically, we propose that any nuanced study of Asia-Pacific game cultures has the capacity to also disrupt and serve as a critique of the residual Techno-Orientalism[3] in many Western approaches to understanding the region's historical and contemporary prowess in post-industrial discourses such as gaming.

With sites such as Tokyo fully placed in the global gaming imaginary and with locations such as Melbourne boasting one of the most active independent gaming scenes, the Asia-Pacific provides an exemplary case study on one of the most buoyant and yet culturally divergent regions in the world. Our aim in locating this study in the region is two-fold: firstly, to situate the depth and diversity of games culture (which we broadly define to include games, game play, and gaming communities) in this region; and secondly, to consider how these gaming cultures in turn provide a lens to view and examine salient geo-political and socio-cultural developments within the region.

Such an approach to the study of gaming cultures provides acuity into the region's reshaping in the imagery of global popular cultures. As Brian

Sutton-Smith observes, gaming cultures are social cultures, thus through the games we play we can learn much about the localized notions of play and community.[4] The study of gaming cultures not only allows readers to gain new approaches to the region's increasingly technological and economic power and how this has translated into global soft power, but also the various contested and transnational gaming communities in the region. We are interested in tracking *both* the continuities *and* the disjunctures. While we are not claiming to offer a definitive or exhaustive portrait of Asia-Pacific gaming in this chapter and via this collection of essays, we do instead aspire towards a partial and provisional mapping of some key debates and hallmark characteristics within the region.

In sum, we first and foremost place an emphasis on negotiating the situated diversity and interdisciplinarity of **gaming cultures**. The appreciation of plurality in and of itself just will not do because it is arguably limited in both its rhetorical reach and pedagogical function. Concomitantly, our focus in this collection is equally on examining the continuities between, and interfaces among, as well as the co-evolution of game **industries—cultures— communities** within the region. At stake here is the task of simultaneously studying the variegated constituencies of regional gaming cultures and using gaming cultures to map the political, economic, social and cultural dis/connections within the Asia-Pacific.

THE LOCATIVE POLITICS OF PLACE: A LUDIC MAPPING OF THE ASIA-PACIFIC

The games industry has matured from a subcultural activity partaken by the likes of *otaku* (media-obsessed fans) to become what is now an integral part of global popular cultures: a phenomenon highlighted by the fact that the games industry revenue now surpasses that of the film industries. Over the preceding couple of decades, and especially since the beginning of this century, the rigor, interdisciplinary nature and depth of gaming scholarship has aptly addressed many issues around new media, narratology, interactivity and active audiences bringing depth to approaches towards creative industries, global studies and the rethinking of popular culture.

More recently, with the rise of crossplatforming and convergent media through Web 2.0, the role of online communities and localized socio-cultural practices such as massively multiplayer online games (MMOs) like *Lineage* and *World of Warcraft* have given emergence to empirical, ethnographic and area studies approaches to gaming communities. Through the lens of gaming cultures we can gain insight into emerging transnational communities as well as helping redefine nation-state boundaries and enclave alliances. Increasingly, the role of locality influences the types of games that are consumed and the types of nation-state associations with certain types of game play. For example, Japan has long had a history of what Testuo Kogawa calls "electronic individualism"[5] which manifests in Nintendo DS and Sony PlayStation Portable (PSP). As historically one of the global gaming centers, Japan has long attracted worldwide interest. However, its significance has started to be challenged by the rise of MMOs particularly prevalent in South Korea.

As a region, the Asia-Pacific is marked by diverse consumption and production patterns of gaming, mobile and broadband technologies, subject to local cultural and socio-economic nuances. Two defining locations—Seoul (South Korea) and Tokyo (Japan)—are seen as both "mobile centers" and "gaming centers" in their representation of a possible future for media practices. Unlike Japan, which pioneered the *keitai* (mobile) 11 revolution and gaming consoles such as PlayStation2, South Korea—the most broadbanded country in the world (OECD 2006)—has become a center for MMOs and attendant industries such as e-sports.

Adorned with over 20,000 *PC bangs* (PC rooms) in Seoul alone and with professional players (Pro-leagues) making over a million US dollars per year, South Korea has been lauded as an example of how gaming can occupy a mainstream position in everyday life. In a period marked by convergent technologies, South Korea and Japan represent two opposing directions for gaming—South Korea emphasizes online MMO games played on stationary PCs in public spaces (*PC bangs*) while Japan pioneers the cult(ure) of mobile (privatized) convergent devices. These two distinct examples are a product of various technological, economic, political, social and cultural factors, which are variously examined in this collection in chapters by Dal Yong Jin and Florence Chee (Chapter 2); Jun-Sok Huhh (Chapter 6); Christian McCrea (Chapter 10); Ingrid Richardson (Chapter 12); and Larissa Hjorth, Bora Na and Huhh (Chapter 14). Gaming cultures provide insight into the ever evolving and contesting formations of the region.

With the introduction of Web 2.0 and as the convergence between SNS (social networking systems) and online games burgeons, it is the Asia-Pacific that can highlight much about twenty-first century formations, transnational communities and socio-cultural enclaves. Through gaming cultures, we can gain insights into the social, cultural and political dimensions of new technologies and media—impacting on how we conceptualize and practise new media and online/offline co-presence.

Furthermore, with key international research associations such as Digital Games Research Association (DiGRA) hosting the *2007 Situated Play Conference* in Tokyo, along with the rise in pervasive location-aware mobile gaming in which online/offline relationships and communities are traversed, the role of place and locality has gained much focus in Game Studies. This reflects some of the broader theoretical concerns around globalization and the "mobility turn" in sociology, anthropology, philosophy and media studies. In general, the role of place has taken on increasing significance as transnational cultural flows of various forms of mobility and immobility of people, capital and media form and transform.

At the same time, however, this is an important juncture in creating and archiving scholarly knowledge on this field. The particular role of the region in the rise of gaming industries is known and yet, due in part to linguistic and socio-cultural differences, much of the discussions have yet to filter into English language global gaming discourses. Many "Western" preliminary studies in the 1990s on the burgeoning field of Asian-Pacific gaming—particularly its online incarnations—took the form of industry reports and marketing forecasts produced by private American and European consultancies for commercial purposes. Accordingly, not only was this information highly specialized, public access to it was limited. Many of these reports did not position gaming within broader socio-cultural and techno-national frameworks. A case in point is the widespread failure to properly anticipate and account for why so many American online games like *EverQuest* would fail at launch in East Asian gaming territories during this period due to a failure to recognize and negotiate myriad culturally-specific protocols informing the seemingly "neutral" aspects of local business practices and game play preferences.

Game studies has gained much attention from researchers as a device that is an integral part of contemporary culture. It seems hard to avoid the ubiquity and pervasiveness of game studies and the games industry. However, much of the research has been directed from an American or European perspective, neglecting one of the most distinct and growing markets globally, the Asia–Pacific. By exploring gaming cultures in the region, insight can be gained into new forms of modernity—cross-cultural consumption and production processes—and how the region is shifting and evolving.

In addition, while there have been many successful anthologies in the realm of Asian consumption and production (such as Chua Beng Huat's *Consumption in Asia*; Robison and Goodman's *The New Rich in Asia*)[6] as well as Internet and mass communications in Asia (such as the excellent anthology on the Internet in Asia by Ho et al. *Asia.com*, or the Japanese focused anthology edited by Nanette Gottlieb and Mark McLelland *Japanese Cybercultures*)[7] there has yet to be a collection that brings together the two converging areas as a publication on gaming cultures would.

Over the last few years, there has been a steadily growing body of publications on digital games. With the exception of a special issue of the scholarly journal *Games and Culture* guest edited by Hjorth, **none** have focused specifically on the Asia-Pacific. Furthermore many recently edited general collections on gaming may be criticized for their residual Eurocentric focus and interpretive frameworks, hence further perpetuating stereotypes around Asian production and consumption of media. It is arguably problematical when socio-cultural differences and contextual specificities are elided or neglected in "global" studies of games.

Edited by Mark J.P. Wolf and Bernard Perron, and published in 2003, *The Video Game Theory Reader* is the first major general anthology in the humanities and social sciences dedicated to the scholarly analysis of digital games.[8] It deservedly remains a landmark publication in many respects, with a follow-up anthology by the same editors planned for publication in 2009.[9] Yet, apart from generalized references to the global cultural significance of Japanese videogames and in-depth case studies that include *Final Fantasy IX*, there is scant focus in the first anthology on Japanese contextual specificities. The collected discussions on "corporealized pleasures" and "postmodern identity patterns" arguably offer important multidisciplinary paradigms for studying games. Nevertheless, the omission of a coterminous critical attentiveness to the socio-cultural contexts of production, circulation and reception invariably risks theorizing games as a transcendental free-floating signifier.

Many other edited collections published since then have focused on offering broad theorizations of games as a key aspect of new media studies (for example, *First Person: New Media as Story, Performance, and Game*) and providing collated overviews of key paradigms specific to game studies (for example, *Handbook of Computer Game Studies*).[10] Many recent publications that survey the field or "state of play" still do not even mention gaming in the Asia-Pacific; they might contain one chapter at best on this topic—for example, *Games Without Frontiers, War Without Tears: Computer Games as a Sociocultural Phenomenon*.[11] This delimited template for edited publications also extends to themed collections on gaming including: *From Barbie to Mortal Kombat: Gender and Computer Games*; *ScreenPlay: cinema/videogames/interfaces*; *Space Time Play—Computer Games, Architecture and Urbanism: The Next Level*; and *The Ecology of Games: Connecting Youth, Games, and Learning*.[12]

On a related note, it is worthwhile pointing out there have been some discernible shifts in sole and jointly authored publications on gaming. Individual texts that focus on aspects of Japanese gaming have historically tended to proliferate, variously affording further information and indeed mystification about the Japanese context, as in books such as Chris Kohler's *Power-Up: How Japanese Video Games Gave the World an Extra Life*.[13] While earlier texts such as Steven Poole's *Trigger Happy: The Inner Life of Videogames* and James Newman's *Videogames* do not extensively discuss Asian themes and play practices, more recent books like Henry Jenkins's *Fans, Bloggers, and Gamers*, Diane Carr et al.'s *Computer Games: Text, Narrative and Play*, and Edward Castronova's *Synthetic Worlds: The Business and Culture of Online Games* are acknowledging and including some ancillary discussion of Asian gaming and contextual specificities.[14] There is undeniable growing international awareness and interest in this field.

At any rate, there are currently **no** games studies collections that focus on the Asia-Pacific region. Moreover, of the studies that do sample locations in the region, **none** to date provide a comprehensive mapping of the socio-technological, socio-cultural, techno-nationalist and economic dimensions needed to fully understand gaming as both a new media and social phenomenon. This chapter highlights and contextualizes this predicament, while the collection attempts to redress this gap and initiate new lines of critical inquiry.

ASIA-PACIFIC REGIONALISM

The Asia-Pacific acts as a particularly salient case study to examine the phenomena of intra-regional and transnational cultural flows. The most significant hub of cultural production within this regional formulation is without doubt in East Asia, specifically the countries of Japan, Korea and China (including Hong Kong SAR). In intra-regional terms, the dominant trajectories of contemporary transnational cultural flows can be mapped from East Asia to Southeast Asia (especially Singapore, Malaysia, Thailand and Vietnam) and the Pacific (especially Australia).

Perhaps one of the most vivid examples of intra-Asian cultural flows is the Korean Wave in the early 2000s, which saw the regional export of South Korea media cultural products, especially in the form of television soaps and family dramas. Online gaming was an irrefutable part of this cultural proliferation whereby Korean-designed online games such as *Lineage* and *Ragnarok Online* made their way to (and presence strongly felt in) China, Taiwan, Vietnam and Thailand. Two important factors in the creation and maintenance of such intra-Asian gaming networks at that time were, firstly, the setting up of joint partnerships with local game servers and service providers (although the current impetus is towards the cultivation of joint venture partnerships), and secondly, the provision of extensive game localization, particularly customizable game content and game play options.[15]

The creation of intra-Asian online gaming networks—particularly, via MMORPGs in the late 1990s and early 2000s, and casual gaming since the mid 2000s—is linked to the coterminous resurgence in the development and expansion of East Asian economies and may be collectively explored as a symptom of Asian modernity. Jim Supangkat has in a separate context referred to the urgency of thinking about Asian modernity in culturally relative terms, whereby the putative reliance on a singular, monotheistic and Eurocentric definition of Modernity is disavowed in favor of thinking instead about Asian "multimodernism."[16] The value of Supangkat's proposition is that it forces us to think not just about multiplicity but also of the *variegated* nature of modernity, its cross-border entanglements and spatiotemporal linkages. At issue here are the cultural politics of proximity, engagement and difference. It follows that the parable of Asia-Pacific gaming deserves to be narrated in relation to the broader story of regional multimodernism.

Game industry developments echo certain aspects of techno-industrial development within the region, particularly the shifts that have taken place over the past decade. Consider the paradigmatic example of China. Previously, development studios of Western and Asian multinational companies focused almost exclusively on using China's cheap labor force to develop games for overseas markets. The situation is quite different these days. China is already renowned for its burgeoning demographic of online gamers. As Peichi Chung notes in Chapter 4, almost half of the worldwide players of the popular MMORPG *World of Warcraft* come from China alone. At the same time, when it comes to gaming, the country is fast becoming an ambitious content producer, and not just act as cheap outsourced labor or serve as avid consumer. It is now emerging as an increasingly significant games producer in its own right, currently focusing on mainly developing games for domestic markets and Chinese-language territories within the region.[17]

In much the same fashion, it is interesting to note that Japanese game developers are now also starting to make a concerted effort to produce and market games for a regional audience. For instance, Japanese games publisher Square Enix entered into partnership with Webstar (an affiliate company of Softstar Entertainment, Taiwan) for its first foray into the online games market in China in 2002 with *Cross Gate*, a MMORPG developed specifically for the Asian market. In Chapter 4, Chung discusses the establishment of another important Japanese-Singaporean partnership in terms of Koei Singapore's development and launch of *Romance of the Three Kingdoms Online*.

As previously discussed, Asia-Pacific regional multimodernism highlights precisely this ethic of proximity, engagement, and difference, which variously also results in points of redefinition and repositioning (as in Chung's discussion of Singapore's game industry positioning *vis-à-vis* Korea's in Chapter 4) and the performativity of inter-cultural engagement and hybridization (as in Benjamin Ng's analysis of Japanese combat games in local Hong Kong cultural production in Chapter 5, and Hjorth's examination of imaginings of Japanese games characters by female cosplayers in Melbourne in Chapter 15). What Ng and Hjorth, in particular, attest to are the different ways in which transnational citations are effectively re-made and re-purposed on highly local and specific terms; such tropes collectively attest to the agency and primacy of cultivating transnational means for local ends.

Accordingly, as Ng astutely observes, it would be too simplistic to regard these flows—and by inference, Japan's continuing primacy and hegemony within regional gaming circles—as outright instances of media imperialism. Richardson's delineation of the phenomenology of portable gaming practices in Australia in Chapter 12 demonstrates that although Japanese paradigms can impact on Australian game play in some ways, Australian gaming is nonetheless ultimately very different in other respects, mainly owing to differing techno-national and socio-cultural constituencies. Indeed, the question of the Pacific—and of the inclusion of "Western" nations such as Australia—always already confounds any seamless tapestry of Asia-Pacific regionalism. The place and voice of Indigenous cultures within this equation further interrogates any such complacency. To this end, the account by Theodor G. Wyeld, Brett Leavy and Patrick Crogan in Chapter 11 about the magnitudes of the Digital Songlines digital storytelling project powerfully highlights the primacy of Indigenous cultural perspectives of place and space; and the authors stress the importance of negotiating cultural specificity as well as issues of cultural heritage and moral rights within new media and gaming contexts.

GAMING INDUSTRIES: A COMPARATIVE REGIONAL PERSPECTIVE

Since World War II, Japan's role as a center for technological innovation has assured a sense of cultural power, particularly in the region. In the wake of Japan's faded imperialism in the Asia-Pacific, NICs such as Taiwan and Hong Kong have acquired an ambivalent awe of Japan's superpower economy and its cultural capital associated with such products as *anime* (animation) and *manga* (comics); while in locations such as Korea the memory of Japanese imperialism still remains fresh. Given the history of Japan's cultural, and more recently technological, imperialism, Japan has often found itself the subject of what Lisa Nakamura pinpointed as a sci-fi "default setting" and various manifestations of what David Morley and Kevin Robins defined as "Techno-Orientalism."[18]

Techno-Orientalism grew out of the West's attempt to grapple with Japan's quick "soft power" rise from 1970s onwards through its production of innovative technologies—from the Sony Walkman to videogames. Indeed, for a long time the residue of Techno-Orientalism shadowed conceptualizations of Japan's continuing power in global technocultures. It has only been recently that Japan's innovation in technology-related industries has been contextualized within a technoculture that no longer "de-faults" to Western precepts or models of culture and society.

Far from the 1970s widely held of the region as being a bloc of satellite NICs (such as Taiwan and South Korea) oscillating around the region's first industrial nation, Japan, we now see a profoundly different picture. Rather than resembling a rigid and highly figurative oil painting cascading with European motifs and colors, the new picture is of an endlessly moving video image in which multiple divergent identities appear and disappear. In this video vignette of postmodernity, in which borders are both eroded and redefined, and transnational flows echo paths well worn, the gaming cultures and communities becomes loci for locality and gestures of propinquity, labors of love and work, and the realities and fictions of modernity. These shifts are reflected in the transformations of gaming cultures and localities in which we see multiple sites such as South Korea and China contesting Japan's stronghold in the region's technocultural cartographies.

As the region's consumption and production patterns have evolved and transformed, so too have the ways in which modernity in the region has been conceptualized. From the Confucius revivalisms of the late 1990s in search of "Asian" values, which were criticized for homogenizing diversity, self-Orientalization[19] and essentialism, the region attempted to think beyond Western and Eurocentric tropes through the lens of "alternative modernities." As Arif Dirlik trenchantly observes, in this search for identity and cultural modernity in an age of mobility and reformation of constructions of nation-state, it was important that the region not deny its own history of cultural imperialism and colonial conflicts.[20]

It is with this in mind that game cultures provide much insight into how the region is not only reconceptualized as geo-imaginary but how this process can reflect upon contemporary global technocultures. Over the last decade since the 1997 economic crisis of the region, the region has transformed itself from a site of technological prowess to ideological power. Given the region's ongoing significance in the creative industries and boasting some of highest technological infrastructure such as broadband, it provides a great example of governmental strategies and industrial IT policies that have informed its movement into this century's "participatory media" such as Web 2.0.[21]

Given the uneven and yet highly significant role played by the region within global gaming industries, it is important to understand this phenomenon within the context of completing and contesting technocultures. In an age of "participatory media" such as Web 2.0 and the rise of UCC (user created content), how we conceptualize local, national and transnational gaming industries is being transformed. These shifts in evaluating the relationships between production, consumption, industry, regulation and representation have taken on various forms as demonstrated by four industry case studies in this collection.

In Chapter 2, Dal Yong Jin and Florence Chee explore the geo-political, economic, cultural and social dimensions of the Korea's creative industries in the form of online gaming. In their critical appraisal, Jin and Chee expose some of the ways in which the online gaming phenomenon has been orchestrated to represent Korea both locally and globally. In Chapter 6, Huhh revisits the pivotal role played by the *PC bang* (PC room) in the rise and success of online gaming in Korea.

In Chapter 4, Chung considers the role of transnational synergies and differences by exploring two models of creative industries—Singapore and South Korea. Unlike South Korea's long history as a manufacturing and agricultural site that quickly embraced technology (hardware and software) as part of broad cultural reforms in 1970s, Singapore's relatively small and multicultural population has focused upon the development of software and intellectual property (IP).

Singapore's "satellite" role in the games industry can also be seen reflected in Sam Hinton's concise study in Chapter 3 on contextualizing the Australian games industry within its "gaming nation" rubric. As an industry set within a milieu in which games are consumed veraciously, Hinton explains why the local industry "is characterized by privately owned independent studios producing primarily overseas IP and ports." However, as Hinton's chapter signposts and Wyeld et al.'s chapter (Chapter 11) demonstrates, the rise in the Australian creative industries has been accompanied by an independent "indie" gaming scene which has sought to provide models for alternative digital storytelling. As Wyeld et al. discuss, games can be used for new forms of cultural heritage and pedagogical deployment. Within the onset of Web 2.0 collaborative and participatory media, these examples of indie and alternative digital storytelling will hopefully continue to grow unabated.

GAMING CULTURES: EVOLUTION AND DIVERSIFICATION

As convergent cross-platforming and trans-media accompanies new forms of UCC media in becoming more pervasive, visible and accessible, the impact upon gaming cultures—as a set of industries, practices, communities and localities—is changing. With the growth in player agency and ancillary discourses—such as cosplay (costume play) to e-sports to LAN gaming to in-game protests—the politics, modalities and rubrics of gaming cultures and genres are transforming. Indeed how we conceptualize "players," as perhaps produsers,[22] requires us to re-evaluate the boundaries of "gaming cultures" as part of a process of evolution and diversification.

From Hjorth's discussion in Chapter 15 of young female game students who have entered the games industry as co-produsers in the form of cosplay to new emerging digital and transmedia storytelling in Richardson's timely study in Chapter 12 on iPhone mobile gaming, notions of agency, empowerment and engagement needs to be redefined. In Wyeld et al.'s aforementioned chapter (Chapter 11), games can provide a site for e-learning whereby younger generations learn and participate in the stories of the Australian Aboriginal "dreamtime." In Chapter 8, the difference between e-participation rhetoric around Web 2.0 and online gaming is exposed in Dean Chan's case study on in-game protesting in China.

In Chapter 5, Ng allows us consider the role of games as a site for cross-media/trans-media storytelling in the case of Hong Kong and its re-imagining of Japan. So, too, David Surman considers in Chapter 9 the transnational adoption of Japanese cute gaming aesthetics and its Techno-Orientalist inflections. This role of games as a space for re-imaging and examining localities and modes of cross-cultural representation is also reflected in Christian McCrea's case study in Chapter 10 on *StarCraft* and the role of memory and game play. In turn, just as "industries" are not self-contained and stable within contemporary gaming cultures, the ways in which we define gaming communities are also transforming.

GAMING COMMUNITIES: CONFLUENCES, CONNECTIVITIES AND MOBILITIES

Is the term "virtual community" a socio-cultural misnomer? In period marked by Web 2.0 and new forms of community, authorship, agency and engagement, notions such as "network" and "community" are being questioned. Moving beyond the debates around "cyberspace" that consumed much of the 1990s,[23] what it means to be online—and its relationship to offline—has shifted. Indeed, the expansion and confluences of games cultures within online community contexts (that are local, transnational and global) begs many questions. What does it mean to think about the Asia-Pacific region in terms of online communities and networks? How is Web 2.0 demonstrating new regional-specific forms of media literacy, creativity, intimacy and labor? And how do these phenomena provide us with new insights into the region in the twenty-first century?

The Internet is the most pervasive and ubiquitous space within contemporary twenty-first century everyday life. While an important feature of the Internet is its role as a "global" technology and social space, its appropriation at the local level is far from homogeneous; a fact that has been increasingly noted in Internet studies. However, it seems that despite the various synergies between Internet and games studies (highlighted by organizations such as the Association of Internet Researchers, AoIR), there is still much to be conducted into the growing phenomenon of online-offline confluences, connectivities and mobilities. In this collection we provide a sample of case studies that aim to address these magnitudes whereby what determines community is the particular social or ludic context and situation players are being challenged with. From Holin Lin and Chuen-Tsai Sun's study in Chapter 13 that explores emerging networking strategies and risk management for Taiwanese adolescent players to Chan's analysis in Chapter 8 of in-game protesting in China, the localized role of online communities is expanded.

The role of multiple contesting localities and subjectivities is explored in both macro and micro dimensions. For example, the role of social performativity is clearly demonstrated by Lin and Sun's focus upon the regulatory processes involved within online communities self-maintenance. In Ng's work, we see the way in which Hong Kong's gaming cultures negotiates itself within the context of consuming and localizing Japanese combat games such as *Street Fighter*. So, too, Hjorth's study in Chapter 15 on cosplaying—and the attendant gendered performativity—demonstrates how young females can negotiate their roles from players to co-producer to produsers to producers *vis-à-vis* Japanese games and the attendant localized forms of gender performativity.[24]

The role of performativity and subjectivity is further discussed by Hjorth, Na and Huhh in their study in Chapter 14 of females who play games in the Seoul in which the gendered history of gaming is highlighted and localized. In Richardson's study in Chapter 12, stereotypes around modes of engagement and disengagement (especially the gendered history of "distraction") are put into question as she reconceptualizes mobile gaming in terms of iPhone and new forms of online, mobile co-presence. These chapters bring into question the way in which games cultures have been discussed, theorized and practiced by presenting alternative models. The various chapters in this collection aim to chart the multiple genealogies of gaming cultures, like the region's geo-imaginary, and contextualize them within a techno-oculture that is both a site for "effect" and "affect."

CONCLUSION: THE ASIA-PACIFIC AFFECT IN THE CARTOGRAPHIES OF GAMING CULTURES

As noted in the introduction, following Webb, one way of understanding the region is in terms of the Asia-Pacific effect. However, in an age of Web 2.0, SNS and UCC, the various technocultural localities might be best defined as the Asia-Pacific "affect." To appropriate and expand Webb's words, the Asia-Pacific clearly also has an affect that informs experiences of it as a "Real thing"—impacting on networks of production, circulation and consumption, as well as emotive registers of performativity, subjectivity and community. Through a sampling of gaming cultures, this book seeks to provide not only insight into the geo-political, socio-cultural and economic dimensions of gaming, but also a way in which to re-imagine the region.

Once a discursive geopolitical rubric, the Asia-Pacific—as a site for contesting local identities and transnational flows of people, media, goods and capital—has come under much radical revision and reconceptualization.[25] This has lead theorists such as Robert Wilson and Arif Dirlik to utilize "Asia/Pacific" as "not just an ideological recuperated term" but an imagined geo-political space that has a double reading as both "situated yet ambivalent."[26] In their anthology *Asia/Pacific as Space of Cultural Production*, Wilson and Dirlik attempt to challenge the "hegemonic Euro-American" construction underpinning the Asia-Pacific to conceive of new ways of conceptualizing regionalism. In particular, they use the configuration "Asia/Pacific" to discuss the region as a space of cultural production, social migration and transnational innovation, whereby "the slash would signify linkage yet difference."[27] Specifically, the diverse and perpetually changing interstitials constituting the Asia-Pacific have been repositioned as a contested space for multiple forms of identity.

According to Arjun Appadurai,[28] a more useful model of regionality could take the form of the "Pacific Rim"—echoing the cartography of the international dateline. In such a model, regionality would take the form of temporal, rather than geographic, clusters. This interrogation of regionality is exemplified in the arguments surrounding the Asia-Pacific, as witnessed in debates around the appropriate term to depict the dynamic and contesting spaces it claims to represent. One can find numerous examples such as "Asia-Pacific," "Asia-Pacific region," "Asia/Pacific," "Asian Pacific" and "Asia and the Pacific."

As Giovanni Arrighi observes in his meticulous discussion of capitalism and modernity in *The Long Twentieth Century*,[29] capitalism can be viewed as four cycles from Genoese mercantile capitalism, Dutch finance capitalism, British industrial capitalism and contemporary American capitalism. According to Arrighi, the fifth form of capitalism, synonymous with twenty-first century modernity, would undoubtedly be East Asian capitalism. In a subsequent essay about the rising power of East Asia globally, Arrighi notes that East Asia has become "the most dynamic world player in world-scale processes of capital accumulation."[30] However Arrighi, like Dirlik, argues that this form of industrialism and power is not nascent. Rather, it is the myopic visions of many Western models of history that seem only to grasp capitalism and industrialism as relatively new forms, neglecting to see that the domination of the "West"—either in the form of the United States or Europe—is part of a much larger process of modernity and mobility.

Against this backdrop of contestation, a rethinking of the region also necesitates a reconceptualization of globalization. In the context of the twenty-first century, this requires us to examine, according to Dirlik, re-orientations towards the new "Global South."[31] Thus, to study the region can help us to understand contemporary global flows and the role gaming cultures play in an age of participatory, crossplatforming and collaborative media whereby rubrics such as "players" and "industries" are transforming. This is no more apparent than in the case of the competing game cultures, practices and communities housed within both the Asia-Pacific "effect" and affect.

NOTES

1. Jen Webb, "Asia-Pacific Art: Beyond the Future," in *Beyond the Future*, eds. C. Turner and M. Low, *Papers from the conference of the Third Asia-Pacific Triennial of Contemporary Art Brisbane, 10–12 September 1999* (Brisbane: Queensland Art Gallery, 2000), 116.
2. Webb, "Asia-Pacific Art: Beyond the Future," 116.
3. For further discussion on Techno-Orientalism see David Morley and Kevin Robins, *Spaces of Identities: Global Media, Electronic Landscapes and Cultural Boundaries* (New York: Routledge, 1995). Also see Lisa Nakamura, *Cybertypes: Race, Ethnicity, and Identity on the Internet* (New York: Routledge, 2002).
4. Brian Sutton-Smith, *The Ambiguity of Play* (London: Routledge, 1997).
5. Testuo Kogawa "Beyond Electronic Individualism," *Canadian Journal of Political and Social Theory/Revue Canadienne de Thetorie Politique et Sociale*, 8 (3), Fall 1984. Retrieved 20 July 2007, http://anarchy.translocal.jp/non-japanese/electro.html.
6. See Chua Beng-Huat, ed., *Consumption in Asia* (London: Routledge, 2000). Also see Robert Robison and David S.G. Goodman, eds., *The New Rich in Asia* (London: Routledge, 1996).
7. See K.C. Ho, Randy Kluver and K.C.C. Yang, eds., *Asia@com* (London: Routledge, 2003) and Nanette Gottlieb and Mark McLelland, eds., *Japanese Cybercultures* (New York: Routledge, 2003).
8. Mark J. P. Wolf and Bernard Perron, eds., *The Video Game Theory Reader* (New York and London: Routledge, 2003).
9. Mark J.P. Wolf and Bernard Perron, eds., *The Video Game Theory Reader 2* (New York and London: Routledge, forthcoming).
10. Noah Wardrip-Fruin and Pat Harrigan, eds., *First Person: New Media as Story, Performance, and Game* (Cambridge, MA: MIT Press, 2004); and Joost Raessens and Jeffrey Goldstein, eds., *Handbook of Computer Game Studies* (Cambridge, MA: MIT Press, 2005).
11. Andreas Jahn-Sudmann and Ralf Stockmann, eds., *Games Without Frontiers, War Without Tears: Computer Games as a Sociocultural Phenomenon* (London: Palgrave Macmillan, 2008).
12. Justine Cassell and Henry Jenkins, eds., *From Barbie to Mortal Kombat: Gender and Computer Games* (Cambridge, MA: MIT Press, 1998); Geoff King and Tanya Krzywinska, eds., *ScreenPlay: cinema/videogames/interfaces*

(London: Wallflower Press, 2002); Friedrich von Borries, Steffan P. Walz and Mattias Böttger, eds., *Space Time Play—Computer Games, Architecture and Urbanism: The Next Level* (Basel, Boston, and Berlin: Birkhäuser, 2007); and Katie Salen, ed., *The Ecology of Games: Connecting Youth, Games, and Learning* (Cambridge, MA: MIT Press, 2008).

13. Chris Kohler, *Power-Up: How Japanese Video Games Gave the World an Extra Life* (London: Dorling Kindersley/Brady Games, 2004).

14. Steven Poole, *Trigger Happy: The inner life of videogames* (London: Fourth Estate, 2000); James Newman, *Videogames* (London & New York: Routledge, 2004); Henry Jenkins, *Fans, Bloggers, and Gamers* (New York & London: New York University Press, 2006); Diane Carr, et al., *Computer Games: Text, Narrative and Play* (Cambridge: Polity Press, 2006); and Edward Castronova, *Synthetic Worlds: The Business and Culture of Online Games* (Chicago: Chicago University Press, 2006).

15. For more detailed information, see Dean Chan, "Negotiating Intra-Asian Games Networks: On Cultural Proximity, East Asian Games Design and Chinese Farmers," *Fibreculture Journal*, 8, 2006. Retrieved 8 August 2008 from http://journal.fibreculture.org/issue8/issue8_chan.html.

16. Jim Supangkat, "Multiculturalism / Multimodernism" in *Contemporary Art in Asia: Tensions/Traditions* ed. A. Poshyananda[Exhibition Catalogue] (New York: Harry N. Abrams, 1996), 70–81.

17. Dean Chan, "Playing With Indexical Chineseness: The Transnational Cultural Politics of Wuxia in Digital Games," *EnterText* 6 (1) 2006: 182–202.

18. See Morley and Robins, *Spaces of Identities*; and Nakamura, *Cybertypes*.

19. Arif Dirlik, "Is There History after Eurocentricism?: Globalism, Postcolonialism, and the Disavowal of History," *Cultural Critique* 42, Spring 1999: 1–34.

20. Arif Dirlik, "Asia Pacific studies in an age of global modernity," *Inter-Asia Cultural Studies*, 6 (2) 2000: 158–170.

21. Henry Jenkins, *Convergence Culture: Where Old and New Media Intersect* (New York: New York University Press, 2006).

22. Axel Bruns and Jason Jacobs, eds., *Uses of Blogs* (New York: Peter Lang, 2006).

23. Nakamura, *Cybertypes*.

24. Judith Butler, *Gender Trouble* (London: Routledge, 1991).

25. Giovanni Arrighi, *The Long Twentieth Century: Money, Power, and the Origins of Our Times* (New York: Verso, 1994); Giovanni Arrighi, Takeshi Hamashita and Mark Selden, M., eds., *The Resurgence of East Asia: 500, 150 and 50 year Perspectives* (London: Routledge Asia's transformations series, 2003); Robert Wilson, "Imagining 'Asia-Pacific': Forgetting Politics and Colonialism in the Magical Waters of the Pacific. An Americanist Critique," *Cultural Studies* 14 (3/4) 2000: 562–592; Arif Dirlik, "Global South: Predicament and Promise," *The Global South*, Winter, 1(1) 2007: 12–23.

26. Wilson, "Imagining 'Asia-Pacific,'" 567.

27. Robert Wilson and Arif Dirlik, eds., *Asia/Pacific As Space of Cultural Production* (Durham: Duke University Press, 1995), 6.

28. Arjun Appadurai, "Grassroots Globalisation and the Research Imagination," *Public Culture* 12(1) 2000: 1–19.

29. Arrighi, *The Long Twentieth Century*.

30. Giovanni Arrighi, "Globalization and the Rise of East Asia," *International Sociology* 13 (1) 1998: 59.

31. Dirlik, "Global South: Predicament and Promise."

Part I

Industries

INTRODUCTION

With the rise of Web 2.0 providing new types of creativity, collaboration, communities and distribution, how we conceptualize models of "industry"—and the agency and empowerment of players—are transforming. This phenomenon is no more overt than in the games industry, whereby the rise of massively multiplayer online role-playing games (MMORPGs) and attendant "playbour"[1] practices are burgeoning. The obvious industry model to be affected by Web 2.0 is undoubtedly online multiplayer games and networked sociality around gaming cultures. The uneven uptake and dissemination of Web 2.0—intrinsically linked to IT policies and technonationalism, as well as reflective of the socio-cultural rituals already at play—have led to ways in which industries are developing. This section provides a snapshot of some of these shifts.

From one of the pioneers in gaming history (Tokyo) to one of the innovators in MMORPGs (Seoul), the region provides some of the most divergent models for gaming cultures and new paradigms for conceptualizing the industry at a local, transnational and global level of consumption and production. Indeed this phenomenon requires us to interrogate issues around agency, participation, empowerment and engagement that underscore the new types of affective, emotional, social and creative labor being deployed between industries and the seemingly creative and collaborative role of individual and communities of players. Undeniably, on both macro and micro, local and transnational levels, what constitutes "industry" is being redefined.

Given the recent global financial economic crisis of late 2008, whereby specters could be felt within the region in the form of ghosts of the economic crisis about a decade ago in 1997, this section's focus upon industry is timely. The financial collapse of 1997 saw key locations such as South Korea left destitute and requiring financial rescue by the International

Monetary Fund (IMF). More than a decade on, the region has seen major reconceptualizations of consumption and production as no longer synonymous with Westernization.[2]

In this section, the three chapters adopt very diverse models for understanding and contextualizing the games industry within broader transcultural industries that shift with regional cultural capital turns. From the deployment of dissimilar methodologies (cultural studies to political economy) to the focus upon different location or case studies (Korea, Australia and Singapore), these chapters provide three of the multi-directional paths of games industries that reflect the contesting technocultures.

In this section we are presented with divergent technocultures—the "broadband center"[3] boasting world class IT policies, South Korea, is sharply contrasted to Australia whereby issues of geography and privatized telecommunication infrastructure have led to many "Internets."[4] These divergent technocultures—and thus models for local, transnational and global games industries—are further renegotiated in the context of Singapore, where Korea's successful technoculture provides inspiration and informs current industry models in Singapore.

Given the inspirational model of its online gaming industry, it is no surprise that this section on industries opens with one of this century's main exemplars, South Korea. South Korea not only dominates the region as a center for online gaming—it has also become part of the global imaginary for a nexus for MMORPGS. Whilst Japan's long history in the rise of twentieth century gaming cultures and technocultures resulted in it becoming a repository for Techno-orientalism, South Korea has now, thanks to its widely broadcasted significance with the production and consumption of online gaming, begun to share the Techno-oriental shadow that haunts some global theories on technocultures.

To avoid Techno-orientalism one must contextualize the technoculture within wider socio-cultural factors. This method is clearly deployed in this section's first chapter by Dal Yong Jin and Florence Chee, which unpacks and sheds new light upon the various layers—political, economic, and socio-cultural—that have played a role in the accelerated rise of the online game industry. Through the lens of South Korea, Chee and Jin reconceptualize the online games industry—and specifically the South Korean government and industry capitalizing and mobilizing the online gaming industry—by contextualizing it within broader socio-cultural factors.

From its innovation in pioneering the world's first graphic MMOG *Kingdom of the Winds* in 1996, Jin and Chee note in Chapter 2 that "Korea has played a central role in the PC-based online game market and digital economy," which is in turn indicative of "the networked environment of virtual capitalism." This chapter, like the other two chapters in this section, explores both the local and transnational factors at play in the constitution of the games industry and how this reflects transnational flows of cultural capital.

Following on from Jin and Chee's comprehensive probing of the South Korean industry, we move to a model that is distinctively different—the Australian games industry. As a relatively small player in the global games industry and yet boasting a disproportionately high number of independent game developers, the Australian context provides a contrasting model. In Sam Hinton's eloquently concise charting of the Australian industry in Chapter 3, we are provided a window onto the "West in Asia."[5] Through his detailed discussion of the "structure and challenges facing the games industry in Australia" contextualized within the history of the local games industry, Hinton paints a very different picture of the Australia of cultural tourist clichés—it is instead a "gaming nation." Far from a technocultural backwater, Hinton highlights that voracious new media acquisition is part of the daily diet for Australian urbans and periurbans. Despite this phenomenon, Hinton observes that various factors have "conspired" to create a "uniquely Australian game development industry that is characterized by privately owned independent studios producing primarily overseas IP and ports."

From the challenges faced by the Australian games industry we move to another satellite industry that has also been overshadowed by the region's big players, Singapore. Like Australia, Singapore has a history fraught with British colonialism as well as a relatively small population and a games industry facing various challenges. In Chapter 4, Peichi Chung confronts some of tests Singapore must address if it is to engage in the global online gaming market. As she highlights, South Korean and Singaporean new media industries are divergent to say the least. While South Korea presents of model of exportation, Singapore is still negotiating its place in the global digital creative industries through fostering collaborations between the local government and multinational game companies. Although similarities can be made between the two locations—boasting high broadband penetration development, IT policies and sophisticated technocultures—the countries present two divergent responses to globalization. Like all the chapters in this section, we are provided with an example of how to reconceptualize notions of industry through the contextualized case studies. As a continuously evolving industry, games present new ways for the creative industries in an age of Web 2.0 and beyond.

NOTES

1. Julian Kücklich, "Precarious Playbour: Modders and the Digital Games Industry," *Fibreculture Journal*, 5, 2005. Retrieved 23 July 2008 from http://journal.fibreculture.org/issue5/kucklich.html.
2. Chua Beng-Huat, ed., *Consumption in Asia* (London: Routledge, 2000).
3. Organization for Economic Co-operation and Development *OECD broadband statistics*. Retrieved 10 December 2006 from http://www.oecd.org/sti/ict/broadband.
4. Most notably a relatively slow connection and download as noted by Hjorth's research into Korean students studying in Australia and how this changes

their relationship to the Internet. See Larissa Hjorth, "Home and away: a case study of the use of Cyworld mini-hompy by Korean students studying in Australia," *Asian Studies Review,* The Internet in East Asia special issue, A. McLaren, ed., 31 December 2007: 397–407.

5. Madanmohan Rao, ed., *News Media and New Media: The Asia-Pacific Internet Handbook* (Singapore: Times Academic Press, 2004).

2 The Politics of Online Gaming

Dal Yong Jin and Florence Chee

INTRODUCTION

The Korean online game market has rapidly emerged as one of the most dynamic in the world. Within a relatively short period of time, Korea[1] has become known for widespread broadband deployment to households, along with a technologically receptive and literate public, which has resulted in the rapid growth in online gaming. Ever since Nexon, a Korean games corporation, introduced the world's first graphic massively multiplayer online game *Kingdom of the Winds* in 1996, Korea has played a central role in the PC-based online game market and digital economy. In 2005, the Korean online game market was worth $1.4 billion, accounting for 56% of the entire Asia Pacific market share. The Korean online game market is expected to continually grow about 20% annually, reaching $2.9 billion by 2009.[2] Due to the rapid growth of users, the structure and dynamics of the interactive game business becomes a key node in the networked environment of virtual capitalism.[3]

Several significant factors, including political, economic and socio-cultural have contributed to the swift growth of the online game industry, which received global attention. Korean developers have been able to outperform major competitors including Electronic Arts (EA), an American developer, publisher and distributor of computer and video games, and Nintendo and Sony, Japanese console/handheld game makers, thanks to the explosion of information technology (IT) business and the subsequent distribution of nationwide broadband networks and booming *PC bang* (Internet cafés, pronounced "bahngs"). The vast popularity of online games in Korea has indeed closely matched the widespread proliferation of information and communication technologies (ICTs), which have facilitated communication and interaction at an unprecedented level. For instance, one of the major results of these governmental and industrial initiatives has been the widespread deployment and adoption of a sophisticated broadband infrastructure to the home in almost all parts of the country, which has greatly contributed to the growth of the online game industry. Through games as well as related activities, Korean youth have used these technologies to nurture friendships through their engagement in activities such as online games, instant messaging and blogging, for example, which assist them in constructing their own tight-knit communities.

With the ever-increasing presence of online games in Korean mainstream culture, the corresponding consequences of games eclipsing other activities have also garnered much attention in recent years to become a very pertinent issue. However, regardless of the swift growth of domestic online gaming as a major part of culture as well as new media, academic research on Korean online games has been correspondingly sparse and limited in scope, with domestic literature tending towards either the celebratory emphasis of positive business development or regulation and media oriented concerns, due primarily to the accelerated pace of development. While such research comprises important contributions to the emerging scholarship of Korean online games, unbalanced accounts foreground readily empirical observations and aggregate data that exclude other possible macro factors, such as political and economic structures and transnationalization of the Korean gaming industry, or micro factors, including more private but resonant problems in the family or social life of those concerned. Therefore, the Korean game industry should be seriously examined in relation to its own socio-cultural circumstances and context *vis-á-vis* the global game industry.

In this chapter, we therefore identify and examine several key factors involved in the rapid growth of online games in the context of broader socio-cultural elements. We provide a critical interpretation of the industry's ownership patterns, finance and markets by exploring online games as well as developing industries in Korea. We map out the forces driving its development by examining government policies and competition among online game companies. We also explore transcultural flows of cultural capital in order to investigate major market players. Finally, we draw upon ethnographic data to link socio-cultural elements contributing to the diffusion of online games in the cultural milieu specific to Korean youth. Our objective is to provide as complete a picture as possible for arriving at a nuanced explanation of the current state of Korean online games, stakeholders and players alike.

For the chapter, we employ political economy approaches and combine them with ethnographic research and in-depth interviews gathered in our fieldwork to strengthen our major analytical framework. In the process, we use primary and secondary sources such as industry reports and government documents, coupled with participant observation in Korean everyday life, Korean PC game rooms and interviews with game players. Such a combination is designed to show the manifestations of policy and culture as experienced on the ground, especially by Korean youth. Through our examination of the Korean online game industry in light of its socio-cultural elements and political economic contingencies, we hope to illuminate some of the underexamined complexities inherent in the conception, development, implementation and reception of online games in a global arena.

THE GLOBAL ONLINE GAMES MARKET
AND KOREA'S DIGITAL ECONOMY

The game (or video and computer games) market, as it refers to consumer spending on console games (including handheld games), personal computer (PC) games, online games and wireless games is a burgeoning new media industry with global revenues rivaling those of film and music.[4] Between 2001 and 2005, the worldwide game market had increased about 30%. It was expected that the game market would increase from its 2005 figure of $27.1 billion in 2005 to $46 billion in 2010.[5] However, the sales of PC and video games already reached an all-time high in 2007 and overall worldwide industry sales soared over the $50 billion mark.[6] A principal driver of the global game market is the expanding console game market, played on a dedicated console, like Sony's PlayStation 3, Microsoft's Xbox, and Nintendo's Wii. Three console manufacturers which have provided game platforms and/or devices have dominated the entire game market in an oligopolistic contest. In the United States, console games constitute 71% of the market at $6.1 billon, and the situation is not that different in Europe (61%).[7] In fact, as of May 2008, the sales of Nintendo Wii, which is a dominant game console, recorded at 675,000 in the United States, and Sony's PlayStation 3 sold 209,000.[8]

In contrast to this global trend, online games, referring to games carried out on a computer network, have been extremely popular and are playing a unique role in Korea's transition towards a digital economy. In 2006, the domestic online game market accounted for as much as 81.5% ($1.77 billion), from 76.2% in 2005, of the total game market ($2.17 billion), including console, online, PC and mobile games. During 2006, the console game market constituted only 6.3%, while mobile games consisted of 10.9%). PC games were 1.2%.[9] The online game market rapidly grew; for example, the market increased by 41.3% between 2004 and 2005.[10] Korean online games[11] (as of March 2007) make up 32% of the world's online gaming market.[12]

The online game industry has expanded its influence in the global cultural market as well as the domestic market. In 2006, Korea exported $671 million in the gaming business alone, compared to only $24.5 million in films and $133.9 million in television, which had been two major cultural sectors leading Korea's increasing cultural penetration in Asia.[13] Korean online game firms played a major role in China's online game market, for instance. In 2005, among 209 online games in China, 91 were from Korea.[14] However, while the largest market for Korean online games is Asia, Korean online games have expanded to other regions, including the United States and Europe. For instance, exports to Japan decreased from 42.6% in 2005 to 32.4% in 2006, while the portion of exports to the United States increased from 15.7% in 2005 to 19.9% in 2006.[15]

Korea's most popular online role-playing games (RPG) as well as casual games have become very popular in other countries. The casual online game *Pangya*, developed by HanbitSoft, set a new record by launching its service in 44 countries including the United Kingdom, France and Germany in recent years. The online game *Wyd* is very popular in Japan, and the online dancing game, *Groove Party*, has been played in China with sales of $4.7 million.[16] In particular, Korean game developer NCsoft dominated the global online game market when they released their medieval fantasy massively multiplayer online role-playing games (MMORPGs), *Lineage* and *Lineage II* in 1998 and 2003, respectively. The games, available in Chinese, Japanese and English language versions had been considered one of the largest commercial MMORPG communities before the emergence of *World of Warcraft*, developed by Blizzard Entertainment in the United States in 2005.[17] As such, Korea promoted online games as the major part of its digital economy, and consequently became a major success in the commercialization of online games in the global marketplace.

UNBALANCING THE ONLINE GAME INDUSTRY

The games industry presents a complicated picture because development, publishing and distribution functions can be combined or separated.[18] This is different from the music and film industries, where those functions are typically integrated into one production label. For games, a single company can perform just one or a combination of these three activities.[19] Because of the difficulty in dividing the game industry, developers and publishing companies are lumped into the same category as development companies by the Korean government.[20]

Over the past several years, the number of Korean online game companies has increased exponentially. When the Korean online games industry was in its infancy, for example, a total number of 694 game companies existed in 1999. However, this number soared to as many as 3,631 companies in 2006. During the same period, the number of game development companies increased 6.7 times from 416 in 1999 to 2,786 companies in 2006, while the number of distributors increased 3 times from 278 in 1999 to 845 in 2006.[21] To offer a comparative perspective for the same time period, Canada had only 170 online game developers.[22] It must be noted that because the majority of Korean game companies often do not work exclusively on online games but also mobile games and PC games, it is unclear as to how many are actually online game companies. However, about 52.5% of game companies are reporting the production of online games, followed by mobile games (27.3%).

Meanwhile, in 2006, Korean development houses mainly comprised small and medium-size venture capital investments, with about 22.5 employees on average.[23] As a reflection of the rapid growth of the online game industry, the total number of employees has swiftly increased from 13,500 in 2000 to 60,669 in 2005, far exceeding the number of workers

(40,116) in the media industry, including newspaper, terrestrial and cable broadcasters and news agencies.[24]

As in many other industries including film, television and mobile technologies, one of the major issues in the online game sector is the concentration of wealth in the industry. Although there were 2,839 development houses, the top eight online companies including NCsoft, Nexon, Neowiz, NHN and CJ Internet, constituted more than 65% of the online game market in 2005.[25] NCsoft made its name with the 1998 launch of a game called *Lineage*, which affords player involvement in combat, siege, political and social systems. Nexon developed *The Kingdom of Winds*, the first online game in Korea. With Neowiz, these three major online games companies accounted for 70% of the top eight online game companies in 2005.[26] This results in much of the people, capital and technology gravitating towards a few leading companies. As emphasized in Kline et al.[27] and Dyer-Witheford,[28] the dominance of online games by a few major companies will continue indefinitely, because game development is an increasingly lengthy, costly and cooperative venture. The escalation of production and advertising costs are a persistent challenge to many small software development companies and often leads to their demise.

Indeed, the cost of developing one game soared from $180,000 in 1999 to $5 to $10 million in 2005. It also typically takes about two or three years to create one game in Korea.[29] An example is GameHi, a medium-size game developer, which spent three years and USD $8 million in the production of its online fantasy game *Dekaron*.[30] This situation is likely to continue in the game development sector, as only a few venture capitalists and large corporations are able to manage the blockbuster level and scope of game development and production timelines.

A related point is that ownership itself is concentrated among a few large corporations. Several major companies have expanded their role in the online game business to compensate for difficulties in financing and marketing experienced by the majority of game developers. Firms involved in international trade, telecommunications and media, such as LG International Corporation and Korea Telecom (KT), have joined the new media sector hoping there will be another windfall. For example, in 2003, KT announced it would invest $100 million in the games market over the next five years, as a publisher. At the time KT announced its plans, the telecommunications giant was already strategically allied with eight game developers. In December 2006, CJ Internet, a subsidiary of the largest multimedia conglomerate in Asia (CJ Group), expanded into the publishing business with 329 employees over five years.[31] In the same year, another large media group, Onmedia, also announced its plan to join the online game industry to leverage its game channel Ongamenet in the marketplace.[32]

The spike in capital flow from many parties, including everyone from small venture capital investors to the largest corporations and media firms, has caused domestic capital in the online game industry to dramatically increase. As Aphra Kerr points out,[33] many countries have consolidated the game industry mainly by partnering with big publishers in order to compete with Sony, Nintendo and Microsoft in their game markets. However, concentration of ownership in Korea presents a very different situation. Some domestic venture capitalists consider online games as one of the most important new media technologies for bolstering the digital economy. Others, such as CJ Internet and Onmedia, consider online games as a necessary industry in which to have a presence. It is this type of media convergence which is expediting the concentration of industry in terms of market share and ownership. It was only a few years ago that games development was often characterized as the ultimate cottage industry for the information age,[34] but this statement has been losing its credibility due to the increasing concentration of the online games industry in the hands of a few large corporations. In the following section, we discuss the effects of transnationalization of the online game industry as it has affected and been affected by the Korean domestic games market.

TRANSNATIONALIZATION OF THE ONLINE GAME INDUSTRY

The effects of transnationalization of the online game industry have been felt profoundly due to continuing foreign interest in large Korean game firms. Along with domestic firms, foreign-based transnational corporations (TNCs) have swiftly invested in the Korean online game industry to profit while participating in the development of cutting-edge technologies. In 2007, Electronic Arts, the largest video and computer game company worldwide, invested $105 million in the Korean game company Neowiz. This investment involved the acquisition of 19% of Neowiz shares for the co-development and global publishing rights of its online games.[35]

The Japanese technology company Softbank already acquired a majority share of the Korean game developer Gravity for $409 million, the largest takeover so far. The Japanese Sega Corporation with Hyundai Digital, a former subsidiary of the Hyundai Group, also made a joint venture in 1996 and worked together on online games from 2001. Foreign investors held about 50% of the market share at major Korean game firms such as NCsoft (41.8%) and NHN (51.4%) in March 2007,[36] in addition to the penetration of the domestic market by subsidiaries of Sony, Nintendo and Microsoft, the world's largest console game makers. With the establishment of such subsidiaries in Korea, these companies have come to dominate the online games market.

As much as online games software from Korea has flourished in other countries, the TNCs have been a formidable force to deal with due to their abilities in generating exponential profits and resources for advanced technology acquisition and development. A few domestic online game companies, such as NCsoft, HanbitSoft and Webzen, have invested in foreign markets. For example, targeting the global game company, NCsoft has established branches and/or joint ventures in Japan, China, Taiwan, Thailand, Europe and the United States However, the majority of domestic online game industries are simply unable to break into foreign markets due to their possession of a relatively small amount of capital. Therefore, it is premature to predict the impact of capital involvement from domestic online games companies on the global market as domestic TNCs.

However, foreign-based TNCs have already benefited from domestic online firms. Dan Schiller points out that while independent capital has spearheaded and cultivated video and computer games, it is the mega transnational conglomerates which commodify the emerging new media sector.[37] Although the number of independent production companies has grown, they absorb high product risks and labor costs for the monopolies, which maintain their control over the critical areas of finance and distribution as in other cultural sectors.[38] All evidence indicates that the transnationalization of the Korean online game industry will continue to deepen the ongoing process of commodification of a new media sector, and domestic companies will also continue deferring to transnational capitals seeking profit.

CONTRIBUTING FACTORS TO GROWTH IN THE ONLINE GAME INDUSTRY

With global presence as well as domestic dominance, online game makers, online gamers, government IT officials and game researchers worldwide have been interested in learning key elements in the rapid growth of the Korean online game industry. Conversely, due to rapid transnationalization and concentration of ownership of the industry, interested parties are simultaneously skeptical as to whether Korea holds the key to the next generation of online games. By analyzing several key underlying and proximate elements such as government policy and social factors, including the levels of broadband penetration, we will provide answers from these fundamental vantage points. Above all, it is worthwhile analyzing the context of the rapid growth in Korean online games, because contextualization provides a process for connecting present circumstances to the social and historical conditions from which online games originated.

To begin, the rapid development of IT and related policy has become the foundation for the growth of online games. As is well publicized, Korea has quickly become the most wired nation in the world, with a sophisticated 70% personal computer (PC) penetration. In early 2008, about 93% of Korean households were connected to broadband services—the highest in the world.[39] The rapid deployment of IT in Korea originated in 1995 when the government enacted the Framework Act on Information, which set up a comprehensive strategy for the Korean Information Infrastructure (KII).[40]

The goal of the KII was to construct an advanced nationwide information infrastructure consisting of communications networks, Internet services, application software, computers, and information products and services, which have greatly influenced the rapid growth of broadband and online games.

The Korean government has also been instrumental in supporting the games industry by providing financial subsidies and incentives to game developers, increasing its investment in an effort to nurture its software industry over the last several years, with plans to continue. The direct influence of the Korean government on the online game industry does not differ much from other new technologies and cultural industries, such as the broadband and film sectors. For example, in 2005, the Korean government announced a plan to invest $20 million to support the development of graphics and virtual reality technologies in the games sector.[41] As part of this plan, the government invested $13.5 million for the growth of the game industry and the creation of a game culture in 2006.[42] Although this amount is inadequate when compared with actual costs, it illustrates the intention of the Korean government to deliver on its promise in keeping with its policy.

INTERNATIONAL POLITICS

Against the backdrop of economic growth are two major historical events, which have served in ways that are not always obvious to steer the direction of online games in Korea. These two events—namely, the Japanese occupation and resultant influence on Korean policy, and the Asian economic crisis in 1997—have clearly promoted the swift development of online games. As discussed, console games are the most popular platform in the global game market. However, Korea is an exception in that online PC games are far more popular than the console variety. A primary reason for the lack of uptake in console gaming has much to do with the platform's origins in Japanese development.

Due to Korea's colonization by Japan in the early twentieth century, as well as its longstanding concern with Japanese cultural invasion, the Korean government had until 1998 banned Japanese cultural products, which included console games, films and music. With the ban lifted, Korea gradually opened the market to Japanese culture, phasing in previously black market products, with console games from Japan making their public appearance in the Korean marketplace by 2002.[43] The historical tension between the two countries has proven persistent and difficult to surmount, as those who anticipated large profits through access to the Korean game market found the endeavour generated a disappointing and negligible amount of revenue for Japanese companies. Through its subsidiary company, Sony experienced a net loss in 2004 and 2005 when it began its sale of PlayStation 2 in Korea, and subsequently delayed its launch of PlayStation 3.[44] With Japanese console makers such as Sony, Nintendo and Sega experiencing such difficulties in penetrating the Korean game market, Korea utilized the opportunity to develop its own domestic online game industry.

The 1997 Asian economic crisis was an unexpected catalyst in the rapid growth of IT, which include broadband services as well as rising Internet start-ups in Korea.[45] This landmark economic recession was also what prompted the rapid development in IT and online games.[46] Since 1998, some 7,700 Internet start ups have been established. Employees laid off during the economic crisis became the main participants in growing Korea's Internet industry. Many middle managers, who had worked for large computer and information companies, including *Samsung* Display Devices, also looked towards smaller-sized private businesses.[47] Many of them joined Internet start-ups, and became grass-roots developers of Internet technologies, including online games software. For example, HanbitSoft, one of the leading online developers in Korea, started its business in 1999 when LGSoft split its game division as part of restructuring of the company during the economic crisis era.[48] A major entrepreneurial activity since the recession has been starting up a *PC bang*, which highlights the trend towards small-scale IT enterprise to offset economic fallout.

ORIGINS OF THE *PC BANG*

The massive growth in the online game sector is partially a result of the rapid proliferation of so-called *PC bangs* along with broadband. *PC bangs* have since evolved into many different places for Internet use for sending e-mails, chat groups, online games and the like at any time.[49] The most popular game during the early days of *PC bang* culture was *StarCraft*. Developed in the United States, it contributed to the rapid growth of broadband connections and the *PC bang* concept which began in 1998.

To put quantity into perspective, there were only 100 PC cafés in Korea during 1997, but by May 2002 this had rapidly increased to 25,000. In 2006 there was a decrease in the number of cafés to 20,986 due to market saturation and the growing access to broadband services in the home. In the present-day however, despite accessibility of broadband in the home, *PC bangs* still play a significant role in facilitating online games culture in Korea by providing ubiquitous and economical access. Many cafés charge very affordable hourly or flat rates for extended use of PCs.[50] Jun-Sok Huhh (2008) also writes about the changes exhibited in Korean business models that have adapted to the dynamics between game publishers and local PC bangs.[51] Interesting developments in real money trade (RMT), micropayments and IP-pricing are just some of the issues that have concurrently affected all stakeholders in the Korean game culture, many of which are still being negotiated in the policy arena.

Meanwhile, the wide availability of broadband has clearly made it easier for Korean firms to attract new casual gamers as opposed to just hardcore gamers.[52] In addition to the *StarCraft* RTS series, in recent years the *Lineage* MMORPGs and *Kart Rider* racing games have also become mainstays in the Korean gaming experience. An increase in the demand for entertainment and network games has stimulated the diffusion of broadband Internet services. According to one survey conducted in the first half of 2002, 81.1% of broadband Internet subscribers were using entertainment related content, and 74.6% were playing network games—twice as high as those of dial-up Internet access subscribers.[53] Our ethnographic data on the role of the *PC bang* in the proliferation of online game play follows in the ethnographic discussion.

PROFESSIONAL GAMERS

Considering the rich atmosphere afforded by Korean online game culture, we cannot ignore the particular manifestation of use cultures emerging from an aggressively integrated glut of multimedia, which serves to mutually reinforce the mainstream online game culture prevalent in contemporary Korean youth. The increasing popularity of e-sports (electronic sports leagues that compete through network games) and the live broadcasting of competitions on cable television networks have expedited the growth of online games, particularly among mainstream Korean youth. E-sports began its first league in 1998 when *StarCraft* became popular in Korea. With the growth of *PC bangs*, e-sports became one of the major activities among teens. In 2001, the first "World Cyber-Games," dubbed the "Olympics of Computer Games," were held in Seoul, where 400 players from 37 countries contended for the $300,000 prize.[54] Mainly due to its commercial effects, several large corporations have joined the league: 278 registered professional gamers in 11 professional teams competed with each other for an annual $5 million in prize money in August 2006.[55] By June 2007, the number of professional gamers had grown to more than 600.

In Korea, the expert professional gamer typically trains for years in order to make it into the major gaming leagues sponsored by large corporations. The Korean gamer-as-celebrity scene is world-renowned and attracts many aspiring celebrity gamers from around the globe, including Canadian Guillaume Patry (who "retired" in his early-twenties). Much of the Korean youth culture is immersed by online games and attendant popular pastimes such as watching professional gaming. This celebration of gamers is quite contrary to the negative connotations of gaming in other parts of the world. The distinguishing factor in the Korean case is support from the populace for what has suddenly become an economically productive activity across many sectors.

Several electronics and telecommunications majors such as Samsung Electronics (Samsung KHAN), SK Telecom (SK Telecom T1), and KTF (KTF Magics), and media companies including MBC (MBC Game Hero), Ongamenet (SPARKYZ) and CJ (CJ Entus), are major sponsors of professional gamers. Considering their convergence with telecommunications and broadcasting, these corporations have come to play a major part in the production of professional game leagues. Due to the popularity of e-sports, even the Korean Air Force has formed its own electronic gaming team and has played in the league since 2006. E-sports are swiftly becoming part of daily life, particularly among the youth.

Moreover, we found the prevalence of a mainstream celebrity gaming culture helps to maintain popularity of games that would otherwise fade into an "old favorite," such as *StarCraft*. In more than one interview, it was mentioned that television broadcasts and associated hype helped "remind" players of the games, and show public strategies that they can try out with friends at the next *PC bang*. Digital cameras and mobile phones of audience members may document the scene for posterity or subsequent reportage on their Cyworld mini-hompy.[56] One cannot look anywhere without seeing a bright, flashy sponsorship logo on the wall, or worn on a jumpsuit by the pro-gamers. With drama similar to that of professional wrestling matches and live color commentary, the *StarCraft* tournament (the game of choice for about half of the 600 professional gamers, as of June 2007) ends with team members of the losing side weeping—all to be rehashed shortly after on game news websites like Ongamenet.

Games have been televised for seven years, with Ongamenet, the largest game channel, reaching three million to four million viewers during 6 to 10 pm prime time, and its competitor, MBC Game, drawing 1.5 million at the same time for its own leagues.[57] Several million viewers watch games over the Internet and on television, captivated by what professional gamers can do. In sum, due to favorable government policies and social infrastructure, online games have made significant leaps in popularity. They have become a major indicator of the knowledge-based information society for which Korean society has been striving, and in this context a unique online games culture has flourished.

CULTURAL INSIGHT

To further our understanding of what is occurring in contemporary Korea with reference to online game culture, we analyze ethnographic data to tie in present-day sociocultural issues with the aforementioned policy context in order to counteract what Larissa Hjorth has argued is a chronic a-contextualization of gaming cultures via Neo-Techno-Orientalism.[58] The goal of our study is a multifaceted explanation of factors that may add up to a greater number of hours clocked by Korean youth online, but are not

accurately summarized as "online game addiction" in the clinical patho-
logical sense.[59]

ONLINE GAME PARTICIPATION IN KOREAN YOUTH

As a cultural group, Koreans have been found to spend a lot more time nurturing social networks than what is common in a country like the United
States.[60] The tendency to nurture one's social relations is very much valued
by Koreans of all ages, but for youth, the choice has been increasingly limited to a select few activities, which include gaming. Between the vice-grips
of schooling, which dominates the better part of the day, and the (sometimes) judgmental gaze of family at home, the adolescent in contemporary
Korea finds little solace aside from that which is associated with online
gaming. For youth, the choice is often between participating in gaming
activities as a part of mainstream everyday life, or stay away at the risk of
alienating oneself from the common activity of the social group.[61] It is not
incidental that almost all the youth interviewed for the study talked about
their online activities in relation to obligation and duty, whether it was their
friends and promised times for logging on or to their guild, clan or band of
blood brothers. It was rare that interviewees talked about any game, in and
of itself, as the motivation for logging on.

PRICE, POLICY, PRESSURE, AND PLACE

Further to our assertions about the many complexities faced by the citizens
of a post 1997 Korean economy, it is important to understand how the *PC
bang* phenomenon came to bear, but also why it has become so popular as
an activity. We explain four key factors that have contributed to the success
of the Korean *PC bang* as: price, policy, pressure and place. On **price**, many
Korean youth are able to meld aspects of their online and offline lives by
using cheap (and therefore accessible) computer stations at *PC bangs*. Gaming venues also command an important place in the courtship of some young
couples due to the cost-effectiveness of socializing at these venues as opposed
to other more costly places.[62] Compared to other "*bangs*" such as *norae
bangs* (Karaoke rooms), *DVD bangs*, and board game *bangs*, *PC bangs* are
still by far the cheapest at 1000 KRWon or less where the other bangs would
cost about four times as much. Secondly, while the Korean **policy** emphasis
on nationwide ICT adoption and usage has created the world's "most broadbanded nation,"[63] this specific prioritization of national resources has set the
tone for the types of ICT-oriented activities people choose for themselves in
their everyday lives. Participation in online games makes sense in this respect,
because the broadband enabled PC is already such an integral part of life for
this segment of the population and is thus more easily rationalizable and/or

consumed between homework, traveling to after school cram schools and the like. Thirdly, the surrounding **pressure** experienced by those currently living in urban centers, such as students embroiled in the demands of their regular and after school activities can often be found in *PC bangs*, using the environment as release valve. However, to call the type of behavior "escapism," is all too convenient, Freudian, and dismissive for our purposes of understanding the situation. Rather, our fourth factor of **place** is a more nuanced consideration that is contextually sensitive to the purpose the *PC bang* has come to serve. Why would those of all socio-economic situations, with access to their own home computer, still pay money to use computers at a *PC bang*? There is certainly more to the story, as the *PC bang* has become a de facto community center and a common place to convene with one's friends, acquaintances, and dates outside the home. An interviewee, Carl, talks about the difference he perceives between playing on a PC at home versus playing at a *PC bang*:

> *F:* Do you have a PC at home you can play?
> *C:* Yeah, sure.
> *F:* But what makes you play at the *PC bang* as opposed to home? What's the difference?
> *C:* The difference is that home is alone and the *PC bang* is with people. When you play the game, you play with [the] computer. The opposite side, the enemy is our computer. In [an] online game, the enemy is other people like me. That makes it more fun. So, *PC bang* can be more together, and you know, Koreans like to be together and doing [sic] something together, so that makes *PC bang* culture. When we play the same [game] at home we feel something empty. When we're together we feel like we can do something [that is] fun.

In addition to being known as a common area for youth, the fallout from the 1997 financial crisis has also cast the role of the *PC bang* as a makeshift unemployment office of sorts, where those who found themselves without an "office" to go to every day routinely spent time at the *PC bang*. Additionally, with *PC bangs* open for 24 hours, it is not uncommon to find people using them as shelters if one was in need of a place to spend several hours during the night.

THE ECONOMICS OF YOUTH AND SELF-DETERMINATION

The economic circumstances of youth in Korea also make earning money online (independent of parental interference) an attractive option. Cross-referencing of census data from the Korean National Statistical Office indicates a 93% unemployment rate in the 15 to 19 age category,[64] causing ripples to occur in older cohorts. This young, relatively inexperienced age group in Korea is culturally and structurally compelled to remain inexperienced in the workforce for a longer period of time than in youth of a similar age in North America.[65] Although those who make money by selling virtual items on sites like the Korean virtual item auction site Itembay.com cannot compete with the professional gamer's income, it is surprising to find out that amateur players can make over USD $100 per week[66] in their online/offline exchanges (whether using Itembay or by making personal arrangements) if they are willing to invest the time.

Castronova has noted that online pursuits allow more meritocratic events to occur to a greater extent than their offline equivalents, and therefore are generally more appealing than offline activities.[67] During the interview, Carl indicates a similar sentiment:

> C: In playing games, we get rewarded more easily than in real life. I feel if I have a high level on the game and if I have good items that people will admire me. We can be the King of some castle.[68] Some people, especially high school students [. . .] are really addicted to the game because they [are] very [involved] in the game, not in real life. Some adults over 30 or 40, some of them have problems in real life, [like failing] in their business. They avoid real life and they just want to satisfy themselves in the game. It's a real problem.

Carl recounted his hardcore freshman days of gaming during which he was ranked 16th on the Korean ladder for *StarCraft* by Blizzard.

> C: When I was a freshman [my family] thought I was crazy because I slept 24 hours after playing 24 hours. It wasn't good for my health [. . .] I had to stop because there is no Internet during army service. But I thought that I had to quit the gaming and I cannot do what I want in the army so I prepared to quit the gaming [. . .] I also earned a lot of money by gaming.

Taking the factors introduced in the preceding insights, it is important to consider contextual reasons along with the readily obvious monetary reasons for why players might spend what some might call an "excessive amount" of time logged on, buying or selling items. One might see how earning money by selling online items might be attractive for many reasons. First, in the already saturated Korean job market the income may provide extra pocket money and an increased sense of independence from one's family (which often many years away and operating within a paradigm privileging collectivism). Second, there seems to be a feeling of productiveness associated with earning a living, especially after compulsory military service when young Korean males are often in a state of uncertainty, and in a state of limbo while searching for a job and/ or finishing post-secondary education. Caillois' point of view in *Man, Play, and Games* is slightly more nuanced in that he explains what we are seeing are those who do not earn as much as more of a frivolous compensation.

Daily competition is harsh and implacable as well as monotonous and exhausting. It provides no diversion and accumulates rancor. It abuses and discourages—for, practically speaking, it provides scarcely any hope of improving one's status by means of one's earnings alone. Therefore everyone seeks to compensate.[69]

Indeed, the practice of selling items may very well be a way that people empower themselves with more agency and a sense of self-worth and associated fringe benefits, alongside significant social practices of youth navigating within a society of conflicting interests. Generally, if a young person in Korea is employed, it is often a low paying part-time job, known as "*urubeit.*" On the other hand, if one chooses, it is quite possible to earn more selling online game items than holding down a part-time job, which, if youth had the time between school schedules, would require the right age, experience, gender and an accepted job application—which would not be required to game online with one's PC.[70]

THE CONTINUING TRANSFORMATION OF ONLINE GAMING

The Korean online game industry has experienced a dramatic growth rate, gaining numbers and blazing trails in the development of business models over several years. The game industry has become one of core businesses in the new media sector, and games software has become a representative of the new media content of the twenty-first century. Korea—one of many small and weak countries until the middle of the twentieth century—has become a major power in today's world of digital technology, and has emerged as a cultural leader in the pursuit of a new kind of empire.[71]

The development of an online game industry has not been without its problems. There are certainly cautionary remarks that are to be made and understood. First, the apparent flourishing of online game capital in Korea is precarious to a certain extent. Despite experiencing dramatic growth over the last decade, the online game industry is now in a phase of stagnation due to increasing competition. Several major online game companies are already experiencing eroding growth. Compared to the previous term, NCsoft recorded a 196% decrease in sales in the first term (January through March) in 2006, and Webzen also announced a net lost of $55 million between 2005 and 2006.[72]

Market saturation has dealt another blow to the online game industry. There is no doubt that the increasing number of users has been the most significant factor in the rapid growth of online gaming; however, the game industry is showing signs of market saturation, in particular, among Korean youth. The major users are nine to 24 years old; however, already more than 80% of them are in the market, and the market cannot expect any increase in users. In addition, the global market is becoming much more competitive, mainly because of the rapid growth of the Asian online game industries. Several countries, including China, have expanded measures to protect and develop their online game industry.

The concentration of ownership in the hands of major corporations and the transnationalization of the domestic market are influencing the online game industry at an alarming rate. Due to the lack of capital and networks, small and medium-size online game developers are depending on large publishers who are rapidly acquiring successful domestic owned developers, as in the North American game industry.[73] Although a few transnational corporations have exploited the majority of small developers, while foreign-based TNCs have enjoyed profits while learning core technologies of game software. Korea has successfully commodified the emerging new media, online gaming; however, the country has already witnessed the same problems that other media have experienced.

In our attempt to illustrate a nuanced picture of online games in contemporary Korea, we also brought to the fore ethnographic evidence of more factors at work than the imperatives of globalization on the online games industry. We show that within Korea, youth were exhibiting an extraordinarily high level of engagement with ICTs and online games in general. The reasons for this engagement, according to the youth however, were nuanced and varied, often being cultural and social. To allow Korean youth to be unfairly labeled as "online game addicts" would be too simplistic and unrepresentative of the complex web of reasons, only some of which have been discussed. However, we hope that the examination of the politics of online gaming in Korea has contributed to present discussions and those to come.

NOTES

1. To clarify, we are speaking of South Korea in this case, hereafter referred to as Korea.
2. Korean Game Industry Agency, *2007 Korean Game Whitepaper* (Seoul: Korea Game Industry Agency, 2007).
3. Stephen Kline, Nick Dyer-Witheford and Greig De Peuter, *Digital Play: The Interaction of Technology, Culture, and Marketing* (Montréal: McGill-Queen's University Press, 2003).
4. Diane Carr, David Buckingham, Andrew Burn and Gareth Schott, *Computer Games: Text, Narrative and Play* (Malden, MA: Polity, 2006). Nick Dyer-Witheford and Zena Sharman, "The Political Economy of Canada's Video and Computer Game Industry," *Canadian Journal of Communication* 30 (2005), 187–210.
5. Pricewaterhouse Coopers, *Global Entertainment and Media Outlook 2006–2010*, [2006]).
6. DFC Intelligence, "Record Game Sales in 2007 are just the Start for the Soaring Video Game Business," Retrieved May 29 2007 from http://www.dfcint.com/wp/?p=209.
7. Pricewaterhouse Coopers, *Global Entertainment and Media Outlook 2006–2010*, 368.
8. Ben Fritz, "Sony's Console Coup," *Daily Variety*, June 13, 2008.

9. Korean Game Industry Agency, *2007 Korean Game Whitepaper*.
10. Korea Game Development and Promotion Institute, *2006 Korean Game Whitepaper*, 2006.
11. In Korea, an online game is generally considered to be a MUD (multi-user dimension, or multi-user dungeon) game. MUD games are role-playing games set in a virtual world of 3-D simulation featuring knights, sorcerers and elves. When MUD games take place through an Internet network, this is referred to as a massive multi player online role-playing game MMORPG. Leo Sang-Min Whang, "Online Game Dynamics in Korean Society: Experiences and Lifestyles in the Online Game World," *Korea Journal* Autumn 2003, 8. The game continues to run as long as there are some players interacting in the game world. Changes in this society take place indefinitely, as long as it has participants
12. Alex Kim, "Time to Set Standard of Online Gaming," *The Korea Times*, February 25, 2007.
13. Ministry of Culture and Tourism, *Cultural Industries Statistics 2007* (Seoul, South Korea: Ministry of Culture and Tourism, 2007).
14. Yong Cho and John D. Downing, "The Realities of Virtual Play: Video Games and their Industry in China," *Media, Culture, and Society* 30 (4) (2008), 515–529.
15. Korean Game Industry Agency, *2007 Korean Game Whitepaper*.
16. Kim, *Time to Set Standard of Online Gaming*.
17. *MMOG Active Subscribers Version 21*, vol. 2007. Retrieved April 3, 2007 from Mmogchart.com.
18. Development entails the design and creation of a piece of game software. This expensive process may be financed either from the developer's own funds or by venture capital, or, increasingly, by advances from a game publisher. Publishing involves the overall management of the game commodity—financing, manufacturing, packing and promotion. Distribution refers to the shipping of the game hardware and software to retail stores. Dyer-Witheford and Sharman, *The Political Economy of Canada's Video and Computer Game Industry*, 187–210.
19. Kline, Dyer-Witheford and De Peuter, *Digital Play: The Interaction of Technology, Culture, and Marketing*.
20. Article 2, Law on Game Industry Promotion.
21. Korean Game Industry Agency, *2007 Korean Game Whitepaper*, 126.
22. Dyer-Witheford and Sharman, *The Political Economy of Canada's Video and Computer Game Industry*, 187–210.
23. Korean Game Industry Agency, *2007 Korean Game Whitepaper*, 271.
24. Korea Press Foundation, *Korean Media Yearbook 2005/2006* (2005). This figure also exceeds several major countries, including Japan (30,000 in 2003) and the United Kingdom (20,000 in 2002), and Canada (6,000 in 2005) see Aphra Kerr, "The Business of Making Digital Games" In *Understanding Digital Games*, eds. Jason Rutter and Jo Bryce (London: Sage, 2006), 36–57.
25. E. V. Lee and S. S. Ryu, "Information Technology Industry Forecast: Contents," *Information Technology Industry Forecast* 12 (2006), 245–277.
26. Lee and Ryu, "Information Technology Industry Forecasts: Contents."
27. Kline, Dyer-Witheford and De Peuter, *Digital Play: The Interaction of Technology, Culture, and Marketing*, 177.
28. Nick Dyer-Witheford, Mapping the Canadian Video and Computer Game Industry, 2004.
29. Joo-Han Kim, Yoon Mi Lee, Min Gyu Kim and Eun Joo Kim, "A Study on the Factors and Types of on-Line Game Addiction: An Application of the

Self-Determination Theory," *Journal of Korean Communication* 50, no. 5 (2006), 79–107.

30. Jin-Seo Cho, "Too Much Competition Drives Game Companies to Limit," *The Korea Times* November 3, 2005.
31. CJ Internet, (2007).
32. S. W. Oh, "Onmedia, Join the Game Industry," *Naeil News* 2007.
33. Kerr, *The Business of Making Digital Games*, 51
34. The Economist, "Babes with Guns: Britain's Videogame Industry," February 22, 1997, 75.
35. Jin-Seo Cho, "US Game Giant EA to Invest $100 M in Korean Game," *The Korea Times*, March 20, 2007.
36. Jin-Seo Cho, "Video Game Big 3 Geared for Battle," *The Korea Times*, February 13, 2007.
37. Dan Schiller, *How to Think about Information* (Urbana, IL: University of Illinois Press, 2007), 124.
38. Vincent Mosco, *The Political Economy of Communication* (London: Sage, 1996), 109.
39. The Information Technology and Innovation Foundation, *2008 ITIF Broadband Ranking* [2008].
40. Ministry of Information and Communication, *Broadband IT Korea Vision 2007* [2004].
41. Min-Hee Kim, "Korea to Nurture Software Industry," *The Korea Herald*, December 2, 2005.
42. Ministry of Culture and Tourism, "Game Industry Policy Exhibition (Press Release)," February 10, 2006.
43. K. J. Lee, "Game Market Watches PS2," *Financial News*, January 29, 2002.
44. Cho, *Video Game Big 3 Geared for Battle*.
45. D. Y. Jin, *Hands On/Hands Off: The Korean State and the Market Liberalization of the Communication Industry* (Cresskill, NJ: Hampton Press, in press).
46. The 1997 economic crisis severely hit the Korean economy on a large scale. Korea suffered unprecedented rates of unemployment and bankruptcies after the crisis. The immediate results of the financial crisis were the suffering of companies and workers. Before and after the crisis, several large conglomerates went bankrupt. When they failed, 3,377 medium-size and small companies collapsed and many workers lost their jobs. By the end of June 1999, the number of jobless reached 1.78 million, the highest in 13 years. This meant the unemployment rate rose sharply, from 2.6% in the fourth quarter of 1997 to 8.5% in the second quarter of 1999.
47. Jim Rohwer, "The New Net Tigers: Korea," *Fortune*, May 2000, 310.
48. K. H. Park, "Online Game Leader must Deserve its Global Leadership," *Seoul Shinmun* January 26, 2007.
49. Heejin Lee, Robert M. O'Keefe and Kyounglim Yun, "The Growth of Broadband and Electronic Commerce in South Korea: Contributing Factors," *The Information Society* 19, no. 1 (2003), 81–93.
50. In-Ho Chung, "Broadband, the Information Society, and National Systems," in *Global Broadband Battles*, ed. M. Fransman (Stanford, CA: Stanford Business Books, 2006), 95–96.
51. Jun-Sok Huhh, "Culture and Business of PC Bangs in Korea," *Games and Culture* 3, no. 1 (2008), 26–37.
52. The Economist, "Invaders from the Land of Broadband: Computer Games," December 13, 2003, 66.
53. Nae-Chan Lee, "Korea's Market-Friendly Internet Policy Spurs Broadband Boom," *The Korea Herald* June 24, 2002.

54. As cited in Kline, Dyer-Witheford and De Peuter, *Digital Play: The Interaction of Technology, Culture, and Marketing*, 190.
55. H. C. Park, "Go to the Scene of e-Sports," *Hangarae Shinmun*, August 1, 2006.
56. Cyworld is a South Korean-based social networking site, which is a combination of social networking, blogging and music and video sharing. According to Hyun-Oh Yoo, CEO of SK Communications, which owns Cyworld, the site now has 20 million users in Korea, which equates to about 40% of the country's total population. Justin Ewers, *Cyworld: Bigger than YouTube?*, Vol. 2007, US News, 2006. Retrieved July 29, 2006 from URL.
57. Bruce Wallace, "Gamer is royalty in South Korea", Los Angeles Times, March 22, 2007.
58. Larissa Hjorth, "Playing at being Mobile: Gaming and Cute Culture in South Korea," *Fibreculture*, no 8 (2006), Retrieved November 20, 2007 from http://journal.fibreculture.org/. Techno-Orientalism was used by westerners to devalue the role of eastern technocultures and Asian "satellite" modernity. From Ma (1999) in ibid.
59. An explanation of this perspective can be found in Florence Chee and Richard Smith, "Is Electronic Community an Addictive Substance? an Ethnographic Offering from the EverQuest Community" In *Interactive Convergence: Critical Issues in Multimedia*, eds. Scott P. Schaffer and Melissa Lee Price, vol. 10 (Oxford, UK: Inter-Disciplinary Press, 2005), 137–155, which looks at the North American case of the online game *EverQuest* and the idea of electronic community.
60. Jaeyeol Yee, "The Social Networks of Koreans," *Korea Journal* (Spring 2000), 325–352. The number operationalized as the proportion of actual ties among possible ones. The heterogeneity increases with network range. Heterogeneity measures are the most direct indicators of the diversity of persons an individual can contact.
61. As explained in Florence Chee, "Understanding Korean Experiences of Online Game Hype, Identity, and the Menace of the 'Wang-Tta'" (*DiGRA*, Vancouver, Canada, Simon Fraser University, 2005), the emotional stakes are even higher for males than females for playing games.
62. So much so, that there are special "couple zones" with workstations that include two computers joined with a loveseat.
63. Larissa Hjorth, "Being Real in the Mobile Reel: A Case Study on Convergent Mobile Media as Domesticated New Media in Seoul, South Korea," *Convergence: The International Journal of Research into New Media Technologies* 14 (1) (2008), 91–104.
64. KNSO, *Economically Active Population 15 Years and Over* Korea National Statistical Office, 2005.
65. There are many socio-cultural reasons for this, such as the dominance of Confucian ideology, which privileges seniority. Consequently, Korean youth typically start their careers later in life than their North American counterparts. Correlating with that characteristic is the common occurrence of Korean youth staying with and relying upon one's parents until marriage (generally occurring in the early or late twenties for females and early to late thirties for males).
66. This figure is derived from my interviews and observations of specific game players. Due to a typical lack of traceability in online/offline deals, statistical data in Korean as well as similar international studies has seemed and continues to be rather inconclusive. As data becomes more centralized, traceability will likely improve.
67. Edward Castronova, *Synthetic Worlds: The Business and Culture of Online Games* (Chicago: University of Chicago Press, 2005); Edward Castronova,

Virtual Worlds: A First-Hand Account of Market and Society on the Cyberian Frontier, Vol. 2002, Gruter Institute Working Papers on Law, Economics and Evolutionary Biology, 2001.

68. In *Lineage* the king of a castle can get taxes from users who rank lower.
69. Roger Caillois, *Man, Play, and Games* (New York: Free Press, 1961), 119.
70. Another significant reason is the prevalence of compulsory military service for most young Korean males during their early twenties. Their normal social environment becomes atomized, their educational trajectories are put on hold, and employment prospects for approximately two years and two months. During this army service, communication with one's friends and family is permitted only by written letters and 45 days of vacation, taken 10 days at a time. The service is viewed as a rite of passage into true male adulthood, with bonuses attributed to one's employment applications only after service is completed.
71. In Hwa Yi, "Korea, the Everlasting Empire in the Online World," *JoongAng Ilbo* July 21, 2006.
72. Hyun Tag Whang, "Gloomy Domestic Game Firms before EC," *Saegae Ilbo* May 6, 2006.
73. Dyer-Witheford and Sharman, *The Political Economy of Canada's Video and Computer Game Industry*, 187–210.

3 Gaming Nation
The Australian Game Development Industry[1]

Sam Hinton

In my wild erratic fancy visions come to me of Clancy
Gone a-droving 'down the Cooper' where the Western drovers go;
As the stock are slowly stringing, Clancy rides behind them singing,
For the drover's life has pleasures that the townsfolk never know.[2]

INTRODUCTION

Australia. For those who don't live here, the word conjures images of red deserts, bounding marsupials and men who wrestle with prehistoric reptiles. This is the stuff of what Russell Ward called the Australian legend,[3] an image born of white Australia that has been chiselled out of the stone of colonial settlement over the course of some 200 years. It's a compelling vision that is reinforced today through tourism campaigns and popular film culture. The Australian cultural stereotype depicted through national sporting heroes and characters like Crocodile Dundee or the late Steve Irwin does not give any hint that beneath the muddy waters of Australian culture lurks a nation of video game players.

It takes only a small amount of research to discover the terrible truth. Australians seem to love new media technologies and have taken up television, video, CD, the Internet and high definition television with gusto. Australians spend more on games than they do on music or video. According to the Interactive Entertainment Association of Australia, the game industry in Australia in 2007 generated some AUD $1.3 billion in sales,[4] with growth predicted to rise as the age of the average gamer continues to climb. The music industry, by comparison, recorded sales of AUD $460 million for 2007,[5] and the video industry reported sales just over AUD $1.2 billion.[6] There's also a suggestion that these sales are not coming from a small affluent segment of the population. According to the Interactive Entertainment Association of Australia (IEAA) some 79% of Australian households have a computer gaming device (in fact, one third of these have four or more gaming devices).[7]

The point is that from a statistical perspective at least, Australia can be described as a nation of gamers. A number of factors have conspired to create a uniquely Australian game development industry that is characterized by privately owned independent studios producing primarily overseas IP and ports. Although fresh locally developed IP is present (*Trainz*, *Ty the Tasmanian Tiger*, *Heroes of the Pacific*, *Heroes Over Europe*, *Puzzle Quest* to name only a few), Australian games companies operate at a significant disadvantage to developers in other countries owing to a number of economic, policy and geographic factors.

This chapter looks at the structure and challenges facing the Australian game industry. I argue that despite the many challenges facing the industry, the development of new technologies that favor independent and small developers, coupled with changes in the economic and political environment, may see the Australian industry well positioned for future growth.

Scott Knight and Jeffrey Brand have compiled an excellent overview of the development of the games industry in Australia for the Australian Centre for the Moving Image's *Game On!* exhibition in Melbourne in 2007/08.[8] It is not my intention to replicate their work here. It is, however, useful to outline the history they present, because it helps put the development of the Australian game industry into context.

The founding game-related company in Australia is almost certainly Melbourne House, a book publisher turned software publisher. In the early 1980s Melbourne House established Beam Software to develop new software titles for the home computer market. Beam concentrated mainly on developing titles for the home computer market. Their first successful title *The Hobbit* was published in 1982 for the Spectrum computer, and is considered to be the world's first graphical adventure game. Later titles from Beam were released for the Commodore 64, and later still, for console systems.

Beam's focus (at least until 1987) on development for personal computer systems was representative of computer game development in Australia more generally. In the early 1980s the computer game market was developing around three technologies—the console, such as the Atari 2600 and the Nintendo Entertainment System (NES), coin-operated arcade gaming, and the personal computer. The personal computer is where the majority of game development in Australia was focussed.

The main reason for this focus was likely development cost and market access. In the early 1980s until the early 1990s personal computers such as the Spectrum and the Commodore 16 and 64 (as well as a number of later models) dominated the home computer market.[9] These relatively inexpensive machines were aimed at the home market and emphasized graphics and sound, and by this subjective measure performed better for game applications than the much more expensive IBM PC, which at the time was considered a business machine and was still largely a text-based two-color machine with graphics hardware added as an expensive upgrade.

In this environment, because of the low cost of hardware and the relative simplicity of the computer systems, game development could be carried out by a small number of people for very little investment. As a result during this period, and up until the mid 1990s, PC game development was much more of a garage industry, and the barriers to entry and costs associated with development were low. First generation companies established at this time in Australia were Beam Software (1980), Strategic Studies Group (1982) and Microforte (1985).

A turning point for Australian game development seems to have occurred in the mid 1990s, when a number of companies were established. Many of these new companies grew as employees of first generation companies like Beam left to start up their own companies. Many of these companies have gone on to establish the core of the present Australian games industry.

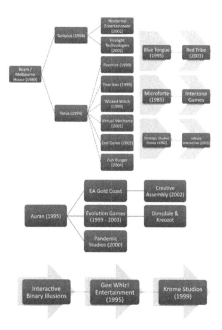

Figure 3.1 Origins of Australian game developers.[10] This Figure shows a "family tree" of Australian developers. The inter-relationship between the companies is quite important for understanding the inter-relationships that have led to the development of a local industry that is generally more collegiate than competitive.

AUSTRALIAN GAME DEVELOPMENT:
AN OVERVIEW OF THE INDUSTRY

The Australian games industry is an interesting beast, although it is quite difficult to pin down. Before going on to look at the Australian industry in any detail, it's important to establish our bearings. To do this it's useful to take a brief foray into the structure of the international industry.

In general terms, the structure of the game industry can be described as consisting of five tiers of production, comprising development, publishing, manufacturing, distribution and retail. Publishers finance game development and work with manufacturers, distributors and retailers to get the games out to the public. Publishers also handle things like marketing, public relations and generally carry a larger burden of the financial risk associated with game development. Manufacturing, distribution and retail handle the process of taking the digital assets of a game, placing them on physical media, packaging and placing in shops for consumers to purchase.

Developers are at the coal-face of the game industry. They are the programmers, artists, sound engineers, testers and project managers who weave together digital assets and ideas to produce a playable game. Developers are also generally at the bottom of the food chain in the game industry. Developers are either owned by publishers (so-called first party developers) or are independently owned and rely on publishers to get their games produced, distributed and sold (third party developers). A very few small game developers are truly independent, and finance their own titles and use the Internet for distribution and payment. In Australia there is a mix of first and third party developers, but since the demise of Melbourne House in 1999, the Australian game industry has had no local games publishing companies.

The production of games is generally divided into four kinds of development, reflecting various delivery platforms: console, PC, handheld and mobile. Aphra Kerr has pointed out that while this taxonomy is a fairly standard way of classifying games in much of the game industry literature, it is one that is becoming increasingly difficult to work with. The standard categories of console, handheld, PC and mobile obscure an increasingly diverse range of support, development and distribution models. Kerr has suggested four alternate categories of console, PC, MMOG and mini-games that are more closely aligned with the production and retail models associated with games. [11] Mini-games, which are small games typically produced for mobile or web-site deployment, are produced in less time by smaller teams and are supported by advertising, sponsorship or pay per download. While these games may be played on a PC, classifying them under the hopelessly broad banner of PC games hides an important dynamic within the industry. At the other end of the scale, the massively multiplayer online game (MMOG) *World of Warcraft* is typically classed as a PC game. Its subscription model puts it in a different category than a more traditional PC title like *Bioshock*. While I have continued to use conventional game classification categories in this chapter, the industry changes that Kerr's taxonomy points to—especially the diversity of retail and production models—have important ramifications for the Australian games industry, which I examine in more detail below.

Console game development, which is presently the main source of income for game development in Australia (see below), is significantly more expensive and convoluted than PC development. Developers who want to make a game for one of the major consoles need to be accredited by the console manufacturer and publishers need a publishing licence with the console manufacturer. In addition to this, developers need to purchase software development kits from the console manufacturer, which can cost many tens of thousands of dollars alone. To add to this, developer margins are slimmer on consoles, as the console manufacturer will take a cut of profits, which they use to offset the cost of console manufacturing. These disincentives for developing for consoles are balanced by the larger market for console games and so the greater likelihood of developing a profitable game.

The financing of game development for most games made by third party developers follows a model very similar to the book publishing industry. If a publisher decides to publish a title, they will pay the developer in non-refundable advances against projected royalties, which the developer can use to pay for development costs (which in game development is dominated by salaries). Royalties only begin to flow to the developer once sales have covered the amount given to the developer in advances. In other words, if a developer is paid AUD $200,000 in advances, the developer won't see anything more until the game has earned the developer at least AUD $200,000. This isn't the same as net profit, because there are various parts of the distribution chain—retailer, manufacturer, distributor and publisher who all take their cut of the profit. If the game is being developed for a console, then console manufacturers also get a cut of the royalties. The percentage of total royalties flowing to the developer varies according to the terms of the contract agreed to by the publisher and the developer, but is anywhere from 10 to 30%.[12] Under these circumstances, a developer who gets a 10% cut of royalties and has received AUD $200,000 in advances would need to see their game make AUD $2,000,000 in sales before they started to see any post-release royalties.

Royalties are often metered out to developers based on the successful completion of parts of the project. These 'milestones' are generally agreed on by the developer and publisher during contract negotiations. If milestones are missed the publisher may increase their involvement with the project, or may decide to pull funding from the project completely, perhaps cutting their losses, perhaps shifting development to another developer. Publishers can also pull out of a game project for other reasons. Red Mile, a publisher and the parent company of the Australian developer, Transmission Games, recently pulled the unreleased *Sin City* game from Transmission. The official reason stated was that Red Mile wanted Transmission to focus on the *Heroes Over Europe* game, due for release in early 2009. While this has few financial implications for Transmission (as the company is owned by Red Mile), it further emphasizes the relative powerlessness of the developer as well as highlighting the precarious nature of their position. For an independent developer putting all their resources into a single title with a single publisher, cancellation of the game can easily send the developer into bankruptcy.

This fraught existence for developers, combined with the economic benefits for publishers of vertical integration has seen many third party developers acquired by publishers. The increasing complexity of games developed for modern systems and the associated costs tend to exacerbate this situation, and there is an ongoing implosion of third party developers into publishers. The publishing industry is also consolidating, with publishers merging like blobs of quicksilver. One merger has seen Activision join with Vivendi to create the largest game publisher in the world.

Because of the complexity of games, developers tend to specialize in certain systems and within certain genres, and publishers will tend to award contracts to developers who have a proven track record with a certain genre. As a result, titles produced by games companies often have a consistent theme—companies that make racing games will tend to make more racing games; companies that make flight simulators will make more flight simulators, and so on.

THE AUSTRALIAN INDUSTRY

Most Australian game developers are privately owned companies, so firm data, especially financial data, is difficult to obtain. The main public sources of data are from reports prepared by the Game Developers' Association of Australia (GDAA), the Interactive Entertainment Association of Australia (IEAA) and the Australian Bureau of Statistics (ABS). Game industry websites such as Tsumea[13] and Kotaku.au[14] also provide valuable insights into the Australian developer industry, and constitute important methods of communication within the Australian game industry.

According to the Tsumea website, in 2008 there were around 70 game development studios in Australia. These studios range from the largest, Krome Studios—with studios in three Australian states and employing 350 staff[15]—to small one or two-person teams. An analysis of game development based on titles reported on company website indicates 46 of these 70 developers accounted for the development of some 523 games across a wide variety of platforms between 1995 and 2008. Around 90% of the games produced in Australia sold in overseas markets,[16] reflecting the smaller market for games in Australia due to the nation's comparatively small population.

A survey of game developers in Australia carried out by the Australian Bureau of Statistics in 2006/07 reported 45 developers with a combined income of AUD $136.9 million.[17] The sample only included businesses with a registered business number. This suggests that many of the 70 game developers listed on the Tsumea site are small part-time operations. Indeed many of them have not released any games at all. Examining some of these studios reveals numerous tiny independent shareware or browser game developers consisting of one, two or three people. Many of these companies may also have ceased operation or are in a period of extended hibernation, from which they may never wake.

The bulk of Australian development is heavily concentrated amongst the top ten game developers—both in terms of revenue and employment According to one source, in 2006 the top eight companies accounted for around 80% of industry income (Insight), or around AUD $109 million. Together, the 45 game developers included in the ABS survey employed 1,431 people, the vast majority of these employed on a full time basis (ABS, Digital Game). Based on reported staffing (gathered from interviews and websites), eight Australian developers account for 75% of game development industry employment. Krome studios (Australia's largest developer) alone employs almost 25% of the Australian game development workforce.

Income from games developed in Australia is predominantly from console games (71.1%), with personal computer titles contributing 14.6% and handheld titles contributing 11.2%. The remaining 3% came from mobile games and other unspecified formats (ABS, Digital Game). According to these figures, Australian development is dominated by production for the mainstream console market with PCs coming a distant second. However, these figures may be misleading. As console development is typically the most lucrative market for game development, income does not represent the number of titles sold, and so should not be taken as an indicator of where development activity is focussed. An analysis of games made by Australia companies between 1994 and 2008, as presented on company websites, shows that console games accounted for 29% of the titles released. The "other" category includes educational games, gambling games and games released for unspecified platforms. The breakdown of games published by Australian developers by title is summarized in Figure 3.2. What is significant here (See Figure 3.2) is the suggestion that there is a lot more mobile and handheld development going on in Australia than the ABS statistics suggest, but that it is less lucrative than console development.

The changing fortunes of Australia's founding game studio, Melbourne House, provides an informative case study of the development of the Australian game industry, and the kinds of challenges faced by developers in Australia. Melbourne House's Beam Software, established in 1983 as aforementioned, had many of its early successes with games developed for home computer systems, relatively cheap computer systems at the home market (the Sinclair, the Commodore 64, BBC Micro and so on). During the late 1980s Beam expanded into the console market, making games for the Super

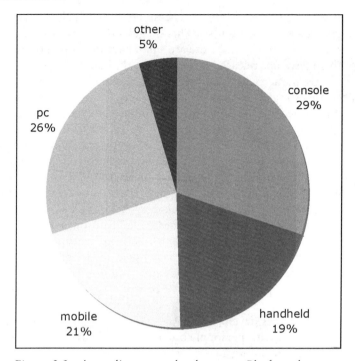

Figure 3.2   Australian game development: Platform by number of titles, 1985–2008.[18]

Nintendo Entertainment System (SNES) and then for other consoles like the Sega Saturn and the Sony PlayStation. The company was publicly listed on the Australian stock exchange in 1996, and acquired by the French publisher Infogrames in 1999. Adam Lancman, then CEO of Melbourne House attributed the need for the acquisition to the increasing complexity of developing games in next generation systems—at the time, the Sony PlayStation 2—and the need for capital to support that kind of development.[19] After the acquisition, Melbourne House's fortunes were linked to Infogrames Australia, which in 2003 was renamed to Atari Melbourne House, following a global re-branding of Infogrames subsidiaries. By 2006 Atari was in significant financial distress, and Atari Melbourne House was sold to Australian developer Krome Studios—Melbourne House had come full circle.

Melbourne House's experience is reflected in a number of Australian developers that have also been acquired by overseas publishers or developers—always on mutually agreed terms. A summary of acquisitions is presented in Table 3.1.

The likelihood of additional acquisitions into the future is quite high, as there are a number of privately owned profitable developers in Australia.

Most Australian developers contract their development services to publishers to produce games that are planned and designed elsewhere. This

Table 3.1 Acquisitions of Australian Developers

Company	Acquired by	New Name	Year
Beam	Infogrames/Atari	Infogrames Melbourne House	1999
BlueTongue	THQ	BlueTongue	2004
Irrational	Take Two	2K Australia	2005
Midway Studios Australia	Krome	Krome Adelaide	2005
Ratbag	Midway	Midway Studios Australia	2005
Atari Melbourne House	Krome	Krome Melbourne House	2006
IR Gurus	Red Mile	Transmission	2007
Pandemic	EA	Pandemic	2007

can be a lucrative strategy for third party game developers, and provides a bread-and-butter income stream. Tantalus' *Pony Friends*—one of the most successful Australian games in 2007, selling more than a million units worldwide[20]—was published by Eidos. Tantalus' involvement with *Pony Friends*—including design—was significant. It is also quite common for development studios to contract to other development companies. Half-brick Studios in Queensland, for example, has been involved in work for titles developed primarily by Krome. Another important way for Australian developers—especially smaller companies—to make money is through doing "ports"—re-writing games released on one platform so that they can be run on a different platform as well. This kind of development work generally involves little design work and is often paid for at a fixed rate by a publisher. The danger of relying too heavily on these strategies for making money is that developers may find themselves losing work through outsourcing to cheaper labor from emerging markets in China or India.

INDUSTRY CHALLENGES

The Australian game development industry faces a number of challenges related to geographic, economic and political factors. Australia's geographic position places it near Asia, which boasts some of the largest games markets in the world, with huge potential for growth into the future. While this market has a great deal of potential, language and cultural differences present a significant barrier for Australian companies. As a result, markets for Australian games tend to be traditional markets—the United States, Canada and Europe—where they compete with well established and (in Canada at least) government supported development industries. The local Australian market for computer games is limited by Australia's relatively small population.

In discussions with Australian game companies, a number of companies noted that publishers are often wary of getting game development work done by Australian companies, due to the distances involved. There is a perception that North American publishers, for instance, are more comfortable using local developers because if something goes wrong with the project, it's easier for a representative to visit the company. Kevin McIntosh, a producer at the Brisbane-based Torus games said in a 2006 interview with the online *PALGN* magazine:

> The distance has worked against us in the past in securing the bigger projects. Publishers feel more secure knowing that a developer is local so they can visit easily and step in to fix a project.[21]

Steve Fawkner from Infinite Interactive noted the same concerns in an interview in 2008.[22] Apparently, even in the high-tech gaming business, face-to-face meetings still trump electronic communication when there's real money at stake.

Another challenge for Australian developers is securing capital to support the development of original titles. As a result, the vast majority of investment in game development in Australia comes from overseas publishers, which can be harder for Australian companies to secure than for companies located in the same country as the publisher. Despite this, there have been a number of successful original Australian titles. Perhaps the most self-consciously Australian of these titles is Krome's *Ty the Tasmanian Tiger*. Transmission Games' World War Two flight simulator, *Heroes of the Pacific*, is another example of a successful original Australian title.

While there have been some notable successes of original Australian titles, there have also been some very significant failures which underline the risks associated with financing game development. Australian developer Auran, which had successes with a number of titles including one entirely original game, *Trainz*, embarked on a major development project in 2005 to develop a massively multiplayer online game called *Fury*. The game was slated as a massively multiplayer online player versus player game. This differed from other MMOs like *World of Warcraft* in its focus on player versus player combat instead of story-based quests set in a world that the player explores cooperatively with other players. *Fury* fell flat on release, first failing to attract subscribers, then continuing to fail to attract subscribers even with a AUD $4 million investment of Chinese money.[23] A desperate attempt to entice players by offering free play and cash prizes was not enough to save

Fury and in December 2007 Auran laid off its entire development team. By August 2008 Auran was forced to shut down the *Fury* servers permanently. The cost of development ran into the millions and essentially cost Auran its game development business.

While capital for the development of original titles can be difficult for Australian companies to raise, a skills shortage in Australia makes it difficult for Australian developers to take on larger more complex projects. Industry leaders believe that the skills shortage is not simply that the industry can't find enough people interested in developing games. What's lacking is people with experience and skills to manage larger, more complex projects. Infinite Interactive's Steve Fawkner believes and sees the skills shortage in Australia as the major problem facing the industry:

> I think our biggest one is the skills shortage. You might hear a lot of developers say that the tax incentives are the biggest issue. They're certainly an issue [. . .] but if we don't solve our skills issue, it ain't going to make any difference if we've got tax breaks, because we haven't got enough people to do the projects.[24]

If Australian game developers face economic issues, the problems they face when dealing with the Australian Government are also significant. At a Federal level, games generally seem to be regarded negatively by Australian policy makers, and are tarred with a stereotypical image of computer games as a solitary anti-social male activity. There does not seem to be much evidence that this perception is changing, despite a concerted effort from the game industry's main representative body, the aforementioned Game Developers' Association of Australia (GDAA). At the state level, recognition of the games industry as a developing industry is uneven. The state governments of Victoria and Queensland have been the first to recognize the potential of game development and have moved to provide various kinds of financial support for game development.[25]

At the Federal level, there continues to be virtually no recognition of the game industry. Two issues in particular have been the focus of attention for the GDAA: the unavailability of tax incentives and the lack of an adult game rating classification. In Australia the film industry has long enjoyed subsidies from the Australian government. In 2006, a new system was introduced to provide eligible film production with a 40% tax incentive. In the same year the GDAA made a representation to the then Minister of Communication, Information Technology and the Arts, asking for the incentive to be expanded to include games. The answer from the government was a firm no. The Minister's response betrayed a fundamental misunderstanding of the nature not only of the game industry, but also of new media industries more generally.

According to the Minister, the games industry would benefit from flow-on effects from the incentives enjoyed by the film industry. This curious perspective presupposes an overlap between the two industries that simply doesn't exist; the Minister might just have well suggested that the print publishing industry would benefit from flow on effects in the same way. As if to underline the Minister's point, when the Sydney-based special effects studio Animal Logic decided to branch into the game industry, they chose to set up in Los Angeles rather than opening an Australian office.[26]

Another factor that reflects the general political attitude to games in Australia is the game rating system, administered by the Australian Classification Board (formerly the Office of Film and Literature Classification). Prior to 1995 there was no classification system for games in Australia. In 1995, as a result of a rash of media outrage and moral panic raised by the games *Mortal Kombat* and *Nighttrap*, the Australian Government moved to institute a classification system for games as an extension of the film classification system.

Currently in Australia there are four classifications for games, ranging from G, suitable for a general audience, to MA15+, which is considered suitable only for people who are over the age of 15. These games are considered unsuitable for people under 15 years of age and are restricted for sale or viewing by under 15s not accompanied by a parent or adult guardian. The problem with this system is the lack of an R classification rating. Any game submitted to the Classification Board that does not fit within the definition of an MA15+ title must be refused classification, which effectively bans them from sale. This is a legal ban and people who are caught trying to import the game can be prosecuted, facing fines and possible imprisonment.

The classification system is applied stringently, and games submitted to the Classification Board for review are routinely refused classification. This usually results in the game publisher modifying the game to make it fit within the MA15+ classification guidelines, and then resubmitting the game for classification. In most cases games resubmitted are given an MA15+ classification. Games that have refused classification include some major releases. Games that have been refused classification (and later given an MA15+ after modification) include *Fallout 3* and *Dark Sector* to name only two major titles released in 2007/08.

The lack of an R rating classification for games stands in stark contrast to film, suggesting a fundamentally different attitude from the Australian Government towards the two kinds of cultural production. An R18+ classification for film implies that some films have content that, while not being appropriate for minors, nonetheless have cultural value that outweighs concerns over the content. The lack of a similar rating for games reflects an attitude that games have no significant cultural value for adults, and are inherently childish. This runs against the Classification Board's own principles that state, in part, "adults should be able to read, hear and see what they want."[27]

Both the lack of Federal Government support for the industry and the need for reform in the classification system suggest that the game industry has not yet been able to overcome its image problem and is not being taken seriously by policy makers. This is difficult to understand given that the local game development industry attracts more than AUD \$136 million annually, and games are becoming an increasingly popular cultural activity. The lack of perceived cultural value in the game industry is also a problem for the industry as it aims for more government support.

Nevertheless, the industry is still developing when placed alongside comparable cultural industries. For example, the game development industry's operating profits in 2006/07 of only AUD \$8.5 million compares to AUD \$92 million for the film production industry in 02/03[28] (which at the time of writing represents the most recent statistics on Australian film), and AUD \$152.1 million for book publishing in 03/04.[29] It is important to note, however, that the film and broadcast industries in Australia do enjoy substantial government support—totalling AUD \$1.2 billion over the period 2000 to 2007. Little of this Federal government support is available to the games industry, and even then, eligible interactive media only garnered 0.3% of the total support for the film industry over the same period.[30]

INTO THE FUTURE

The Australian games industry will be likely to encounter changing market conditions as international and Australian developments change the technological, economic and social spaces in which the industry operates.

One of the major developments may well be the increasing importance of online distribution. Games have been sold online for a long time. Shareware and web-based downloads have been an important way of recouping some costs of development for small independent developers. However, in more recent years, online purchasing of games has been available through dedicated online systems designed specifically to manage payment and delivery of game content.

The first of these systems, Steam, was released by game developer Valve Software in 2002, but achieved its highest visibility with the release of Valve's flagship game *Half-Life 2*, in November 2004. Although *Half-Life 2* was available as physical media for purchase in retail outlets, it required activation using the Steam network after installation or it could not be played. The title could also be downloaded and purchased online via Steam.

While PC-based online distribution systems like Steam show potential for growth, the most valuable market for games is the console market. The current generation of consoles—the Sony PlayStation 3, Microsoft Xbox 360 and Nintendo Wii—are all network-capable, providing their owners with a port that can be plugged into a home broadband connection. Once connected to the Internet, each of the three platforms links the player into proprietary online environments[31] which players can access to download patches, previews and game content.[32] Payment for this content is done by way of a point system on the Wii and the XBox 360 (which can be purchased with credit card or with game cards bought through bricks and mortar retail outlets). On the PlayStation 3, payments are made by transferring funds to the PlayStation Network account via credit card. Once credit has been transferred to the online environment, players can use their credit to make their purchases.

I use the phrase "game content" when referring to purchasing from these online environments because it is intentionally broad. One of the features emerging from online distribution is new modes for the release and sale of games. While many games are available for purchase and download online, genres of games that are episodic or which provide additional content for a small fee are becoming more popular.

Episodic games are games that are released in parts. Each part extends the original game and may cost less than a full game to purchase. The value of this system for developers and publishers is quite clear: It allows for the production of smaller games that can be produced more quickly than a full game and which can be withdrawn from the market if they are not successful. Episodic games that prove successful can entice players to spend more on the game than they would if the game were released in one package. Another feature of games linked to online purchasing systems is the availability of premium content—material that is not in the basic game, but can be added by paying an additional small fee.

The impact of online distribution is already becoming clear in the music industry, which, due to the smaller size of content, probably provides a good indicator of what we might be able to expect for games and other media assuming bandwidth continues to grow with prices remaining the same. While physical media is still the major source of music purchasing in Australia, it is the speed at which online distribution is growing that draws attention. In 2007, some 17.6 millions music tracks were digitally delivered to Australia users, a 60% rise over the previous year (ARIA). Overall in Australia, in 2007, just under 10% of total music sales were online, double the amount from 2006.[33]

Already we are beginning to see rapid uptake of online game purchasing. Sony reported in 2007 that its PlayStation Network has more than 9.8 million accounts, and that something in the order of 17 million DVDs worth of data had been distributed across the network. What's more surprising is that this represented a registration rate of only 45% indicating there are many people with PlayStation consoles who have not yet connected to Sony's online system.[34]

The move to an online distribution and purchasing system for gaming is likely to have a significant impact on the shape of the game industry. By moving into online distribution and thereby doing away with manufacturing, distribution and retail, publishers are able to assert more control over the game production cycle while reducing costs. However, the number of publishers with the ability to establish and support large online purchasing and distribution systems will likely be somewhat smaller than present, and the savings associated with online distribution will marginalize publishers who do not distribute games online.

If online distribution does prove to be a major source of change in the game industry, then there are significant ramifications for the Australian industry. While publishers stand to gain the most from online distribution, opportunities are opened up for developers, too—especially small developers looking to take innovative original titles to large mainstream audiences. Because the Australian game industry is made up of a lot of small independent developers, online distribution potentially represents a new world of opportunity.

One of the major benefits of online distribution for small developers is the possibility of higher royalties flowing from game sales. As previously noted, game developers can expect to see only small portion of the royalties from game sales, and only after any advances have been covered. With lower costs for distribution, manufacturing and retail, the publisher can be more lavish with developer royalty payments, making development much more viable. Additionally, because costs of distribution are lower, publishers are more likely to give smaller titles a chance—there is little risk associated with distributing a virtually unknown new game.

Alongside the possible ramifications of online distribution for the Australian market, the changing demographics of the game market also opens potential benefits for Australian developers. An important emerging market for games is mobile/handheld and casual games. In some ways mobile and handheld games are like the golden days of early PC gaming. Games can be made by small teams, and do not require a large amount of initial investment capital. Developers building games for Apple's iPhone, for example, can develop a game using a free SDK, and get 70% of sales revenue.[35] This is a very enticing prospect for small independent or garage developers, and has attracted interest from a number of well established game developers.[36]

There are a number of Australian developers who have specialized in the development of mobile or handheld games. Australian Developers like Firemint, Iron Monkey, Kukan, Wicked Witch and Viva la Mobile are among the most prolific Australian development studios and have all established game development strategies that focus almost entirely on the mobile phone and handheld market. Australian developer Firemint has released *The Sims DJ* for the iPod Touch, and is developing at least one game for the iPhone as well.

While technological change will have significant and potentially positive impact on the Australian game development industry, other factors will also play a major role in determining the fate of the Australian industry. Economic factors will continue to play a role. The reliance of overseas investment in Australian game production means that a downturn in the

global economy could make obtaining development contracts more difficult for Australian developers as international sources of funding shrink.
Furthermore, like the film industry (and export industries more generally),
Australian developers benefit from a weak Australian dollar. Favorable
exchange rates for US currency make Australian game development more
attractive to US investors simply because it costs less to produce Australian
games. If the Australian currency maintains a high value against the green-
back, it will also be difficult for Australian developers to pick up overseas
publishing deals.

Finally, policy decisions are likely to play an important role in the continued viability of the Australian game industry. Despite their present reluctance to embrace the industry, it seems likely that it will only be a matter
of time before the Australian Government responds to demands of support from the Australian game development industry. Game players will
get older, and more representative of the general population. More people
will play games as the industry matures and begins appealing to a broader
cross-section of the society and even politicians themselves will increasingly become game players. The challenge for the games industry is not just
in getting the Australian Government to support the industry, but also in
making sure any such support is carefully targeted.

A number of game developers are wary of government subsidies that
could make Australia an attractive site for overseas publishers to establish
a base, and with their multi-national power, effectively kill off the local
game development industry. In Canada, government subsidies for the game
industry has attracted a great deal of investment, but much of the game
industry investment has come from international companies like Electronic
Arts and Ubisoft who have established large publishing and development
studios in Canada.[37] In Australia such overseas investment would make it
even harder for local studios to attract skilled staff, and some of the larger
studios—like Krome—could be swallowed up by international publishers
coming to roost in a tax-friendly Australia.

CONCLUSIONS

Australia is a nation of gamers. We enjoy games, and while they seem at odds
with romantic ideas about drovers and the "real Australia," they are nonetheless a growing cultural and economic phenomenon that should not continue
to be ignored by policy makers, lest they fall out of touch with the electorate.

It is probably this interest in games, coupled with a desire to not just consume, but also to produce, that has led to the development of the Australian
game industry. It is an industry that is in many ways unremarkable—its size
and prosperity pale to insignificance beside the economic backbone of the
Australian resources industry; the titles produced in Australia are similar to
titles produced in other countries like the United States, Canada, France and

the United Kingdom, although they are fewer and generally smaller. What is remarkable about the Australian game industry is that it exists at all. Much like the native fauna and flora of the Australian continent, Australian game developers have had to learn how to make the most of a difficult environment. As this environment changes, new opportunities and challenges will appear which no doubt local developers will make the most of.

Technological change is rapid and uncertain, but it appears that a number of developments—such as online distribution and the rise of mobile and casual gaming—represent significant shifts in the industry globally that may have beneficial consequences for Australian game developers. More inscrutable even than technological change, global economic conditions are also likely to have a large impact on the fortunes of the industry. The Australian government certainly has a role to play in the future of the Australian game industry, although what role and how it should best be played is a matter for careful consideration.

NOTES

1. I would like to thank Jodie Vaile for her assistance in compiling and collating statistics on Australian game companies and their titles.
2. Andrew Barton Patterson, "Clancy of the Overflow," in *Poetry in* T. Inglis Moore (ed) *Australia: v1 from ballads to Brennan* (Sydney: Angus and Robertson, 1964), 108.
3. Russell Ward, *The Australian Legend* (Melbourne: Oxford University Press, 1966).
4. Interactive Entertainment Association of Australia, "Skyrocketing Sales for Australian Gaming Industry in 2007." Retrieved 19 September 2008 from http://www.ieaa.com.au/news/pdf/Sales%20figures%202007%20Release.pdf.
5. Australian Recording Industry Association, "ARIA releases 2007 wholesale music figures." Retrieved 19 September 2008 from http://www.aria.com.au/pages/ARIAreleases2007wholesalemusicsalesfigures.htm hereafter cited in text.
6. Australian Film Commission, "Get the picture: video." Retrieved 19 September 2008 from http://www.afc.gov.au/gtp/wvanalysis.html . Although it should be noted that games cost more than albums, and so sales figures do not necessarily reflect popularity. In 2007, 32 million music CDs were sold, and an additional 17.6 million online purchases were made. Over the same period, Australians purchased some 15.4 million games. In 2007 Americans purchases 231.5 million games, which on a per capita basis is very comparable to Australia (0.76 for the United States compared with 0.77 for Australia).
7. Jeffrey E. Brand, "Interactive Australia 2007: Facts about the Australian computer and videogame industry," Interactive Entertainment Association of Australia (2007). Retrieved 19 September 2008 from http://www.ieaa.com.au/research/Interactive%20Australia%202007.pdf.
8. Scott Knight and Jeffrey E. Brand, "History of Game Development in Australia," Australian Centre for the Moving Image (2007). Retrieved 19 September 2008 from http://www.acmi.net.au/global/docs/games_history_australia.pdf.
9. Jeremy Reimer, "Total share: 30 years of personal computer market share figures," Ars Technica (2005). Retrieved 19 September 2008 from http://arstechnica.com/articles/culture/total-share.ars/.

10. This image was taken from the Tsumea website at http://tsumea.com.au/ and is reproduced here with the permission of Souri, the author of the image.
11. Aphra Kerr, "Spilling Hot Coffee? Grand Theft Auto as contested cultural product," in *A Strategy Guide for Studying the Grand Theft Auto Series*, ed. N. Garretts (Jefferson, North Carolina: MacFarland Press, 2006). Retrieved 19 September 2008 from http://eprints.nuim.ie/archive/00000436/.
12. There is no precise figure here. Various sources provide a range of figures, but there seems to be a strong consensus that 10% is at the low end of the royalties scale, and 30% is at the high end. See, for example Allan Behr and Katherine M. Wallace, "Negotiating Development Contracts," International Game Developers Association. Retrieved 19 September 2008 from http://www.igda. org/articles/behr-wallace_contracts.php and Erik Bethke, *Game Development and Production* (Piano, Tex: Wordware Publishing, 2003), 16.
13. Tsumea. Retrieved 19 September 2008 from http://tsumea.com.au/.
14. Kotaku Australia. Retrieved 19 September 2008 from http://www.kotaku. com.au/.
15. Mark Bozon, "IGN Interviews Krome Studios," article on IGN.com posted 15 August, 2008. Retrieved 19 September 2008 from http://au.wii.ign.com/ articles/899/899438p1.html
16. Insight Economics. "Australian Electronic Game Industry Profile," November 2006. Retrieved 19 September 2008 from http://www.gdaa.com.au/docs/ GDAA_Industry_Profile_Report_221106.pdf hereafter cited in text.
17. Australian Bureau of Statistics. *Digital Game Development Services, Australia, 2006–07.* (Canberra: Commonwealth of Australia, 2008). Hereafter cited in text.
18. These figures should be used as a general guide only. The numbers were obtained by examining the websites of 70 companies identified as Australian game developers, and recording the number of games each developer has published. Some developers do not list all their titles, while others list titles they participated in producing, which may lead to double-counting.
19. Jason Hill, "House of fun no more?" *The Age* Screenplay Blog, posted 17 July 2006. Retrieved 19 September 2008 from, http://blogs.theage.com.au/ screenplay/archives/gaming_culture/002580.html.
20. Jason Hill, "Developing Dreams," *The Age* Screenplay Blog, posted 30 April 2008. Retrieved 19 September 2008 from, http://blogs.theage.com.au/ screenplay/archives//009324.html.
21. Luke van Leuveren, "Torus Games Interview," article on the PAL Gaming Network posted on 26 October 2006. Retrieved 19 September 2008 from, http://palgn.com.au/article.php?id=5564 .
22. Glen McLeod-Thorpe, "Part Two of Our Steve Fawkner Interview," article on the PAL Gaming Network posted 15 September 2008. Retrieved 19 September 2008 from http://palgn.com.au/article.php?id=12740 hereafter cited in text.
23. Jason Dobson, "Auran gets $3.2mil CDC investment for Fury," article on Gamasutra posted 30 March 2007. Retrieved 19 September 2008 from http://www.gamasutra.com/php-bin/news_index.php?story=13347.
24. McLeod-Thorpe, "Part Two of Our Steve Fawkner Interview."
25. In Victoria, the State Government's key body for supporting the industry is Multimedia Victoria (http://www.mmv.vic.gov.au/) which has assisted the industry through providing developers with console development kits, helping game studios attend overseas game exhibitions and trade shows, funding a motion capture studio at Deakin University, and by providing financial support for the Games Developer's Association of Australia and local games industry conferences and events.

The Queensland Government has provided similar incentives through the Information Industries Bureau (http://www.iib.qld.gov.au), offering support for Queensland developers to attend trade shows overseas and in Australia. A package announced in 2003 provided AUD$800,000 in government funding over four years for the game industry, much of it to support industry promotion activities noted above. Queensland Minister for Small Business, Information Technology Policy and Multicultural Affairs, "Smart State kickstart for $25 million games fund," ministerial press release, 7 November, 2007. Retrieved 19 September 2008 from: http://www.cabinet.qld.gov.au/MMS/StatementDisplaySingle.aspx?id=43428.

26. Jason Hill, "The Logic behind tax breaks," *Sydney Morning Herald* Screenplay blog, posted 16 June 2008. Retrieved 19 September 2008 from http://blogs.smh.com.au/screenplay/archives//018877.html.

27. Commonwealth of Australia. "Guidelines for the Classification of Films and Computer Games." (Canberra: Attorney General's Department 2008). Retrieved 19 September 2008 from http://www.comlaw.gov.au/ComLaw/legislation/legislativeinstrumentcompilation1.nsf/framelodgmentattachments/6C888688A3BBD40ACA2574120004F72A

28. Australian Bureau of Statistics, "8679.0—Television and Film Production, Australia, 2002–03," (Canberra: Commonwealth of Australia, 2004).

29. Australian Bureau of Statistics, "1363.0–Book Publishers, Australia, 2003–04," (Canberra: Commonwealth of Australia, 2005).

30. Australian Film Commission, "Income and expenditure of federal film agencies (actual dollars)." Retrieved 19 September 2008 from http://www.afc.gov.au/gtp/govtfunddata01.html. It's not clear how or whether this support is included in ABS income calculations for the film industry, but in 02/03 government support amounted to AUD $173.3 million, AUD $81 million more than the industry's net operating income for the same period.

31. PlayStation 3—PlayStation Network; Wii—Wii Shop Channel; XBox 360—Xbox Live.

32. These console-enabled environments alone demand further study because they have implications for the use of media in the home that goes well beyond gaming. On the Xbox 360's online environment (XBox Live), it is also possible to purchase movies, TV shows and music videos that are downloaded to the XBox's internal hard disk and can then be viewed using the machine. This, coupled with the machine's ability to play back high definition DVDs, indicates that there is a lot more going on with game consoles than just games—but this is beyond the scope of the present discussion.

33. International Federation of the Phonographic Industry, "Music Market Data for 2006," May 2007. Retrieved 19 September 2008 from http://www.ifpi.org/content/library/music%20market%20sales%20data%202006.pdf.

34. Kazuo Hirai, "PlayStation Business Review", Sony Computer Entertainment, 2008. Retrieved 19 September 2008 from http://www.sony.net/SonyInfo/IR/info/Strategy/pdf/presen_03.pdf.

35. Apple, "iPhone Developer Program—3. Distribute Your Application." Retrieved 19 September 2008 from http://developer.apple.com/iphone/program/distribute.html

36. Most notably, the major PC title *Spore* released an iPhone version of the game, *Spore Origins*. Other industry figures like John Carmack (of Doom/Quake fame) have noted interest in developing for the iPhone.

37. Nick Dyer-Witheford and Zena Sharman, "The Political Economy of Canada's Video and Computer Game Industry," *Canadian Journal of Communication* 30 (2005): 187–210.

4 The Dynamics of New Media Globalization in Asia

A Comparative Study of the Online Gaming Industries in South Korea and Singapore

Peichi Chung

INTRODUCTION

In an age of globalization, convergence occurs across various levels.[1] Within global markets, economic and technological convergence operates conspicuously, while being challenged by social and cultural divergence. This is particularly the case in the global world of online gaming. In debates surrounding globalization and notions of nation-state, two poles can be found—on one side, theorists argue that global flows are eroding traditional nation-state boundaries; on the other side, theorists posit that globalization is further etching borders, creating "enclave" societies. These debates are especially prevalent in the stage of transnational gaming companies and their relationship to state and IT techno-national policies.

This chapter engages in the theoretical debate of the competition between nation-state and transnational media companies. The purpose is to study the complexity of globalization by examining the dynamics of online gaming industries in Asia. This chapter moves beyond two poles of analysis and proposes a contextualized research framework to understand globalization at a full scale. John Urry mentions that globalization reflects complex network systems that are non-linear and fluid.[2] As each network has different factors contributing to the global emergence of its own, the presentation of globalization varies at the local level. For instance, in certain globalization processes, the government plays a pivotal role in determining whether a country should move toward integration, disintegration or fragmentation.[3] While most of the time globalization blurs national boundaries and leads to the rise of transnational states,[4] transnational states often work with transnational corporations to create global hegemony. With convergence technology, globalization also becomes a culture of speed.[5] The feature of immediacy in information technology guarantees the metropolis success in the global economy.

In order to address the disparity of views on globalization, this chapter will focus upon two divergent examples of new media industries in the region—South Korea and Singapore. While South Korea shows a model of a new media industry that exports its local product globally, Singapore presents a model of new media industry that is based upon collaboration between the local government and multinational game companies. Singapore and South Korea are two countries in Asia that achieve high broadband penetration development. By discussing these two examples, the chapter aims to examine the type of globalization practices that the countries have created. In turn, this chapter will sketch out the meaning of cultural globalization and evaluate the influence of convergence technology in the emerging new media economy of Asia.

The chosen case studies exemplify two leading Asian tigers that are basking in the success in digital development. Both countries are known globally for their booming digital industries, denoted by their high ratings in digital creation and literacy.[6] In 2007, South Korea was listed as number nine, and Singapore was number eighteen, in the list of countries with highest broadband penetration rate.[7] The significance of the digital development in both South Korea and Singapore is that various social groups are able to reclaim alternative social space in the society. For instance, South Korea is strong in online gaming sector and mobile communication. Both technological platforms offer new spaces of sociality for the youth to gain social capital and engage with the politics of individualism.[8] In Singapore, the digital development opens up space for digital media artists to reconstruct their social position as independent entrepreneurs. These artists become cultural producers representing voices from the local digital media art scene of Singapore.[9] The result of this emergence is that new media technology becomes a site of cultural practice that allows new media artists to participate in the state's development of a homegrown creative industry.

The chapter is divided into four sections. First, the chapter will focus on the theory of globalization and the role of cultural policy in the global information economy. I will then discuss cultural policies in the establishment of online gaming industries in both South Korea and Singapore. Secondly, the chapter evaluates the influence of South Korean cultural policy based upon the discussion on the process of globalization among local firms in its domestic online gaming industry. Thirdly, the chapter examines the globalization process of Singapore by comparing and contrasting the industry structure to that of South Korea. I discuss the industry dynamics shaped by actors such as the Singapore state, transnational media companies, local firms and international creative talents. Lastly, the chapter concludes with discussion on the phenomenon of the state market as a response to the concept of global complexity in the theory of globalization.

The study is based upon in-depth interviews that were conducted in Seoul, South Korea, and Singapore from 2006 to 2007. Fieldwork data includes 20 interviews with government officials, managers of online gaming companies and public interest groups in South Korea. It also covers 26 interviews with government officials, local digital media artists, international game programmers and managers from local and transnational game companies in Singapore. Pseudonyms are used to protect the privacy of the interviewees in this chapter.

GLOBALIZATION AND CULTURAL POLICY

Most of the literature in media production discusses the emergence of a media industry from the perspective of organization.[10] The success of a media industry has been based upon the productivity of transnational media corporation or small and medium sized media companies. Such focus is discussed at length in the context of the United States (particularly California), United Kingdom, Canada, France and Australia. In traditional media industries, local firm and production labor are important players in establishing a successful media city in either France or the United States.[11] For instance, Hollywood represents the most successful example of global media conglomeration. The worldwide box office success of Hollywood since the early 2000s confirms the power of the six US film studios in attracting viewers across various cultural backgrounds in the global film markets.[12]

In creative industries, government, small media firm and creative talent become emerging actors in the new media production system. As creative talents are increasingly mobile due to globalization, small firms also become alternative media institutions that are compatible to compete and collaborate with transnational media companies by producing value added products in the global market. The emergence of both global creative talent and small new media firms reflects positive changes in the existing power structure between transnational media companies and the local state. In the global culture industry, big media corporations dominate the market and create successful branding effects. However, media experiences from consumers in different regions still reflect the importance of local characteristics in media audience consumption in the global market.[13]

There is a lack of focus on the context of Asia where the development of new media industries involves state and its collaboration with local firms, transnational media companies and creative talents. One of the challenges that the state faces in today's media globalization is that citizens predominantly engage their media consumption activities in deregulated, privatized and liberalized environments. In an age of the "prosumer," people produce and consume products and services outside the monetary system.[14] As the global market structure is changed from the sole dominance of transnational corporation or transnational state to a much diverse situation, citizens now are no longer passive consumers. They produce media messages by writing news blogs to participate in civic journalism. Consumers nowadays become both active producers and users. They engage in productive content creation through acts of produsage.[15] The freedom exercised in online publication and sharing of creative content challenges the existing power structure in either state or corporate control.

Globalization scholars argue that the social and economic forces determining where capital flows and how labor markets develop are increasingly being characterized by *denationalization*.[16] The essence of globalization is global capitalism, which has superseded the nation-state of globalization.[17] The state now faces challenges from two sides: From a top-down view, the state has a weakening role in national development because its decision making is now bound by compulsory regulation determined by multilateral entities. From a grass-roots position, the state also receives restrictions from various social actors as they are grouped into broad categories encompassing non-governmental organizations that closely participate in government activities.[18]

Cultural policy is a mean of governance that shapes a particular type of media industry for citizens. The government establishes social contract with the public through media regulation.[19] The all-pervasive role of the media industries has far reaching effects on artistic, cultural and government practices; cultural policy often works to reflect social interactions in a society.[20] According to Toby Miller, cultural and artistic activities fostered by the state often maintain various identities that constitute its citizenship.[21] The formation of cultural citizenship through cultural regulation can have several purposes. That is, cultural policy that promotes establishment of a cultural economy based upon advertising leads to a form of citizenship based upon purchase of commodities.[22] The advertising can also encourage certain form of nationalism through promotion of the collective consumption of certain commercial products in the society.[23]

In South Korea, cultural policy achieves cultural regionalization through the popularity of the Korean Wave.[24] This phenomenon has seen in Korean products such as TV dramas and films taking on forms of cultural capital in the region.[25] The Korean state has played a significant role in developing broadband services in the ICT industry.[26] The advanced Internet infrastructure benefits the Korean online gaming industry in a way that the majority of online users play games easily with broadband access either at home or at *PC bangs* (PC rooms). It is argued that the massive growth of the online gaming industry is a result from the growth of *PC bangs* with broadband.[27] *PC bangs* not only offer a socializing place for gamers to meet online and offline. They also work closely with Korean game publishers to form business.[28] In all, through fostering and supporting domestic media industries such as television, film and ICT, the South Korean government has secured a role for Korean products in the construction of regionalization in Asia.

The Korean Wave is a result of the local media industry responding to media liberalization—this is exemplified in case of the success of Korean online game products in Asia. The country smoothly moves from the global technological innovation center to global cultural "soft power" with the fast spread of consumer support of South Korean digital media products in the

Asia-Pacific.[29] These cultural trends, and the corresponding market convergence, reflect a response in the region to the role of globalization from the
1990s onwards.[30] For the Korean policy makers, integrating film, television
and online game businesses into global market was the only solution for
Korean media industries to survive in the country's trend of globalization.[31]
Even as early as 1994, South Korea was establishing cultural policy that
addressed globalization; symbolized as the beginning of the South Korean
globalization (*segyewa*) policy by President Kim Young Sam.[32] While the
transnational companies started to invest in Korean film industries in mid-
1990s, it became pivotal that the Korean government collaborated with the
domestic film companies to promote local film industry.

In the online gaming sector, two specific cultural policies contribute to
the development of online gaming industry in South Korea: the military
exemption program and the e-sport promotion policy. Both policies were
employed by the Ministry of Culture and Tourism, a government agency
that designs the cultural policy of Korean Wave. The first military exemption program began in the mid-1990s when the online game industry was
at its early stage of development. This policy allowed talented programmers and engineers to serve their military services in private game companies.[33] The training they received in game companies provided young
talents industry experiences before they entered the workplace. This policy
also benefited the industry by offering timely supply of game talents to the
online game industry. E-sport promotion is another cultural policy that
shows the government's intent to engage with the online gaming industry. In Chapter 2, Jin and Chee mention that the increasing popularity of
e-sports and professional gamers attract the attention of the mainstream
Korean youth. The government follows these public trends and supports
efforts to establish a game market base through the promotion of healthy
game culture in the local Korean society.

In addition, Korea's policy on the local new media industry was strongly
informed and supported by sophisticated government IT policy that insisted
on high investment in IT infrastructure and offered funds to Internet Service
Providers. The government's neoliberal policies created deregulated environment that allowed fierce competition among domestic telecommunication
companies. As these companies improve their services to gain customer support, the well developed broadband services also lead to the rapid growth
of e-commerce. *PC bangs* provided a key role in distribution networks of
online game companies in the domestic market. This stable network contributed to the growth of Korean game companies like NCsoft and Nexon
as revenues collected from the domestic market in Korea provided these
companies with a veritable backbone to enter the global market.

Figure 4.1 shows the impact of the government's IT policy on the online
game market in Korea. The figure also shows that online games such as *Lineage*, *Fortress 2 Blue* and *Mu Online* reached higher numbers of concurrent
users when broadband penetration reached a higher amount of Internet

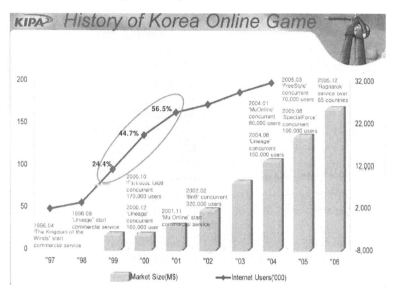

Figure 4.1 History of Korea online games. Source: NIDA (National Internet Development Agency, www.nida.or.kr).

users from 1999 to 2006. That is, in 1999 when the Internet penetration rate reached 24.4%, the online game market was set to exponentially expand. The online game market size rapidly increased from a total worth value of $29 million to $160 million, when the penetration rate reached 56% in 2001 that constituted more than 22 million Internet users in Korea. The rationale for the government to focus on the technological aspects of the online gaming industry is revealed in the following interview:

> The government assumes that whenever broadband technology is ready, the game market will be there. Our ministry focuses on the technological side, developing the infrastructure including broadband and wireless broadband in the future. We also build up specific industry technology like gaming engine and computer graphics. We do R&D to help the game industry. We try to trigger the demand part of the industry. Our support includes not only game industry, but also digital content industry and IT industry (Dr. Chong. Deputy Director. Software Industry Promotion Division. Ministry of Information and Communication, interview with the author, June 12, 2006).

In Singapore, cultural policy focuses upon economic expansion in order to make the country competitive both in the region and globally. The government concentrates on both the economy and technology with particular focus on attracting foreign talent and overseas capital to Singapore. This use of cultural policy started in 1985 when the government showed the first attempt to acknowledge the significance of art and culture in its political agenda.[35] The Singaporean government prioritizes the nation's economic prosperity and intends to use culture, art and creativity to build up the nation's competitive ability in the global economy.[35]

In 1989, the advisory council in the economic committee of the Singapore government produced a report that set up the blueprint for cultural policy in the country. The outcome was that National Art Council (NAC) and National Heritage Board (NHB) were established to direct the development of aspects of the arts in Singapore. In the 1990s, the government adopted a much rigorous attitude to pursue economic potential of the arts by setting up media-related office of the Media Development Authority (MDA). Combining efforts from official agencies such as Economic Development Board (EDB), Information Development Authority of Singapore (IDA), MDA (Media Development Authority) and NAC (National Art Council), the Singapore government designed *Renaissance City Report*, *Renaissance City 2.0*, *Design Singapore* and *Media 21* to promote media industries in film and music, media, design and arts and entertainment since the late 1990s.

These policies reflect strategies of globalization and regionalization that the Singaporean state uses to extend the country's economy. Singapore is the first country in Asia that releases its creative economy policy as a national cultural policy.[36] These policies incorporate Asian values into the creative cluster, however, the main goal still focuses on the use of Asian brand to create a "gateway" for international companies to come to Singapore and integrate into the creative economy of Asia.

In digital entertainment industry, one of the most notable cultural policies in the development of digital media industry is the government's plans to attract international media companies to Singapore. The government used schemes from the Economic Development Board (EDB) to attract foreign direct investment from overseas media companies to invest in the local filmmaking business.[37] In addition, the *Interactive & Digital Media 2015 Singapore* scheme is another policy that aims to generate 10,000 new jobs and create $10 billion worth of value by the year of 2015. The strategies that EDB uses to establish its online game industry includes: (1) attract top tier interactive and digital media companies to set up offices in Singapore, (2) attract international talents to quickly build up the talent base of the online game industry, and (3) encourage collaboration between international game companies and local game companies to strengthen network dynamics of the local industry.

THE ONLINE GAMING INDUSTRIES

The burgeoning South Korean online gaming industry was established by efforts on behalf of the government to support strong IT policy and free market competition. In 2006, the Korean online game market reached a total of $550 million dollars for market revenues.[38] The export of the Korean game continued to increase to $671 million and online games accounted for 89% of the total volume exported. Chapters 2 and 6 demonstrate that *PC bangs* play an important role in facilitating the mass popularization of online game culture in Korea. In 2004, the *PC bangs* alone accumulated $1,398 million dollars revenue, making up 39% of the domestic game market.[39] One of the dominant gaming genres for Korean game players is, without doubt, the massively multiplayer online role-playing game (MMORPG). With the recent market shift from MMORPG to casual games, a space has been provided for new game companies to emerge onto the online game industry in Korea. For instance, the success of new games such as *Special Force* from Neowiz and *Kart Rider* from Nexon[40] demonstrate that the Korean market still continues to grow after 10 years of development in the online game sector. In 2004, Korean online games contributed around 51% of the total online games in China with a total of 154 games in the Chinese market. The distribution of Korean games also spread across Europe and the United States, despite the fact that the country's main market still centers upon Asia for regional distribution.

South Korea reaches market saturation with few game firms occupying the majority share of the domestic market. Jin and Chee describe that in 2005, the top eight online companies included NCsoft, Nexon, Neoiz, NHN and CJ Internet, constituting 65% of the online game market. This development has resulted in a self-generating globalization process when less competitive Korean game companies began to sell games overseas and search for potential market outside of country. Such need for overseas market reveals a different type of local effects that South Korean game companies respond to the trend of globalization. As most media industries in Asia explore their overseas market due to their lack of ability to compete with Western media companies and their products, the case of South Korea demonstrates the emergence of a regional production center mostly based upon industry dynamics such as government policy and firm competition at the local level. Even though foreign investment is important to most major game companies in Korea, local game companies maintain their competitive ability with their expertise in content creation and network knowledge know-how. These companies form joint venture with transnational corporations including Electronic Arts, Softbank, Shanda and Sega Corporation. Foreign investment allows local Korean game companies to internationalize their product services to the global market.

The industry value chain in South Korea reflects a particular dynamic relationship among game developers, publishers, *PC bang* operators and the game players. South Korea's regulatory framework encourages firm competition and foreign direct investment. While the Korean state does not directly involve in the production and consumption process of game development, foreign-based companies receive less restriction in conducting business compared to other Asian countries such as Singapore and China. As foreign games from the United States and Japan still receive wide popularity from the Korean gamers, Korean game companies compete with successful foreign titles including *Starcraft, Counter Strike, Diablo* and *World of Warcraft* in the domestic market.

In Chapter 6, Huhh mentions that the diffusion of *PC bangs* was contributed by the popularity of *Starcraft* in 1998. Korea's largest online game company, NCsoft, benefited from the first mover effect of its successful title *Lineage* during the early stage of the company's development.[41] In addition, the *PC bang* model also contributes to the popularity of the MMORPG genre in South Korea due to the long hours that users spend in playing games in *PC bangs*. The director of Korean Association of Game Industry,[42] Mr. Jang, describes the industry structure in the following interview:

> Our industry structure sees the publisher on the top, followed by the first party and second party. Under the publisher, the first party is in-house developer. The second party is the subsidiary company or the investment company. The third party is the independent development company. The current trend is that those publishers usually have all of them. But since now the number of companies that try to develop, distribute and publish games is actually decreasing, this means that the industry is growing and becoming mature by gradually separating these roles between publisher, developer and investor. Merger and acquisitions among local firms is also good for stability for this market (Mr. Jang, Director, Korean Association of Game Industry, Interview with the author, June 16, 2006).

In Singapore, the government's sudden turn to culture and arts in 1990s—and the introduction of specific scholarship schemes to develop the creative industry since 2000s—have ensured that the companies in Singapore have grown and flourished in a relatively short period of time. The industry structure of Singapore shows the division of two sectors: multinational game companies (MNCs) and small local game companies (SMEs). As the local online game industry relies on the multinational companies (MNCs) to transfer industry know-how, local game companies also compete with the MNCs in obtaining creative talents and applying government funds.

More than seven MNCs—including Lucas Films, Electronic Arts, Koei, Ubisoft, 10 Tacle and RealU—have set up studios in Singapore. These companies are international game companies from the Unite States, Japan, France and Germany. The MNCs established their regional offices in Singapore due to the potential markets in China and India. The EDB offers high investment to these multinational media companies with agreement that these companies will transfer technical know-how to local talents so that, in the long run, these local talents can become entrepreneurs to set up small to medium sized online game companies in Singapore.

The industry development model in Singapore connects the local game industry to the global industry value chain. By linking with transnational media companies, the online gaming industry works as a satellite city that provides services to major digital media markets in the world. Most of the transnational companies in Singapore have established stable distribution networks in their global businesses. The established publishing network allows local game companies to develop products that are cross platform from console, personal computer, mobile or online game. The result of this industry development strategy is that in 2008 the game development studio of Koei in Singapore launched its first developed-in-Singapore game, *Romance of the Three Kingdoms Online*. This game is the online version of Koei's historical strategy game, *Romance of the Three Kingdoms* series. This leading Japanese game company has published eleven editions of this game across various platforms in PC, PlayStation, Wii, Nintendo DS and Sega. In 2005, the company set aside USD $1.8 million to set up its development studio office in Singapore and completed its first project in 2008.[43]

Compared to South Korea, the government of Singapore has much active involvement in creating the industry dynamics between local firms and multinational companies. Media Development Authority (MDA) takes charge of the participation of multinational companies in the local game industry. As the government expects to measure the industry growth by adding the economic contribution of these companies to the country's GDP and employment rate, local government offices have clear division of duties in correspondence with multinational game companies. For instance, the Economic Development Board (EDB) looks for multinational companies that bring in direct foreign investment to Singapore. The Information Development Authority of Singapore (IDA) watches over the infrastructure to ensure adequate technological development of content. Media Development Authority (MDA) focuses on content production and looks for resources to match make multinational companies with local companies. The main goal of the government involvement is to assist the growth of the domestic industry and to build up the economy. The information officer of MDA explains the collaborative process among the government offices and multinational companies in the following interview:

> EDB is set up to deal with foreign enterprises. MDA works with foreign companies once they come in. We also work with local game companies to actually produce games for Korea and Japan . . . Most of the MNCs come in to Singapore with big project that actually can make all these things. They have expertise . . . In the case of Lucas Film, EDB brought them in. EDB will deal with IDA if what Lucas Film needs relates to infrastructure. MDA will get involved if Lucas Film wants

to work with small companies on animation or Media Corp on project (Mr. Chan, Interview with the Author, May 10, 2007).

The synergy effect between the local state and multinational companies creates a particular space for local game companies in both developing and publishing sectors. There were about 30 game companies in Singapore in 2008.[44] While seven were international companies, the remaining were local game companies developing games for the global markets or publishers releasing foreign games to the nearby South East Asian regions. Due to the limited market size of Singapore and the preference of Western games among local gamers, most of the local game developers consider MNCs industry players at a different level. As the local game companies do not directly compete with MNCs such as Electronic Arts or Lucas Films, they focus on niche market in the global scale and produce games for consumers outside of Singapore.

For instance, the first made-in-Singapore game, *Dropcast*, was completed in 2007 by a medium size local game company, Mikoishi. This company uses different strategies to enter markets in Asia. The first game of this company focuses on action puzzle games for Nintendo DS platform, while *Steam Iron*, is a real-time strategy game specifically for the South Korean market. The company positions itself in the global industry value chain working with multinational game publishers. In additions, *Dropcast* was launched by American publisher, THQ; and *Steam Iron* was launched by Korean top tier publisher, Nexon, in 2008. The founder of one of the local companies describes her company's industry position and the role that local game companies play in the gaming industry of Singapore as follows:

> I do not have buyer[s] from Singapore. Most of my buyers are from the United States, Japan and Korea . . . Local game companies are finding out ways to set up a gaming industry here. We are not huge multi-national companies with a lot of support in infrastructure. Let alone a whole technical studio and technical tool in another country. Like Lucas Film for example, Singapore does not have to re-invest the tool. They don't have to build engine. EA Canada has been building games for thirty years. They can just grab things to come here. But Nexgen, Boomzap and Mikoishi [local game companies] start building from zero . . . The government support from MDA is helpful to us in our early days. We used government funds to build prototypes. But now we also need concrete chain. The issue of market needs to be addressed (Ms. Chang, Interview with the Author, May 29, 2007).

In all, as the global MMORPG market is already occupied by successful titles such as *Lineage* and *World of Warcraft*, local game companies position themselves as global independent game developers producing titles that are not yet explored by the established global game companies. This game development pattern shows a contrast to the South Korean game industry as most of the industry value chain in South Korea is formed by local game companies. In addition, due to the lack of art and audio talent in the local industry, Singaporean game companies outsource projects to companies in Philippines, Malaysia, Thailand or Eastern Europe. The CEO of one local game company explains the interdependence of his company with other companies in the international production system in the following interview:

> Our company outsources to Eastern and Western Europe. We find partners through Internet I listed my name in gamasutra. In the site there is a section for the contractor. So we build up online friendship. Our art style is fusioned between East and West. It's a bit of Japanese and Western art in between. It is targeted for Western markets . . . We try to find our unique space. The Japanese and Korean are beginning to have their own styles. Chinese game artists too. So we thought we try to merge this style and that's how the concept of merged (Mr. A. Yap, CEO, Interview with the Author, May 15, 2007).

The outsourcing strategy that local companies apply creates a hybrid space for games that are made-in-Singapore. Both the developed-in-Singapore game and the made-in-Singapore game involve the participation of local creative talents producing games that are circulated in the global market. The *Romance of the Three Kingdoms Online* reflects a strong Japanese influence on the creative concept, while *Steam Iron* shows an attempt by the local company to incorporate elements that would appeal to Korean casual gamers in its content creation.

CASES OF THE GLOBAL COMPLEXITY

This section contextualizes global complexity with the emphasis on local companies in South Korea and multinational game companies in Singapore. The South Korean case suggests an outgoing globalization process based upon the collective performance of South Korean game companies in global market. The case of Singapore indicates an incoming globalization process from multinational game companies that go to Singapore to set up regional studios in Asia. Both globalization flows result in trans-border cultural exchange because of the corporate motive to achieve market expansion. The South Korean globalization shows a state market created at the global level. The Singaporean case reveals globalization and its influence on a state-supported industry at the local level.

Table 4.1 shows the respective global market that each major South Korean online game company has achieved. The global territories that these companies have reached show the globally integrated network that

Table 4.1   The Global Markets of Top Tier South Korean Online Game Companies.

Name of the Company	Major Markets	Successful Titles
NCsoft	China, Japan, Taiwan, Southeast Asia, Europe, America	*Lineage I and II, Guild War*
Nexon	Japan	*Maple Story, Kart Rider*
Webzen	Taiwan, China, America	*Mu*
Actozsoft	China	*Legend of Mir 1, 2 & 3*
Neowiz	US, Japan	*FIFA Online* (Collaborated with Electronic Arts); *Special Force*

Korean game companies have collectively achieved in Japan, China, Taiwan, Southeast Asia and the United States. The market performance of these companies indicate that Korean games tend to enter Asia markets easily compared to their attempts to enter markets in the United States and Europe. For instance, Nexon is particularly successful in Japan among all the Korean game companies. Webzen have entered the markets of Taiwan, China and the United States with its title, *Mu Online*. Actozsoft became popular in China. Neowiz collaborated with Electronic Arts to create *FIFA Online* and therefore entered the markets of the United States and Japan. Mr. Seo from Webzen explains the overseas success of Korean companies in the following interview:

> The successful games in Korea are guaranteed for the success in China, as Chinese people try to follow Korean people's action. Nowadays, a number of Korean games are still popular in China . . . The areas occupied by Korean Wave are successful regions for online game as well. Unlike America and Europe, our companies have difficulty entering those markets . . . There is a similar pattern of spread between Korean Wave and online game. Successful markets in Korean Wave helps our company to rapidly transform from a Korean company to become a global company (Mr. D. Seo, Head of Strategy and Planning Team, Webzen, Interview with the Author, June 15, 2006).

The interview shows that the Korean online gaming industry shows a similar pattern of globalization to the Korean Wave in television and cinema. As the Korean Wave in television shows the country's transnational mobility in reaching markets in Japan, China, Hong Kong, Taiwan, Southeast Asia, North Korea, Iraq and the United States,[45] this pattern of spread shows that online game content benefits from the pre-existing industry structure. Korean online game companies also present a comparable exportation pattern by entering international markets that have consumers who share similar cultural background and social rules.

The Korean transformation from a local media industry into a global media production center is seen in the strategies that companies use to approach different markets. In China, Korean games that contain Chinese graphics and narrative style receive wide success among the Chinese users. Korean companies are able to apply localization by either outsourcing to Chinese developers or maintaining partnership with Chinese distributors. The collaboration between Korean online game company, Actozsoft, and Chinese distributor, Shanda, contribute to the success of *Legend of Mir 2* in China. As Shanda occupies major Internet café distribution channels in China, Actozsoft has benefited from the success of its game and thus established strong brand recognition in the Chinese market. Another example of successful localization in the overseas market is Webzen. The following game consultant descries the strategy of the company as the following:

> Many Korean companies make the branches in China and hire Chinese people. The good example is Webzen. The company made the Chinese branch and they make the game for only Chinese market, not Korean market. They hire Chinese graphic artists. When I first saw the game from Webzen, I thought this game was not Korean game. Chinese graphic artists reflect their taste for this game (Mr. S. Park, Game Consultant, Interview with the Author, June 4, 2006).

In Japan, most of the Korean online game companies work with local companies to establish their branding reputation in the Japanese market. Korean online game companies publish titles in Japan because of the mature market in console game. Some companies set up branches in Japan in order to maintain service to the Japanese customers, while others, such as Nexon, chose to purchase Japanese companies to enter the market. As a transnational organization, Nexon, aggressively markets its own name, Nexon Japan, in order to enter the Japanese market. By purchasing small companies in Japan, Nexon maintains its own IP and such a strategy has proved to be effective in the case of two games, *Maple Story* and *Kart Rider*, which have been released in the Japanese market.

In the United States, most of the Korean games fail to enter the market. The only exceptions are titles produced by NCsoft. NCsoft chose different subscription model to promote *Lineage*. While in Korea the company heavily relies on *PC bang* distribution channel, the company changed to traditional subscription method in the package game market. NCsoft even steps ahead of other Korean online game companies by developing titles that mainly target the US market. The title *Guild War* is developed based upon the tastes of the American users. By entering the US market, NCsoft presents the potential of Korean company to compete with MNCs in the global gaming market. The manager of the international business team at the NCsoft describes the marketing strategies of NCsoft as a global company in the following interview:

> The most important marketing strategy for NCsoft was the focus on specific regions and users for each product. For example, in Korea the level-up system with items was very popular, but in North America and Europe quest was much more important factor for success. In China and Southeast Asia, players tend to like PVP (player vs. player) and the competition between two players . . . Because players have differences, we select regions to sell games. We also give much responsibility for the decision making to each regional branch. If we need to make global decision and regional interest and global interests are in conflict, we give top priority to the global one . . . We are a global company (Mr. Yun, Manager of International Business Team, NCsoft, Interview with the Author, June 15, 2006).

Unlike the case of South Korea that concentrates on the collective performance of local game companies in the global market, globalization has been central to the corporate performance among multinational game companies in Singapore. According to PricewaterhouseCoopers report on *Global Entertainment and Media Outlook*, the online game market in Asia is expected to grow from $3,715 million in 2008 to $5,178 million in 2011.[46] As the broadband subscribers in Asia will increase from 151 million in 2008 to 243 million people in 2011, the online video game subscribers are also expected to rise from 40 million in 2008 to 62 million in 2011. Due to higher broadband and PC penetration in the region, the Asia-Pacific region has the largest online game market in the world. Among the 8 million players worldwide, 3.5 million players of the most popular MMORPG online game, *World of Warcraft*, are in China. The online game market in Asia will rise rapidly for the potential of growth on the countries of China and India. Singapore therefore becomes the gateway of Western multinational game companies to enter the markets in Asia.

The multinational game companies have generated two levels of industry dynamics in Singapore: firm and creative labor. In firm dynamics, multinational game companies increase corporate collaboration in the local industry to the global level. As the MNCs have different countries of origin, firm dynamics in the local industry receives organizational influence from the United States, France, Germany and Japan. Local talents who work for MNCs have learned different management styles and organization cultures from these companies. The exposure benefits local talents to gain knowledge on developing and publishing games in the international business framework. The general manager of one of the world's leading game companies describes the influence of MNCs in shaping the local gaming industry of Singapore as follows:

> We have a very big role here. I have different hats. We help the government to promote the industry . . . We work with schools, speaking, student exchange, internships. We have internships here with kids . . . As a company, we do a lot with the local community. In the United States, we give 10 million dollar donation to the USA film school. Then it is our responsibility for helping to build economy here. We move our headquarters here, 170 people, 90% of them are Singaporeans. We create jobs. We do a lot of involvement with many groups, different organizations. We have tours and talks to try to help people here little by little (Mr. Thompson, Interview with the Author, November 7, 2007).

One significant reason for MNCs to set up studios in Singapore is that MNCs come to Asia to better understand the market. Due to the complexity of market preferences in Asia, Western MNCs face challenges to understand the rules of licensing and distributing in each country. These MNCs also need further knowledge to discover approaches to develop more appropriate content for the market. The previous interviewee further mentions the strategy that his company applies to meet the market demand in Asia:

> Our biggest challenge is to figure out how to make more appropriate content for this market. In India, we need a cricket game. In China, we need an online role-playing game. In Japan, we need a Japanese horror action game. As a media company, we need to be in all key categories . . . But it does not mean that we need to go from scratch, spend a hundred million dollars to make a new engine. We just need to let our games to be on PC and it needs to be online. We can work with partner[s] to localize our content to make our product relevant to the market.

Some of the MNCs respond their need to localize content for the Asian market by hiring creative talents from the region. Some others outsource projects to studios in nearby countries such as Thailand, China and Malaysia. The CEO of one German game company describes his reason of hiring multinational team in his Singapore office as follows:

> In Singapore, we started with a multinational team recruited from Indonesia, Philippines and Singapore. The reason for us is that Singapore offers a good location because the game industry is international. We can reach out to the world from here. It is a great location to produce international titles. We also have an opportunity to access Asia in many respects. First, we can access the talent pool, possibly the future distribution and Asian markets. All these considerations convince us

to move our studio from Germany to Singapore (Mr. Goodman, CEO, Interview with the Author, November 5, 2007).

This trend of easy access to talent pool in the region creates a secondary industry dynamics related to the presence of international creative talent in the local gaming industry. As the development of an online game varies greatly from the development of a console game, MNCs that already domi-nate the existing console game market need experienced developers from Asia to begin its online gaming business. These Asian programmers assist the MNCs to localize their contents and offer technical knowledge to cre-ate a system that supports hundreds of thousand users to play game in the online setting. The following interview shows the reason for a Korean game programmer to move to Singapore to work for MNC:

> My company needs online game experience. Most of them [MNCs] never made online game. They don't know how system affects users and how users will react to the system. They want graphics, close data. They also want to know what has to be done in the first line, the second line . . . Most of the Western developers are trying to bring the stand-alone game play and experience to online game. But the mechanism for MMORPG game is totally different . . . They [MNCs] do not have the server technology to take on hundreds of thousand people at the same time. That is why I came here—to transfer my skill and experience (Mr. Sam, Interview with the Author, November 22, 2007).

As a result, globalization takes place at the local level when Asian game developers migrate to Singapore to work for MNCs. These Asian game developers become cultural producers who create contents for MNCs to enter the market in Asia. The collective effort of game development leads to a hybridizing production process in the industry context of Singapore as these Asian developers standardize the elements of game design in MNC setting. They blur the boundary between Western and Asian games. The following Korean programmer reveals her observation on the gradual loss of national representation in a standardized online game due to the collec-tive effort of game localization and standardization contributed by global creative talents:

> Now it is very difficult to tell any difference between console game, PC game and games across different platforms. If you look at [MNC] games, they are exactly the same on PC, PS2 and Consoles. If you look at any game from console game to online game, it is very hard to tell any difference. For movie, you have to be a Korean filmmaker to make Korean films. But for game, there is no difference after all. A German programmer can make game for *Lineage*. Korean developer can make game for North America. American companies can also make game for Asia (Ms. Hu, Interview with the Author, November 15, 2007).

CONCLUSION

In conclusion, the globalization process is clearly complex in the context of South Korea and Singapore. The two cases in this chapter show the various factors contributing to the shaping of online gaming industries in the two countries. On the industry level, the case of South Korea shows that local game companies play the key role in creating the economic success of online game industry. The globalization process of the industry is resulted from fierce competition among local firm competitions in a developed broadband economy. The government's development on the technological infrastructure provides an environment for local game companies to practice their corporate strategies to maintain service in the local market. These practices to meet with the demand from sophisticated hardcore gamers has led to remarkable industry growth on a global scale. By contrast, in Singapore, the influence of globalization is shaped by the local state and MNCs. The government actively participates in the upgrade of industry clusters in the online gaming sector by bringing in multinational game companies to the local industry. The industry dynamics are formed as a local effect of global corporation when MNCs expand their corporate operation across national borders to search for new markets and local partners for their corporate expansion in the online gaming sector in Asia.

Both sites together reveal the theme of competition between the local state and the MNC in the traditional globalization debate. On the theory level, globalization means state involvement in creating a market for its local new media industry in the context of Asia. Globalization reflects the work of multinational companies forming their "globally integrated network" around the world. Globalization is a reflection of the emergent systems resulting from the dominance of MNCs in the global market and are sometimes complex and far from achieving equilibrium. There is always possibility to engage with the various practices of complexity that determine the patterns of power struggle between people, corporations, societies and media industries across various geographies. The industry development models in the online game industries of South Korea and Singapore respond to Urry's idea with their self-organizing "practice of complexity."[47] That is, while the Korean case shows the local effect in creating industry dynamics, the Singaporean case points to the global influence in forming the local online game industry. Both cases confirm the progressive nature of government involvement in the industry setting in Asia-Pacific region. The government uses effective industry policies to update the country's national competitiveness in the online gaming sector so that local firms can integrate to the global market and contribute to the national development. The models presented in this study reveal strategies for both online game industries in the use of new communication technology to maintain political autonomy in the globalization process. They also reflect the possibility of a state market that can be created at the global scale by the industry involvement of the state, local firms, MNCs and creative talents.

NOTES

1. Henry Jenkins, *Convergence Culture: Where Old and New Media Intersect* (New York: New York University Press, 2006).
2. John Urry, *Global Complexity* (Cambridge: Polity Press, 2003).
3. M. Simai, "The Challenging State System and the Future of Global Governance," in *Globalization: Critical Concepts in Sociology. Volume II: The Nation-State and International Relations*, eds. R. Robertson and K. White (London: Routledge 2003), 64–90.
4. William Robinson, *A Theory of Global Capitalism: Production, Class, and State in a Transnational World* (Baltimore: The Johns Hopkins University Press, 2004).
5. John Tomlinson, *The Culture of Speed: The Coming of Immediacy* (Los Angeles: Sage Publications, 2008).
6. Organization for Economic and Co-Production Development. (2006). "Top 25 Countries in Household Broadband Penetration." Retrieved on July 20, 2007. http://www.websiteoptimization.com/bw/0704/.
7. Internet World Stats. (2008). Broadband Internet Top World Countries with Highest Broadband Penetration Rate in 2007. Retrieved on April 20, 2008. http://www.internetworldstats.com/dsl.htm.
8. Larissa Hjorth, "Being Real in the Mobile Reel: A Case Study on Convergent Mobile Media as Domesticated New Media in Seoul, South Korea," *Convergence: The International Journal of Research into New Media Technologies*, 14(1) 2008: 91–104.
9. Peichi Chung, "The creative industry of Singapore: Cultural Policy in the Age of Globalization," *Media International Australia: Incorporating Cultural Policy*, 128, 2008: 31–45.
10. David Hesmondhalgh, *The Cultural Industries* (Los Angeles: Sage Publications, 2007).
11. Allen Scott, *The Cultural Economy of Cities* (Los Angeles: Sage Publications, 2000).
12. Toby Miller, Nitin Govil, John McMurria, Richard Maxwell and Ting Wang, *Global Hollywood 2* (London: British Film Institute, 2005).
13. Scott Lash and Celia Lury, *Global Culture Industry* (Malden, MA: Polity Press, 2007).
14. Alvin Toffler, *The Third Wave* (New York: Bantam Books, 1980).
15. Axel Bruns, *Blog, Wikipedia, Second Life and Beyond: From Production to Produsage* (New York: Peter Lang, 2008).
16. David Audretsch and Charles Bonser, *Globalization and Regionalization: Challenges for Public Policy* (Boston: Kluwer Academic Publishers, 2002).
17. William Robinson. *A Theory of Global Capitalism: Production, Class, and State in a Transnational World* (Baltimore: The Johns Hopkins University Press, 2004).
18. Robinson, *A Theory of Global Capitalism*, 66.
19. Terry Flew. "The Social Contract and Beyond in Broadcast Media Policy," *Television and New Media*, 7(3), 2006: 282–305.
20. Tony Bennett, "Acting on the Social: Art, Culture and Government," *American Behavioral Scientist* 43(9), 2000: 1412–1428.
21. Toby Miller, "The National Endowment for the Arts in the 1990s: A Black Eye on the Arts?" *American Behavioral Scientist* 43(9) 2000: 1429–1445.
22. Justin Lewis and Toby Miller. *Critical Cultural Policy Studies: A Reader.* (Malden, MA: Blackwell Publishing, 2003).
23. Stuart Cunningham, "Cultural Studies from the Viewpoint of Cultural Policy," in*Critical Cultural Policy Studies: A Reader,* eds. James Lewis and Toby Miller (Malden, MA: Blackwell Publishing, 2003), 13–22.

24. Youna Kim, "The Rising East Asia 'Wave': Korean Media Go Global," in *Media on the Move: Global Flow and Contra-Flow*, ed. Daya Thussu (London: Routledge, 2007), 135–151.
25. Doobo Shim. "Hybridity and the Rise of Korean Popular Culture in Asia." *Media, Culture & Society* 28(1): 25–44 (2006).
26. Jin Dal Yong, "Socioeconomic Implications of Broadband Services: Information Economy in Korea," *Information, Communication & Society* 8(4), 2005: 503–523.
27. See Chapter 2 by Jin and Chee in this volume. Hereafter cited in text.
28. See Chapter 6 by Huhh in this volume.
29. Larissa Hjorth, "Being Real in the Mobile Reel: A Case Study on Convergent Mobile Media as Domesticated New Media in Seoul, South Korea," *Convergence: The International Journal of Research into New Media Technologies*, 14(1), 2008: 91–104.
30. Shim, "Hybridity and the Rise of Korean Popular Culture in Asia."
31. Jin Dal Yong, "Cultural Politics in Korea's Contemporary Films under Neoliberal Globalization." *Media Culture and Society* 28(1), 2006: 5–23.
32. Jin, "Cultural Politics in Korea's Contemporary Films under Neoliberal Globalization."
33. Jung Hyun Wi, *Business Strategy of Online Game* (Seoul: Jeu Media, 2006). In Korean.
34. Terrance Lee, "Creative Shifts and Directions: Cultural Policy in Singapore," *International Journal of Cultural Policy* 10(3), 2004: 281–299.
35. Lily Kong, "Cultural Policy in Singapore: Negotiating Economic and Socio-Cultural Agendas." *Geoforum* 31, 2000:409–424.
36. Audrey Yue, "The Regional Culture of New Asia: Cultural Governance and Creative Industries in Singapore." *International Journal of Cultural Policy* 12(1), 2006: 17–33.
37. Kong, "Cultural Policy in Singapore: Negotiating Economic and Socio-Cultural Agendas."
38. Ministry of Culture and Tourism & Korea Game Industry Agency. *The Rise of 2007 Korean Games: Guide to Korean Game Industry and Culture.* (Seoul: Ministry of Culture and Tourism. 2007).
39. Ministry of Culture and Tourism & Korea Game Development & Promotion Institute. *2005 The Rise of Korean Games: Guide to Korean Game Industry and Culture.* (Seoul: Ministry of Culture and Tourism, 2005).
40. Larissa Hjorth, "Playing at Being Mobile: Gaming and Cute Culture in South Korea." Retrieved 20 October 2006, *Fibreculture* 8, 2006 http://journal.fibreculture.org/issue8/issue8_hjorth.html (2006).
41. 50% to 60% of the revenue of NCsoft came from *PC bang* transaction at the beginning stage of the industry development.
42. The Korea Association of Game Industry is a non-profit organization composed of most major players in the online game industry in South Korea. The organization had about 25 members, constituted by top tier and second tier major companies at the time of interview.
43. Economic Development Board. "KOEI Has Set up a Game Development Studio in Singapore." EDB Singapore Database. Consulted on October 2, 2008.
44. Media Development Authority. *Singapore Media Fusion: Games.* (Singapore: Media Development Authority. 2008).
45. Kim, 2007.
46. PricewaterhouseCoopers. *Global Entertainment and Media outlook: 2007–2011* (New York: PricewaterhouseCoopers LLP, 2007).
47. Urry, *Global Complexity.*

Part II

Localities

INTRODUCTION

The chapters in this section collectively play out Doreen Massey's focus on how "locality" must always be understood in terms of the spatial and temporal organization of social relations.[1] Massey reminds us that a place's specificity—as well as the associated sense and sensibility of its contemporaneity—must be understood as a complex interweaving of historical and present-day social relations. At the same time, she is careful to avoid romanticizing and essentializing an insular politics of locality; place distinctiveness is crucially posited as coterminous with place-interdependence.[2] The processes of forming identity and forging self-identification are fundamentally relational. Massey's theoretical formulations provide important cues for negotiating the situated localities of Asia-Pacific gaming. These game cultures may develop distinctively localized expressions and national characteristics; yet, at the same time, they can evolve collaboratively and symbiotically within and across national boundaries. The three chapters in this section explore some of these generative tensions and patterns.

In Chapter 5, Benjamin Wai-ming Ng considers the intricate politics of locality via his robust and empirically rich study of the diverse ways in which *Street Fighter* and *The King of Fighters*, two iconic Japanese arcade and combat games, have been played, localized and hybridized by Hong Kong players, fans, and businesses alike. He paints a vivid cross-media portrait of the dynamic force of intra-Asian cultural flows and localization processes in forging East Asian popular culture. For over the past two decades, the impact of Japanese combat games has been strongly felt in Hong Kong comic books, films and fashion—even earning fashionable citations in local pop music and television programs.

Ng emphasizes that it would be erroneous to interpret these cross-border engagements purely as the exertion of Japanese pop cultural imperialism. His analysis of the effect of such Japanese combat games on the evolution of slang and other social vernacular in Hong Kong illuminates the depth and scope of localization and hybridization practices. Nevertheless, these conjunctures are not necessarily homogenizing or equalizing. As Ng discerns, they paradoxically belie the hybridization and transmission of class-based languages and practices from the bottom-up, while simultaneously demonstrating the maintenance of social class differentiation and stratification.

Place distinctiveness is the focus of Jun-Sok Huhh in Chapter 6. A vivid experiential account of what you see, hear and smell in the *PC bang* (PC room) is powerfully established—and its not inconsiderable appeal evoked—from the outset of this chapter. The primacy of place is two-fold here, focusing on both the actual site of the *PC bang* as well as its irrefutable significance and role within Korean gaming culture.

Huhh's detailed analysis of the evolution, development, and impact of *PC bangs* as core gaming locales substantiates his argument that they are not just significant but fundamentally *central* to the cultivation and phenomenal growth of online gaming in Korea. He identifies and discusses a broad range of divergent factors salient in the rise of *PC bangs*, including the 1997 Asian financial crisis, the Korean government's implementation of extensive broadband policies and infrastructure, and the mass popularization and gamer uptake of two key networked games, namely, *StarCraft* and *Lineage*. Huhh also highlights the significance of multi-pronged collaborative arrangements, chiefly between *PC bangs* and online game publishers, game guilds, e-sports and real-money trading (RMT) respectively.

His insightful analysis of the business and culture of the *PC bangs* crucially never loses sight of the fact that these are, at base, social sites for *playing* games. To this end, Huhh proffers a compelling comparison of *PC bangs* to gaming arcades to emphasize the social constituencies of (game) play, a theme which is powerfully encapsulated in his description of the collaborative social gaming that takes place at *PC bangs* during elaborate in-game castle sieges known as *GongSungJun* in Korea.

Melanie Swalwell offers an alternate perspective on the social modalities of gaming in another part of the Asia-Pacific region. In Chapter 7, she presents reflexive "snapshots" of the activities and experiences of not-for-profit Lan gaming groups in Australia and New Zealand. Her in-depth interviews with the administrators of five Lans over a period of time provide illuminating insights into the organization, maintenance, dynamism and subsequent decline as well as ultimate dissolution of these gaming groups.

Although there are important differences in comparing not-for-profit collectives and business practices respectively, Swalwell's study of Lan gaming nonetheless dovetails with Huhh's assessment of the *PC bang* in that they make highly persuasive cases for negotiating the virtuality of networked gaming as both a *context* and *conduit* for maintaining offline sociality. Swalwell even goes so far as to clarify that the discernible decline in Lan gaming cannot be directly attributed to the rise of online massively multiplayer gaming. Indeed, Lanning continues to take place, albeit currently on a much smaller scale. Her prognosis clearly has a broader application. Swalwell's study attests to the historical presence and future possibility of temporary and contingent coalitions of gamers and social gaming paradigms in the Asia-Pacific.

NOTES

1. Doreen Massey, *Space, Place, and Gender* (Minnesota: University of Minnesota Press, 1994).
2. Doreen Massey, *Power-Geometries and the Politics of Space-Time* (Heidelberg. University of Heidelberg Press, 1999).

5 Consuming and Localizing Japanese Combat Games in Hong Kong

Benjamin Wai-ming Ng

INTRODUCTION

As a gaming superpower, Japan has dominated the world market in arcade games, home console games and handheld console games since the mid-1980s.[1] Globalization and localization often come hand in hand, and thus it is not surprising to see different regions consume Japanese games in their own ways.[2] As John Fiske points out, just as readers can become "active readers" by adding new meanings to cultural products,[3] Hong Kong game players, businessmen and artists have been turning Japanese games into "Hong Kong-style" game culture and other forms of hybrid culture in terms of the rules of playing, the making of crossover cultural products as well as specific languages translated, used or created.

This chapter examines the consumption and localization of Japanese combat games in Hong Kong through a case study of *Street Fighter* (SF) and *The King of Fighters* (KOF), two of the most popular arcade games as well as combat games in the world. Both games have had a strong impact on Hong Kong popular culture and the Hong Kong entertainment industry. Hong Kong artists and players have been selectively and creatively incorporating elements of Hong Kong commercial movies, martial arts novels and comics, as well as lower-class slang and behavior into these two Japanese combat games. Examining the history of SF and KOF in Hong Kong, the making of new rules and jargons by Hong Kong players, and the adaptation of these two games into Hong Kong comics from historical and ethnographic perspectives, this chapter aims to deepen understandings of the dynamic force of localization and transnational cultural flows in forging Asian popular culture.[4]

THE RECEPTION OF JAPANESE COMBAT GAMES IN HONG KONG

Playing Japanese combat games is a collective memory of Hong Kong people who were born after the 1970s. The history of combat games in Hong Kong can be traced to the late 1970s when the two pioneering combat games, namely *Heavyweight Champ* (Saga, 1976) and *Warriors* (Vector-beam, 1979), were introduced to Hong Kong. *Boxing* (Nintendo, 1984), Nintendo's first combat game, and *Urban Champion* (Nintendo, 1985) were well received in Game and Watch (Nintendo's handheld game console) and Famicom (Nintendo's home console) respectively. However, combat games did not create a commotion in Hong Kong until the introduction of *Street Fighter* (or SF1, Capcom) in 1987. James Newman, a British game researcher, argues that "the pleasures of videogame play are not principally visual, but rather are kinaesthetic."[5] This idea is particularly true in the case of SF1. Despite its primitive program, rough character designs and unsophisticated graphics, SF1 won the hearts of the players with its innovative control system (such as the use of separate keys for punching and kicking and the joystick for choosing direction, jumping or hiding) that later became the model for other two-dimensional combat games including KOF series and Samurai Spirit series. *Street Fighter's* mass appeal also helped popularize *hissatsuwaza* (literally "sure-kill technique," the most powerful fighting skill) among young people in Hong Kong.[6] Game players in Hong Kong added elements of Chinese martial arts to SF1 by perpetuating the rumor that there is a hidden *hissatsuwaza* called *yiyangzhi* (single *yang* finger), a term borrowed from popular Hong Kong martial arts novels by Jinyong (1924~). There was a time when Hong Kong game players were absorbed with finding and discussing this hidden move. This shows that the localization of Japanese combat games started from the very beginning of their introduction to Hong Kong. Players, through their own imagination, turned *Street Fighter* into a Chinese martial arts game.

Street Fighter 2 (SF2), launched in 1991, created an unprecedented arcade game craze in Hong Kong. Regarded as the most commercially successful combat game in the history of videogames, SF2 represented a breakthrough in control system, stage and graphic designs, drawings and music.[7] It became the most popular arcade game in Hong Kong in the early 1990s. Many small-sized game centers had nothing but SF2 games. The queue was always long for the game. SF2's competitions were held frequently by various organizations in different parts of Hong Kong. Local game magazines focused their reports on SF2. Characters and terms of this game were adopted in Hong Kong comics, movies and Cantonese pop music.[8] For example, the Hong Kong comic artist Situ Jianqian, used Ryu, Ken and Chun Li, the three major characters of the SF series, in his comic, *Supergod Z: Cyber Weapon* (1993). After receiving a warning letter from Capcom for copyright infringement, Situ changed their names, but kept the character designs (Figure 5.1).[9]

Likewise, elements of SF have been adapted into Hong Kong cinema. *Future Cops* (1993, directed by Wangjing) copied the story and characters from SF2. Aaron Kwok and Ekin Cheng, two top Hong Kong movie actors, played the role of Ryu and Ken, respectively. Even the fighting tactics of this movie followed the game closely. Jumping on the bandwagon of the SF craze in Hong Kong, this movie pocketed 1.8 million HKD at the

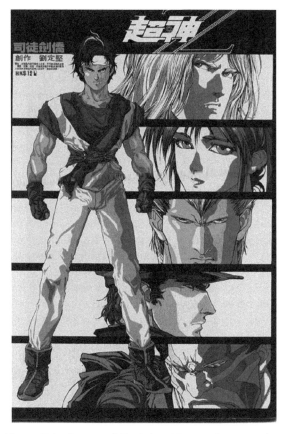

Figure 5.1   Supergod Z: Cyber Weapon borrows the
main characters from SF2.

box office. *The Avenging Fist* (2001, directed by Lau Wai-keung) made a
crossover of SF2 and *Tekken* (Iron Fist, a representative three-dimensional
Japanese combat game developed by Namco). In *Kung Fu Hustle* (2004,
directed by Stephen Chow), a martial arts master used the "fireball throw-
ing fist," a *hissatsuwaza* of Ken and Ryu in SF.

Hong Kong businessmen and game players, without the permission
of Capcom, created a number of modified versions of SF2 with stronger combat ability. SF merchandise such as figurines, t-shirts, posters,
music CDs and card games, licensed or not, flooded the market. The
main characters of SF, including Ryu, Ken, Chun Li and Gouki, became
household names and cyber icons. A Hong Kong young man was hospi-
talized for chemical poisoning, because he used hair spray too much and
too often to copy Ryu's hairdo. Chun Li was one of the most favorite
characters for "cosplay" (or "costume play," a Japanese-English term
coined to refer to the dressing of animation-comic-game or ACG lovers
as their favorite ACG characters). The characters and story of SF2 also

appeared in Hong Kong pop music and TV programs. The media-mix of SF2 promoted the fusion of Japanese and Hong Kong elements in making Hong Kong popular culture.

Having reached the peak of its popularity and influence in Hong Kong in the early 1990s, the SF craze began to cool down. A brief revival occurred in 1997 when SF3 was launched. SF3 enhanced combat ability and added new characters. Besides the original SF series, Capcom also introduced SF-related series, such as Young SF series, EX SF series and SF vs. KOF series for arcade games. After the launching of SF EX3 in 2000, Capcom announced that it would cease the production of SF arcade games. However, SF has not disappeared from Hong Kong. Die-hard SF fans turn to play SF games adapted for PS2 and PS3 as well as continue to play old SF arcade games (in particular SF2) and participate in SF tournaments. In October 2007, Capcom shocked the game community by revealing its plan to launch SF4 in 2008. SF4 is basically a 2-D game with some 3-D graphics and its opening animation is in Chinese ink painting style. Introduced to Hong Kong game arcades in May 2008, it received a moderate success, but did not bring back its old glory (Figure 5.2). It is because new-generation game players prefer 3-D combat games such as *Gundam vs. Gundam*, *Virtual Fighters* and *Tekken*

Figure 5.2 Game players are trying SF4 with great interest. Taken in September 2008, Hong Kong.

to 2-D combat game classics. As a result, SF4 is largely popular among older generation players who find the game nostalgic. In 2009, SF4 will be adopted into PS3 and X-Box360, but people do not have a high expectation on its market performance and cultural impact. Mr. L., a 29-year-old die-hard SF fan, said: "I have been playing SF for the last 19 years and I myself am excited to see the return of SF in 2008. However, I do not think SF 4 will make a great impact in Hong Kong, because it is basically a 'back to SF2' game. It alienates younger players who are used to the SF3 system and characters and only draws attention of older players who played SF2 a decade ago."[10]

In the late 1990s, *King of Fighters* replaced *Street Fighter* as the most popular combat game in Hong Kong. Developed by SNK, a Japanese game developer specializing in combat games, from 1994 to 2005, KOF had been introducing a new series annually. When KOF was first launched in Hong Kong in 1994, its response was overwhelming. Many game players found the team format (three fighters vs. three fighters) adopted by KOF more exciting than the individual fighting format used in SF. KOF reached its peak in the late 1990s, and in particular the KOF 96, KOF 97 and KOF 98 created a commotion. Many local organizations and game centers organized KOF tournaments. Its main characters, such as Iori Yagami, Kyo Kusanagi, Mai Shiranui and Laqia, became well-known among young people in Hong Kong. The character design of KOF has had an impact on Hong Kong youth fashion and comic design. For example, the so-called "MK look" fashion style is under the influence of the KOF character designs.[11] In recent years, "MK look" has penetrated Hong Kong street fashion, gangsters movies, action figures and martial arts comics. The demand for KOF character goods, both imported and locally made, were fierce and included Hong Kong editions of Japanese KOF comics and guide books, action figures and weapons designed by the Hong Kong comic artist Situ Jianqian, as well as KOF comics, magazines and guide books published in Hong Kong.

The popularity of KOF began to decline in the new millennium, but it remains one the most popular combat games at game centers in Hong Kong (Figure 5.3). For example, Fight Club, an unofficial KOF fan-club founded in 2001, has developed into the largest game organization in Hong Kong with 30,000 members.[12] It runs a very active forum on the Internet and organizes KOF tournaments. The main reason for the decline of KOF is that it had been using the same circuit board for more than a decade, making the game inferior in graphic and sound effects when compared to their Capcom and Namco counterparts. Besides, the quality of KOF deteriorated after the bankruptcy of SNK in 2000. In 2000, SNK merged with the Korean game maker Playmore to become SNK Playmore. In celebrating the tenth anniversary of KOF and rekindling people's interest in the game, in late 2005, SNK Playmore introduced KOF 11 that used a brand new circuit board. It has also developed the home console game market by introducing the first three-dimensional KOF game, *The KOF: Maximum Impact* for PS2 and

Figure 5.3 Even now, some game centers in Hong Kong highlight KOF. The photograph was taken by the author in Tai Po, Hong Kong in 2006.

SNK vs. Capcom for X-Box. In 2009, SNK Playmore will launch KOF 12, the next-generation KOF arcade game that uses a new high-functioning circuit board developed by Taito. Mr. T., a 30-year-old KOF fan, believes that KOF 12 will have an impact in Hong Kong. He stated: "I have been playing KOF since 1998 and am never get tired of it. It is because each generation of KOF has something new in terms of story, character and the control system. KOF12 is going to be a major breakthrough and I am really excited about it. I think KOF12 will be better received than SF4 in Hong Kong because there is no discontinuity among KOF players."[13]

Hence, 2008 and 2009 are exciting years when both SF and KOF are trying to make a comeback. Capcom and SNK Playmore may be a bit too upbeat about their latest combat games and the retro-gaming effect, overlooking the fact that combat games have entered the age of 3-D technology. SF4 and KOF 12 are basically 2-D games with some 3-D graphic effects, and thus are less appealing to younger game players. In Hong Kong, SF 4 was launched in May 2008 and KOF12 will be introduced in April 2009, Game experts, game magazines and game players are not very enthusiastic about them. They are, in a sense, like *Rambo 4* or *Rocky 6*, made as a tribute to the classics and to target the older fans.

In retrospect, from the earliest SF1 to the latest SF4 and KOF12, the twenty-one years of Japanese combat games in Hong Kong have become an integral part of the collective memories of Hong Kong players. The SF and KOF series will enter the Hall of Fame in the history of games in Hong Kong.

Although these two games are now past their prime, they remain popular and influential within and outside the world of games in Hong Kong. The history of the two games demonstrates the interplay of Japanization and localization in consuming Japanese games and enriching local culture in Hong Kong.

JAPANESE COMBAT GAMES AND HONG KONG ARCADE GAME CULTURE

If games are a form of text, then game players in Hong Kong are "excessive readers" (in John Fiske's terminology) who actively interpret the text in their own ways based on their life experiences.[14] The games themselves are imported from Japan and their functions are built-in, and thus have little "cultural discount" by nature,[15] but Hong Kong players and artists have used different tactics to play, interpret and use Japanese combat games in their own ways. Since the early 1990s, Hong Kong players have established a unique arcade game culture by setting rules and jargons almost exclusively used among themselves in Hong Kong.[16] These rules and jargons were created during the age of SF and reinforced by the players of KOF and other combat games. They have gradually been adopted into non-combat games and even the daily life and vocabulary of the young people. Hence, consuming Japanese games in Hong Kong is not a form of cultural imperialism, because we have witnessed the making of a dialectical nexus between global (Japan) and local (Hong Kong) in terms of ongoing cultural hybridization.[17] From the perspective of cultural globalization, hybridization should not be interpreted as a degradation of authenticity. It is indeed a value-added cultural interaction that gives local meanings and dimensions to foreign cultural products.

The majority of combat game-related jargons borrow from the languages of the lower class and some are considered indecent and coarse by the society. The background of the players and the running of game centers are accounted for the influx of the lower-class language into the arcade game culture in Hong Kong. In the 1980s and 1990s, most game centers in Hong Kong were small-sized and financially weak. They preferred SF and KOF games because of their small size and high return rate. These game centers were mostly located in the old districts where rents were cheap. Hence, most players came from low-income families and many were students and manual laborers. The image of game centers perceived by the officials, teachers, parents and the press was relatively negative, associated with smoking, excessive noise, gang activities, and drug dealing. Unlike their Western counterparts,[18] few people in Hong Kong recognized the educational and cultural values of games. Playing at game centers was regarded by the public in Hong Kong as a form of entertainment for lower-class and uneducated males.[19] As young people from poor families could not afford a game console or PC, they played at game centers. Consciously or not, the players introduced their languages into arcade games. Table 5.1 lists the jargons added into the Hong Kong arcade game culture during the heyday of SF in the early 1990s:

Table 5.1   Cantonese Jargons Created or Adopted by SF and KOF Players in Hong Kong

Jargons	Original Meanings	Derived Meanings	Popularity and Uses
"Da-bau-kei" （打爆機） or "bau-kei" （爆機）(literally "exploding the machine")	"Da-bau" （打爆）is a coarse Cantonese expression that means breaking or destroying.	Completing the entire game program such as destroying all enemies or reaching the destination.	It has become a popular term for young people in Hong Kong. Many terms have been derived from it, such as "bau-kei-wong" （爆機王） (a skillful player who often wins the game), "bau-kei-kung-loek" （爆機攻略） (the tactics to win the game) and "bau-kei-wa-min" （爆機畫面） (the picture with congratulatory notes displayed on the screen when the player finishes the game).
"Da-dai-lo" (打大佬) (literally "beating up the big brother")	"Dai-lo"(大佬) means the elder brother. It also applies to the gang leader.	Fighting with the last (usually the strongest) opponent.	It has become a jargon for all games. Many terms have been derived from it, including "Chung-dai-lo" (中大佬) (the strong opponent in the middle of the game), "yan-chong -dai-lo" (隱藏大佬) (hidden opponent, usually extremely powerful) and "lam-mei-dai-lo" (臨尾大佬) (the last opponent).
"Chek-chau" (隻揪) (literally "one to one weapon-free combat) or "dan-tiu" （單挑）(literally "challenge by an individual")	A gang slang that means one to one combat.	One to one competition.	This term has been used for a long time and is later applied to SF and other combat games.
"Cheo-bo" （出波）and "cheo-sing" (出昇)	Both terms are coined by Hong Kong players, and refer to the tactics, "bo-tung-chun" (波動拳) ("fireball-throwing fist') and "sing-lung-chung" （昇龍拳） ("rising-dragon fist", used by Ryu and Ken in SF.	Any flying weapon and hitting tactic.	They have become jargons for combat games.
"Bug-kei" （bug 技）	A term coined by Hong Kong players to refer to tricks.	Using the bugs in the program as tactics to play.	The program of KOF has many bugs and thus its players have developed many "bug tactics." This term has become a jargon for all games.
"Da-Kwai" （打龜）(literally "hitting the turtle")	A term coined by Hong Kong players to refer to the defense tactics.	A kind of "bug tactic" that only plays defense.	KOF, due to its design problems, can easily use this defense tactic. This term has become a jargon for all games.
"Hissatsuwaza" (必殺技) (literally "sure-kill technique")	A Japanese term originally applied to the strongest tactic in martial arts.	The killing tactic and weapon used in combat games.	This term has existed for decades, but the SF series popularized it. It is now a common term used in daily conversation whether or not it is related to games.

Hybrid game jargons are creatively coined by Hong Kong players as a localization device to retain their Hong Kong locality while consuming Japanese games. There are three different patterns in linguistic hybridization in the making of game jargons in Hong Kong. First, the application of terms from Chinese *kung fu* to game tactics. Second, the use of underground slangs to refer to actions and characters in games. Third, the combination of English, Cantonese and Japanese to create new terms. These three patterns demonstrate the rich cultural imaginations of the lower class to domesticate Japanese games into their own local culture.

In addition to game jargons, Hong Kong players have also established a set of unwritten rules for arcade games. Many of the rules were started from SF and then reinforced by KOF and other arcade games. Failing to follow the rules may cause language or physical abuse. Table 5.2 lists major rules established by Hong Kong players in playing Japanese combat games.

Influenced by the rules, languages and behaviors of the worlds of the lower class, the martial arts and the underground, the making of game jargons and rules by SF and KOF players in Hong Kong demonstrates the fact that playing arcade games, like watching soccer, is largely a subculture for lower-class males. For example, the common practice of "tiu-kei" (challenging) shows that young people use competition to improve and show off their skills, like the way martial arts students often do (Figure 5.4).

Figure 5.4 Challenging and competing with strangers in KOF is common. The photograph was taken by the author in Shatin, Hong Kong, in 2006.

Table 5.2　Rules Set by the Players of Japanese Combat Games in Hong Kong

Jargons	Meanings	Rules	Popularity and Uses
"Kan-kei" （跟機）	Booking for the next game.	Somebody puts a coin or token at the top of the machine to book for the next game. When the current player finishes his game, he must give up the machine to the next player.	Similar behaviors existed in Hong Kong in the late 1970s, but were not common. The popularity of SF1 made this rule standard practice at game centers.
"Tiu-kei" （挑機）	Challenge other player (usually unknown to each other).	When someone is playing the game, the challenger inserts money to the same machine or the nearby machines to challenge. The current player has to stop his game against the computer and must take up the challenge.	This behavior began with SF1 and became prevalent in SF2 and KOF. It has become a common practice for arcade games that have the challenge function built-in.
"Joeng-round" （讓 round）	Giving up one round for the weaker player so that both players can play longer.	For three-round match like SF, the first round winner loses the second round to his opponent on purpose so that both players can play the final round and the weaker player does not feel offended.	This rule started with SF1 and soon applied to other three-round games. Refusing to obey this unwritten rule will result in fighting. For example, on 17 December 2007, a game player was beaten up by his challenger because he did not give in the second round in playing KOF02. A similar case occurred on 17 February 2008 between two players of SF3.
'Wat-kei" （屈機）	The use of unfair tactics in the game	It is an unsportsmanlike behavior that uses "bug tactics" to defeat the opponent. This is a taboo in playing arcade games in Hong Kong.	This behavior appeared in SF2 and became more common in KOF. Nowadays, this term has become a common term used to describe any kind of unfair behavior or unsportsmanlike attitude. In 2008, this term appeared in the public examination in the subject of Chinese language. The Examination Board of the government was criticized by the media, teachers and parents for using game slang in public examination.

"Joeng-round" (giving in one round), "kan-kei" (booking for the next game) and the ban of "wat-kei" (using bugs to win) are like underworld rules to reduce unnecessary arguments and confrontations. The use of the lower-class language and behavior in playing Japanese combat games in Hong Kong is a cultural representation of social class identity among game players. In Pierre Bourdieu's conceptualization, the ideas of class status, habitus, cultural capital and symbolic violence are manifested in cultural and social activities.[20]

Interestingly enough, from my own fieldwork in Japan and interviews with Japanese game players, I did not find similar rules among arcade game players in Japan. A Japanese player explained that Japanese culture puts emphasis on harmony and thus most players only play with the machine by themselves or with their friends, adding that Japanese players try to keep a distance from others and usually do not challenge strangers. Accordingly, there is no need to set the rules that restrict players from hogging machines or that ban the use of bug tactics. Another reason, from my observation, is that playing at game arcades is a socially acceptable behavior in Japan and players come from different sectors of the society. Thus the rules and languages associated with the lower class and the underground are not incorporated into the games in Japan.

The fusing of elements from Hong Kong low class into Japanese games should not be interpreted as a corruption of "Japanese-ness" or authenticity, but indeed a hybrid culture that enriches the content of and adds new dimensions to Japanese games in transnational cultural flows. "Made in Japan, Played in Hong Kong," Japanese combat games have been localized and hybridized by Hong Kong players.

JAPANESE COMBAT GAMES AND HONG KONG KUNG FU COMICS

While the making of new rules and jargons in playing Japanese games represents a kind of localization of Japanese culture from below (consumers, not producers), the adaptation of Japanese games in Hong Kong comics is the localization of Japanese culture from outside (Hong Kong, not Japan).

Hong Kong comics are famous for their *kung fu* stories and actions. By nature, they are similar to Japanese combat games. Both are about righteous heroes fighting evil. In addition, the relatively culturally odor-free SF and KOF make them easier to be indigenized outside Japan.[21] Therefore, adapting SF and KOF into Hong Kong comics is relatively easy for Hong Kong comic artists. Many of them are lovers of Japanese combat games themselves. The making of Hong Kong comic editions of SF and KOF is a smart business idea, since there are a large number of faithful supporters of these games in Hong Kong. According to my count, from 1991 to the present, Hong Kong comic artists have produced at least 66 Hong Kong comic editions of SF and KOF. Many have been serialized and enjoy a good circulation. While borrowing their main characters and fighting skills from SF and KOF, these Hong Kong comics have also added local elements to make them a hybrid culture. We have witnessed the crossover or fusion of Japanese combat games and Hong Kong *kung fu* comics.

In 1991, the Hong Kong comic artist, Xu Jingchen, published *Jietou bawang* (*Street Fighter*, 100 issues), the first Hong Kong comic edition of

SF. This comic was an instant success and its first issue sold 50,000 copies. However, it did not acquire the copyrights from Capcom and thus was an unlicensed publication. Since Xu was not under the supervision of Capcom, he could freely add many new elements to SF in terms of storylines, characters, and fighting skills. For example, unlike the original story in the game, in this comic, Ryu and Chun Li are lovers and later marry. The comic reaches its climax when all SF major characters, including friends and enemies, come to attend their wedding banquet. Hong Kong readers like this development because it follows the tradition of Hong Kong martial arts novels of combining romance and action. This comic keeps the main characters and fighting skills of the game, but adds a large number of new characters and Chinese martial arts tactics to enrich the story and action, turning the Japanese combat game into Hong Kong-style *kung fu* comics. Of all the new characters, the most noteworthy is Zhan Hu ("Fighting Tiger") who is obviously borrowed from Wang Xiaohu, the protagonist of the classic Hong Kong *fung fu* comic, *Long hu men* (School of Dragons and Tigers) in terms of character design and martial arts. More precisely, Zhan Hu is the middle-aged version of Wang Xiaohu. In early years, Xu Jingchen worked under Huang Yulang and Ma Rongcheng, the two most influential masters of *kung fu* comics in Hong Kong. No wonder he has applied the storytelling and drawing techniques of Hong Kong *kung fu* comics throughout his work. Due to copyright reasons, *Jietou bawang* was forced to cease its publication. However, Xu Jingchen soon created another comic, entitled *Super Fighter* (120 issues). This comic keeps the main characters of SF, but gives them new names to avoid legal responsibility. For example, Chun Li becomes Qing Hui. This kind of "proxy signifier" is a linguistic strategy or code commonly used in cross-media and cross-cultural adaptation. As in Levi-Strauss's discourse on the use of linguistic signs as metonymies, both the author and the reader can read the writing on the wall and will not be confused.[22] For example, the Cantonese pronunciations of Qing Hui and Chun Li are very close and the Chinese dressing of Qing Hui also reminds readers of Chun Li.

After *Jietou bawang* and *Super Fighter*, Xu Jingchen turned to draw licensed editions of SF comics, including *Street Fighter 3* (155 issues), *Young Street Fighter Zero 3* (40 issues), *Street Fighter EX2Plus* (38 issues) and *SF vs KOF* (2001, 27 issues).[23] Due to the supervision of Capcom, these licensed comics are closer to the original game than his previous works. Even the names of fighting tactics are adopted from the game. Although the degree of creativity and localization are compromised, Xu continues to add new plots and tactics to his comics. For example, in *Street Fighter 3*, Ryu creates a new tactic, called *Chun Li wangqingzhang* (The fist of forgetting the love of Chun Li) in memory of Chun Li. This plot seems to have borrowed from the Jinyong's martial arts novel, *Shen diao xia lu* (The Legend of the Condo Heroes) (Figure 5.5).[24] Moreover,

Figure 5.5 Ryu creates a new fist tactic in memory of
Chun Li in the Hong Kong comic, *Street Fighter 3*.

he continues to borrow the character Wang Xiaohu (renamed as Wanghu)
from *School of Dragons and Tigers*.

Likewise, in *SF vs. KOF*, the plot of the baby monk that he added might
have borrowed from Ma Rongcheng's *Zhonghua yingxiong* (The Legend of
Chinese Heroes), a classic of *kung fu* comic. The drawing of fighting scenes
and background follow the Hong Kong comic tradition. In his drawing
of *hissatsuwaza*, Xu's comics keep the original names, but change them
into Chinese *kung fu* instead of simple and straight forward free kicking
tactics as designed in the original games. The language used is colloquial
Hong Kong-style Cantonese with some indecent expressions, such as "*da-
zan-keio*"—(beat him up till he becomes handicapped). Although Xu's SF
comics are so different from the original game, Hong Kong game players
cum comic readers do not mind the changes. On the contrary, they are
excited to see the differences. It shows that in cross-cultural media adaptation, sometimes consumers care less about authenticity, and are concerned

more about whether the new media can give new life to the work.[25] Hu's turning of SF into Hong Kong-style comics is considered very successful in this respect.

Many other Hong Kong comic artists also drew their own editions of SF comics. According to my count, in the 1990s alone, there were at least 15 comic editions of SF made in Hong Kong, including Guang Binqiang' *Street Fighter 3 Third Strike* (28 issues) and Yu Jianpei's *Street Fighter 92* (12 issues). Most of them were unlicensed publications and did not last long. Like Xu's, they were all drawn in the Hong Kong *kung fu* comic style and added many new characters and stories.

Hong Kong comic editions of KOF have been published since 1995. Situ Jianqian, the artist of *Supergod Z: Cyber Weapon*, is famous for turning KOF into Hong Kong comics. His works in this regard include *KOF Z* (2000, 45 issues), *KOF 2000* (40 issues) and *KOF 2002* (56 issues). In particular, his first KOF comic, *KOF Z*, sold about 50,000 copies per issue, making it the bestselling Hong Kong comic edition of KOF. From the beginning, Situ has acquired the copyrights from SNK and therefore his comics are relatively faithful to the original. Nevertheless, he has added Hong Kong elements in his comics in terms of drawing and character. For example, there are some new supporting roles who have Hong Kong-style nicknames, such as Dasha 大傻 (big fool), Datouwen 大頭文 (Wen, the big-head) and Xixiong 細雄 (Xiong, the little).

Xu Jingchen, the most famous SF comic artist, also produced a popular KOF comic, *KOF 99* (38 issues). Its first issue sold about 40,000 copies and the rest between 20,000 and 30,000. Deng Yaorong is the artist of *KOF 96* (36 issues), *KOF 97* (52 issues) and *KOF 98* (44 issues) and his *KOF 96* sold about 40,000 copies at its peak. In recent years, the most active Hong Kong artist of KOF is the team of Yong Ren and Cai Jingdong who created *KOF 2001*, *KOF 2003* (2004, 8 issues), *KOF Maximum Impact* (2005) and *New KOF 2006* (2007). All of these KOF comics made in Hong Kong have incorporated local elements. For example, in *KOF 2003*, Hong Kong is the major background and the venue of the KOF tournament is the Hong Kong Convention and Exhibition Centre in Wanchai (Figure 5.6). Its language is very colloquial that contains some indecent expressions, such as *"chun"* 寸 (arrogant) and *"da-dou-fei-hei"* 打到飛起 (beat one up to the air).

In brief, Japanese combat games and Hong Kong martial arts comics are perfectly and creatively mixed into a hybrid cultural form, namely, Hong Kong comic editions of SF and KOF. The localizing and synergetic tactics employed by Hong Kong comic artists show the creativity of Hong Kong artists and have added new life to Hong Kong comics. They are redefining Hong Kong comic in terms of the new relations between locality and universality, Chinese and Japanese, as well as tradition and modernity. Hong Kong comics have been transformed from *kung fu*

Figure 5.6 Fighting in the famous tourist spot, Golden Bauhinia Square, located in front of the Hong Kong Convention and Exhibition Centre (*KOF 2003*).

comics about local gangsters to combat comics involving top fighters from the whole world.

ISSUES IN TRANSNATIONAL GAME INTERACTION

If the world is becoming a "global village," this global village must have different tribes. Japanese games have gained global popularity, but they are interpreted and played differently by players according to their own social and cultural backgrounds. Through a study of the reception and adaptation of two representative Japanese combat games in Hong Kong, this research is one example of how Japanese games have been localized abroad. It deepens understanding of two important issues regarding cultural consumption and localization in an Asian context.

The first issue involves looking at how individual consumers interpret and consume cultural products in order to add new meanings to them. A historical review of SF and KOF in this chapter shows that Japanese games have been localized by players in Hong Kong for more than two decades. Like *kung fu* comics, gangster films and soccer, playing arcade games, in particular its combat genre, is largely a subculture for lower class young males in Hong Kong. Male players like combat games, because they are congenial to the Hong Kong *kung fu* and street cultures.[26] For instance, they worship heroism based on eye for eye attitude and brotherhood. Players cannot change the system, but can modify the rules and vocabulary.[27] The idea of the passive mass as slaves to the cultural industry is not applicable to SF and KOF players in Hong Kong.[28] Consumers have creatively added new meanings and contents in consuming popular culture.[29] Hong

Kong players have borrowed terms, rules and techniques from Hong Kong martial arts novels, movies and the underground world for Japanese combat games, and domesticated them so that they can fit in their mode of thought and behavior.

The second issue looks into how cultural importers (or recipients) make use of foreign elements to create their own culture. Japanese combat games have influenced Hong Kong comics, movies, fashion and character goods. This study focuses on how SF and KOF are adapted into Hong Kong comics. Hong Kong SF and KOF comics are forms of hybrid culture that mix Japanese games with Hong Kong *kung fu* comics.[30] This crossover is a kind of hybridity that enhances cultural creativity and vitality.[31] Since 1991, Hong Kong comic artists have been drawing their own editions of SF and KOF in the typical Hong Kong comic style. Names, places, martial arts, language, drawing and format have all been localized. For example, free kicking in Japanese games become Chinese *kung fu* in Hong Kong comics. Many characters borrow from representative Hong Kong *kung fu* comics or movies as well as the storylines and plots from bestselling martial arts novels. Colloquial Cantonese including foul languages and gang jargons are used in these comics. SF and KOF have been transformed into various kinds of hybrid cultural products and in some cases the Hong Kong feel is even stronger than that of the Japanese. Besides, this study suggests that the localization of Japanese games is mainly initiated by Hong Kong artists, businessmen, players and consumers, and not by Japanese companies. Hence, neither glocalization nor cultural imperialism is applicable to describe the nature of the reception of Japanese games in Hong Kong.[32]

This study of consumption and localization of Japanese combat games in Hong Kong shows the powerful tactics of cultural consumption, cultural appropriation, localization and hybridization in transnational cultural flows in Asian gaming contexts, an important theme that deserves more in-depth investigation in game studies.

ACKNOWLEDGEMENTS

The chapter is substantially modified and expanded from an article he published in *Game Studies*, 6 (1) October 2006. This study was supported by a grant from the Research Grant Council of Hong Kong (Project No: CUHK4680/05H).

NOTES

1. The electronic game is one of the most globalized but little-studied forms of Japanese popular culture. Writings on Japanese games focus on their educational, psychological, historical and social aspects. Scholarly studies from cultural and comparative perspectives are relatively few. See "Journal Articles: Academic Research into Computer Games," *Computer Games* at

http://www.game-culture.com/journals.html. However, in recent years, Japan's dominance has been challenged by United States in the home console market. Japan is also lagging behind the United States, Korea and Taiwan in online games.

2. For a historical and comparative study of the reception of Japanese videogames in different parts of Asia, see Benjamin Wai-ming Ng, "Videogames in Asia," in *The Video Game Explosion: A History from Pong to PlayStation and Beyond,* ed. M. Wolf (Westport: Greenwood Press, 2008), 211–222.

3. John Fiske, *Understanding Popular Culture* (London & New York: Routledge, 1989), 32.

4. Data about SF and KOF were gathered from newspapers, magazines and Internet, interviews with game players, arcade game shopkeepers, and editors of game magazines as well as on-site observation and participation.

5. James Newman, "The Myth of the Ergodic Videogame," *Games Studies* 2 (1) 2002: 2

6. "Hissatsuwaza" (literally "sure-kill technique") is a term used in traditional Japanese martial arts and was later adopted into Japanese games. According to my own memory and interviews with game players, this term was first used in Hong Kong in the 1980s as a game jargon and then has become a common term used frequently by Hong Kong youngsters since the 1990s. See Tin-fai So, *Internet Dictionary* (Hong Kong: PC User, 2002). In 2005, there was a popular Cantonese song with this title sung by Leo Koo.

7. Steven Kent, *The Ultimate History of Video Games* (New York: Three Rivers Press, 2001), 446.

8. Dawei Chen, "Lun Xianggang wuxia manhua de tuibian" (On the Changes of *Kung Fu* Comics in Hong Kong), in *Chuantong Zhongguo wenxue dianzibao (E-Journal on Traditional Chinese Literature)* 115. Retrieved 5 April 2002 from http://www.literature.idv.tw/news/news.htm.

9. Jianqian Situ, "Preface," *Supergod: Cyber Weapon* (Hong Kong: Freeman Press, 1993).

10. I conducted this interview with Mr. L on 3 September 2008 in Hong Kong, asking him about his game history and his expectation of SF4.

11. "MK Look" is the abbreviation of "Mongkok look." It refers to the outrageous street fashion style of the youngsters (and even gangsters) wandering in the Mongkok district in Hong Kong, characterized by golden hair-dye, earrings, tattoos and dark color tight shirts and jeans.

12. Hingyu Wong, "The Strongest Underground Combat Game Organization," *Eastfinder* 671, 1 December 2004: 112–115.

13. Interview conducted on 11 September 2008 in Hong Kong.

14. Fiske, *Understanding Popular Culture*, 150–154.

15. C. Hoskins and R. Mirus, "Reasons for the US Dominance of the International Trade in Television Programs," *Journalism of Communication*, 38 (1988): 500–501.

16. Besides my own knowledge about videogames in Singapore and Hong Kong as a game researcher in Singapore (1996–2001) and Hong Kong (2001–present), I have asked game players in Japan, Malaysia, Taiwan and Mainland China—via the Internet—about their game cultures. It seems that they all have their own arcade game cultures that are different from that of Hong Kong. The rules and jargons created by Hong Kong players, according to my online survey, can also be found among Cantonese speakers in Southern China and Malaysia due to strong Hong Kong influence in these regions.

17. John Tomlinson, "Cultural Globalization and Cultural Imperialism," in *International Communication and Globalization: A Critical Introduction*, ed. A. Mohamadi (London: Sage, 1997), 170–190.

18. Patricia Greenfield, *Mind and Media: The Effects of Television, Videogames and Computers* (Cambridge: Harvard University Press, 1984).

19. For a study of the language, behavior and value of Hong Kong male game players, see Wai-lok Tam, *Japanese Video Games in Hong Kong: A Study of Subordinate Males as Consumers*. MA thesis, Department of Japanese Studies, National University of Singapore (2001). The general public has biases against game culture. For instance, the police and district councils in Hong Kong have identified game centers as the crime hotbed. Spot inspection by the police is routine. District councils of old districts, such as Mongkok and Shamshuipo, have published reports on crimes associated with game centers.

20. In his analysis of modern sports, Pierre Bourdieu states that different sports reflect the specialized taste of various social classes and even in playing the same sports, different social classes perform in their own ways. Pierre Bourdieu, "Sport and Social Class," in *Rethinking Popular Culture: Contemporary Perspectives in Cultural Studies*, eds. C. Mukerji and M. Schudson (Berkeley & Los Angeles: University of California Press, 1991), 357–373.

21. Iwabuchi Koichi coined the term "culturally odorless commodities" to refer to the universality of Japanese videogames, animation and electronic goods. See Koichi Iwabuchi, *Recentering Globalization: Popular Culture and Japanese Transnationalism* (Durham: Duke University Press, 2002), 24–28. The characters of SF and KOF are from various parts of the world, using different martial arts. "Japanese-ness" is not particularly strong in these two games. See Steven Kent, *The Ultimate History of Video Games* (New York: Three Rivers Press, 2001), 446.

22. Edmund Leach, *Levi-Strauss* (London: Fontana, 1970), 48–49.

23. Chilang Liu, "Xu Jingchen qianwan tui jieba" (Xu Jingchen spending millions to promote his *Street Fighter* comics), *Easyfinder* 506 (Hong Kong, 2003), 136.

24. Shenjing Ba, "Cong youxi manhua shuoqi" (Discourse on Games and Comics), *Diannao shangqingbao* (Journal of Computing Communications), 7 (2001). In the novel, the protagonist, Yang Guo created *Anran xiaowun zhang* (Palm of Sadness) in memory of his love Xiao Longnu.

25. For instance, the best-selling Hong Kong comic, *The Ravages of Time* (by Chan Mou) is adapted from *The Legend of the Three Kingdoms*. Although this comic differs from the classic in terms of story, characters and historical views, Hong Kong readers do not really mind the differences and indeed are thrilled to see how the comic artist creates something new based on the tradition.

26. Due to the differences in values, censorship, legal and educational backgrounds, combat games are less popular in Southeast Asia than East Asia. For example, in Singapore, the most popular genre for arcade games is big-sized games like car racing. See Benjamin Wai-ming Ng, "Japanese Videogames in Singapore: History, Culture and Industry," *Asian Journal of Social Science* 29 (1) 2001: 148–151.

27. Michel de Certeau, *The Practice of Everyday Life* (Berkeley: University of California Press, 1984), xi–xxiv, 29–40.

28. Theodor Adorno, *The Cultural Industry: Selected Essays on Mass Culture* (London & New York: Routledge, 1991)

29. Fiske, *Understanding Popular Culture*, 28.
30. It reminds me of the study conducted by Massey on the youth culture in a jungle in Mexico. She regarded the natives playing Western video games in the jungle as a hybrid culture. See Doreen Massey, "The Spatial Construction of Youth Cultures," in *Cool Places: Geographies of Youth Cultures*, eds. T. Skelton and G. Valentine (London and New York: Routledge, 1998), 121–125.
31. Nestor G. Canclini, *Hybrid Cultures: Strategies for Entering and Leaving Modernity* (Minneapolis: University of Minnesota Press, 1995).
32. Glocalization is coined by Roland Robertson to describe the business strategy used by multinational companies to modify their products according to the specific needs of different overseas markets. See Roland Roberston, "Glocalization: Time-Space and Homogeneity-Heterogeneity," in *Global Modernities*, eds. Mike Featherstone, Scott Lash, and Roland Robertson (London: Sage, 1995), 25–44.

6 The "Bang" Where Korean Online Gaming Began
The Culture and Business of the PC *bang* in Korea

Jun-Sok Huhh

INTRODUCTION: A HIDDEN FACTOR OF KOREAN ONLINE GAMING

If you visit any urban street of South Korea (henceforth Korea), you would be fairly surprised that there are so many signboards named "*PC bang*" or "Game bang" on the streets. If you think these places are ordinary Internet cafés, you should go inside one of them. You immediately cannot miss the unique atmosphere of such places. In contrast to the Internet café, visitors to *PC bangs* (PC rooms) are mostly playing online games at each networked computer. There are few who are web surfing or doing office jobs.

Another intriguing point to notice is that players are talking to one another while playing. It is not a cool and quiet place, but a hot and boisterous playground. Some *PC bangs* even provide "seats for couples," which allow two lovers to play a game together side by side. In Korea, *PC bang* is one of most popular places for dating among young couples; this aspect is elaborated on in Chapter 14. It is not unusual that many visitors call at *PC bangs* with their friends to play online games.

If you look at the visitors more closely, you can certainly find that a few of the players seem to be geeky. Here is a typical picture: They look more relaxed than others. Ashtrays already full of cigarette ends may be placed in front of them. They lean deep against their chairs with their two hands busy on mouse and keyboard. They are talking a lot with their co-players—sometimes with those seated beside them, and at other times over the chatting window on their screen. They are diehard massively multiplayer online role-playing game (MMORPG) players, who are mostly headquartered in the *PC bang* and who represent one of most elite sectors of the Korean online gaming population.[1]

Korea has one of largest online game markets in the world. The factors determining the rapid growth of gaming are multiple and varied. Some experts argued that the high rate of broadband penetration was helped by the high proportion of apartment living, while others said that the unique cultural relationship Korea has toward the Internet and community informed the success of online gaming.[2] Dal Yong Jin and Florence Chee emphasized the geo-political and economic forces that have cultivated the mainstream success of Korean online gaming.[3] In this chapter, I aim to bring to light a hidden and unappreciated factor, namely that the *PC bang* provides a dedicated place for playing online games outside one's home. It can be asserted from the outset that aspects of *PC bang* culture may be likened to arcade gaming in the late 1970s and early 1980s. Like the arcade, the *PC bang* is a kind of offline playing field for computer gaming where people visit the place to enjoy playing games with their friends face to face. On one hand, *PC bang* is a legitimate successor to arcade gaming; on the other hand, it is a part of a new breed of online gaming culture engendered in Korea.

The *PC bang* has played a critical role in shaping and forming the socio-cultural context and business for Korean online gaming. Despite the high accessibility of broadband available in homes, many Korean players still prefer going to *PC bangs* than staying comfortably at home. This chapter addresses the unique and localized characteristics of the *PC bang* in the rise and evolution of Korean online gaming. First, I briefly discuss the proliferation of the Internet in Korea and the transformation of the Internet café into the *PC bang*. The second section is a description of the game that ignited Korean online games, *StarCraft*. The third section deals with the cultural specificities of the Korean *PC bang* and highlights the importance of the physical space that provides the context and meaning of online-offline experiences in online gaming. The fourth section illustrates the business relationship that the *PC bang* has with online game publishers. The final section summarizes the discussion and comments on the contemporary milieu of the *PC bang*.

THE "BANG" OF GAMES: PROLIFERATION OF THE INTERNET AND TRANSFORMATION OF THE INTERNET CAFÉ IN KOREA

To non-Koreans, the notion of the *PC bang* is often misinterpreted as a local version of the Internet café. As a matter of fact, the early *PC bang* was fairly similar to the Internet café. Introducing online gaming to *PC bang*, however, made a big change in that the motivation of visiting was changed from the convenience of Internet connection to seeking the fun of online gaming. The rise of Korean gaming culture needs to be understood accordingly in the context of the spread of broadband Internet connection in Korea.

The first Internet connections in Korea were introduced in 1994. Apart from the high-speed connectivity offered by universities or research laboratories, most individual users were connected to the Internet via dial-up modems. At that time, ordinary networks mainly consisted of text-based BBS services, not graphical Web browsers. The Internet was limited to few enthusiasts only.

In 1997, the government eliminated the long-term monopoly of Korea's only telecommunications company, Korea Telecom (KT). In that same year, competitors such as Hanaro Telecom—which started its main business with Asymmetric Digital Subscriber Line (ADSL) broadband connection service—were established. For Hanaro, this choice of business was strategic because it believed that the broadband connection business would have more competitive advantages than voice-call service. While the voice-call market was already saturated with KT capturing more than 90% of voice-call users, broadband connection represented an unexplored realm in telecommunication services of Korea at that time.

Concurrent to this industry development, the government viewed broadband connection as a stepping-stone for advancing in the so-called "information era." In addition to various kinds of national campaigns celebrating the possibilities of the Internet, the Korean government gave Hanaro a head start by prohibiting KT from entering the broadband market, at least for one year.[4] Later, this provided a foundation for sound competition between the two companies in broadband markets that, in turn, contributed to the fast and widespread development of the Internet.[5]

The first commercial Internet cafés providing faster online connection began to emerge in 1995. This was a far cry from the 22,000 *PC bangs* that now grace most second-level buildings in Korea's capital, Seoul; these earlier examples tended to be located near universities to service students who tend to be early adopters. These early Internet cafés offered little more than a place for Internet connection and office-related jobs such as document printing. The number of Internet cafés remained insignificant until 1998, when two critical events redefined the role of technology in Korean everyday life. In the wake of the 1997 economic crisis of the Asia-Pacific region that saw Korea bailed out by the International Monetary Fund, 1998 heralded not only the strong implementation of broadband policies by the Korean government aforementioned but also the introduction of *StarCraft*.

Without the demand for content such as online games, there would not have been any actual demand for a faster connection in spite of the strong drive by Korean government. *StarCraft* served as a catalyst for creating an explosive growth for broadband connection. Although broadband connection was not necessary for playing the game, early Korean Internet users considered broadband connection indispensable when playing *StarCraft*.[6] At that time, some players blamed their defeats in networked matches on allegedly poor connection speed.

Positive feedback generated by *StarCraft* and broadband connection in turn created further opportunities for both Internet cafés and game developers. One prominent example was an MMORPG named *Lineage* by NCsoft, launched in February 1998. It was the first generation of online games that took advantage of high-speed Internet connection. The spectacular success of *Lineage* helped to forge a receptive environment for online gaming in general. Once the uncertainty about the online game business was lifted, a big rush to make MMORPGs began in late 1999 in Korea (see Table 6.1).

Table 6.1   Trend of Game Developers and Publishers in Korea 1999–2004

Type of Company	Year					
	1999	2000	2001	2002	2003	2004
Developer	416	952	1,381	1,774	2,059	2,567
Publisher	278	547	736	859	921	1,001

Source: Korea Game Development and Promotion Institute (KOGIA), Game BaekSeo [Game White Paper] (Seoul: KOGIA, 2005), 118.

It should be noted that there was a clear co-evolution between the growth of Korean online gaming and that of the *PC bang* during the early years. As shown in Table 6.2, the growth rate of *PC bang* businesses between 1998 and 1999 was remarkable. This growth was informed by the fact that newly proliferating Internet cafés in 1998 offered their visitors a more comfortable and conducive environment for online gaming. The ambience of the place quickly altered from a quiet library style into an open, frenetic coin-operated setting, with most selling snacks and beverages. Food delivery was also allowed for customers. The pricing policy of *PC bangs* encouraged their visitors to play longer; the more you stay on, the lower the hourly charge gets. It was not a coincidence that the Korean word "Game bang" became interchangeable with *PC bang*.

Another clue to the cultural transformation of the Internet café into the *PC bang* can be found in its business trends after 2000. It is intriguing that the number of *PC bangs* has still remained high even after broadband connection penetrated people's homes on a widespread basis. If the convenience

Table 6.2   Trend of *PC bang* and Broadband Subscription in Korea 1998–2005

	Year							
	1998	1999	2000	2001	2002	2003	2004	2005
PC Bang	3,000	15,150	21,460	22,548	21,123	20,846	20,893	20,786
Broad-banded-Household (thousand)	-	370	4,020	7,810	10,080	11,178	11,921	12,190

Source: The datum on *PC bang* is from KOGIA, *Game BaekSeo*, 118, and the datum on broadband subscription in Korea is from National Internet Development Agency of Korea (NIDA), Internet Jawon Tonggye [Internet Resource Statistics], available at http://isis.nida.or.kr.

of broadband had been the only—or most significant—motive for visiting the *PC bang*, then business theoretically should have declined from about 2000 onwards with the advent of domestic broadband connectivity. However, as can be noted from Table 6.2, the vigor in the business operations of *PC bangs* has changed little in spite of widespread use of home broadband. This phenomenon suggests that what attracts players to the *PC bang* is not its technological aspect (i.e., broadband access). In short, the *PC bang* was far from just a convenient site for broadband connection, rather it represented a place for fostering the culture of Korean online gaming.

IGNITING THE *PC BANG*: *STARCRAFT*

StarCraft's contribution to Korean online gaming is irrefutable. Before 1998 when Blizzard's *StarCraft* came to Korea, electronic gaming had been under a dark shadow in Korean culture. The game business in Korea started around the early 1980s with the illegal copying of Japanese arcade games. It remained officially illegal to import Japanese products until early 2001. All games operating in arcades were pirated versions orchestrated by local reverse engineering. Arcade games gained some popularity among the youth; most parents tended to take the media effects approach toward gaming, especially viewing it as seriously undermining children's education. The Korean government initially considered computer gaming not as a legitimate leisure activity or an industrial sector to be nurtured, but as a matter of regulation for preventing its side effects. Unfortunately, in Korea, the popularity of arcade games was too ephemeral for electronic gaming to enter into mainstream culture. It was not until 1998 that gaming was on the lips of ordinary Korean people again.

This long-term state of depression in electronic gaming was broken in a single strike by a game named *StarCraft*. The sales record of the game in Korea was estimated to be 3.5 million copies—more than half of the worldwide sales volume of 6 million from its launch in 1998 to 2002.[7] With the advent of *StarCraft*, young people en masse were quick to abandon popular leisure activities such as billiards, arcade games and Korean checkers. It is now well-known that interest in *StarCraft* in Korea went far beyond the casual playing of the game and generated another game-related sector, namely, e-sports that made computer gaming both a sporting event and a spectator sport.

Why were Korean players so fascinated by *StarCraft*? To begin with, this science fiction real-time strategy (RTS) is undoubtedly well designed. Nevertheless, the quality of game play alone is insufficient for explaining its exceptional popularity in Korea. This game was originally published by a division of LG Electronics, LG Soft, in 1997. Because of the financial crisis, the company could not evade the huge wave of severe downsizing. A managing staff of LG Soft at the time, Young-man Kim, made a bold decision to establish a new game start-up based on *StarCraft*, namely HanbitSoft. He secured the copyright of the game in the process of abolishing his division. The first thing that HanbitSoft did was to distribute free copies of the game at the newly proliferating *PC bangs*. At that time, the *PC bang* was a focal point among the young who could not find their first jobs and the unemployed who had been sacked due to widespread corporate downsizing. As the only thing they had enough time for was the time for leisure, this newly introduced content was swiftly absorbed among them. The national economic crisis of 1997 thereby played an awkward but critical role in the success of *StarCraft*. There are no precise metrics for sales volumes in the *PC bang* sector, but around 30% of total sales in Korea are estimated to be from purchases at *PC bangs*, which amount to 1.5 million copies.

LOCATING THE *PC BANG*: COMPLEMENTING ONLINE GAMES WITH THE OFFLINE

As previously noted, the motivation or reason to visit a *PC bang* did not lessen even after home broadband was easily available. This trend poses a seeming paradox: If you could enjoy playing games in the comfort of your home with fairly low costs, why bother to venture out to play the same online games? Why does the *PC bang* continue to be so compelling to many young Koreans? What does the *PC bang* offer to the Korean gaming population?

TWO VIEWS ON ONLINE GAMES: SUBSTITUTE VS. COMPLEMENT

Compared with other gaming forms, online games forged new gaming territories by increasing the capacity of the game to include many players. Departing from the experience of single-player or limited multi-player games, these games engendered new modes of game play and a sense of community precipitated by online relationships. Massively multiplayer online games are not limited to interaction with a computer or with a few other players only, which in turn makes the social sphere of gaming salient. Some critics go further to consider online game as a platform to construct entirely new relationships among players.[8] They see online games realized in massively multiplayer forms as a substitute for, or alternative to, real world relationships. Real world relationship is history-dependent in that people cannot choose their lives fully by their own will. The possibility to regenerate another alternative life by one's own decision is open in online games or virtual worlds. According to this view, other single-player or limited multi-player games are not genuine social gaming in that they are too hard-wired to the pre-designed software that controls all the fundamental experiences of gaming. This kind of games represents either the consumption of narratives prescribed by game developers or the computer-mediated recreation of traditional games such as Chess. By contrast, the online gaming experience on massively multiplayer formats is unique in that a large part of game play is determined by interactions among players in the games. Also, massively multiplayer online games give players the freedom to choose their in-game identities. In this sense, online games serve as a *substitute* to real world player interactions.

Although interface designs have sought to create feelings of contact in online relationships, contact via the Internet is still a mediated and indirect experience. Gaming interactions in the virtual world are inevitably informed by offline experiences and by the real world context. Therefore, we take our offline experiences and pre-given identities into the world of online game play. At the same time, playing online games—surrounded by other players in the offline context—creates particular relationships, and online and offline synergies, that cannot be underestimated. In this sense, online games still serve as a *complement* to real world experiences. A well-known example preceding online games is arcade gaming. Arcade gaming was the first popular computer-mediated experience that made use of real world contexts of competition. Many children might have fond memories of winning the highest score in their local arcade.[9] Arcade gaming was a new experience created by new computer technology, but the motivation of fun was a very old one.

The *PC bang* has its cultural roots in pre-Internet society. It is a contemporary equivalent to old arcade gaming, and these two cultures share the core mechanism for enjoying fun, the offline physical context that complements computer-mediated gaming. As a space for forging emerging online gaming culture, the *PC bang* re-enacts the fun of the arcade age—and, equally important, the fun of the shared arcade space. The *PC bang* therefore functions as an important offline social context for online gaming, and it makes use of playing practices that have their genealogies in communal and competitive arcade gaming.

PC BANG AS ARCADE GAMING

A typical example of online-offline synergy in the *PC bang* is the small-scale local *StarCraft* contests that were very popular in Korea during the late 1990s and early 2000s. Nowadays, Korean e-sport is a symbol that represents the mainstream popularity of online gaming in Korea.[10] The interesting fact is that e-sport was not organized in a systematic way, but sprang spontaneously from below. Before the official coining of the e-sports industry, many *PC bangs* in Korea often sponsored local *StarCraft* contests in their own towns. While Battle.net—an official service provided by the developer to make online matches among players easier—was a reliable large-scale scoring board for the competition, players often desired to contend and compete directly in the same offline space. These early local town-scale contests founded what would become the burgeoning e-sports industry in Korea. Despite growing interest in competitions in Battle.net, Korean players still choose to play *StarCraft* with other players while sharing the same physical and cultural environment. The King-of-the-Town motivation of arcade gaming is still prevalent in local matches of *StarCraft*. Even today, the professional gaming leagues ("pro-leagues") still hold their preliminary elimination contests in *PC bangs*, which remain the ground for aspiring e-sports superstars.

In Korea, one of the favorite leisure activities for young people is playing online games with their friends at the *PC bang*. As Chee observed, *PC bangs* operate as "third spaces" in between home and schoolwork.[11] It is not unusual for schoolchildren to drop by their local *PC bang* with their classmates to play casual online games. Despite their ability to access the games at home via fast broadband connection, it is the physical, offline social space of the *PC bang* that compels them to return. The ongoing popularity of *PC bangs* demonstrates the significance of the offline social setting in maintaining online game play.

THE *PC BANG* AND MMORPG PLAYERS

Generally, Korean MMORPGs have placed too much emphasis on in-game fighting among players. More often than not, this bias has given rise to misunderstandings by non-Korean players and game critics, resulting in underdeveloped arguments about Korean gaming.[12] In contrast to MMORPGs made in the West such as *EverQuest* and *World of Warcraft*, Korean games are thought to be less crafted and less complicated in their narratives and game play. However, such readings miss the point of online gaming as a social activity where players bring to the game offline forms of socializing. The crucial point is that the so-called dearth of prefabricated content in Korean games lends itself to players importing their own modes of play and socializing in the game space. Most Korean online games have evolved along this path whereby credence is given to users' participation in the virtual showdown.

This aspect is clearly evidenced in the phenomenon of *GongSungJun*—a massive territorial warfare between two guilds in *Lineage*. Basically, this is a grand combat between two guilds of players in the attempt to secure the ownership of a castle or a province in the game. *GongSungJun* in *Lineage* effectively initiated an imaginative way of playing MMORPGs. Many gamers in Korea say that *GongSungJun* may be the most addictive online gaming experience in their lives. It is the offline element of gaming at the *PC bang* that created the core of game play in *GongSungJun*. At the day of grand battling, most of guild members, numbering around thirty or forty, gather in a *PC bang* so that more coherent group play can be coordinated. A commander and the squad leaders direct their teams not via online communication but by verbal and proximate physical communication. It is spectacular to see players going all out in front of their PCs with live voice direction at their backs.

Since the early years of *Lineage,* quite a few *PC bangs* have supported their own star guilds in that MMORPG. These guilds are given considerable discounted usage fees and special allowances such as the exclusive occupation of the *PC bang* when *GongSungJun* is carried out. These guild members provided stable revenue for *PC bangs*. In addition, in-game grand battling carried out at *PC bangs* were perfect for publicity and promotional purposes.[13]

So-called real-money trading (RMT) also originated from the promotional strategies of *PC bangs*. In 2000, as the competition among *PC bangs* increasingly intensified, some of them invented novel promotional tools for attracting more clients. At first, they purchased in-game items of popular games such as *Lineage* from their expert customers, and offered new customers these items for nothing. The birth and rise of RMT in Korea directly resulted from local trading between *PC bang* owners and their visitors. This in turn initiated the rapid growth of the famous secondary market for in-game items and currency in Korea. The experience of RMT at *PC bangs* provided the chance for players to be familiar with RMT. At the early stage of RMT, *PC bangs* afforded one of the strongest buying powers in the Korean RMT market.[14] Around 2001, some *PC bangs* started turning themselves into so-called gold farming shops that specialized in producing and selling in-game items for RMT. Because many players were on the receiving end of RMT, the trend was viewed favorably, which undoubtedly ensured the prospering of RMT.

COOPERATING WITH THE *PC BANG*: BUSINESS BETWEEN *PC BANGS* AND GAME PUBLISHERS

As the *PC bang* has been a critical part of Korean online gaming, it is not surprising that there has existed close partnership between online game publishers and *PC bangs*. As previously noted, *StarCraft* is the first best-selling game in Korea. Single-player games and games with limited multiplayer content sold as standalone CD-ROM packages could not match its success. In contrast to the subsequent slump in sales for such games, MMORPGs distributed exclusively online have been highly popular after *Lineage* came on the scene. Ever since then, online game publishers have become the main business partners of *PC bangs*.[15] As Table 6.3 shows, the largest revenue portion for online game publishers came from the *PC bang* sector. What is the business model for the *PC bang*? What pricing methods do publishers harness for eliciting profits from this sector?

Table 6.3   Revenue Profile of NCsoft by Business Sector 2000–2004

Type of Sector	Year				
	2000	2001	2002	2003	2004
PC bang	39,386	61,370	53,331	48,005	74,703
Individual user	10,738	43,558	74,726	88,603	133,523
Other affiliates	4,479	8,336	4,680	1,681	573
Loyalties	1,296	9,327	21,873	28,248	36,977
Total	55,900	12,2593	154,610	166,537	245,776

Note: The data are US dollar in ten thousands.

Source: NCsoft, *Fact Sheet*, available from http://www.ncsoft.com/kor/nccompany/ir_data_report04.asp

IP PRICING: THE SOLUTION FOR THE *PC BANG*

At a glance, there appears to be no compelling reason why a customer would buy a game at a *PC bang*. A player who would play an MMORPG at a *PC bang* might not only have to pay the game's subscription fee but also the additional charge by the *PC bang*. Granted the *PC bang* has unique cultural and social attraction for online game players, nonetheless there is little equivalent budgetary incentive. If it had not been for an inventive pricing policy—namely, IP pricing—by game publishers, *PC bangs* might not enjoy such huge popularity.

IP pricing means that the game publisher charges a price according to the number of fixed IP addresses used by each affiliated *PC bang*. With this policy, for example, a player could enjoy *Lineage* at *PC bangs* without paying a monthly subscription for an individual user account. In the beginning, this approach was only exercised by a select few *PC bangs* that made use of free playing as a promotional attraction. It was NCsoft that introduced IP pricing for gaming at the *PC bang*. NCsoft utilized IP pricing to secure a larger player base for its mega-hit game, *Lineage*.[16] With the extreme popularity of the game, IP pricing swiftly became the standard in pricing online games at the *PC bang*.

On the one hand, IP pricing helped online game developers and publishers to have a more stable source for profit. As Table 6.3 shows, during the early years, earnings from *PC bangs* had been the biggest part of revenues for game publishers. In addition, IP pricing made it possible to predict the demand for a game under development more accurately than before, which helped fund the costs of developing games.

On the other hand, IP pricing was a mutually beneficiary option for both players and *PC bangs*. The hourly price of playing at a *PC bang* was slightly higher than the per hour price of a monthly subscription. IP pricing, however, allowed customers at *PC bangs* to have more flexibility and advantages over an individual monthly subscription. At *PC bangs*, players can avoid the constraints of monthly pricing. Owners of *PC bangs* could also profit from IP pricing given the minimal profit margins stemming from the gap between user pays and charges by game publishers. From 2000 to 2004, the average monthly charge at an IP was about USD $50.[17] If the IP of a *PC bang* was conservatively estimated to be occupied for 10 hours per day, monthly revenues from an IP would amount to about $450 considering the average hourly price charged at a *PC bang* is $1.50. Even with other operational expenses, the costs of managing *PC bang* overheads were relatively small, thus ensuring a good income.

The success of an online game obviously depends on the number of players it has. "Network effects"—a compound phenomenon whereby the more players you have, the more players you will attract—is a key factor in the business of online gaming.[18] In this respect, it is interesting that the strategic choice for implementing network effects was the player in the *PC bang* rather than individual user or subscriber. The charge set by game publishers was cheaper at the *PC bang* compared to individual accounts. The *PC bang* was therefore the starting point not only in the cultural sense but also in a business one.

MICRO-PAYMENT AND CONFLICT OF INTEREST

Circa 2002, the MMORPG-saturated Korean online game market showed signs of stagnation. Numerous MMORPGs following *Lineage* had been launched since 1999, but the share of two games, *Lineage* by NCsoft and *Mu Online* by WebZen, consisted of around 70% of the entire market. Some companies tried to find another way to penetrate this state of oligopoly by differentiated styles of games. Among these trials, so-called casual games emerged as the next online gaming trend from 2003 onwards.[19] The casual game emphasizes the competitive dimensions of multi-player experience—rather than the typical massiveness as witnessed in *Lineage*. Since casual games are basically free, profits for publishers are via micro-payments by players for in-game cash, in-game items, and so on. It is not hard to imagine that this changing trend in the industry caused a conflict of interest between *PC bangs* and game publishers. Unlike the typical MMORPG with subscription, there was no nominal price for playing such a game, which rendered IP pricing for *PC bangs* irrelevant. However, the game publishers could not simply abandon IP pricing as the *PC bang* still provided a large portion of game publishers' total revenues.

A typical incident in this new configuration was demonstrated in 2005 with the conflict between an online game publisher Nexon and *PC bangs*. Nexon is one of the giants in the Korean gaming market with its strong lineup of casual games such as *B&B* and *Kart Rider*. Nexon took a hardened attitude to force *PC bangs* into the same IP pricing for its casual games as applied to the MMORPG. *PC bangs* were, of course, fiercely against this policy. They claimed that players would not visit *PC bangs* to play such free casual games. The implementation of IP pricing would seriously encroach on their potential income. The early stages of confrontation escalated into collective refusal by *PC bangs* to comply with Nexon's policy.

However, this collective action did not last long as individual *PC bangs* quietly decided to pay the charge set by Nexon. With the popularity of Nexon's *Kart Rider* surpassing the registered subscriptions of *Lineage*,[20] *PC bangs* had no other option but to obey Nexon's policy. Nexon also backed down by implementing a series of reductions in its charges for IPs at *PC bangs*. Interestingly, even after IP pricing was established for free-to-play games, the profitability of the *PC bang* was not seriously damaged. This is another clue in the culture and business of *PC bangs* in Korea that has continued to remain popular despite shifts in the industry and game play.

Today's relationship between two institutions in Korean online gaming—*PC bangs* and game publishers—is heading toward a more cooperative future. Some recent games based on micropayment models do not charge in *PC bangs* any more, with a few publishers even sharing their revenues from selling virtual assets with *PC bangs*. For example, *Special Force*, another popular online game by Neowiz, sought to intentionally emphasize cooperation between game publishers and *PC bangs*. Neowiz considered the *PC bang* as not just a revenue source but as a strategic partner to entice players to pay more in online games. To enhance this scenario, Neowiz added various exclusive in-game items that could only be purchased at *PC bangs*. A growing number of publishers are taking similar strategic approaches by giving extra bonuses to users purchasing virtual assets at *PC bangs*. This kind of cooperative approaches is emerging as an alternative strategy at the *PC bang* for micro-payment-based games.[21]

CONCLUSION: ANOTHER SPECTER NAMED *PC BANG*?

This chapter has outlined some of the key characteristics informing the culture and business of the *PC bang* in Korea. The *PC bang* is definitely a distinctive form of business in that it puts much more emphasis on online gaming and its association with offline socializing, as arcade games once did. It evolved from a convenient spot for high-speed Internet connection to a dedicated place for online gaming. The *PC bang* has functioned as a complementary social space for playing online games, clustering indirect online relationships into a direct offline experience. In this sense, it is the arcade upgraded in the age of the Internet and it infers a cultural mixture between online interaction and offline communication. The *PC bang* has also been a crucial collaborator in the business of online gaming, as demonstrated by the cooperative role it has played with game publishers in IP pricing. With the recent rise in free-to-play casual games and the implementation of micro-payments, the relationship between the game publisher and the *PC bang* has taken on a new dimension, which may be not as cooperative as before.

In 2006, there was a serious threat to the Korean gaming industry that occurred with the scandal of *Sea Story*. Played on an electronic gambling coin-operated machine, *Sea Story* basically served to blur boundaries between gambling and gaming in Korea.[22] The aftermath was even more destructive than the scandal itself. The huge success of *Sea Story* has induced some *PC bangs* to be transformed into illegal online gambling houses. These *PC bangs* are even mutually syndicated via secretive Internet networks that provide gamblers with a larger-scale environment. The implementation of regulations against such undesirable deviations from the original *PC bang* has not been perfected and seems impossible to ensure henceforth. Another critical threat came from Hangame.com, the gaming division of Naver.com, which is the largest Internet portal in Korea. The popular online Go-Stop games in Hangame.com have been used as an illegal gambling platform.[23] Some of *PC bangs* changed their titles to "Hangame *PC bang*" which served as actual gambling spots for gambling addicts. This is even more problematic in that the gambling contents are unsuitably supported by one of largest game companies in Korea.

Unfortunately, if the present rapid turnover trend continues, many *PC bangs* will no longer be recognizable as a culture supporting online-offline gaming and socializing. Returning to the earlier arcade discussion, arguably the *PC bang*, an original and integral part of the culture and business of Korean gaming history, could become another sad specter. Like the arcade, the *PC bang* could possibly become a place of, and in, the past. If the *PC bang* vanished, it would affect the future direction of Korean gaming culture. If a culture loses its uniqueness and history, what would remain for further evolving? Maybe, it's game over?

NOTES

1. A nice description of the *PC bang* culture and other Korean gaming scenes is included in Rossignol's reportage. Jim Rossignol, "Sex, Fame and PC Baangs: How the Orient Plays Host to PC Gaming's," *PC Gamer UK*, April, 2005: 169–186.
2. Michael Kanellos, "Consumers: Gaming Their Way to Growth," *Cnet News.com*, June 25, 2004. Retrieved 20 December 2007 from http://news.cnet.com/2009-1040_3-5239555.html; Dave Kosak, "Why is Korea the King of Multiplayer Gaming?" *Gamespy.com*, March 7, 2003. Retrieved 20 December 2007 from http://archive.gamespy.com/gdc2003/korean; Mark Russell, "Gaming the Online Games," *Newsweek*, 18 October 2004.
3. Dal Yong Jin and Florence Chee, "Age of New Media Empire: A Critical Interpretation of the Korean Online Game Industry," *Games and Culture*, 3 (1) 2008: 38 58.

4. Izumi Aizu, "A Comparative Study of Broadband in Asia: Deployment and Policy," paper presented at GLCOM Colloquium No. 13 (GLCOM, 2002). Retrieved 20 December 2007 from http://www.glocom.org/special_topics/colloquium/ 20020529_bb_in_asia.

5. Notwithstanding the government's role in promoting the Internet, the role of the Korean government in the development of Korean online gaming has been more limited than one might presume. In Chapter 2, Jin and Chee highlight Korean government's direct intervention in the games industry. But its interest lagged definitely behind the more significant and spontaneous success of *StarCraft* and *Lineage*. The government's role in promoting Korean online games industry, and thereby directly influencing the success of online games in Korea, is highly debatable.

6. Moreover, the introduction of a low, monthly, flat pricing policy of ISPs for broadband connection also encouraged online gaming to flourish.

7. Tong-hyung Kim, "'StarCraft' developer eyes online games," *Korea Now*, April 16, 2005. Retrieved 20 December 2007 from http:// koreanow.korea-herald.co.kr/SITE/data/html_dir/2005/04/16/200504160021.asp.

8. *Snow Crash* (New York: Bantam Spectra, 1992), a science fiction by Neal Stephenson, provided a path-breaking momentum for this kind of approach. Among many so-called online Metaverses that Stephenson boldly imagined, *Second Life* is a forerunner in that it considers socializing in virtual world as a kind of substitute of real world. For further detail, see Cory Ondrejka, "Changing Realities: User Creation, Communication, and Innovation in Digital World," working paper (SSRN, January 16, 2005), http://ssrn.com/paper=799468.

9. Lincoln Ruchti illustrated this point persuasively by showing the enthusiasm of 1970s and early 1980s arcade gaming in the United States in his documentary film *Chasing Ghosts: Beyond the Arcade* (Glenham, NY: Men at Work Picture LLC, 2007). Many ordinary people remember these times as the "Golden Age" of computer gaming, which speaks of the importance of gaming experiences in the offline context.

10. Ahn-Jae Lee, "e-Sports as a Growing Industry," Industry Report (Samsung Economic Research Institute, 2005), http://www.seriworld.org/01/wld-ContV.html?mn=B&mncd=0201&key=20051004038500.

11. Florence Chee, "The Games We Play Online and Offline: Making *Wang-tta* in Korea," *Popular Communication*, 4 (3) 2005: 225–239.

12. Evaluations of *Lineage* by Western game reviewers were mostly harsh. Popular gaming webzine Gamespot.com rated it 5.5 out of 10. See Ron Dulin's review on the game (*Gamespot.com*, January 9, 2002).

13. Jun-Sok Huhh and Sang-Woo Park, "Game Design, Trading Markets and Playing Practices," working paper (Gamestudy.org, 2005). Retrieved 20 December 2007 from http://gamestudy.org/eblog/2005/12/04/game-design-trading-markets-and-playingpractices.

14. Gamestudy.org, "Hanguk MMORPG, Munje-ui HyunJang-ul Jikyeboda [Korean MMORPG, What Are Problems?]," Interview with Documentary Director Il-Ahn Kim (Gamestudy.org, 2005). Retrieved 20 December 2007 from http://www.gamestudy.org/bbs/zboard.php? id=w&no=16.

15. Park and Gillespie pointed out piracy protection as a contributing factor to the *PC bang*'s success in Korea in "PC-bang" Brought a "Big-bang": The Unique Aspect of the Korean Internet Industry," paper presented at ASPAC Conference (ASPAC, 2004). Retrieved 20 December 2007 from http://mcel.pacificu.edu/aspac/papers/scholars/parkb/park.htm. This assertion, however, is not supported by actual fact. Initially, the online game in general is less at risk from piracy than the PC-based stand-alone game. Moreover,

there is no specific reason why *PC bang*s did not support a piracy industry if it had been profitable. As we have witnessed in various examples, no stand-alone games, with the exception of *StarCraft,* have gained from such regulations in piracy.

16. Jung-Hyun Wi, *Online Game Business Junryak* [Business Strategy of Online Game] (Seoul: Jewoo Media, 2006), 83.
17. Wi, *Online Game Business Junryak*, 103.
18. David Evans, Richard Schmalensee and Andrie Hagiu, *Invisible Engines: How Software Platforms Drive Innovation and Transform Industries* (Cambridge, MA: MIT Press, 2006), 285.
19. The casual game in Korea is not a poker-like or puzzle-like game but an easy-to-learn arcade-style action game. Sometimes, game developers call it the "mid-session" game.
20. Larissa Hjorth, "Playing at Being Mobile: Gaming, Cute Culture and Mobile Devices in South Korea," *Fibreculture*, 8, 2006. Retrieved 20 December 2007 from http://journal.fibreculture.org/issue8/issue8_hjorth.html.
21. But the relationship between two might not be as intimate as before. For example, Neowiz made a deceptive move for *Special Force* to make a premium charged service named *GunPang* for *PC bang.* Underlying conflict of interest cannot easily vanish in so far as the business model of micropayment persists.
22. Tong-hyung Kim, "Overseas Travel Ban Slapped on 34 over "Sea Story" Probe," *The Korea Times,* August 25, 2006. Retrieved 20 December 2007 from http://times.hankooki.com/lpage/200608/kt2006082518131110440.htm.
23. Michael Ha, "Online Gambling Sites Mushrooming," *The Korea Times*, June 9, 2008. Retrieved 10 June 2008 from http://www.koreatimes.co.kr/www/news/nation/2008/06/117_25599.html.

7 Lan Gaming Groups
Snapshots from an Australasian Case Study, 1999–2008[1]

Melanie Swalwell

Will people continue to go to Lans, do you think, when the speed of playing on the Internet catches up to what can be achieved at a Lan?
(Question posed to the author at a seminar, 2000).

holy crap all the old peeps . . .
we should all get together in like a gathering of people and computers
. . . now what do they call such events?!?
(Post to Lan A's messageboard, 2007).

A form of networked gaming, Lanning is the practice where gamers play multiplayer games with and against each other, over a Local Area Network (LAN). A Lan ensures that players experience fast gameplay and low ping times. Lan gaming is conducted on both a small scale, such as in peoples' homes or after-hours in an office, and a larger scale, such as at festival-type events—often known as Lan parties—devoted to getting many players onto a Lan. Examples of large Lan events include: QuakeCon, an annual event held in Dallas, Texas and sponsored by id software; xLAN, an annual Auckland event which also serves as the New Zealand qualifying tournaments for the World Cyber Games; and the large Dutch Lan Event, Campzone, studied by Jansz and Martens.[2] Internationally, there is significant diversity between Lans. At a standing Lan such as that found in an Internet or Lan café, computers and networking equipment will be supplied. By contrast, at many smaller or temporary Lans, the network lasts only for the duration of the Lan, and players must bring their own computers along to play on. In this chapter, my interest is in *Lan groups*, that is, groups of people who meet regularly, perhaps every month or two, to Lan.

To date, only a handful of projects have inquired into Lanning. Lan gaming receives a brief, early mention in Sandy Stone's reflections on those in the communication industry who play "technosocial games."[3] Jansz and Martens' aforementioned 2005 research at Campzone was based on a questionnaire inquiring into players' motivations. Beate Geissler and Oliver

Sann's project "shooter" is a visual contribution to the discourse on Lanning: Made in the artists' studio, "shooter" consists of a video and series of photographs of Lanners at play, the latter showing deep concentration on the faces of players.[4] Other researchers have taken advantage of players' physical co-location at LANs to conduct research: Bart Simon considers the phenomenon of case modification, noting the importance of the spectacular public display of mods at Lans in Montreal.[5] In another study, Catherine Beavis et al. approached gaming in Lan cafes as presenting informal learning and teaching opportunities for young people.[6]

I have long been interested in the not-for-profit, and extremely social nature of, Lan gaming groups. In 2003 I published "Multi-Player Computer Gaming: 'Better than playing (PC games) with yourself,'" an article situating the Lan phenomenon and theorizing the complex intertwining of, and negotiations between, the range of different materiality and reality statuses that gamers undertake in the course of playing a game. I argued that the bodily-aesthetic sense of being—in some sense—both "here" (in material space) and "there" (in virtual, games space) was particularly foregrounded in Lanning.[7] The current chapter is conceived as a companion piece of sorts to this article: While it focused on tensions between the "here" and the "there," this chapter attends to Lans' temporal and historical development, which I think of in terms of the "then" and the "now."

The chapter hones in on several Lans in two locations within Australasia to present a fine-grained analysis of Lan gaming culture and the ways that this has developed and changed over time. Focusing on specific places gives the "local" in Local Area Network an extra meaning. The chapter presents "snapshots" of five Lan gaming groups at different historical moments. These are, roughly: 1999, when I began research with a large, Sydney Lan; 2004, when I conducted research with the admins of five Lans in Australia and New Zealand; and 2008, the time of writing.

Two things motivated me to revisit Lan groups. The first was a comment made by Frank, a founding admin of the Sydney Lan group I had been following for some years. In 1999, he had explained his uncertainty over how formal he should make the group: While he could see potential for turning a profit from Lanning, he was reluctant to do this as he felt it would stop being *fun*. This dilemma between business and fun seemed to me to be a key aspect of both the Lan groups' attraction and its success, and the issue was one that he and I revisited in subsequent discussions.

The second provocation for this research was a 2003 market analysis report by IDC Asia-Pacific, a market research company servicing the region. This stated that while Lan events are more popular than online gaming in Australia, the viability of these events is low, given their lack of a business model and their reliance on volunteers and sponsorship to run and promote the events.[8] Lans were clearly in a period of transition by the middle of the first decade of the twenty-first century, as a range of efforts to grow the online gaming market were stepped up throughout the Australasian region.

However, this report's view of Lanning's "viability" was overly simplistic. Apart from not gelling with the facts—new Lan groups were continuing to emerge and Lanning had not been sidelined by broadband—the report also seemed cynical to me, telling industry, or parts thereof, what it was perceived it wanted to hear: If Lanning was in decline, this would presumably mean greater market share for commercial network gaming providers. While such agendas are perhaps not uncommon in these types of market forecast reports, it made a reconsideration of Lan groups seem timely.

In 2004, I resumed formal research with Lan organizers, building on earlier ethnographic work I had conducted with one Lan group (Lan A). Using a mixture of methods, I attended Lans wherever possible, for participant-observation and informal discussions with gamers, and followed up with in-depth, semi-structured interviews with the organizer(s) or administrators (admins) of Lans. I spoke with the admins of 5 Lans, 3 in Australia (Lans A, B, and C) and 2 in New Zealand (Lans D and E). The questions motivating the research were: What impact has the proliferation of various types of online networked gaming had on Lanning? As volunteer networks, how will Lans fare over the middle to longer term? What relations do Lans have with more commercial enterprises who target gamers as a market? Have Lans themselves adopted elements of this mode of address of gamers? Finally, having fixed many of the technical problems that routinely afflicted Lans in their early years (e.g., problems with power, etc), how much else has become "fixed," over time? How organized and "official" do Lans need to be? How do admins—whose contributions of time and effort are considerable—keep it fun?

In this small scale study, my aims were to: a) contribute to a better understanding of the issues faced by the volunteer/not-for-profit network gaming sector, at a time when the number of commercial and non-commercial options for gaming in the region were multiplying; b) chart examples of the interaction of different (volunteer and for profit) game services; and c) document the Lan groups that existed during this period, from the perspectives of organizers. Much of the material in this chapter derives from the interviews I conducted with the admins in 2004. This now historic material is supplemented by more recent observations from the admins. The chapter concludes with a roundup of the groups' current status.

[2004]

INTRODUCING THE LANS

The mixture of online and face-to-face interactions, and DIY (do it yourself)/gift economy origins of Lan groups make them fascinating subjects of study. At a Lan, not only is a players' avatar visible to another player of a game, but the players are themselves co-located in physical space, a feature which contributes significantly to the distinct sociality and culture of Lanning. In the early days of Lan groups, it was common to hear stories of players giving freely of their time and expertise to help others access the Lan—time they could have spent gaming—even to the extent of partially disassembling a computer and rebuilding it on the spot, using whatever components were at hand. Though many players seem to be more aware of networking and so there are fewer networking issues these days, this sharing of know how continues to operate on other levels.

All of the Lan groups I approached operate on a volunteer basis. Two of the five groups have been operating continuously for many years, with Lan A celebrating its tenth year in 2004. Two are relatively new, though some of the admins of these groups have been involved in other groups previously. One group (Lan C) is very new, evidence that new Lans continue to be set up. As one admin said: "there are a lot more little Lans popping up all around the place, and actually whereas they used to do it in the garage, they're actually giving it a name, and advertising for other people to come along" (Lan A). Different groups enjoy different levels of organizational status, with groups variously set up as companies with admins as directors, totally informally, or with an auspicing arrangement where the official side of things (bookwork, taxation arrangements, etc.) is taken care of by retail sponsors. Lan E dissolved its structure when its venue and hosting arrangements changed a couple of years ago: The admin alluded to the potential for problems with this, when remarking on the openness and non-exclusivity of the group:

> That's our sort of, our niche. It kind of sucks in a way [though], because you never know what's going to happen. Someone could come along, ruin the scene for everyone by doing something illegal, showing rude things to kids, that sort of stuff, so there's a bit of a risk there because we are completely off the record. There's no legal organization that runs it or anything like that. We've got no protection, so we're hoping that no-one is going to turn up and do something stupid. It's worked out so far.

Most of the groups have a venue by now that is secure, though Lan A is temporarily without a home while their regular site undergoes refurbishment. Typically Lans have had to move around over time, to find venues that could adequately provide for the numbers of interested gamers. Lan D currently has a very interesting arrangement where they are operating out of a museum, while Lan E moved into Lanplace some years ago, a purpose built gaming venue in a Wellington office suite which is the envy of many Lanners. Lanplace is unique: It has been set up by a successful ISP entrepreneur/gamer, Shame Cole, as a gift of sorts to the game community for helping to make his former business, Paradise.net, such a success. The former Managing Director with a one-third share, Cole reportedly earned $10 million from the sale of Paradise.net to TelstraSaturn, in 2000.[9] Lan E's admin commented: "[Lanplace] is massive. I would be surprised if there is anywhere else in the world that has this kind of freedom and ease of use . . . There's nothing else quite like this anywhere else, I'm sure." The network is purpose-built and the whole environment is very flash: "[players] just need to turn up with their computer. They hook into hundreds of thousands worth of networking equipment . . . Everyone's got their own individual halogen lines they can adjust and it's a fancy, flash set-up." It also means that organization is minimal for the admins, and while players and admins alike sometimes get nostalgic for the 'old days':

> The days of assembling a network out of bits of switch and whatever—they're long gone, thankfully . . . We [used to] run around helping people to get onto the network, replacing cables, setting up this and that, and it was a big job, and collecting money as well. Now all that kind of stuff is handled by the staff at Lanplace, so we can just turn up and participate in the games with everyone. Of course we have to pay now. (Lan D)

I was interested in whether the move had also brought compromises, for the group's independence, for instance:

> yeah, it gave us less flexibility, because we immediately couldn't give away $1000 video cards or whatever every few months. But at the same time, people just turn up, plug in, and you are in this incredibly nice place with fancy air conditioning, big screens and projectors, network PlayStation 2 set up for the projectors. It was a no-brainer. We were definitely keen to get it off the ground . . . The other thing is that everyone used to take their monitors . . . Back in the old days I had to actually lug my monitor and my cables and my PC whereas nowadays you just take the PC because you can hire a monitor of varying sizes there.

PATRONAGE

Patronage is something that has changed for many groups over the years, and is a subject that most admins have clearly given thought to. Online gaming has eaten into the support base of Lans to an extent, but no admins saw this as being too detrimental. The admin of Lan D noted that while a lot of gamers do play massively multiplayer online games, lots of them turn up at the Lan as well.

> There are definitely some who defected entirely to this alternate reality and sit at home playing—that happens . . . But it's swings and roundabouts really. Like people end up meeting each other through a massively multi-player game and they might bring them to the next Lan for example, so that might replace the user that we lose to the massively multi-player.

The admin of Lan A reported that some of the states in Australia are only seeing Lans happen once or twice a year now rather than monthly; "it's really, really backed off." I asked her whether the decline might be attributable to the considerable effort involved in physically packing up computers and transporting them to a venue for the day (compared to playing at home online), and she agreed, suggesting that this was particularly a factor for older gamers.

> Yeh. It's a big age thing. I mean we've got constantly new people coming through and the new people that come along tend to be mostly teenagers. And then we still get people who have never been before who are in their twenties and thirties. The ones that used to come who are in their thirties and forties don't come anymore.

She felt, however, that the decline in attendance amongst older gamers was also attributable to a kind of boredom:

> The content and mission in games is the same as it used to be. There's nothing innovative coming out now. It's just better graphics, better sound—that's really the only changes—so that's not enough I think to get the big interest it used to have.

RULES, CODES OF CONDUCT, FILE SWAPPING

Surfing various Lan groups' webpages at the start of the project, I was struck at the growth in, and prominence of, rules, disclaimers and codes of conduct. These cover, variously, acceptable language and behavior, file swapping and the carrying of weapons, amongst other things.

Lan A has always had a code of conduct:

> Frank [one of the founding admins] is a very careful, business-minded person so from day one we had an agreement on the website, so that if you come along, you are agreeing to that. I don't know how many people even bother reading it. I know I did when I first went . . . but the 15-year-old boys, they're not going to sit there and read a big long agreement and disclaimer. They go along, and they are told they are doing something wrong.

When I asked Admin E about the Lan network being used for things other than just playing games, he noted that

> There's always been an element of that . . . It's just that instead of people maybe stealing albums of MP3, which was probably the biggest 'in' thing when it started, you've got to watch for people who might be stealing movies or something like that. It's still technically, the same kind of issue.

As has already been mentioned, he is concerned at the possibility that a younger Lanner could unwittingly be exposed to explicit or gory content at a Lan. However the issue that probably resonates most is file swapping, because of the copyright implications. Continuing on from her point about the sameness of many games, Admin A thinks that boredom is again a significant factor: "There are no new breakthroughs in gaming, so it's a habit for everyone that comes along to a Lan [to swap files]. They may not play games as much as they used to, but they'll still go there and just do other things." Yet the image of Lans as huge swap meets where copyright protections on the latest AV items are circumvented is not an entirely accurate one. It's important to consider what is being downloaded—often it's not the latest things at all, but some of the oldest. As Andreas Lange has noted, with a lack of comprehensive digital game archives, gamers have in many cases been the ones responsible for preserving old games.[10] This point was brought home to me during one of my visits to this Lan, when an admin I was speaking with was downloading material at the same time. When he experienced problems with it, I asked him what he was downloading.

> Oh, something for the kids (laughs). I got it off one of the guys. It's a simulator for one of the old game systems. And it's all the different games, so it runs on the computer. So even though the X-Box is the latest game system, sort of thing, they can still play all those old games, and they still enjoy them. Because, I mean, something that you ultimately discover is that there are games that just look fantastic, but they're really garbage to play. If something's missing that gameplay element, it's just no fun at all. You can have the prettiest graphics in the world, but if it's just not a good game, you don't want to play it ultimately.

Another point that needs to be borne in mind about file swapping at Lans is that some file swapping is quite legitimate: Games patches and trailers are just two examples here of files that are intended to be digitally disseminated.

Admin A recognizes that file swapping is a concern, but notes also that:

> It's a hard situation because we can't control what [players] do there—if we see it we can say 'don't do that' and 'you can get out, bye bye, you've agreed to our disclaimer which says you can't do that here.' We don't condone it, we don't set up anything ourselves that allows it. We have looked at a lot of different ways of blocking; we block net access now, so people can't be downloading anything illegal so then we feel that we're protecting ourselves and it's for virus protection also, a lot of different reasons. But we can monitor the network as technology improves; we are learning ways of monitoring computers. But as far as copyright goes, I mean, how can we police that?

Indeed beyond the (now) standard disclaimers and codes of conduct, Lan A provides quite elaborate information on the risks of file swapping. Their webpage warns that: "File sharing is becoming riskier and riskier at Lans, with more malicious gamers and malicious virii [sic] causing problems." They further advise gamers to check all file shares to make sure they don't have any before leaving home, and if they do need to share something at the Lan, recommend using FTP. "If you need to use Windows File Sharing, please make sure you don't allow write access, and it's preferable that you password the share so only those you give the password to can access your shared folders."

ORGANIZERS THEMSELVES

The question of admins' commitment to the regular and time consuming organization of Lans is a major factor affecting Lan groups' evolution over time. It was something I found myself pondering as I helped dismantle Lan D's network. Bending down to pull yet more duct tape off the carpet, I realized (somewhat guiltily, having left the night before to get some sleep) just how much work admins put into a 24-hour event. An admin from Lan E explained to me that though there had once been five organizers of their Lan, there are now only two. "Well, there's kind of three, but our third organizer doesn't go that much anymore. He kind of drifted away from it and he's not one of the original ones. He started a couple of years ago." The first admin to leave was, as he put it, "the classic Lan defector":

> Broadband had just become the 'in' thing, people were playing with very low ping times on servers and he had it. And he decided if he could get a low ping at home, why bother going to a Lan anymore, so as a result of him not wanting to go anymore there was no point in him remaining an organizer, so he was the first one to leave.

For many other admins, however, it's "real life" that gets in the way of their ongoing commitment. This is the situation with Lan A, the longest running group of the five. One of the three directors has moved interstate for family reasons (he participates in organizational matters by email as and when he can); another wanted the experience of working in another country (he says it's temporary and he intends to return); the other is married and has a very demanding job, keeping him busy. A long time Lanner at this group, the (now) sole admin finds that she is the one holding it together.

> I just sort of stepped in and took up the slack where I was needed—so real life does come in—and we're all getting older, so as our age changes, our priorities change as well—we just don't seem to have as much time to—we're not as gung ho about it as [we were] in the beginning. That lustre fades on anything after a while.

Lan E's admin expects that when some of the younger gamers "start thinking more about dating and trying to mold themselves into the person they think a prospective partner might like" that they will also notice some drop in player numbers. "It's perfectly legitimate . . . and one of the reasons that we need to start attracting more users to Lans because I can only imagine that that trend is going to be negative for attendance."

ORGANIZATIONAL CONSIDERATIONS

How "official" and organized do Lans need to be? Most Lans seem to position themselves somewhere along an organizational continuum, trying to find an acceptable position between ensuring that they are properly set up so that admins are not personally liable for any accidents, for example, while retaining a degree of looseness.

Lan A has a company structure but, as the organizer says:

> We keep it casual. I think that's how it will always be . . . You could very easily turn Lanning into a money-making business, I think. If you wanted to go in that direction you could make it streamlined and official and have employees all having specific tasks. [But] the people who tend to do this sort of thing hate that commercialization and rebel against it . . . it would destroy it I think.

Later she put it thus: "we are officially protected without making big rules and a big fuss and seeming like a corporation." This relaxed approach carries through to the Lanners themselves. Over time, very serious gamers (and the "CS [Counterstrike] kiddies," as they're termed) have tended to drift off to another Lan.

From this casual and relaxed Lan, it was the complete lack of organization of another Lan that prompted the admins of Lan D to start their own: "We could see the shortcomings of [that Lan] and wanted to try and fix them." "You know, it's not really a proper Lan group. There's no real organization . . . its really just a group of gamers getting together and setting up some tables and playing some games." While they recognize that the admins of this other group were doing the best they could, the admins of Lan E felt they could do much better:

> I mean they have power problems, they have network problems, they have a committee that really is flawed, completely flawed. They have so many members on it and no one even makes a decision. They just bounce stuff backwards and forwards rather than actually getting the problem solved and getting issues dealt with. I mean you try and talk to one guy and he's got to send an email out to twenty other guys, and

then maybe you'll get an answer back, or it'll be too late, or you'll get one guy that disagrees. It's just a nightmare.

Lan B's organizational ethic sets them apart, and they pride themselves on their distinctiveness: The admin's tagging of his posts "The strangest LAN crew in the [region]" is just one example of this. The admins see a large part of their role as organizing an *event*. "We put on events . . . If we are sitting there, you know, running an event going 'This is going terribly,' there is no enjoyment in it at all. There is no real point in running it." They spice up their Lans with party celebrations, by running novel competitions and awarding original trophies. Their brown paper bag competitions deserve a mention here: These involve players forming into pairs, with one putting a large paper bag over their head so they can't see what they're doing; they then receive oral guidance from their teammate about where to move, shoot etc in a game of *Quake*. Lan B's admin discusses their ethic in terms of a tension between experimentation and fixity:

> Gamers more or less, they stick to one thing. That would probably be the best way to describe it. You know, people have been playing *Counter-strike* for years now, I mean the original one came out in 1998. I remember playing it in a small net café and going this is great, we should really try this, and it's still going absolutely huge now. People will play that and play nothing but that. They don't really want to experiment with something that's new and that sort of goes against what we're about, because after the admin, we are gamers too. We like to experiment; we want to try new, fun things, unorthodox competitions and such. Keep things interesting where people can sit there and go, 'yeah, I remember Lan 8 where we did blah blah blah.' People, if they don't want to experiment, they won't join that server and they won't enjoy themselves. So we really have to push the idea that it's not your average event.

RELATIONS WITH COMMERCIALS

Given that all five of these Lans are run on a not for profit basis, I asked the admins about their relations with more commercial enterprises. Most deal with sponsors, though this isn't necessary anymore for Lan E, since they moved into Lanplace. Lan C's sponsorship arrangements are also greatly simplified by being dealt with through the computer shop which auspices their group. Lan D is probably the most involved with sponsors. One of the admins of this Lan had very successfully used his position as manager of an electronics store to leverage sponsorship. As he said:

> If I wasn't where I am we wouldn't have [lots of these sponsors]. A lot of these supply companies, they won't deal with the public. So by dealing

with me, they're actually just dealing with one of their customers. Realistically they sort of look at it as if I'm sort of doing a job for them.

These admins reason that their aim is to leave Lanners with the feeling that the suppliers are trying to look after them, so that gamers might then think it's worthwhile to save up and buy the company's game to support them, in turn. Rather than seeing sponsors as "just this blank, huge corporation making millions of dollars," they hope that gamers might think "hang on a minute, I was just at a Lan last weekend, and the company that makes that game sponsored $500 worth of prizes for the gamers. I might just go and buy that [game]." In addition to the usual posters and prominent placement of logos (on websites, name tags, etc.), they foster such a climate through thanking sponsors by name over a microphone during the Lan, making sure that they get some kudos at the event.[11]

By contrast, the admin of Lan A commented on how relaxed sponsorship arrangements are. Because there are more Lans now asking for sponsorship, companies are now budgeting for sponsorship, making it "more business like," but it's still "extremely casual."

> You sort of contact them and say, I'm from blah blah, we do this, would you give us something? In return, they usually say, in return could you put some posters of the game or company or whatever up on your walls at your event, put an ad on your website and then get back to us afterwards and let us know what you did with the things we gave you to give away.
> [. . .]
> There's no official agreements—nothing in writing—it's just very casual.

In years gone by, Lan A has occasionally run events for game companies, for product launches and the like. Frank confided that the need for these events to be slick—unlike the Lan events—was a disincentive to doing too many of them.

RELATION TO ONLINE

The question of online gaming's relation to, and effect on, Lanning elicited considered reflections from admins. While most agreed that some gamers had given up Lanning in favor of online gaming, for most it wasn't a clearcut either/or issue. The admins of Lan D all play online, but said that "You can only sort of go so far and play so much before basically it becomes boring." The verdict resounding amongst the four admins from this group was that "online gaming is practice for Lans"; just like in other sports, "you want to be able to eyeball them when you blow 'em away." This sentiment was echoed by others—like the admin of Lan A, who explained:

I think the whole point of the Lan is that you are there with other people. You can play—you've always been able to play these games over the Internet, well, for many, many years. People just like the Lan because it's the real thing. You are there. You are sitting next to the person that you just killed (well, you know what I mean!). You're there with them, you can yell out at people. It's interactive, whereas on the Internet you're closed behind your little space, in your own privacy, wearing your speedos and nothing else (or whatever), you can get out on a Lan and actually see the people you are playing and nothing will replace that. I think the draw to that will always be there in some capacity—it may grow over time.

It is likely that the slower uptake of broadband in Australasia relative to other geographic regions has played a role in the development of Lan groups here. In 2004, Australia and New Zealand were 18th and 22nd in the world in terms of broadband penetration.[12] In Australia, IDC attribute this slower rate to:

> . . . the lack of availability of ADSL in many areas up to more recently, [the] high costs [of] associated services [like] installation and subscrip-tions, download caps, and a mood within the population that there is a lack of compelling content to attract them to high speed services.[13]

In New Zealand, these figures include at least 30,000 customers of the major provider, Telecom, on their Jetstart service, which operates at sub-broadband speeds of 128Kbps over DSL lines.[14] Restrictions on bandwidth are frustrating to gamers, particularly in New Zealand. An admin of Lan D argues they are not getting a good deal by international standards:

> Just to put things in perspective in New Zealand we get 256K down-load, 128K upload. You only get 10Gig for a month, which is not bad. That costs us about $69. If you go to Japan or you go to England, $29 gets you a 2Meg connection, so 2000K connection, and no cap what-soever. Realistically what we want now . . . is double that, just to get enough bandwidth to play some of these bigger games, because they are getting bigger and bigger and they require more power and band-width to run (Lan D).

On the subject of networked consoles, the admin of Lan E opined that, "X-Box Live is having [no effects on Lanning] so far . . . I don't know anybody else apart from me who has got it." Indeed, far from being seen as a threat to Lanning, consoles were credited with potentially broadening the market for games, a development that was welcomed. Lan A has, in the past, run 'X-Lans' (four Xboxes networked with the split screen views from these projected up on several screens), incorporating the consoles into the structure of the Lan event. Some of the other groups also have consoles set up at events, with a projector offering players a break from PC games. Though Lanning is all about PC games, there is no snobbery about consoles. Players readily acknowledge the qualities of console games, especially the graphics, welcoming moves to enhance interoperability between consoles and PCs: After all, "X-Box is virtually a computer now" (admin, Lan A), and PlayStation 2's and PCs can play "Need for Speed" against each other (admin, Lan D).

LOOKING AHEAD

The pressures and constancy of running a Lan are undeniable, and this has been a theme of my discussions with admins from Lan A over several years. Some of these admins feel an uneasiness between what the group could become, the reality of running the Lans, and the ideal they started out with—that it should be fun. One of Lan A's original directors (then working overseas) mused on this in email correspondence with me in 2004:

> Things have changed a bit over the last year or so. The Lan scene changed from one of competitive gaming to a bunch of people that want to leech :) However, [Lan A] has been pushing back with a fairly hectic gaming schedule to try and push for games . . .
> I am missing [the Lan] a bit, but not that much . . .

Another admin from this group had told me the year earlier that "a lot of games have become too much like each other" and that "what's missing is the next defining thing." Asking the admin currently running this Lan whether it's still fun for her, she hesitates slightly: "Well, when I'm there, yes. Leading up to it I grumble and groan, and complain . . . because I have to get up at six in the morning to go there. I think we all do." Things change though when she's there, particularly if it's going well:

> We're all pretty pumped if we've had a great day, the console ran smoothly, nobody complained about anything . . . I think nobody likes the lead up to it, the thought of having to do all that work, but everybody grumbles about the things they have to go and do. We feel like we have to now . . . for me especially, I regard it as a responsibility now rather than a hobby.

When asked what it would be comparable to, she replies:

> I don't know. Maybe a child's sports team. Parents who maybe get in there and coach a little league team. Similar to that—it becomes something you have to do. It starts as something cool, fun and gradually over

the years it becomes another thing you have to go and do. You still do it. You don't hate it. You don't have the same enthusiasm any more, I don't think. It's more a chore in your life. You still do it happily, though.

Others also report feeling responsible, that they have a "duty of care" for the thing they have had a hand in creating (admin, Lan E). Admins of the newer lans were more optimistic and so more reluctant to be drawn on how long their involvement might last, how long they thought the group might be sustainable for. As one admin from Lan D put it: "That's something I don't really want to answer because I don't even want to think about not organizing lans or not gaming. I enjoy it too much." Another from this Lan said, "If everything was getting too much I'd never stop going to Lans and gaming or anything like that. But if it ever got to the point where . . . I'd be looking at still being involved, but bringing other younger guys in, passing the experience onto them . . ."

As it happens, that is one option under consideration by the admins of Lan A. A prominent Lan, I asked what one does with it when it's reached the current point? The admin currently running it thinks there are two options:

[Some] days I think to myself—these guys [the other admins] aren't as interested anymore obviously or they'd be here . . . sometimes I think I should sort of say to the guys hey, if you guys aren't going to get in here and do something, then maybe you should consider the options, because you can't expect our team of people to do all this voluntarily and just keep going, feel like we have no direction, and you guys don't do anything for us anymore. But, I mean, it runs itself. The team we've got now are pretty loyal, pretty into it. I don't think anyone is going to disappear anytime soon. So the two biggest options I think we've got are a) close it down, or b) hand it over to younger people who do have that drive to make it huge and keep it going. Basically the fun wears off, and as you get older, I think, that would be the best option—that's what I'd like.

In a brighter moment, she continues:

I think it can evolve to a new generation . . . There's no reason why [this Lan] can't or any Lan can't keep on going, keep on earning that interest. Things may need to change. We might look at getting a smaller venue and going back to the core a bit and having a limited player list. I think that would be a good idea personally. If you can limit something it creates more of an interest. If people think they can't get in, there's more of a rush for it, so these are some of my ideas . . .

She argues, too, that they need to advertise: "We're competing now, against other Lans and if we do want to survive as a big [Lan], we're going to have to do something . . . because we've got competitors." If some of these changes can be made, she is optimistic that the Lan will not only survive, but also improve.

Another quite pragmatic strategy employed by Lan B has been to take a break: When I spoke to one of the admins, they were just preparing to relaunch the Lan after a year or so of inactivity. They said:

> Yeah we are looking at restarting public events. We basically—we had other things, we had uni, and we had full-time jobs and stuff and we had a lot on our plates and it sort of took a back seat for a while. More or less the reason was we could go to [another Lan]. I was basically really good friends with another admin and I was helping him run events and we were just, almost every second week, we were helping run events. [Plus] we were sort of taking a break from it for a while, just actually being players, as our target audience. Probably about a month, a month and a half ago we thought yeah let's bring it back. It's looking a little bit shaky at the moment. We actually had to postpone, but . . . we'll get a couple of ideas together and hopefully start it off again.

Admins of the much newer Lan D, when asked how they'd like to see things develop, look forward to the possibility of a dedicated venue in their region, like Lanplace in Wellington: "To have our own venue, that's fully set up. Cover costs, make a little bit on the side." In addition, they argue that there is a need for a national level body for computer gaming in New Zealand, similar to those that other sports enjoy, in line with their view that gaming is a sport. This would be a sign that gaming was being taken more seriously, they argue, and would provide some support for the best players to compete internationally at the World Cyber Games, for instance.

[2008]

In 2004, at the outset of this research, I was aware that the Lan scene that had existed for a number of years was undergoing change. While the report that provoked my inquiry implied that Lans would decline due to their lack of a business model and in the face of increased online gaming options, in 2004 Lan groups did not look to be in decline, nor was a "swapping" of gaming practices—from Lan gaming groups to online gaming—particularly prominent. Lans continued to generate significant levels of interest, and new Lans were being set up, a situation that continues today. Yet simultaneously, the veteran admins of Lan A had for some time been reporting high levels of fatigue, aware they lacked the energy required to take the Lan into the future. Four years later, the situation looks quite different.

Shortly after my interview with the admin of Lan A, the group found itself—as expected—temporarily "homeless" while their regular venue was refurbished. They ran a few smaller Lans in another venue during this period, however, this became "too annoying," according to Frank. Their final event was held in late 2005. In early 2007, the following message appeared on the Lan's website, replacing all the news, messageboards, and other Lan paraphernalia once hosted there.

The Last Post
Hello everybody!

OK, this is the post to let everyone know that [the Lan] has actually officially closed its doors. Just in case you hadn't figured that out already.

I would like to thank everyone who made [the Lan] what it was. There are way too many people to even think about listing you all here.

Now all that said [sic], we don't want to see [the Lan] just disappear, so if you have a game related idea for what you could use the [Lan] name, website, etc. then drop me an email . . . and we will have a chat.

Thanks again to everyone.

When the closure was announced, much anguish was expressed on the Ausgamers' messageboards: Many gamers were lamenting the loss—what would they do without this Lan? Now, some two and a half years later, the occasional notice appears advertising a social get-together. Or a thread will begin expressing nostalgia for the old days and light-heartedly suggest a get-together, as in the epithet cited at the beginning of this chapter. Greetings and news is exchanged often about who has gotten married, had a child, gone overseas, etc. The company that was the legal entity behind the Lan has now been wound up. Apart from these periodic (on- and off-line) social catch-ups, Frank related that, "no one has come forward with any good ideas for [the Lan], so even the site may just disappear sometime soon." For his part, Frank is now working for a mobile games network provider, uniting his e-business skills with his interest in games: "it's nice to be back in games, even if I no longer play them :-). " Acknowledging that he is "over running events," he notes, "there are still a couple [of Lan groups] going on in Sydney but they are few and far between really."

Four years on, Lan B has not relaunched and the group's website is now defunct. Chatting with the admin of this group, he cited reasons to do with work, specifically shiftwork making it difficult for he and his fellow admin and co-worker to get days off together. He also volunteered that, "the (long overdue) onset of broadband and file sharing has stopped a few people from going to lans." However, he and his mates—"mainly friends that we met while running the event"—still get together in each other's houses and Lan when they can: "It's more of a spur of the moment thing when we're all available, and the good thing is that we know how to run it so we're never short of power boards or network cables."[15] I was curious as to what the games of choice were at these Lans; specifically, I wondered whether admins citing "the role of broadband" might be code for a general move towards MMORPGs (in line with comments from two of Lan A's admins about there being a certain exhaustion amongst lanners with particular game genres). This admin assured me that for him and his friends this was not the case:

> nah, we find that MMORPGs at lans (public and private) were exactly the same as playing at home and there's no social aspect to it—it's just not as fun. We still play the same kinds of games, mainly FPS. We still play games such as the original "Ghost Recon" which was a huge hit with our crew when it was in its heyday.

While others—Lanners and admins alike—have also expressed versions of this view that there's nothing like "being there," this admin's comment also provides an answer to the question I was asked in a seminar, as to whether players will continue to go to Lans when the speed of Internet play matches that of Lans. Evidently, when they have the choice, these players prefer playing face to face at a Lan.

Lan C did not make it past the start up phase of running a few events. One of my original informants opined that this was due to "non-attendance, the age of broadband and antisocial/lazy personalities . . . Gaming as a whole is done online, people don't go to LANs to play 'World of Warcraft' and broadband (even if it is rather slow and unappealing in Australia) takes care of any file sharing people might do." He felt that a different outcome might have been possible had things been differently managed, but didn't want to dwell on what might have been.

Responding to my inquiries in 2006 about a hiatus in Lan D's events calendar, one of its admins wrote that:

> [Our Lan] has been a bit quiet as of late our working lives seem to have taken over and switched into overdrive. [I have had to move and have been] either on courses or working flat out to bring my knowledge up for the past 12 months or so. [The other main admin] has been flat tack as well with the [electronics] store as well as now planning for a new addition to his family of wife and cat with a baby on the way (while still remaining adamant that this won't affect his gaming).

At that time (2006), these admins were sharing the knowledge and skills they had gained from running Lans with a group based in Wellington. They stated:

> We're currently . . . providing backup support and advice for a 200-person event . . . with the view in the future to take this to a 300+ event. As this is the group's first event of this size (they have run several 40 to

50 person events) we are just there in the background offering advice and support where they need it, obviously there are considerations in running an event of 200+ people that never arise in a smaller event so trying to help them to have a smooth first run.

As for Lan D itself, it is still in suspension.

Lan E has also closed its doors or rather, Lanplace closed its doors. Its former admin explained:

> The venue was expensive to run and Shane wasn't getting enough business to justify its continued operation. Without the Lanplace venue and the general waning interest in regular LAN events (we were getting as few as 25 people to events, compared with averaging 70 to 80 in its heyday), the organizers unanimously agreed to let the old dog die with Lanplace.

Lan E's final Lan event was held in November 2006. It was also the last ever event at Lanplace.

CONCLUDING THOUGHTS

This chapter has presented "snapshots" of five selected Lan groups, at different moments in time. In collaborating with admins, I have been concerned to allow their voices to come through as much as possible. This is not only because admins are articulate commentators on game culture, or because their explanations reveal the behind-the-scenes tensions their groups have faced. In their own voices, admins speak of gaming's significance, its place in peoples' lives, and the changing landscape its cultural formations occupy with an eloquence and ambivalence that are missing in many accounts. Such richly nuanced reflections provide readers with a chance not only to understand the Lan group phenomenon as an important late twentieth/ early twentieth-first century game cultural form in Australasia, but also to appreciate what these Lanning groups meant to those who ran and attended them, in all their complexity, considerations that are crowded out by the instrumental demands of industry reports, for instance.

A word about the fate of these Lans is in order: I have avoided pronouncing on the decline of Lanning in general, though clearly all five of the Lan groups profiled here have stopped running regular events. While it would be possible to impose a number of narratives to make sense of these changes, my view is that this would be premature: There is still an ongoing commitment and "investment" in the voluntary Lan group sector on the part of players and admins. This seems particularly true in regional centers: A regional Lan a few hours south of Sydney continues to hold events, albeit less regularly now,[16] and discussions continue about setting up a group in western New South Wales (a few hours west of Sydney). Possibly the closer social ties in regional centers—Lan D raised funds for flood relief at one of its early events—or the still-poor quality of broadband available to some rural gamers will contribute to the longevity of such Lans. As a practice, Lanning is not dead, though the "golden years" of Lan groups do seem to be over. It seems likely that Lan groups will become less regular and smaller in size, with one-off or annual Lan party style spectaculars for the most part catering for those who still want to Lan.

NOTES

1. This research was made possible by a grant from Victoria University of Wellington's New Researcher's Fund. An earlier version of this paper was presented at the "Other Players" conference, Center for Computer Games Research, IT University, Copenhagen, December 6–8, 2004.
2. Jeroen Jansz, Lonneke Martens, "Gaming at a LAN event: the social context of playing video games," *New Media and Society* 7.3, (2005): 333–355.
3. Sandy Stone, "Split Subjects, Not Atoms: or, How I Fell in Love with My Prosthesis," in *The Cyborg Handbook*, eds. Chris Hables Gray, Heidi J. Figueroa-Sarriera, Steven Mentor (New York, London: Routledge, 1995), 401.
4. Beate Geissler and Oliver Sann, "shooter." Retrieved September 20, 2008 from http://www.lifeisgood.biz/shooter/.
5. Bart Simon, "Geek Chic: Machine Aesthetics, Digital Gaming, and the Cultural Politics of the Case Mod," *Games and Culture* 2, (2007): 175–193.
6. Catherine Beavis, Helen Nixon, Stephen Atkinson "Lan Cafes: cafes, places of gathering or sites of informal teaching and learning," *Education, Communication & Information* 5.1 (2005): 41–60.
7. Melanie Swalwell, "Multi-Player Computer Gaming: 'Better than playing (PC Games) with yourself,'" *Reconstruction, an interdisciplinary cultural studies community* 3.4 (2003). Retrieved 20 September 2008 from http://reconstruction.eserver.org/034/swalwell.htm.
8. Jun-Fwu Chin, Linus Lai and Foad Fadaghi, "Australia Online Gaming Forecast, 2002–2007" (Market Analysis), *IDC Asia/Pacific* (Singapore, April 2003), 10.
9. Noel O'Hare, "The Game of Our Lives," *The Listener*, October 26 (1995): 16–22.
10. Andreas Lange, paper presented at "'Level Up': Digital Games Research Association Conference" (DIGRA), Utrecht, Netherlands, 4–6 November, 2003.
11. An X-Box sales rep I met at group D's Lan was very impressed with the Lan group, having never seen anything like it before. I found it remarkable that someone selling gaming gear had such little awareness of the practices of consumption in the games community.
12. Paul Brislen, "New Zealand slips a place in broadband uptake race," *Computerworld*, 30 October, 2003. Retrieved September 20, 2008 from http://www.computerworld.co.nz/news.nsf/0/9FA5804ABFC13B93CC256DCD0014CEAD?OpenDocument; Howard Dahdah, "Study: Australia's broadband uptake steady, DSL outweighs cable," *PC World*, June 25, 2004. Retrieved September 20, 2008 from http://www.computerworld.com.au/index.php/id;261863431;relcomp;1.
13. Chin et al., "Australia Online Gaming Forecast," 4.

14. Chris Barton, "NZ lagging behind in broadband uptake," *New Zealand Herald*, March 9, 2004. Retrieved November 1, 2004 from http://www.nzherald.co.nz/storydisplay.cfm?storyID=3553598.

15. It is not unknown for existing office networks to be used in a similar way outside of office hours, for low hassle Lan gaming with friends and/or colleagues.

16. In forum discussions on the future of this Lan group (which was not part of this study), one of the admins wrote:

> There is no doubt a core of people will always be interested in a solid days gaming in a LAN environment but it is up to everyone to get their mates they play with online or at other LANs to make it to [an event]. History has shown us that people will always leave as they move on with life, some may come back but only through the influx of new people attending [events] will it not seem "stale."

Part III

Genres and New Rubrics

INTRODUCTION

How we experience, imagine and re-imagine games—as part of a set of practices, cultures and processes—is undoubtedly being shaped by "participatory media" such as Web 2.0 in which convergence is met by divergence.[1] Within contemporary culture, we can witness convergence occurring across various levels—technological, industrial social, economic, and cultural. As players become produsers[2] in the world of game cultures, and as discourses such as "game art" (i.e., machimina) merge and evolve with new media practices, the genres and rubrics that determine and define gaming are being contested. As media consumption and production spaces and practices transform within the first decade of the twenty-first century, it is gaming that will provide us with new ways of imaging, constructing and representing our stories, experiences, memories and politics. So, too, game worlds can help us connect to both new and older forms of engagement, agency and empowerment as we partake in the so-called "participatory media" proffered by contemporary culture.

In this section we are provided five different examples for reconceptualizing the role and possibilities of gaming as a vehicle for politics, storytelling and experiences of embodiment. However, it is important not to fetishize the newness of game cultures, but rather—like the study of new media[3]—to view it as transforming already existing practices. The convergence that is gaming cultures, must be understood with broader histories of mediated intimacy, telepresence and play that both rehearse and rewrite older methods and processes of locality. As an influential theorist in the field of media-archaeology Erkki Huhtamo has argued, the cyclical phenomena of media tend to transcend historical contexts, often placating a process of paradoxical re-enactment and re-enchantment with what is deemed as "new."[4] For Jussi Parikka and Jaakko Suominen, the procedural nature of media archaeology means that "new media is always situated within continuous histories of media production, distribution and usage—as part of a longer duration of experience."[5]

We begin this section with Dean Chan's reconceptualization of political agency within online games in China. As he argues in Chapter 8, these types of online politics need to be understood with "a historicized, situated analysis of Chinese techno-sociality." He details the rise of these in-game protests and interrogates how we must consider notions such as e-participation and democracy in an age of multiple Internets and online communities. Through this case study, Chan reflects upon the particular social networks that constitute Chinese netizenship and how online protest can be not only "a new protest strategy," but more importantly, be "constitutive of 'a new field of struggle.'"

We then move to the role of games in constructing, maintaining and challenging "geo-imaginaries" within the global consumption and production flows. In David Surman and Christian McCrea's chapters, the notion of the region as a geo-imaginary comes to the forefront. Here we are reminded of the politics of the work of Koichi Iwabuchi[6] and Anne Allison[7] in "imagining" and consuming cultures such as game pioneers, Japan. Rather than deploying an unreconstructed form of Techno-Orientalism, both chapters highlight the author's grappling with the politics of global gaming cultures and how they participate—upon various levels—in constructing "imagined communities."[8] But unlike the unreflexive Techno-Orientalism that has operated around western consumption of Japanese culture, and to a lesser extent "Asia," both authors reflexively confront their own assumptions and preconceptions in consuming games such as *Pokémon* and *StarCraft*. For Surman, his consumption of *Pokémon* is about confronting fetishized Occidental models that persist. As he convincingly argues in Chapter 9, by situating the "complex rhetoric of the design" within a socio-cultural context in a global gaming imaginary, we can begin to reflect upon it as more complex phenomenon "that oscillates between the poles of Japanese 'cute' (*kawaii*) and American 'cool.'"

For McCrea, *StarCraft* provides a curious space informing all his gaming experiences. In Chapter 10, McCrea complicates the notion of the "magic circle" of the game space by posing the role of memory and specters of embodiment. As he enters into diverse and divergent gaming spaces, the residue of *StarCraft* remains. Like the formative experience of a culture, *StarCraft* operates like his country of origin through which all other countries/games are experienced. As a country that immersed itself within the pleasures and experiences of *StarCraft* on a scale unimaginable in other contexts, South Korea is an integral part of the "magic circle" and game worlds of *StarCraft*. As a country the author has never visited, here we see another version of the "imagining" *vis-à-vis* cultural consumption of a country. As he reflexively observes, "all of my computer and video game play—and likely my theorization of it—now retains a memory of *StarCraft*." Like Surman, McCrea highlight how games play to local, transnational and global cultural flows that operate to imagine and re-imagine cultures. Here we are reminded that games are cultural as they are embodied worlds—they become part of our memories, feelings, emotions and knowledge.

The subsequent chapters explore the socio-cultural spaces of game communities through two different case studies. In Chapter 11, Theodor G. Wyeld, Brett Leavy and Patrick Crogan provide us with an example of games as a storytelling vehicle that seeks to keep the Australian Aboriginal cultural heritage accessible to younger generations. In this chapter, we see the role games can play as educational devices that allow experiences, memories and knowledges to be imparted to new generations of Australians. Through the Digital Songlines (DSL) digital storytelling project, a 3D computer game was developed and made to replicate the modes and mores of Australian Aboriginal spirituality, known as the "Dreamtime," in which knowledge practices are embedded in movement and appreciation of the landscape.

The potentiality of games to afford different types of experiences, memories and knowledges is also evoked in Ingrid Richardson's exploration of the often-overlooked space occupied by mobile gaming and specifically, the relatively new convergent frame of the iPhone. As a relatively new technocultural frame for mobile gaming, Ingrid Richardson explores the possibilities, potentialities and realities of this new mode of "sticky games and hybrid worlds." Drawing on case studies conducted in Perth and Melbourne with 32 game students, Richardson delicately unpacks some of the phenomenological or "socio-somatic" implications for gaming worlds within this new embodied media. Richardson persuasively conceptualizes iPhone "as a 'serious' mobile game console that may potentially bridge the gap between the mobile phone and more dedicated handheld game devices such as the DS and PSP."

As all of the chapters highlight, the capacity for games to provide new ways of seeing and experiencing the world, as well as a device for implementing emerging forms of storytelling and political action, is immeasurable. In turn, we must redefine the perimeters that we sketch for the cartographies of game cultures as they develop into new forms of genres and rubrics.

NOTES

1. Henry Jenkins, *Convergence Culture: Where Old and New Media Intersect* (New York: New York University Press, 2006).
2. Axel Bruns and Jason Jacobs, eds., *Uses of Blogs* (New York: Peter Lang, 2006).
3. Jay Bolter and Richard Grusin, *Remediation: Understanding New Media* (Cambridge, Mass.: MIT Press, 1999); and Erkki Huhtamo, "From Kaleidoscomaniac to Cybernerd: Notes Toward an Archaeology of the Media," *Leonardo*, 30 (3) 1997: 221–224.
4. Huhtamo, "From Kaleidoscomaniac to Cybernerd."
5. Jussi Parikka and Jaakko Suominen "Victorian Snakes? Towards A Cultural History of Mobile Games and the Experience of Movement," *Games Studies:*

the international journal of computer game research, 6 (1) December 2006. Retrieved 20 April 2007 from http://gamestudies.org/0601.
6. Koichi Iwabuchi, *Recentring Globalization: Popular Culture and Japanese Transnationalism* (Durham, NC: Duke University Press, 2003).
7. Anne Allison, "Portable monsters and commodity cuteness; *Pokémon* as Japan's new global power," *Postcolonial Studies* 6: 3, 2003: 381–398.
8. Benedict Anderson, *Imagined Communities: reflections on the origin and spread of nationalism* (London: Verso, 1983).

8 Beyond the "Great Firewall"

The Case of In-Game Protests in China

Dean Chan

China is a world leader in jailing "cyber-dissidents"—currently 48 according to Reporters Without Borders [in 2008]. To Westerners living in largely democratic countries, it is hard to understand how liberation, empowerment, and optimism can coexist alongside suppression, censorship, and compromise. Yet all of these words are equally and simultaneously appropriate in describing what is happening on the Chinese Internet.

—Rebecca MacKinnon[1]

INTRODUCTION

Technology does not have a unidirectional impact on society. The technological determinist view and teleological assumption that the People's Republic of China (henceforth China) is being fundamentally democratized by and through the Internet needs to be interrogated. As Lokman Tsui eloquently puts it, "Technology is never isolated from a context but is always enmeshed in social constructs consisting of models of thought intertwined with habits, beliefs, and values in a specific culture."[2] Yet, at the same time, the techno-social enmeshment in this specific cultural context is not necessarily seamless or unproblematic. A case in point is the presence of the so-called "Great Firewall" of China, which is a comprehensive Internet content filtering and blocking system that serves as a censorial device and functions as a state-controlled bulwark against unwarranted external influence. Rebecca MacKinnon's epigraphical statement goes some way towards encapsulating the ambivalences in the status quo, while simultaneously gesturing towards the need for reflexive qualification and ongoing assessment of staid precepts, particularly in relation to democracy and the Internet in China.

Scholars such as Guobin Yang and Jack Linchuan Qiu argue that the question of the Internet's democratizing impulse in China needs be reformulated. For Yang, a more productive line of enquiry is to analyze the co-evolution of the Internet and civil society in China, specifically, "how they interact in ways that shape the development of both."[3] For Qiu, the onus is instead on teasing out the social, political and economic meanings implicit in "the paradox of rapid Internet growth under authoritarian circumstances." The Internet is not "a superimposed agent of change" in Qiu's formulation but "a conduit through which existing propensities of the Chinese society . . . are set free."[4]

Yang's and Qiu's approaches are not incompatible. Both are, in essence, arguing for a historicized, situated analysis of Chinese techno-sociality. Together, they animate and substantiate my focus in this chapter on analyzing the emergent phenomenon of protests taking place within online games in China. This focus echoes Qiu's proposition that "[u]ser networks at the grassroots constitute the most innovative source of change in China's virtual landscape" and recognizes that techno-social channels like online gaming provide a "kaleidoscope for the examination of the intricate interplay among a myriad of social forces in the networks of Chinese netizens."[5] This hermeneutical approach presupposes that the technological medium of the Internet is continually modulated by socio-political and cultural contexts. In-game protests correspondingly offer a lens to view salient developments in contemporary Chinese techno-sociality. Yang agrees that online protests have special significance for the evolution and development of "popular protest in China, where the mobilization of organized protest is relatively infrequent because of state sanctions"[6]—and, MacKinnon would add, because of the prospects of being jailed for committing acts of cyber-dissidence. I fully acknowledge the irreducibility of these competing tensions. Like Yang, I am interested in online protest not simply because it represents "a new protest strategy"; rather, it is ultimately constitutive of "a new field of struggle."[7]

THE IDIOMS OF GLOBAL IN-GAME PROTESTS

The focus of this chapter is on China; however, analyses of Chinese in-game protests can ill-afford to ignore the broader contexts for such activities. Indeed, a new global genealogy of activism and mass mobilization is unfolding in virtual worlds in the form of in-game protests.[8] Online games are not just spaces for play and social interaction; they have also become sites for different types of collective group action and social engagement.

Over the past decade, large-scale player congregations have taken place in the North American online servers of massively multiplayer online role-playing games (MMORPGs) such as *Ultima Online, EverQuest, Star Wars Galaxies*, and *World of Warcraft*. The protests were sometimes aimed at deliberately crashing the servers in forceful collective expressions of player grievances over issues such as recurrent customer service problems and the introduction of inadequate new character classes.[9] Mostly, however, they were a way for players to vent their frustrations and rally against the game operators. In 1997, players angry at persistent software problems in *Ultima Online* assembled at the in-game castle of "Lord British," the avatar of Richard Garriot, creator of that game world—and stripped naked.

At the same time, however, in-game protests cannot be simplistically celebrated as unfettered expressions of player agency. In 2005, another nude protest took place. The protest was sparked when the game developers made some changes to the "Warrior" character class in *World of Warcraft*. Many warriors found that these changes placed unfair restrictions on their virtual activities. Consequently, disgruntled gnome warriors (and many curious onlookers who had read news about the planned protest that was posted on online forums) assembled at the Ironforge Auction House in the Argent Dawn server and stripped down to their underwear, simultaneously flouting in-game social protocols and creating a public spectacle. However it was not so much the in-game nudity that proved problematic for the game administrators. Instead, it was the prospect of an over-crowded server as more and more people logged on to see the spectacle. Tim Guest reports on the response of one Game Master (GM), who issued a stern warning to the assembled warriors: "Gathering in a realm with intent to hinder game play is considered griefing [deliberately ruining or disrupting the game for other players], and will not be tolerated."[10] The GM's warning was backed up with classic bureaucratic management-speak: "We appreciate your opinion, but protesting in-game is not a valid way to give us feedback."[11] As Guest wryly notes, the "totalitarian boot" eventually came down and those "who persisted with their naked frolics (as well as a few innocent bystanders) had their accounts temporarily suspended."[12] The overburdened server eventually crashed.

Other virtual world protests have been more specifically directed at social justice concerns arising from in-game politics. When a server administrator of *World of Warcraft* banned the formation of a gay-friendly guild within this MMORPG in 2006, some players sent their avatars to in-game heterosexual weddings to protest against the game company's discriminatory policy of allowing only certain public displays of sexual orientation.[13] These protestors, like those in *Ultima Online*, might well have been motivated by consumer rights (in the sense of wanting equitable and unrestricted access to participate in consumer culture) as much as political rights. Guest nonetheless attempts to put the consumer's motivation to protest into perspective—specifically that of a gamer's perspective:

> Consumers don't usually rally against changes in products. When the Coca-Cola Company introduced 'New Coke,' no one campaigned in the supermarket aisles. They just didn't tend to buy the cans. But if Coca-Cola owned your whole world, and it wasn't just the taste of the drink they altered: it was your job, your house, or even your ability to walk—you might complain.[14]

Guest astutely identifies the core reasoning that effectively—and affectively—blurs the putative boundaries between consumer choice and consumer rights for MMORPG players. In other words, what is at issue here is the irrefutable investment—*both* financial and emotional—that players have made in subscribing to these games and often spending not insignificant amounts of time in grinding (or levelling up their avatars), socializing, and acquiring game items. The central paradox inherent in many virtual world protests is that they are simultaneously products of, and responses to, the relentless commodification and corporatization of everyday life. It is perhaps inevitable that consumer rights issues inform many MMORPG protests given the commodified basis of this medium, which is after all only accessible via paid subscription. These are, in essence, privatized commercial spaces. However, the root causes and subsequent unfolding of events clearly differ from case to case; the myriad situations are, in effect, interpellating the gamer-consumers and hailing them into agentive action in considerably different ways.

Accordingly, I propose that the socio-political exigencies informing and compelling the exercise of such consumer rights warrant situated analyses. Indeed, if anything, the varied paradigms of MMORPG protest emphasize the importance of maintaining interpretive approaches that are equally attentive to both the nature and actual site of the activism. This chapter mainly focuses on in-game protests and virtual world mass mobilizations that have taken place in the China since 2005. My two chosen case studies concern protests that have been prompted by and revolve respectively around the themes of patriotism and public morality. The aim in this chapter is to gain a better understand of these in-game protests as an emergent facet of MMORPG culture and, in particular, to gain insight into the specific socio-cultural context in which they occur.

NEGOTIATING IN-GAME PROTESTS IN THE CHINESE CONTEXT

In response to their government's plan to introduce a scheme to limit online gaming at cyber cafés to three-hour sessions in 2005, a small group of *World of Warcraft* players in China staged a dramatic in-game protest: Their digital avatars committed mass suicide in the virtual world. Many Western commentators have remarked on this event as yet another sign of China's oppressive and authoritarian regime. "If the Chinese government can monitor *World of Warcraft* players, then Azeroth (where the game takes place) is in some sense a little bit totalitarian, too," suggests Chris Suellentrop in a *Wired* article.[15] This all-too-familiar refrain is emblematic of a key trope in emergent Western Techno-Orientalist discourses about gaming in China—that is, Chinese ludic space as always already inscribed by and co-extensive with government control. This trope substantiates the moral imperative to judge and castigate China's governance in the name of upholding liberal definitions of democracy and individual freedom. Such rhetoric contrasts sharply with Techno-Orientalist discourses on Japanese and Korean game cultures, which, as discussed in Chapter 1, are usually characterized by a paradoxical fetishistic admixture of fascination and revulsion, fear and desire, fantasies and phobias. Techno-Orientalist discourses on Chinese gaming are equally fetishistic, but in a decidedly different way. Discussions about Chinese gaming tend to inevitably dovetail with indictments of China's governance. Governmental clampdowns on Internet gaming and addiction are regularly cast as irrefutable evidence of the heavy-handed operations of an authoritarian Chinese regime. Within this charged context, gaming becomes an index of social freedom; games offer yet another battleground for ideological struggle.

Suffice it to say that such perspectives mask a degree of presumptiveness about the putative freedoms supposedly available in game spaces outside of China. Indeed, the curtailment of social freedoms and player agency can manifest in Western MMORPGs in myriad ways as previously discussed. Henry Jenkins discerns that many Western discussions of the Internet and gaming in China somewhat erroneously describe the rise of digital access and consumer culture as intrinsically liberating forces that will cultivate democratic aspirations behind the repressive government's back.[16] In point of fact, however, the Chinese government has been actively nurturing the domestic rise of consumerism since the 1990s: "The goal has been to facilitate economic and technological change without promoting political destabilization."[17]

There is a broader historical context for these developments. The introduction of market-based economic reforms in 1978 under Deng Xiaoping effectively marked China's transition from a planned economy to a socialist market economy. Stephanie Hemelryk Donald and Michael Keane observe that Western political commentators have attempted to characterize China's post-1978 transition under various formulations: post-socialism, state capitalism, even social capitalism.[18] The ruling Communist Party of China (CPC), in attempting to differentiate its social and economic reforms from contemporaneous changes in the Central European post-Communist regimes, eventually settled on developing the "socialist commodity economy" and conscientiously cultivating "socialism with Chinese characteristics."[19] The latter slogan continues to serve as the official term for the economy of the PRC; and it is essentially, posits Wang Yu on behalf of the CPC, "Chinese socialism in tune with China's reality."[20]

This compound ideological reorientation had other concrete effects, particularly in the fields of mass media and communications. Donald and Keane track parallel developments in the management of Chinese media systems to the point whereby the current favored model appears to be "a hybrid form of governance that has been termed 'authoritarian liberalism'— a combination of economic liberalism and political illiberalism."[21] This has in turn resulted in a model of governmentality whereby

> Chinese people have been allowed an increasing freedom to choose, to consume, and to be self-regulating, but where the authoritarian spectre of the disciplinary state remains as a fallback strategy of governance should civic freedom lead to anti-government uprisings.[22]

For Michel Foucault, the conception of a "regime of governmentality" is integral in highlighting the complex and complicit relationship between a government and its citizenry in maintaining the status quo.[23] This is a useful proposition to explore in relation to the Chinese Internet and its user-citizens or netizens (*"wangmin"*). For Qiu, the Chinese regime of governmentality has a direct bearing on the ways that local netizens are constructing their online identities. He identifies the two dominant tropes essential to this process of collective identification: "(1) the rise of a predominant culture of consumerism that characterizes much of the larger society and (2) the persistence of online nationalism with increasing affinity to state agenda."[24] Both processes of cultural identification, argues Qiu, "have been utilized by the state apparatus since the beginning of Deng Xiaoping's reform and opening-up period and are likely to remain central to the transformation of China in the long run."[25]

The actual number of netizens under discussion here needs to be put into clear perspective. According to the China Internet Network Information Center (CNNIC), there were 253 million Internet users in China by the end of June 2008 (increasing by 91 million from the same time last year), while the Internet penetration rate had reached 19.1%.[26] Most netizens in China (68.6%) are young people under the age of 30.[27] This majority demographic is driving the current use of the Internet in China primarily as a source of entertainment. This group is also linked to the proliferation of certain types of Internet entertainment, chiefly, online music, video, and games. 58.3% of Chinese netizens play online games; and of these, the proportion who play role-playing games is 53%—or 78.15 million players.[28] Given the sheer number of gamers, and the aforementioned constituencies of their particular socio-political environment, the scope for virtual world mass mobilizations and in-game protests is both immense and irrefutable.

THE RHETORIC AND PRACTICES OF IN-GAME PROTESTS IN CHINESE MMORPGS

In-game protests in Chinese MMORPGs offer a lens to view aspects of contemporary Chinese techno-sociality. The two case studies to follow encapsulate the complicated entanglement of social, political and economic values that undergird such events; and the two cases are respectively focused on the themes of patriotism and public morality.

(i) On Patriotism

The first case study comprises two interconnected incidents that took place in 2006 in the online game *Fantasy Westward Journey*. Based on *Journey to the West*, one of the Four Great Classical Novels of Chinese literature that is perhaps best known for chronicling the adventures of the Monkey

King, the game was the most popular MMORPG in China at that time. *Fantasy Westward Journey* had over 25 million registered player accounts and a peak concurrent user (PCU) count of up to 1.3 million players during first quarter of 2006, with an average concurrent user (ACU) count of 458,000 players.[29] The first incident in question concerned the virtual imprisonment of a player's avatar and the dissolution of his guild by the game operators. This in turn allegedly led to the second incident involving a mass virtual world protest over what was believed to be the flagrant display of a symbol of Japanese militarism, the Rising Sun flag, within the game.

On July 4, 2006, the game administrators placed a player's high level avatar (which, at Level 144, was only 11 levels shy of the maximum) in the game's "Great Tang Permanent Incarceration Prison," effectively curtailing the avatar's freedom and participation in the virtual world. The player had named his avatar "Kill the little Japs." He was asked by the administrators to change his alias on the basis that it was "politically sensitive," but he adamantly refused:

> I began playing this game two years ago. When I first applied to NetEase, you did not say that my alias was unacceptable! But now you come and lock up my ID. This is obviously depriving me of my private assets. Over these two years, I have spent more than 30,000 RMB on game point cards, and I have also spent more that 10,000 RMB on equipment trading.[30]

At issue here is the player's obvious and considerable investment in what Julian Kücklich terms "playbour," namely, the convergence between play and labor that often transpires in online gaming.[31] Nevertheless, this affective expression, should not elide the inter-ethnic politics and tensions at the heart of this particular case. The player in question had also founded a guild with about 700 members, making it one of the top five ranked guilds in the game. The guild was named "The Alliance to Resist Japan." On July 5, all the guild members received emails from NetEase, the game's operator, informing them that their guild had violated the rules of the game and it would be dissolved. NetEase alleged that the guild subsequently instigated a mass protest within the game, presumably as an act of retaliation.

On 7, July 2006, thousands of players congregated in an area in the game known as the Summer Palace. Attention was focused on one building, namely, the "Jianye city government office." The *Beijing Evening News* reported that almost 10,000 players had gathered to protest what they perceived to be a Japanese Rising Sun flag represented on the wall of the Tang Dynasty government office.[32] It must first and foremost be noted that this flag, with sixteen rays emanating from a red sun against a white background, was originally the war flag of the Imperial Japanese Army (1870–1945). Although banned after World War II during the Allied Occupation of Japan, the flag has been re-adopted as the emblem of the country's Maritime Self-Defense Force since 1954. Nevertheless, this flag is still regarded as a potent symbol of Japan's historical militarism, particularly in some Asian countries such as China and Korea that experienced Japanese wartime aggression.[33]

The gamers taking part in the protest believed that Japanese expansionism was alive and well, encroaching quite literally on their gaming turf. The visual evidence of the Rising Sun flag in *Fantasy Westward Journey* compounded rumors circulating via the Internet that a Japanese company was taking over NetEase and making changes to the game, including turning Chinese statues of lions (a symbol of patriotism) into pigs.[34] Given this, it is perhaps unsurprising that the mass protest took place on a date with socio-historical significance, particularly in terms of Sino-Japanese relations. July 7 is the anniversary of the 1937 Marco Polo Bridge Incident, a battle between China's National Revolutionary Army and the Japanese Imperial Army, which effectively marked the beginning of the Second Sino-Japanese War (1937–1945).

NetEase strenuously denied rumors that it was being bought by a Japanese company and that the game content included pro-Japanese propaganda, maintaining that the Rising Sun motif was actually based on a classic Chinese painting *Sunrise in the East*.[35] The company acknowledged the depth of patriotic fervor underpinning the protest in their official response:

> In changing the name of an individual player or handling the case of an individual guild, we do not want to cause any unhappiness to people. We do not want such an incident to affect the patriotism of everybody. But this is a game. When we operate this game, we follow the state's regulations on Internet administration and we are monitored by the National Internet Supervisory Bureau. People come here to experience joy, and we therefore emphasize health, relaxation and happiness and we should not bring in politically sensitive topics. The experience of history tells us that patriotism should be expressed rationally under the grand theme of protecting the interests of the nation and the people. Patriotism requires passion, but it requires rationality even more so. Passion and rationality form our correct way of expressing our patriotism.[36]

At first impression, such rhetorical maneuvering is not dissimilar to the bureaucratic logic and language espoused by the GM at the nude protest by gnome warriors discussed earlier in this chapter. It may be argued that the statements by NetEase and the GM are equally didactic. Nevertheless, the circumspect focus on the issue of patriotism in NetEase's statement warrants further consideration. As Henry Jenkins notes, the most striking aspect of the protest march in *Fantasy Westward Journey* and the company's subsequent response to it is "the degree to which all involved saw issues of national honor and patriotism at stake in this dispute."[37] He recognizes that the protest was not "a struggle over an in-game asset: It was a struggle about how the game fit within larger debates about Chinese nationalism and about the country's relation to Japan," its neighbor which is described by Jenkins as "the country's former military foe and current economic rival."[38] He identifies two important inter-related contexts that frame the protest:

> One can understand NetEase's development of a multiplayer game based on a classic of Chinese Literature as part of this larger push towards the use of games to promote national culture (as well as define the company brand against competition from Korean and Japanese licensed games). At the same time, the player's response also reflects the internalization of these same policies—an effort to police games of content that might run counter to the patriotic spirit the government seeks to promote.[39]

Indeed, if anything, Jenkins's analysis illuminates the impact of cultural policy on production and consumption contexts, particularly when that policy dovetails so transparently with the rhetoric and ideology of nation building, as in the case of China. His reading of the protest highlights the importance of negotiating the cultural history and socio-political context relevant to this particular situation. Qiu's previously cited analysis of the relationship between Chinese governmentality and collective identification among Chinese netizens is relevant here. The two incidents comprising this protest respectively allude to salient aspects of consumer culture and online nationalism—which are, aptly enough, the two key tropes discerned by Qiu. It follows that the protestors most likely responded to the events taking place in *Fantasy Westward Journey* because the incident as a whole spoke so directly to core issues that tend to compel collective identification among Chinese netizens.

It is not so much the veracity of what was actually being represented on the wall but what the protestors believed it stood for that is ultimately significant. As part of his incisive examination of the representational politics in the *Fantasy Westward Journey* protest, Carlos Rojas contends: "Like the digital flag, the on-line protests are virtual copies of real-life political protests, which themselves function (like flags) as symbols of abstract ideals."[40] It is crucial to retain Rojas's point about the potency of the visual sign in this incident, where both the digital flag (in the game) and the actual flag (in "real life") are equally functional as a powerful symbol of abstract ideals. Michael Billig's 1995 book *Banal Nationalism* provides a useful point of reference here. He uses the term "banal nationalism" to refer to everyday representations of the nation that construct and enforce a sense of national solidarity among the citizenry. His oft-cited example of banal nationalism, which encapsulates the latent power inherent in a certain representation of the flag, proves to be uncannily prescient: "The metonymic image of banal nationalism is not a flag which is being consciously waved with fervent passion; it is the flag hanging unnoticed on the public building."[41] As in the case of the *Fantasy Westward Journey* protest, it is precisely the seeming banality of metonymic images and their quotidian mundanity, which utterly belies their ideological force and their capacity to prompt people into patriotic action.

(ii) On Public Morality

The second case study originates in a love triangle. The incident began in April 2006 when a man posted an impassioned open letter on an Internet bulletin board denouncing a student he claimed was having an affair with his wife. The situation quickly escalated. In an article for the *International Herald Tribune*, Howard W. French reports that the open letter prompted an immediate response from hundreds of netizens. He provides a vivid one-line chronology of the snowballing chain of events:

> Within days, the hundreds had grown to thousands, and then tens of thousands, with total strangers forming teams to hunt down the student's identity and address, hounding him out of his university and causing his family to barricade themselves inside their home.[42]

Zixue Tai, Qiu and Guobin Yang have analyzed the proliferation of Internet-mediated mass mobilizations in China.[43] The cases on record are remarkably diverse and span the gamut from making public demands for an investigation into a campus murder cover-up, to joining forces to conduct an exposé on the secret lives of celebrities. Participants are often galvanized by, and act upon, some shared moral imperative. French goes so far as to describe these incidents as "morality lessons [which] are administered by online throngs and where anonymous Web users come together to investigate others and mete out punishment for offenses real and imagined."[44] These events largely originate in online forums or bulletin boards and eventually spill over to offline contexts, often with profound consequences. Tai, Qiu and Yang are in agreement that such mass mobilizations are constitutive of a new online-offline dialectic and continuum in Chinese techno-sociality.

The incident in April 2006 shared the foregoing traits but possessed two other significant features: (1) a strong connection to online gaming; and (2) the occurrence of a large-scale in-game protest that expanded the scope of the mass mobilization. The original letter was posted on the bulletin board of the MOP game forum, and eventually resulted in the public naming and shaming of the Yanshan University student responsible for initiating the affair. Roland Soong opines that it would have been "just a personal adulterous affair" but for the fact that the accused student was at that time "a renowned WoW [*World of Warcraft*] player under the name Zxxs."[45] The public posting of the letter on the game forum was thereby a strategic gambit. The personal affair was at the very least intended to become a game community affair.

In order to come to terms with the artful persuasiveness of the initial letter, I will be quoting the first two paragraphs in their entirety and offering an examination of their rhetorical techniques. The first paragraph proffers an introduction by way of creating a self-portrait of the devoted husband:

> Let me introduce myself. I used to be the demon warrior "Xianzi Ke'er" in WoW District 2's Maiwei Audio-Visual server alliance. I joined this game in order to accompany my wife in real life. She played the role of a human preacher with the pretty name "Dim Moon." Because I am relatively busy at work—there are probably very few people in this game who work—I was basically anonymous except to a few friends. After all, I entered this game in order to be with my wife, and fancy equipment does not interest me. I just wanted to be with my wife so that I can continue to take care of her in the virtual world. Dim Moon has left her job for about three years. She was not happy in her original work environment. Since I was moderately successful at work, I agreed that she can remain home. I always thought that it was the duty of the man to provide for the family. I also enjoyed the feeling that I can support the entire family. So I was glad to do so. I thought that Dim Moon liked it too, because she was not a competitive person in real life and I want her to be happy. If the events to be described below did not occur, I think I would have continued to feel this way for my entire life.[46]

The informal, conversational tone creates a conspiratorial air for this testimonial. The content is similarly modulated with care. "Xianzi Ke'er" paints a portrait of himself as a dutiful provider, someone who has "real life" work responsibilities but is nonetheless happy to play games to accompany his wife. Within this narrative, masculinist presumptions are adroitly framed as paternalistic care. The testimonial is also notable for the way in which gamer identity is seamlessly folded into the vernacular of social life. Social identity and gamer identity are cast as being mutually constitutive. The incipient sense of this continuum of identification is developed to even greater effect in the second paragraph, which focuses on "Dim Moon" who is the more avid gamer of the two.

> The Maifu Alliance's Sentinel Guild is a good group. They are united and strong. The students at Yanshan University who founded this group put in a lot of effort, and Dim Moon was one of them. Within the RAID group, she is seldom absent as the preacher. Occasionally, when I see my wife show a happy smile during game play that is seldom seen in her real life, I must honestly say that I am jealous while being happy that she has so many friends in the virtual world. Dim Moon is a preacher who does not worry too much about appearances, because she

values friendship as the most important thing. So she gets along with people. She likes RAID, she hates PK [Player Killing] and she is too lazy to bother with money. Many friends sell of [sic] good stuff, and they always remember to share some of the profits with her. Among those, the Sentinel Guild's president Tongxu got along with her quite well.[47]

"Tongxu," the guild president, was the student accused of having the affair with his wife. The context for how they met and eventually got together is clearly established. "Xianzi Ke'er" characterizes his wife via her gaming preferences and practices. These are the manifest game world premises by which one player gets to know and ultimately judge another player. The intimation here is clear: What you are like as a player is essentially coterminous with what you are like as a person. After this paragraph, the tone and mode of address in the letter noticeably shifts. Readers are made to feel more and more like voyeuristic participants in an unfolding narrative. Eventually, the moment of confrontation arrives:

> Our conversation was frequently interrupted by our tears. I understand that a woman who feels that her life is empty and lacking in excitement might be attracted by the game world, she left home quietly, she answered the call of the game guild, she let her body loose after being kissed forcibly after a meeting . . . that time, the principals were Dim Moon and you, Tongxu.
>
> After thinking for a long time, I asked myself: Is this woman still the woman that I loved deeply? The woman whom I planned to buy a house immediately and have children? I am not a procrastinator. At that I really could not choose between six years of time and two days of betrayal. So I contacted you, Tongxu.[48]

The online posting had transformed by now into an open challenge to "Tongxu" to come forth and explain his guilt. Within three days of the posting, more than a million searches for information about this affair were made on Baidu, China's leading Internet search engine.[49] At the MOP game forum, the page views were coming in at 30,000 per hour with 2,000 comments per hour.[50] "Xianzi Ke'er" eventually requested for the posting to be removed from the game forum because of the overwhelming response.

There were also significant developments taking place concurrently within the *World of Warcraft* game world. Shortly after "Xianzi Ke'er's" posting, a number of alliances among players began to appear in Area 2's Mawei Audio-Visual server. Within a few hours, they had formed a splinter guild called Sentinel Comforters, consisting of more than a hundred people who were united with the single goal: the outright condemnation of the Sentinel Guild's president "Tongxu."[51] The mass rally culminated in a dramatic mass suicide staged by the protesting guild members. It is important to recognize that this was not just an act of open criticism by some members of the Sentinel Guild. Instead, it was a very public sign of their total loss of respect for the guild president. As discussed in Chapter 13, within MMORPG culture, respect for the guild leader is absolutely essential in maintaining the guild's harmony and prosperity. The research in the chapter by Holin Lin and Chuen-Tsai Sun shows how the perceived integrity of the guild leader is an important attribute for commanding both online and offline respect. "Tongxu" had evidently lost respect among his immediate gamer peers. It was not long before his real life identity was revealed. Public condemnation mounted to the point where he felt sufficiently pressured to eventually withdraw from Yanshan University where he was studying.

This case study shows other important dimensions in Chinese MMORPG protests—their variegated role in facilitating, supplementing and expediting mass mobilizations. The particular incident at hand also accounts for why this might be possible by highlighting the present magnitudes of online-offline sociality among Chinese gamer-netizens. At this juncture, it is worth recalling the previously cited CNNIC data about youths and gamers being the core demographics in China's burgeoning netizen population. The sheer number of netizens present online at any given time may be a significant point in and of itself. Accordingly, Yang surmises that the frequency of online protests in China's highly monitored and controlled networks might not be a paradox.

> One crucial feature of the virtual sphere might explain the frequency of online protest: At any given time, thousands of people are online, perhaps for political purposes, but most likely for fun. These *netizens* (or *wangmin* in Chinese) can slip into action as occasions arise, over a campus murder cover-up, a school house fire, a deadly accident at a coal mine, a corrupt official newly exposed. The more outrageous the incident, the more likely it is to arouse the virtual crowd, always lurking and always alert. Once aroused, the networked crowd can rapidly fill the web with queries, information exchanges, debate, protest, and organized activity, at times even achieving the power of public opinion.[52]

Yang's reasoning is persuasive and applicable to the particular case at hand. Indeed, if anything, this case study demonstrates how the "transboundary interactions between online and offline realms were an important mechanism driving the information politics."[53] This particular case study also puts into clear perspective the observation by Yang that "information politics is central in China's online activism, involving both the release of testimonial and factual information and struggles over information channels."[54] He asserts that the public dissemination of testimonial information, in particular, helps to "make the need for action more real for ordinary citizens."[55] Such is the rhetorical force and power of persuasion at work in the impassioned online testimonial that sparked this particular incident.

CONCLUSION: TOWARDS A NEW SOCIAL MOVEMENT?

The forms of gamer protest are evolving, with online mass mobilizations either spilling over or connecting to offline activism in many different ways. But is it possible—or, indeed, viable—to think of gamer activism as a new social movement?

Matthew Chew proposes that gamer activism is a tangible sign of a fledgling socio-political consciousness, which is in turn constitutive of a nascent "Virtual-World-Oriented Social Movement (VSM)."[56] He treats various gamer protests, both online and offline, which have taken place in China between 2003 and 2007 as evidence of an emergent sociology of radical activism. Much of the discontent originates in disputes between gamers and game companies over virtual property. Key issues include theft and dispute over in-game items among players, use of hacked virtual property, and loss of property as a direct result of game company negligence or game server fault. Other sources of complaint include technical instability (chiefly, frequent game crashes and persistent lag) and the termination of individual player accounts as a punitive measure often taken by game companies to remove suspected hackers or perceived troublemakers from the game world.

Chew believes that Chinese gamers are becoming increasing sensitized to, and aggrieved by, an emergent general perception of "the corrupted, authoritarian rule of virtual-worlds" by game corporations.[57] Disagreements between gamers and game corporations have at times taken a violent turn, ranging from the vandalizing of a game company office, to the self-immolation of a disgruntled gamer at online games operator Shanda's office in Shanghai. At the same time, Chinese gamers are beginning to take their grievances to the judicial courts. In 2004, a gamer won the first virtual property dispute case against a game corporation. Chew surmises that gamer rights protection will eventually offer a framework for collective action that "offers integrity and continuity across protests, turning largely NIMBY (not-in-my-backyard) protests erupted independently in different games into an incipient movement."[58] Current developments in gamer awareness of consumer rights and rights protection are proposed as two key signifiers of a nascent public collective action.

Chew's prognosis may be premature. It is important to emphasize that gamer protests are, for the most part, highly contingent coalitions and transitory mass collaborations. They are not necessarily long-term collective actions. Besides, not all protests are fixated on game-specific concerns. More significantly, the case studies traversed in this chapter underscore how in-game protests may at once *circumnavigate* and *exceed* the putative parameters of game culture. I do nonetheless concur with Chew's identification of discernible changes in gamer awareness as a social index of developments in the Chinese public sphere, both online and offline. To borrow the words of Yang, "the condition and fate of the Chinese virtual public sphere depends as much on its internal dynamics of private pleasures and public concerns as on the changing political, social, and technological environment."[59] The myriad forces—technological, historical, political, cultural, and social—conditioning and compelling in-game protests as discussed in this chapter are thereby indexical of the forces that simultaneously act out and act on developments in the contemporary Chinese public sphere.

NOTES

1. Rebecca MacKinnon, "Cyber Zone," *Index on Censorship*, 37 (2), May 2008: 82.
2. Lokman Tsui, "Introduction: The Sociopolitical Internet in China," *China Information*, 19 (2), 2005: 183
3. Guobin Yang, "The Co-Evolution of the Internet and Civil Society in China," *Asian Survey*, 43 (3), 2003: 408.
4. Jack Linchuan Qiu, "The Internet in China: Data and Issues," Working Paper Prepared for *Annenberg Research Seminar on International Communication*, 1 October 2003: 18.
5. Qiu, "The Internet in China," 3.
6. Guobin Yang, "The Internet and Civil Society in China: A Preliminary Assessment", *Journal of Contemporary China*, 12 (36), August 2003: 469.
7. Yang, "The Internet and Civil Society in China," 475.
8. Artist-activists are also starting to use online game spaces for staging protests. A prominent example is American artist Joseph DeLappe's *Dead-in-Iraq*, which is a memorial and protest project that takes place in *America's Army* (2002), the free-to-play online multiplayer game developed by the US Army as a promotional and recruitment tool. As part of this ongoing project that commenced in 2006, DeLappe periodically logs into *America's Army* with his digital avatar named "dead-in-iraq" and, using the in-game text messaging system, he types in the name, age, service branch and date of death of US service persons killed in Iraq since the war started. For a further discussion of DeLappe's work as well as other examples of in-game activist art projects, see Dean Chan, "*Dead-in-Iraq*: The Spatial Politics of Game Art Activism and the In-Game Protest," in *Joystick Soldiers: The Politics of Play in Military Video Games*, eds. Nina Huntemann and Matthew Payne(New York: Routledge, forthcoming). Such in-game interventions by individuals need to be acknowledged as part of the emergent genealogy of in-game protests, however the focus of this chapter is on collective or mass-mobilized protests occurring in virtual world environments.
9. Ed Halter, "Playing dead," *Arthur Magazine*, 23 July 2006: 43.
10. Tim Guest, *Second Lives* (London: Arrow Books, 2008), 212–213.
11. Guest, *Second Lives*, 213.
12. Guest, *Second Lives*, 213.
13. Halter, 43. For a detailed analysis of this case and the debates surrounding it, see Matt Peckham, "Sounds of Silence: Sanitizing Expression in Brave New Worlds," *Computer Gaming World*, 261. Retrieved 17 July 2008 from http://www.1up.com/do/feature?pager.offset=0&cld=3149452.
14. Guest, *Second Lives*, 212.
15. Chris Suellentrop, "Global Gaming Crackdown," *Wired*, 14 (4), April 2006. Retrieved 15 January 2008 from http://www.wired.com/wired/archive/14.04/law.html.

16. Henry Jenkins, "The Chinese Columbine," *Fans, Bloggers, and Gamers: Exploring Participatory Culture* (New York and London: New York University Press, 2006), 222–225.
17. Jenkins, "The Chinese Columbine," 223.
18. Stephanie Hemelryk Donald and Michael Keane, "Media in China: New Convergences, New Approaches," in S.H. Donald, M. Keane and Y. Hong, *Media in China: Consumption, Content and Crisis* (London and New York: Routledge, 2002), 3–17.
19. Donald and Keane, "Media in China," 5.
20. Wang Yu, "Our way: Building Socialism with Chinese Characteristics," *Political Affairs*, January 2004. Retrieved 7 September 2008 from http://www.politicalaffairs.net/article/view/36/1/1/.
21. Donald and Keane, 5.
22. Donald and Keane, 6.
23. Michel Foucault, *Discipline and Punish: The Birth of the Prison*, trans. Alan Sheridan, (London: Penguin Books, 1991, 1st. pub. 1975).
24. Qiu, "The Internet in China," 14.
25. Qiu, "The Internet in China," 14.
26. China Internet Network Information Center (CNNIC), *Statistical Survey Report on the Internet Development in China: Abridged Edition* (Beijing: CNNIC, July 2008), 10.
27. CNNIC, *Statistical Survey Report on the Internet Development in China*, 12.
28. CNNIC, *Statistical Survey Report on the Internet Development in China*, 24–25.
29. Henry Jenkins, "National Politics within Virtual Game Worlds: The Case of China," *Confessions of an Aca-Fan: The Official Weblog of Henry Jenkins*, 6 August 2006. Retrieved 15 January 2008 from http://www.henryjenkins.org/2006/08/national_politics_within_virtu_1.html. PCU and ACU figures are generally considered to be more reliable than the number of subscription accounts in gauging gamer usage. This is because a single player may have multiple accounts—and particularly in the East Asian context, players typically rely on a range of micro-payment options and often play games in cyber cafés.
30. Cited in Roland Soong, "Freedom of Identity, Speech and Assembly on the Internet," *EastSouthWestNorth*. Retrieved 11 August 2008 from http://www.zonaeuropa.com/20060710_1.htm.
31. Julian Kücklich, "Precarious Playbour: Modders and the Digital Games Industry," *Fibreculture Journal*, 5, 2005. Retrieved 23 July 2008 from http://journal.fibreculture.org/issue5/kucklich.html.
32. The original Chinese language news article is translated in Soong, "Red Rubber Ball."
33. Even during the 2008 Beijing Olympics, Japanese fans were encouraged not to display the "rising sun" flag at sporting events. See Naoto Okamura, "Japan fans warned not to fly naval flag," *Reuters*, 8 August 2008. Retrieved 5 September 2008 from http://www.reuters.com/article/topNews/idUST35118820080808.
34. Jenkins, "National Politics within Virtual Game Worlds."
35. Jenkins, "National Politics within Virtual Game Worlds."
36. Soong, "Freedom of Identity."
37. Jenkins, "National Politics within Virtual Game Worlds."
38. Jenkins, "National Politics within Virtual Game Worlds."
39. Jenkins, "National Politics within Virtual Game Worlds."

40. Carlos Rojas, "The Meaning of the Inoperative Community," *Blogcritics Magazine*. Retrieved 23 July 2008 from http://blogcritics.org/archives/2006/07/27/075757.php.
41. Michael Billig, *Banal Nationalism* (London: Sage, 1995): 8.
42. Howard W. French, "Mob rule on China's Internet: The keyboard as weapon," *International Herald Tribune*, 1 June 2006. Retrieved 23 July 2008 from http://www.iht.com/articles/2006/05/31/business/chinet.php.
43. Zixue Tai, *The Internet in China: Cyberspace and Civil Society*, (New York: Routledge, 2006); Qiu, "The Internet in China"; and Yang, "The Internet and Civil Society in China."
44. French, "Mob rule on China's Internet."
45. Roland Soong, "The Most Famous Pervert in China," *EastSouthWestNorth* Retrieved 11 August 2008 from http://zonaeuropa.com/20060417_1.htm.
46. Soong, "The Most Famous Pervert in China."
47. Soong, "The Most Famous Pervert in China."
48. Soong, "The Most Famous Pervert in China."
49. Soong, "The Most Famous Pervert in China."
50. Soong, "The Most Famous Pervert in China."
51. Soong, "The Most Famous Pervert in China."
52. Guobin Yang, "Mingling Politics with Play: The Virtual Chinese Public Sphere," *International Institute for Asian Studies (IIAS) Newsletter*, 33, March 2003: 7.
53. Guobin Yang, "Activists Beyond Virtual Borders: Internet-Mediated Networks and Informational Politics in China," *First Monday*, 7, September 2006. Retrieved 23 July 2008 from http://firstmonday.org/Issues/special11_9/yang/index.html.
54. Yang, "Activists Beyond Virtual Borders."
55. Yang, "Activists Beyond Virtual Borders."
56. Matthew Chew, "The Gamer Rights Protection Movement in China" [PowerPoint Presentation], Paper presented at *Chinese Internet Research Conference*, 13–14 June, The University of Hong Kong, Hong Kong, 2008. Retrieved 9 September 2008 from http://www.slideshare.net/CIRC/chewmattewthe-gamer-rights-protection-movement-in-china-2.
57. Chew, "The Gamer Rights Protection Movement in China."
58. Chew, "The Gamer Rights Protection Movement in China."
59. Yang, "Mingling Politics with Play," 7.

9 *Pokémon* 151
Complicating *Kawaii*

David Surman

INTRODUCTION

This is an essay about the experience of encountering *Pokémon* in the first couple of years after the release of the videogames here in the United Kingdom. The dichotomous paradigms of "cute" and "cool" that shape the zeitgeist of *Pokémon* motivate academics to discuss the culture and reception of the game. I argue that by looking closely at the art of *Pokémon* we can begin to understand the complex rhetoric of the design, that oscillates between the poles of Japanese "cute" and American "cool."

Three summers ago, one of my colleagues hosted a barbeque for faculty, friends and family at his large house in the countryside. In a rare glimmer of Welsh sunshine, it was a treat to see everyone having that special kind of fun, pinned somewhere in between total relaxation and best behavior. Caught half asleep in my chair, a little voice called out and asked, 'Do you like *Pokémon*?' A young man aged around 6 years had been directed by a knowing parent to talk to me, the computer games design faculty member. Substantially older and much more self-conscious about announcing my interests, "of course," I tentatively replied. Though this was something of an understatement; I had been following *Pokémon* avidly from its first arrival in the late nineties; I knew the game inside out, and rarely had an opportunity to talk about it (I certainly wasn't part of the core demographic). What followed was an interrogation, maybe even a trial. My Poké-team, play style, knowledge and progression each charted under oath. Every word was met with a lightning riposte, both critical and superlative. It turned out I was pretty good, but I didn't know my "tanks" from my "sweepers," and I had been compromising a competitive team with too many cute-but-weak *Pokémon*. With a churlish smile, I accepted his criticisms.[1]

I was left with my thoughts as the conversation came to a close. To date I had worn my *otaku*-dom like a badge of honor, a relatively resolved doxa from which my knowledge of *Pokémon* could be played. Away from 6-year-old Jude's electric scrutiny, I began to realize that I had neither the time nor the consciousness to fully apprehend all that the *Pokémon* universe had become. Nor could I comprehend the current *Pokémon* game in the same way he had. Yet in what seemed like an instant, the particular style of the game had expedited our conversation to a deep level. We were two seasoned adventurers taking for granted talk of terrain, made buoyant by shared experiences. To players of *Pokémon*, this immediacy is natural; the game asks of us all the same thing—to commit a certain amount of thought, to inhabit its universe in a certain way.

I want to consider some of the issues that permeate that garden conversation with my young friend, not because we achieved any great meaningful insight into the game, but precisely because such exchanges *aren't* unique. Some of what I suggest here is relevant to the broader church of Japanese games design, and perhaps to the medium at large. It has become clear that committed conversations are a core part of the culture surrounding, penetrating and issuing from the game. There is a "big conversation" happening around virtually all successful videogames, comprising forum chatter, various kinds of fan-based creativity, complementary retailing, bar-room banter and playground chants. *Pokémon* is particularly characterized by a reflexive emphasis on communication (*tsūshin*) which is keenly promoted by spokespersons and designers at Game Freak.

This ubiquity has lead critics including Koichi Iwabuchi[2] to question the "Japanese-ness" of *Pokémon*. He argues that the ubiquity of character media like *Pokémon* relies on the removal of the cultural traces connected to its production source, Japan. In this "odorless," culturally neutralized form, *Pokémon* is able to succeed commercially and internationally in a way that distinctively Japanese media cannot. This principle underpins the ambiguous nature of Japanese media power in the twenty-first century, wherein the culture evoked by the commodity carries only a tenuous connection to the source. Citing Hoskins and Mirus,[3] Iwabuchi writes that

> in contrast to the American dominance of world film markets, Japan's success derives from its exporting of "culturally neutral" commodities whose country of origin has nothing to do with "the way [that they work] and the satisfaction [that a consumer] obtains from usage." Hoskins and Mirus contrast the ease of export of culturally neutral commodities with the much greater difficulty of exporting products that are culturally embedded.[4]

In a myriad of ways, we are collectively "playing *with* videogames"[5]; but when the reciprocity between game and player is finely tuned to provide maximal capital growth, eliciting vast amounts of constituent labor from players (and even some non-players), we need to ask the question—what do games want from us? How does game form interpellate the playing subject? Iwabuchi's final remarks situate *Pokémon* as propagating a consumerist ideology: "Even if the origins of cultural products become increasingly insignificant and difficult to trace, the 'Japaneseness' of *Pokémon* still does matter with regard to Japan's collusive role in generating cultural asymmetry on a global scale."[6] Such a sober view contrasts with the prevailing optimism of suggestions that, through *Pokémon* and other "soft" cultural commodities, Japan is enjoying a new international visibility and that the demand for such commodities in turn disseminates Japanese aesthetic and cultural values to an international audience.[7]

Iwabuchi notes that as *Pokémon* was being prepared by Nintendo of America (NOA) for international distribution, requests for designs of *Pokémon* to be changed were put forward, but ultimately rejected by the Japanese producers.[8] NOA's reformat of *Pokémon* for Western audiences is well understood and documented,[9] yet the refusal to compromise on the original designs implies that this Americanization is not totalizing, but rather negotiated, and that the visual style is significant insofar as the character design is protected. This chapter takes seriously the point at which commodity and design concept collide, and looks to those character drawings in close detail to better understand what they can tell us about *Pokémon* aside from popular assumptions and the archetypal discussion of fandom and fads.

In asking such a question, this chapter posits design analysis as a complement to the ethnographic focus seen in the majority of *Pokémon* studies, and in so doing hopes to illuminate a burgeoning blind spot in the current academic research on Japanese videogames more generally. I refer to the examination of their visual styles, rhythms, animations, forms, material contemporaries and technological antecedents—fears of exoticism and misinterpretation have stalled the formal scrutiny of Japanese videogames, including *Pokémon*.

This chapter takes a long hard look at *Pokémon*, one of the largest and most profitable media franchises in the world. We can encounter *Pokémon* in virtually all major media forms, including animation for television, film, theme-park and a huge variety of merchandise. At the root of the *Pokémon* universe is a series of videogames, created for Nintendo's handheld devices, first the GameBoy and later the DS. *Pokémon* games have appeared on a variety of other hardware systems, and often take the characters from the franchise into new gameplay contexts, emphasizing a different facet of the largely consistent and continuous *Pokémon* universe. I am focusing on the two complementary versions of the first game, *Pokémon Red* and *Pokémon Blue*, released between 1996 and 1999 across all major territories. These games feature the "primary generation," that is, the first 151 *Pokémon* (there are now over 400 at last count).

From humble origins in Japan, *Pokémon* is now a global phenomenon. It has elicited considerable scholarly interest in recent years, and those in the English-speaking world have committed to the interpretation of *Pokémon culture* and its impact on children. Another body of literature has been produced by the anti-*Pokémon* movement, which is predominantly made up of religiously motivated figureheads and parenting groups who are concerned by the perceived occult dimensions to the game.[10] It is ironic that literature coming from the religious critics employs (albeit attenuated) close analysis as a strategy to undermine and criticize the game, when conventional scholarly analysis of these games hesitates from speaking about them in such a piecemeal way. For example, in condemnation of the game content, John Paul Jackson writes that:

> As players pit their *Pokémon* against one another, they are encouraged to use rage, poison, fire, etc. Furthermore, they can attack by sending a curse of amnesia, confusion, paralysis or sleep. Even species classified as outside the psychic category can attack with psychic powers such as hypnosis, mind reading, teleporting, and inflicting headaches on others.[11]

It is important to make a counter move toward this close description, in order to fully penetrate through to the inner workings and deep play. In the past few years, activity in the research around *Pokémon* culminated in the publication of two books, *Pikachu's Global Adventure: The Rise and Fall of Pokémon*, an anthology of essays edited by Joseph Tobin,[12] and later Anne Allison's monograph *Millennial Monsters: Japanese Toys and the Global Imagination*.[13] Considered together, these two publications comprise a substantial contribution to the academic interpretation and analysis of *Pokémon*. The study of the political economy of *Pokémon* is exhaustive, and the authors rightly position the game in the context of East Asian modernity and globalization, as part of the mass media "recentring" around Japan's "soft power."[14] Both volumes however shy away from any direct discussion of the artistic ambition or visual style of the game series. The tendency in academia is to understand *Pokémon* through its social effects, though at the same time hesitating from scrutinizing what is issuing from the cartridge to the LCD screen.

The game's original designer Satoshi Tajiri is often quoted talking about his original ambitions for *Pokémon*, mainly emphasizing what motivated him and how he negotiated with Nintendo over time. In fact, when he is mentioned it tends to be through recourse to his original statements about the game's concept. To give an example, one particular anecdote is crucial to how the method with which the majority of scholars interpret the aesthetic of *Pokémon*. Tajiri recalls the urbanization of his childhood playspaces, and the loss of those overgrown, muddy hideaways that children love to explore. In particular, the process of redevelopment deprived children of the excitement of catching bugs in the wild corners of the town. This anecdote chimes with the sentiments of animation film director Hayao Miyazaki, who likewise sourced one meaning of his work in the accelerating loss of the countryside to burgeoning urban sprawl. Bracketed by recourse to these same anecdotes, Allison summarizes that:

> Tajiri has said that he had two major motivations in designing *Pokémon*. One was to create a challenging but playable game that would pique children's imaginations. The other was to give kids a means of

relieving the stresses of growing up in a postindustrial society. Born in 1962, Tajiri shares the opinion of many in his generation that life for children today is hard. In this academic-record society, the pressure to study, compete, and perform starts as early as birth . . . In Tajiri's mind, the rewards of millennial Japan have come with a loss to humanity.[15]

While these stories give us a motivation for the game concept, they don't take us very much further when trying to understand the imagery of *Pokémon*—its characters, environments, patterns and grammar. Furthermore, one could suggest that the paradigmatic focus on Tajiri's explanation creates a totalizing myth—of how gameplay in *Pokémon* recuperates his lost childhood experience for contemporary children. Reference to the conceptual beginnings of *Pokémon*—what we might call the *narrative of its development and play*—displace the problem of talking about the representational grammar and ludic patterns of the game. In his discussion on such modern myths, Roland Barthes remarks, "The fact that we cannot manage to achieve more than an unstable grasp of reality doubtless gives the measure of our present alienation: We constantly drift between the object and its demystification, powerless to render its wholeness."[16] Unwilling to challenge this quandary, it seems a cursory reference to Tajiri's intention is sufficient for many scholars to determine the goings-on of *Pokémon*. For a game to have such a massive impact on digital visual culture, it must be more than a triumph of collective nostalgia and contemporary marketing. This chapter points out the centrality of *style*[17] in the *Pokémon* universe, and how its visual grammar, more than the collective nostalgia of its concept, play a crucial role in its widespread dissemination.

A chapter-length study doesn't provide the kind of space needed to undertake a comprehensive study of the aesthetic of *Pokémon*, so this chapter focuses on the work of artist Ken Sugimori, who provided the vibrant designs for the original one hundred and fifty one *Pokémon*. The same artwork illustrates the infamous *Pokémon* cards, scourge of children's pocket money—a separate game which shadowed the sudden boom in the popularity of the videogames and *animé* around the turn of the millennium. Sugimori doesn't appear in the current scholarly literature on *Pokémon*; this oversight betrays the orientation of the field toward more cultural and contextual analyses of videogames, since the work of contributing artists is conceived critically as less important than a presiding vision of the gameplay, and of game culture. In current Game Studies, game art assets— including pre-visualization material, animation and sound design—are often relegated as secondary considerations, yielding to contemporary efforts to qualitatively define the elusive "aesthetic of gameplay," autonomous from its surrounding audiovisual elements.

This chapter follows closely my research into the form and context of Namco's *Katamari Damacy* (2004) and the sequel *We Love Katamari* (2005), and the strong continuity I argued for between Japanese videogames and contemporary art.[18] Continuing that comparison, I will look closely at the ways in which Sugimori's illustrations play a major role in the collective unconscious of *Pokémon*. In this respect Sugimori is to Tajiri's *Pokémon* what Sir John Tenniel's illustrations are to Lewis Carroll's *Alice Adventures in Wonderland* and *Through the Looking Glass*. The text and image are interleaved together in the imagination; Tajiri's gameplay and Sugimori's art sit together in that moment of first exposure.

KEN SUGIMORI, *PULSEMAN* AND VISUAL STYLE

In his essay "An Introduction to Otaku Movement," Thomas Lamarre suggests that the consumptive practices of the *otaku* incorporate a specific method of viewing in which parts of the character design are perceived in preference to the whole, because of the sub-cultural continuities they signify.[19] In these discrete parts—*neko* (cat) ears, angel wings, priestess robes, a sleek fringe—an epistemology of fan knowledge manifests to stabilize a given design within a long stylistic continuity to which *otaku* culture is deeply committed. Lamarre writes that:

> As they compulsively replayed videos of such favorite series as *Macross*, they [the *otaku*] began to perceive differences in animation styles within and between episodes. The result was a new attention to what might be considered flaws, inconsistencies or trivial details by other viewers.[20]

The mimetic stylistic tradition of *mangaka* and the close scrutiny of the otaku produce two complimentary sides to a singular dynamic—intertextuality of style produced at points of both production *and* consumption. He adds that:

> these apparently insignificant details become part of the viewing experience, making the experience of viewing akin to scanning for information, rather than reading a story . . . In effect the peripheral becomes central; or rather there is a breakdown in the visual ordering of central and peripheral that results in a non-hierarchical visual field of information.[21]

Lamarre's identification of a widespread sensitivity to style in the *otaku* reception of *manga*, *anime* and videogames is important, as it reinforces the need to examine closely the visual fields created in these media, and in so doing critically reflect on the considerations made by fans. Since we still live in the trailing zeitgeist of *Pokémania*, it's hard to objectively see the artistic impact it has had; how do we separate fad from legacy? Surely this anxiety explains the absence of any reference to Sugimori in the literature on *Pokémon*. One of Tajiri's close friends, Sugimori continues to work as an artist and design consultant for Game Freak, the second-party developer for Nintendo founded in 1989 by Satoshi Tajiri.

The story of how *Pokémon*'s characteristic visual style developed begins in an earlier Game Freak project, *Pulseman* (1994) that featured on the SEGA Mega Drive[22] console.[23] *Pulseman* was only released in Japan, though a surge of interest in Game Freak vis-à-vis *Pokémon* has created a new market for the resale of *Pulseman* cartridges on auction-websites like eBay. The relatively unknown Pulseman game features many elements in common with Capcom's flagship franchise and current mascot *Mega Man* (a.k.a. *Rokkuman*, Rock Man). The background story describes how an ingenious computer scientist named Doc Yoshiyama creates a powerful female artificial intelligence, "C-Life," and like Pygmalion and Galatea, he falls deeply in love with her. In fact he falls so madly in love that he downloads his consciousness into the computer system, and in that virtual Eden they make love, producing *Pulseman*. He is a human machine hybrid, able to live in the "everyday" world as a material being, with the power to channel and transform into powerful bolts of electricity (the letter S of his namesake is depicted as an jagged lightning bolt on the title screen). After a period of time Doc Yoshiyama emerges from his own computer system; obviously corrupted by the experience he declares that he is now the evil Doc Waruyama, and establishes a terrorist cell named the "Galaxy Gang" who spread a wave of cyber-crime across the globe. *Pulseman* must therefore fight his father-creator, and preserve the world.

At the time of its release, *Pulseman* was praised in the Japanese gaming press for a sophisticated graphic style that pushed the boundaries of the SEGA hardware. Satoshi Tajiri and Ken Sugimori also worked alongside Junichi Masuda, the musician who would later score the theme music to *Pokémon*. The game was unanimously praised in well-known magazines such as *Famitsu* for its excellent character design, animation, sound and gameplay, and frequently compared to the SEGA classics *Sonic the Hedgehog* (1991) and *Ristar* (1994). When critics say that *Pulseman* is one of the best-looking games produced on the Mega Drive system, what are they specifically referring to? The answer to such a question helps us to leverage the importance of Ken Sugimori to the legacy of *Pokémon*.

The style of *Pulseman* signifies a long genealogy of character designs that operate at the core of Japanese contemporary visual culture. Beginning proper in the 1960s with Osamu Tezuka's *Astro Boy* (*Tetsuwan Atomu*, 1952) and Shotaro Ishinomori's *Cyborg 009* (*Saibōgu Zero-Zero-Nain*, 1964) *manga*, these characters feature in science fiction narratives as heroes fighting against faceless, sometimes occult, sometimes corporate forces. In their design, what is most immediately apparent is the consistency of both the silhouette and the palette; red, black and yellow appear repeatedly across this range of characters. Earlier still, Osamu Tezuka's social commentary *manga Ma-Chan* (1946) featured the same color scheme, penned in the period immediately after the Second World War. Tezuka's early interest in Disney animation practice suggests that the palette most probably has its origins in the early "living color" Mickey Mouse designs of the 1930s, whose iconic image had become a mainstay in the modern world. Philip Brophy writes: "While Disney's work had by the 1950s grown progressively more idyllic, Tezuka's work grew equally more somber and reflective."[24] Echoing these Disney antecedents, *Pulseman* shows off a pair of large cartoony white gloves in the attract sequence of the game, which betray Sugimori's awareness of the tropes distilled in the tradition of the robot boy.

While there is no explicit connection between such characters and their narrative universes, the intertextuality of form signals the concern for tradition and expressions of respect held between designers from 1960 to the present. Beginning with *Cyborg 009*, we see how the lead-character Joe Shimamura (a.k.a. "Cyborg 009") has the trademark "cow's-lick" fringe, which often occludes one of his eyes. The motif of sleek black hair and a windswept fringe appears in the recurrent character of "Rock" (*Rokuro Makube*) in the *manga* and *anime* works of Osamu Tezuka. As a kind of shorthand developed over time through its repeated use, the fringe signifies a delinquent character, of complex moral and ethical standing, and even more complex allegiance. Unlike the youthful "Kenichi" archetype used by Tezuka, whose face is always shown clearly, with optimism and transparent emotion, Rock is a complex, shadowy character—perhaps Tezuka's most complex archetype. While he is perpetually depicted in the body of a young man, as "Detective Boy Rock Holmes" in the eponymous *manga*, or as "Mamoru Hoshino" in *Captain Ken* (1950), his personality and themes have matured over the years, most notably becoming a sadistic and cynical terrorist in the film version of *Metropolis* (Rintaro, 2001) where Rock features as the adopted son of "Duke Red" (himself another Tezuka archetype).

SILHOUETTE

Pulseman doesn't have hair, recalling the super-*sentai*-styling of warriors like *Kamen Rider* and the *Power Rangers*; his helmet covers the majority of his head and face. The brow of the helmet cuts down at a sharp angle between the eyes, creating a pointed nose, and then curves up and back to create an elegant shark-fin, finally curving back round the head to a ducks-tail flick at the back. This elaborate construction is doubly coded, first for its sci-fi excess, but second, when considered *in silhouette*, Ken Sugimori's design bears a strong similarity with that of heroes *Astro Boy* and *Cyborg 009*. In shadowy repose, the difference between successive generations of characters is minimized. The recurring form of the silhouette, like a plot of land inherited by many individuals, is cultivated in texture and color to create a sense of the contemporary, while staying the same in perimeter and shape. The shadow form of the character is the "permanent trait,"[25] which the color therein forms the impermanent, changing aspect. In an interview with *Computer and Video Games* writer Stuart Bishop, Sugimori writes of the development process: "First we select an insect and after that we add essential elements to the insects to make it more like *Pokémon*, such as adding some hard shape to it, to be more like steel."[26] The history and precedent of existing designs weigh in on that choice of shape, making subsequent *Pokémon* stylistically continuous with their brothers and sisters. This is subtly expressed in silhouette. The shadow of a character actually became an ad-break featurette in the animated TV show, where audiences were asked to identify silhouetted *Pokémon* before the interval, and were given the answer afterwards.

Shadows play an important part in the appreciation of Japanese character design, and reflection on their value recalls the well-known essay by Junichirō Tanizaki, *In Praise of Shadows* (*In'ei Raisan*), first published in 1933. In that essay, he talks about the beauty of tarnished, worn objects, which hold a special appeal to the Japanese. He writes:

> Of course this 'sheen of antiquity' of which we hear so much is in fact the glow of grime. In both Chinese and Japanese the words denoting this glow describe a polish that comes of being touched over and over again, a sheen produced by the oils that naturally permeate an object over long years of handling—which is to say grime. If indeed 'elegance is frigid,' it can as well be described as filthy . . . we do love things that bear the marks of grime, soot, and weather, and we love the colors and the sheen that call to mind the past that made them. Living in these old houses is in some mysterious way a source of peace and repose.[27]

To see the texture of an object that has been handled signifies powerfully the relationship between the object and its attendant owner. That appealing patina lurks in the finish of Sugimori's concept drawings for *Pulseman*, and in the primary generation of *Pokémon*. Specifically, the designs consist of a black inked outline into which color is added with either watercolor or an acrylic ink wash. Sugimori is careful to allow for variance in the tone with areas of white in the primary generation drawings depicting subtle highlights. While the color is finely textured his approach means that it is not overly rich, and creates a patina that is very attractive to the eye. Existing only as illustration for the game and *Pokémon* cards, Sugimori's process is not compromised, but maintained through to publication. In this respect Sugimori's original design and concept drawings are at odds with the animated and merchandise-based manifestations of *Pokémon*, which rely on their shiny, bright surface to signify newness and compete for consumer attention. Regarding his process, Sugimori says:

> First I put white paper in front of me and draw a picture, and then I put film paper on top of it. Then I try to copy the pictures underneath, and try to make it more professional. And I do this over and over to

practice [sic], then try to make it satisfactory. I also try to adjust the picture by taking the size of eyes and stuff, and try to make the picture more perfect by doing it over and over.[28]

This qualitative difference between Sugimori's work and that of his assistants has lead some fans to bemoan how Sugimori has been "sidelined" in recent years in favor of newer artists whose work more closely resembles the animated and merchandized *Pokémon*.[29] This kind of commentary recalls Lamarre's suggestions about *otaku* appreciation, where heavily invested fans scrutinize and compare contributions to the corpus of material making up the *Pokémon* universe at any one time. Sugimori's character designs for the 151 *Pokémon* deliberately use this complex texture and use of tone to describe form, and in so doing eschew the "Superflat" aesthetic of glossy magazine forms.

One important juncture exists between the humor and idiosyncratic emotion of the character designs and the artistic process. Sugimori comments that: "Many of the *Pokémon* characters first became loved because they were funny, that's why many people have supported it. And I'm sure that younger people will still support the *Pokémon* because it's funny."[30] While Sugimori's designs are accepted as some of the finest character design in games art to date, there are a number of peculiar ones which lead Kat Bailey to recently compile a list of the "Top 5 Lamest *Pokémon*."[31] At the top of the lame list is one of the primary generation, "Mr. Mime"—*Pokémon* number 122. Bailey writes that, "Mr. Mime makes you shake your head and question what reality we actually inhabit. Surely proto-human-clown-mime *Pokémon* don't arise in any ordinary universe."[32] Nintendo's official website describes Mr. Mime as "a pantomime expert that can create invisible but solid walls using miming gestures" (www.pokemon.com).

HETA-UMA

Designs by Sugimori such as Mr. Mime evoke a complex reaction, for what they are and how they are depicted. We can see the skill in their construction, after overcoming the immediate weirdness of their design. This response recalls King Terry's[33] *heta-uma* movement. Frederick L. Schodt writes that:

> Terry's influence vastly exceeded his actually output as a cartoonist, for he appeared in Japan when formalism and realism were under attack, not only in comics, but society at large (deliberately amateurish comedy and music shows, for example, were wildly popular on television). Terry became the guru of a revolutionary art movement known in Japan as *heta-uma*, or "bad-good," which invigorated the comics world and subverted that of traditional illustration.[34]

Heta-uma aesthetics are premised on Terry's observation that,

> everyone starts as a "bad" artist and tries to become good. But simply becoming "good" is not enough. Artists who try too hard to become "good" begin to emphasize technique over soul, and then the life goes out of their drawings; their spirit fails to keep up with their technique.[35]

In the culture of *Pokémon*, the iconicity of Sugimori's designs for *Pokémon* such as Pikachu, Bulbasaur and Charmander elevate them to a point beyond criticism. In characters like Mr. Mime and Jynx, I suggest that Sugimori draws upon the surreal humour of *heta-uma*, in concert with his illustration technique, to create designs which oscillate between the poles of good and bad, and which under closer inspection reveal a complex genius at work. The knowing creation of such "diversity" plays into the core theme of *Pokémon*, "communication" (*tsūshin*), in that it invites the "big conversation" between players to scrutinize and work through new *Pokémon* as they are released as part of successive games.

Beyond the still image, gesture and animation play an integral role in *Pokémon* and its antecedent *Pulseman*. Reviews of *Pulseman* collectively say that the game feels fast, but very solid, and responsive. When you look at how the game is put together, and pay particular attention to the character and environment on-screen, certain qualities are apparent. There is a conscientious use of "keys." Animator Richard Williams rhetorically asks:

> Question: what is a key?
> Answer: the storytelling drawing. The drawing or drawings that show what is happening in the shot.[36]

As *Pulseman* falls through the air, we are given a pose that conveys something of his personality, his motivation, maybe even his agenda. When we see him gesture just before the title screen explodes, we are given another little snippet. Sugimori's use of keys enables him to encapsulate story information in the design of the character, and in so doing transcend with the design the conundrum of how best to convey a narrative in videogame design.[37]

TOY, REPOSE, COUNTER-POSE

Accompanying silhouette and *heta-uma*, the "key" is crucial to appreciating the richness of Sugimori's 151 initial *Pokémon* designs. As both concept artist and animator, Sugimori has a complex appreciation for the key drawing, and all of the designs are keys, in that they contain the basic orthographic information about the character (the rudiments of its appearance) while at the same time giving an impression of their personality and demeanor. When you look across all 151 designs there are three emergent categories of pose, which subtly determine the story and how it is evoked. These categories are useful in that they help us gauge the changing meaning of *Pokémon* as they evolve.

I refer to the first stage as the "toy" stage, and you might compare it to a cuddly toy, or a toy dog. The vast majority of *Pokémon* that have three stages of evolution see their first stage in this pose. The "toy" emphasizes irresistible cuteness, and the status of the *Pokémon*-as-object. The ratio of head to body is usually equal, and the short arms or legs are outstretched as if stuffed. In this stage the pupils of the *Pokémon* eyes are often widely dilated to maximize cuteness, and its gaze is ubiquitous. It strongly connotes a "to-be-looked-at-ness," and also a "to-be-held-ness" emphasized by the lack of orientation in the movement of the design. It sits as an object, subject to our merciful attentions. It recalls the Willendorf Venus, an ancient fetish sculpture, optimized to fit into an owner's hand; in its vulnerability and lack of orientation (for instance, as conveyed by crossed-eyes) it strongly connotes an unseen owner. In the bipedal upright *Pokémon*, arms are often outstretched as if in the gesture of inviting and accepting a hug. Teetering forward, the arms also evoke the image of a baby taking its first steps. The original three, Bulbasaur, Charmander and Squirtle, are what I would categorize as classic "toy" *Pokémon*.

The second category of *Pokémon* designs features those that are in "repose." In this second category, which usually refers to *Pokémon* which are in their second stage of evolution, but which can also include "younger" and "older" *Pokémon*, the character has grown larger and so the limbs are subtly posed. Yet, as in the bodies of adolescents, these characters contain either a frigid elegance or an awkwardness. In aesthetic terms, they are reminiscent of the "odalisque" archetype in Orientalist art, the languid house-servants who return our gaze over a naked shoulder. The eyes of "repose" *Pokémon* are smaller and more focused and often address us directly, though their bodily gestures betray the vestiges of immaturity or quirkiness. The recurrent visual elements of the *Pokémon* in repose recall the ambiguity evoked by the fringe of Tezuka's Rock archetype.

In Sugimori's design for the plant-*Pokémon* Oddish, we see the perfect expression of a "toy" *Pokémon*, connoting pure cuteness, minimal and spherical, with a head of bright green leaves. Eventually Oddish evolves into the larger Vileplume, and the design shifts from toy to repose. Vileplume carries a large peculiar bloom on the top of its head, like a teetering sombrero. From under its tilted "hat" the *Pokémon* looks directly at us, its red eye shining out from the shade. Its gesture remains open as in Oddish, as does the smile, but the tilting gesture of the plume suggests an added quality of ambiguity, a complex rhetoric evoked by the plant life Sugimori references. In the second state of the "big three," now Ivysaur, Charmeleon and Wartortle, there is an interiority and seriousness to their expression. In a Japanese art historical context, these designs evoke the ancient statues in

Tōdai-ji Temple, of "Kōmoku-ten,'Kōmoku-ten, the guardian of the west of the four guardian kings, symbolizes the *un* of A-*un*. His expression is that of the spirit of power in reserve."[38]

"Counter-pose" is the final category of *Pokémon* I have observed, and is largely limited to the final evolutionary stage of the character, or to legendary *Pokémon*. I take the term "counter-pose" from the Italian *contrapposto*, which means "counterpoise." As in the classic example, the counter-pose describes how the pose of the character simultaneously conveys a sense of relaxation and dynamism, and in so doing seats power firmly within the creature. In the final forms of the big three, Venusaur, Charizard and Blastoise, each stands in counter-pose, subtly orientating their weight onto one leg to suggest a potential movement, while looking through, or away from, the viewer. The eyes are the most resolved and human-like, and challenge the authority of the *Pokémon* trainer, alluding to the fact that at the end of the evolutionary chain emerges the proposition of *Pokémon* as autonomous from their trainer.

In this relatively simple introductory account, one can see how the initial designs created by Sugimori play a role in generating the big conversational zeitgeist among children and avid players around the world. The artistic direction of the character design creates a conceptual space in which opposing poles and qualitative differences can co-exist, where conventional binaries are triangulated by multiple possible associations (*jan-ken-pon*). As overlapping registers of complexity, the lines of logic that run through the primary generation of *Pokémon* interface with value considerations associated directly with Sugimori's artistic technique. The key pose, texture and *heta-uma* patina that runs through the collection dynamically complicates their emotional and nostalgic register. Sugimori's original designs transcend the fad fashion cycle in that they suggest an intense worldly logic on their own terms (as style evoking consistency, begetting plausibility), and this in turn naturalizes the integration of the game into everyday regimes of work and play. Pikachu is the only *Pokémon* able to transcend these categories, since it is only he (in the course of the *anime* at least) who does not succumb to the commodifying force of Poké-ball capture. Anne Allison writes that he is "the only *Pokémon* to remain outside a ball in the story—and therefore the currency of equivalence into which all the other monsters are convertible—Pikachu never gets "pocketed." Always more monster than thing, it is forever visible and cute . . ."[39] Most importantly, cuteness (*kawaisa*) does not explain in a complete way the visual coding of *Pokémon*, but is something set into a context by evolution in the game, and the comparison of *Pokémon* along lines afforded by the Poké-dex archive. Cuteness figures centrally in the ideological explanation of *Pokémon*, but like the myth of the designer's concept, *kawaii* has overshadowed the deep play at work in the game, and the changing charisma of the Pocket Monsters.

THE POKÉDEX: ART, EVOLUTION AND SERIALITY

In *Pokémon*, as you cumulatively "catch 'em all," your captive creatures are registered in a digital diary of sorts, the *Poké*-dex. Your mentor Professor Oak charges you with the task of traveling the world hunting for new species of *Pokémon*. This device contains a great deal of statistical and novel information about your *Pokémon*, and over the course of the series, the amount of information and its presentation has become more abstract. Allison makes several critical insights into the Poké-dex and Poké-balls, the device with which *Pokémon* are captured. Comparing Disney illusionism to *Pokémon's* reflexivity, she writes that:

> *Pokémon's* artifice, by contrast, is fully exposed. Tajiri Satoshi, the main designer of the game, for example, speaks of how he aimed to create an "interesting new game" that mixed genres: portraying battles (as in action games) but with the "lines" of information and stories favored in role-playing games. The result is that *Pokémon* are represented on screen both figuratively (bodies with flying sparks, attacking vines, venomous poison) and computationally (by an analytic grid that measures the powers, strengths, and attack strategies of each party). This gives pocket monsters a double epistemology, known to players through sight (their material appearance out of the Poké-ball) and through data, or their statistical profile.[40]

Allison goes on to deftly examine the millennial capitalism at work in *Pokémon* as commodities, partially gifted, and then partially exchanged, in the course of play. However, let's hesitate on her observation that *Pokémon*, once they are codified by the Poké-dex, become explicitly double coded, signified through abstract numeric data and through audiovisual representation. *Pokémon* are either over-determined or absent altogether. Like Schrödinger's cat in a box, when *Pokémon* are in their balls, are they there—alive or dead? The simple spheres, as seen on their HUD of the game screen, express an essential truth about all *Pokémon* in the game, and about the game more generally—it's absent, cold, mass-reproduced, infinite seriality. If we know anything from the analysis of Sugimori's artwork, it's that nothing is ever that simple—the distancing effects of serialization must be in some internal tension with some aspect of the game form. I will return to this suggestion briefly.

Recently I argued for an appreciation of the serialized aesthetic in accordance with Marc Steinberg's notion of "New Seriality" present in the works of artist Takashi Murakami.[41] I compared Murakami's oeuvre to *We Love Katamari*, the game that essay discussed at length, where seriality took the form of long winding series of virtual commodities which you had to recover to form large constellations. By rolling the "katamari," a giant ball of things, you quickly were picking up others, and in the process the katamari grows. I suggested this rapid process of caricatured consumption could in turn be read as an allegory of the *otaku* predicament in millennial Japanese (and perhaps global) culture. In *Pokémon*, the experience of seriality is much less immediate and not part of any explicit commentary by the games designer, as was in the case of Keita Takahashi the designer of *We Love Katamari* at Namco.

The full measure of seriality in *Pokémon* comes as a consequence of a long period of play, where you have explored a substantial amount of the game, and labored to gain a particular, rare *Pokémon*, of which there are many. In the course of attempting to capture a *Pokémon* with a particular demeanor, you will invariably catch several. While there are subtle nuances to the *Pokémon* in their statistical depiction, their representation remains the same for each of the apparent clones. For example, four grumpy Raticates tremble nervously in your options menu as you circle tirelessly trying to find the elusive Abra you want so much. In your storage facility back at the local Poké-center, countless more sit in spherical stasis, alongside itinerant rows of Pidgies, Magikarp and Caterpies. This seriality is the symptom of long term play in *Pokémon*, an aggregate of failed and successful hunts, in which the player must discern which lucky pocket monster (from this relativizing hub) gets to receive the dedication of play that will ultimately personalize and make it.

The two epistemologies that Allison therefore identifies work simultaneously, but then, after a point, they function one after the other. Long term play (over a period of many tens of hours) produces the kind of independent *otaku* vision noted by Lamarre that covets the statistical over the representational, since it orientated more toward the game than the story, and as such makes clear the structures of power and competition. The distillation of value, from images to abstractions, is natural to all long-term play of games, and it is in these diminished play experiences that games reveal some of their more complex, nuanced (and unanticipated) meanings.[42] In this respect, *Pokémon* are transformed into everyday objects, ready to be arranged as a form of strategy or tactic with which we can play. The Poké-dex, a mosaic of collected *Pokémon*, is perhaps the definitive mechanic at work in the modern Japanese videogame. As you explore the island worlds of the various games of the franchise, you are able to observe, catch (and in some games photograph) the *Pokémon* inhabitants. They are collected and schematized into a systemic representation that reflexively highlights the comparative and iterative processes through which both they were designed by the production team and acquired by the player.[43]

Pokémon are serialized into the logic of the Poké-dex, which transforms the longstanding game conventions of serialization, which had previously been seen as limitations, into the fundamental mechanism of the game. As Jean Baudrillard suggests, the serialization of form is synonymous with the mechanization of production.[44] To look at serialized objects is to understand the mutual intelligibility between the agendas of production and consumption. The industrialization of post war Japan can be uniquely understood through the proliferation of consumer culture and pop cultural forms from the late 1960s onwards. Large cultural shifts are metonymically expressed in the form and content of animated television series, soaps, toys, comic books and so on.[45]

Though Murakami's concept of "SuperFlat" is a discourse more than a coherent theory, it can help in explaining the presence and persistence of some of the tropes of game world production and consumption—in particular the repetition of assets with little or no variation, a "mass-ornamental" aesthetic[46] synonymous with the release of *Space Invaders* (1978). For example, consider the sequence of identical aliens attacking in waves; subtle differences in pixel placement mark the identity of the different rows of invaders. The impact of mass production, media convergence and consumerism define the serial aesthetic. Mark Wolf has highlighted the contiguity of this early game aesthetic with the rise of abstraction in North American Abstraction of the 1960s, also implying that it is an accidental, technologically driven appearance:

> Although their simplicity was due to technological limitation and not the result of deliberate artistic choices, the minimal, often abstract graphics of early video games fit in rather well with trends in the art world during the 1960s . . . Early video game graphics, with their points, lines, and blocks of color, often on a black background coincided with minimalist, abstract styles of art.[47]

The concept of abstraction does not sufficiently account for the way in which the trope of repeated, serialized form functions in gameplay. Sugimori has described how simplistic graphic elements impact on gameplay. The question of realism and simplicity he describes recalls King Terry's *heta-uma* paradox, of knowing when something sits at the prime point between contradictory poles:

> The basic graphics may simultaneously limit and enhance gameplay, for example if a map is very realistic, it might become more complicated, and then it would be hard for players to understand where to go next. However, an unrealistic map may not work as a good guide, so some of the realistic graphics may cause some limitations to the games. That's why we have kept these graphics more simple this time, and also in the battle scenes, if we had made the back of the battle scenes more realistic, it might point out where the battle was and so when you draw, you have to be more precise. That's why we didn't make it complicated.[48]

In his analysis of Murakami's *DOB series*, Marc Steinberg suggests that the expressive potential of the work does not sit within particular elements, but rather in the relationship between works in a series, each bearing minor variations, and dominant consistencies, "in subsuming the transformations between objects into a single plane of experience—the picture plane—become sites where the logic of relation, as an ontologically consistent yet invisible in-between, attains expression."[49] The evolved sequences and variations of *Pokémon* echo this sentiment, in that they show subtle continuities of form, which also simultaneously change to take those forms in new directions. Precisely because of the subtle and seemingly irrational changes in *Pokémon*, it can be conceived in terms of Steinberg's "new seriality." He suggests that:

> we think of seriality itself not so much as a typology of objects as a typology of the relations between objects. It is not the objects themselves that have changed in our era as much as it is the relations between them that have changed (it is these changes that in turn allow for the possibility of new products, and new trends; the change in seriality precedes the change in series).[50]

The serial aesthetic is the *aesthetic of convergence*, a reading of the space between things and the hum of interest they generate collectively. They are unified by conceit or style, not necessarily ontology (see, for instance, the shift from Apple Computers to 'i' branding). In a history of videogames form, the serial aesthetic is *de rigeur*, immanent to the processes of the medium. Assets (created items, textures, characters, sounds—all elements of the diegesis) are serialized from the outset (see *Space Invaders*) due to hardware limitations, replicating graphical information meant smaller memory usage and thus greater efficiency of form. Memory and storage capacity in games have grown exponentially, and while hardware limitations are always there, serialization has become so central to game form that it is maintained and endorsed as a component of the medium's aesthetic heart. Moving through a gameworld often amounts to a percussive disclosure of serialized forms, and this is one of several pleasures situated in the space between play and repetition. The game design process is inculcated with the role serialization plays in the structuring of gameplay, since it structures difference into the experience. It demarcates like for like, constructing an immediate signifier for social groups, bring cohesion to created assets. Subtle differences *within* the series then add complexity and depth. For instance, from early games design till present, color cycling has been used to stage differences within the gameplay.

In *Pokémon*, this simple color cycling is used to pick incredibly rare "shiny" *Pokémon*, which are collectively defined by their striking difference from the norms of color. Iterative changes and subtle variations in one aspect of the aesthetic become a cue for a complex set of assumptions regarding changes in time, place and difficulty. *Pokémon Red* and *Blue* came onto the original GameBoy at a time when the home console market had grown in processing power exponentially. The tiny 8-bit processor of the GameBoy was a technological step backwards, and yet, because *Pokémon* negotiated new serialized relations between the game object and others, including cards, merchandise TV cereals and film, it achieved considerable success. Steinberg writes:

> If the emergence of series is inseparable from the industrial era, it should come as no surprise that the form this seriality takes has changed with our postindustrial or information-capitalist times. Where for Baudrillard the relation between objects—along with the variation in color or shape which differentiated them—played out within one object type (a toaster), in other words *within* the series. What is important now is rather the connections *between* series. It is the creation of relations between vacuum cleaner series and the car series, the pencil series and the toaster series that defines the shift in relations under information-capitalism. In short, it is the age of branding and convergence.[51]

The serial aesthetic is synonymous with the onset of modernity; it is the industrialization of aesthetics. For Barthes, the onset of industrialization was evidenced in the decline of the eighteenth century Dandy, the narcissistic figure preoccupied by detail and decoration through ritual embellishment of "authentic" original clothing. Detail would later provide the bourgeoisie with a means to subtly customize clothing and express distinction without disrupting the democratic ethos of industrialized aesthetics. The Dandy, connoisseurs of detail, could not recuperate the aura when clothing was no longer characterized by its uniqueness, and therefore not fit for the higher purpose of pageantry, "all forms of behavior which bear witness to the profoundly creative, and no longer simply selective, idea that the *effects* of a form have to be thought through, that clothing is not simply an object to be used but is a prepared *object*."[52] Sugimori's designs, like the figure of the Dandy, signify most intensely precisely because of their contradistinction from the perfect commodity of the Poké-ball. Avid collection of the rare "shiny" *Pokémon* enables players to give character to their assemblage/team of Pocket Monsters, to occupy a highly desirable minority amongst the player base.

CONCLUSION: *POKÉMON* NUMBER 151

The serialization of *Pokémon* is seen by many scholars as thorough and resolved, and certainly, in many of its tropes (such as the Poké-ball), *Pokémon* are perfectly shifting between streamlined commodity and cute fetish. I want to return to an earlier question about possible contradictions that exist in the serial commodification of *Pokémon*. Earlier I identified three categories in Sugimori's designs, the toy, the repose, and the counter-pose. I suggested that in the *Pokémon* defined as counter-pose, the story contained in Sugimori's key drawing evokes a complex agency.

The final Poké-dex entry in Sugimori's primary generation is the aggressive MewTwo, *Pokémon* number 151. MewTwo was the hardest original

Pokémon to catch, and required huge effort to bring him under your control. Once you had him, his psychic power would devastate any in the competition, but this was so totalizing that in play against friends a separate rule would arise whereby it would be agreed that MewTwo wouldn't be used. The same goes for many of the Legendary *Pokémon*, including the three legendary birds, Moltres, Zapdos and Articuno. In the design of these counter-pose *Pokémon*, Sugimori often evokes the monster design of the Japanese *tokusatsu* (special effects) film and television series, especially those since the 1950s, including Godzilla. He gives those monstrous yet familiar silhouettes from the past renewed agency in the form of eyes and expressions that cut through the viewer. Counter-pose *Pokémon* like MewTwo take a long time to find capture and care for. Third stage evolved *Pokémon* like Blastoise take a great deal of time to grow from humble beginnings. In these final forms, the serial commodification of *Pokémon* is problematized by the personal narrative of play, which amongst players is taken for granted.

The first category of *Pokémon* I identified, those of the toy style, lend themselves to easy and immediate commodification. Their combat weakness makes them an easy capture in the game, and their appearance strongly connotes the inevitability of acquisition. The vast majority of them occur in the earliest stages of the game, and this fact perhaps tells us the most about why many scholars have assumed that the commodity metaphor of *Pokémon* is so totalizing. It takes time to get to the end of the game, a great deal of time. In these final phases of gameplay, the full implications of design and evolution are revealed, in parallel to the dénouement of the narrative. To fully appreciate the implications of the work of key artists like Sugimori in franchises like *Pokémon*, scholars must commit to playing games to their conclusion and beyond. The textuality of a game is individuated by play. A commitment to engaging with the ancillary artistic materials previsualizing and surrounding games is important, but also to the deeper structures of the games themselves need greater attention, since they provide a rich seam for new critical enquiry.

ACKNOWLEDGMENTS

This paper was originally presented at the *IE2007 conference* in Melbourne, Australia. I am grateful for the comments and suggestions of Barry Atkins, Dean Chan, Larissa Hjorth, Robin Hunicke, and Christian McCrea during the development of this chapter.

NOTES

1. I have argued elsewhere that "[o]ne could even say that through the lens of play, the novice gamer and expert gamer are experiencing different media texts, individuated by their implicit competency . . . Competency of play is yoked to the textual richness of the gameworld." David Surman, "Pleasure, Spectacle and Reward in Capcom's *Street Fighter* Series," in *Videogame,*

Player, Text, eds. B. Atkins and T. Krzywinkska (Manchester: Manchester University Press, 2007), 204–21.

2. Koichi Iwabuchi, "How 'Japanese' is Pokémon" in Pikachu's Global Adventure: The Rise and Fall of Pokémon, ed. J. Tobin (London: Duke University Press, 2004), 53–79.

3. Colin Hoskins and Rolf Mirus, "Reasons for the US Dominance of the international trade in television programs," Media, Culture and Society, 10, 1988: 499–515.

4. Iwabuchi, "How "Japanese" is Pokémon," 56–57.

5. James Newman, Playing with Videogames (London: Routledge, 2004).

6. Iwabuchi, "How "Japanese" is Pokémon," 74.

7. Midori Matsui, ed., The Age of Micropop: A New Generation of Japanese Artists (Tokyo: Parco, 2007).

8. Iwabuchi, "How "Japanese" is Pokémon," 70.

9. Anne Allison, Millennial Monsters: Japanese Toys and the Global Imagination (London: University of California Press, 2006).

10. Christine R. Yano, "Panic Attacks: Anti-Pokémon Voices in Global Markets," in Pikachu's Global Adventure: The Rise and Fall of Pokémon, ed. J. Tobin (London: Duke University Press, 2004), 108–38.

11. J. P. Jackson, Buying and Selling the Souls of our Children (London: Kingsway Publishing, 2000).

12. Joseph Tobin, ed., Pikachu's Global Adventure: The Rise and Fall of Pokémon (London: Duke University Press, 2004).

13. Allison, Millennial Monsters: Japanese Toys and the Global Imagination.

14. Koichi Iwabuchi, Recentring Globalization: Popular Culture and Japanese Transnationalism (London: Duke University Press, 2002); Joseph S. Nye, Soft Power: The Means to Success in World Politics (New York: Public Affairs, 2004).

15. Allison, Millennial Monsters: Japanese Toys and the Global Imagination, 201.

16. Roland Barthes, Mythologies (London: Verso, 2000), 159.

17. For my expanded theory of game style in videogames see David Surman, "Style, Consistency and Plausibility in the Fable Gameworld," in Animated 'Worlds,' ed. S. Buchan (London: John Libbey, 2006). This chapter follows closely my research into the form and context of Namco's Katamari Damacy (2004) and the sequel We Love Katamari (2005), and the strong continuity I argued for between Japanese videogames and contemporary art (see ff. 18).

18. David Surman, "Notes on Superflat and Its Expression in Videogames," Refractory: a Journal of Entertainment Media 13 (2008). Retrieved November 10 2008 from http://blogs.arts.unimelb.edu.au/refractory/2008/05/23/notes-on-superflat-and-its-expression-in-videogames-david-surman/

19. Thomas Lamarre, "An Introduction to Otaku Movement" EnterText 4 (1) 2004: 151–187.

20. Lamarre, "An Introduction to Otaku Movement," 158.

21. Lamarre, "An Introduction to Otaku Movement," 159.

22. SEGA Genesis in the United States.

23. An excellent fan-authored page detailing various aspects of Pulseman can be found at: http://volteccer.jvmwriter.org/index.shtml; a Japanese-language resource can be found at http://vc.sega.jp/vc_pulseman/.

24. Philip Brophy, "Ocular excess: a semiotic morphology of cartoon eyes," Art and Design, 12 (3/4) 1997: 29.

25. David Surman, "Animated Caricature: Notes on Superman, 1941–1943," EnterText 4 (1) 2004: 67–96.

26. Stuart Bishop, "Game Freak on Pokémon!" Retrieved September 20, 2008 from http://www.computerandvideogames.com/article.php?id=91965.

27. Junichirō Tanizaki, *In Praise of Shadows* (London: Vintage Books, 2001), 20.
28. Bishop, "Game Freak on *Pokémon!*"
29. SATURNINEBEAR, "Art Of Pokémon Part 2". Retrieved September 20, 2008 from http://www.pojo.com/features/Jan2003/Poke-26/art_of_pokemon_ii.htm.
30. Bishop, "Game Freak on *Pokémon!*"
31. Kat Bailey, "Top 5 Lamest Pokémon." Retrieved September 20, 2008 from http://www.1up.com/do/feature?cId=3169539
32. Bailey, "Top 5 Lamest Pokémon."
33. Schodt writes that "Japanese manga are a wellspring of ideas for illustrators, graphic designers, and not surprisingly, for more than a few fine artists, many of whom dabbled in manga themselves. The one artist illustrator whose work exists in a continual symbiotic relationship with manga is Teruhiko Yumura, a.k.a. King Terry, Terry Johnson, and Flamina Terrino Gonzalez." Frederick L. Schodt, *Dreamland Japan: Writings on Modern Manga.* (Berkeley: Stone Bridge Press, 1996), 140.
34. Schodt, *Dreamland Japan*, 141.
35. Schodt, *Dreamland Japan*, 141–142.
36. Richard Williams, *The Animator's Survival Kit: A Working Manual of Methods, Principles and Formulas for Computer, Stop-Motion, Games and Classical Animators* (London: Faber and Faber, 2001) 57.
37. In this respect, *Pokémon* can be compared to Jonathan Blow's independent game *Braid* (XBLA, 2008). *Braid* relies on vast tracts of text and an almost fauvist painterly style to connote a seriousness and narrative density. In the final version of the game however, the final animation contains very few keys and those that are present only convey extremity. While the lack of dress elements can be seen as part of the games overall impressionistic flavor, the burden of narrative exegesis in *Braid* ends up as so much text on the screen, in a game which otherwise emphasises temporality and almost constant movement.
38. Gichin Funakoshi, *Karate-Dō Kyō-Han* (Tokyo: Kodansha, 1973), 246.
39. Allison, *Millennial Monsters: Japanese Toys and the Global Imagination*, 227–228.
40. Allison, *Millennial Monsters: Japanese Toys and the Global Imagination*, 213–214.
41. Surman, "Notes on Superflat and Its Expression in Videogames."
42. Surman, "Animated Caricature: Notes on Superman, 1941–1943."
43. Allison, *Millennial Monsters: Japanese Toys and the Global Imagination*, 213–214.
44. Marc Steinberg, "Characterising a New Seriality: Murakami Takashi's Dob Project." *Parachute* 110 (2003): 90–109.
45. The wish fulfillment of the magical cat Doraemon, who can summon anything you need from his magic pocket, perhaps best expresses the direct way in which Japanese popular culture bore the weight of both post war frustration and interest in a potentially renewed sense of modernity.
46. Siegfried Kracauer, *The Mass Ornament: Weimar Chapters* (London: Harvard University Press, 1995), 75–88.
47. Mark J. P. Wolf, *The Medium of the Videogame* (London: Routledge, 2001), 30.
48. Bishop, "Game Freak on *Pokémon!*"
49. Steinberg, "Characterising a New Seriality: Murakami Takashi's Dob Project," 102.
50. Steinberg, "Characterising a New Seriality: Murakami Takashi's Dob Project," 93.
51. Steinberg, "Characterising a New Seriality: Murakami Takashi's Dob Project," 92.
52. Roland Barthes, *The Language of Fashion* (Oxford: Berg, 2006), 67.

10 Watching *StarCraft*, Strategy and South Korea

Christian McCrea

INTRODUCTION

Even academics and theorists working on computer games rarely speak of pleasure in their research, perhaps out of a historically ingrained inclination to objectivism. After a decade of having various iterations of the US-made game *StarCraft* and its expansion *StarCraft: Brood War* (hereafter collectively referred to as simply *StarCraft*) installed on every computer I have owned, a pretense of such objective distance is impossible. The visual and sonic texture of play has stained my subconscious far beyond that attributable to obsession. To a lesser or greater extent, all of my computer and video game play—and likely my theorization of it—now retains a memory of *StarCraft*. I do not read the associated novels or know the game lore in depth, nor could it be said that I care for science-fiction or real-time strategy games beyond *StarCraft*. I am not particularly skilled at its play, and often cheat in matches against the computer despite having played scenarios hundreds of times.

As the years ticked on, I became peripherally aware that South Korea and *StarCraft* were locked in a sort of symbiotic relationship. As I played online, I faced fewer and fewer English speaking opponents and an almost overwhelming number of Korean players sitting in what I would later know as *PC bangs* (Commercial PC-use rooms, or Internet cafes). It often happened that mid-game, a mutual fascination emerged; mine with the relationship between game and state, and theirs with futility of an erratic English-speaking player attempting to fight deeply honed Korean strategies. I would learn in time that my stakes were incompatible with victory, as I would change strategies before they were perfected, or simply play unproductively and at cross-purposes. I would build a uselessly large number of structures at the expense of actual troops, which would inevitably result in players asking me what I was thinking, shifting my time in the game from at first being strategic to slowly becoming more social. I would hoard resources and risk defeat. In 2002, I stopped playing against human competition and began to experiment with the production of gameplay areas—or "maps," which finally led me to stop playing for long periods at a time as I concentrated on work and research.

My *StarCraft* then changed again. I began to download and watch broadcasts of matches from Korean e-sports (electronic sports) leagues and follow pro-gamers (professional players), watching their strategies unfold. So it was as a lapsed obsessive that I came to read accounts and reactions to matches I had seen. An extraordinary three-round match at the 2004 Ever Ongamenet Starleague Semi-Finals between "Boxer" (Lim Ho-Ywan) and "Yell0w" (Hong Jin-Ho) altered my experience of games entirely. The tournaments had been growing more complex in their organization and presentation, with several tiered systems and matches making even avid watching a tactical experience.

So it was with some surprise that I caught myself attempting to read South Korean culture in the texture of strategy. Boxer subverted the play methods built up over six years and deployed a usually unsuccessful strategy to an embarrassing, crushing success, three short matches in sequence. That the strategy worked three times in a row testified to its perfect timing and his dedication to training. The broadcast cut to Boxer's reaction, wracked by sorrow by having to short-circuit the drama of extended play and so convincingly defeat a friend. This was no longer about *StarCraft*. Two years later, a blog site dedicated to commentary on Korean professional *StarCraft* culture, "*Sense of Star,*" written by "Mariencielo" used a picture of Boxer at this precise moment, and even began its commentary with the Robert Frost poem, "The Road Not Taken," to emphasize the drama of Boxer's decision.[1]

The context for these intensities is to be found in the qualities of the game itself. *StarCraft* (developed and produced in 1998 by the company Blizzard) is a real-time strategy game in a science-fiction setting, allowing players to occupy the role of a unseen figure, guiding a growing army through problems of resource management, tactical warfare and conflict planning. The game is played largely over personal computer (PC), and lets players pit themselves either against the computer, or against other players from around the world.

In this chapter, I undertake a close study of *StarCraft*; more precisely, what is visible on both the surface of *StarCraft* as a text and *StarCraft* as deep phenomena, specifically aiming the study at making sense of South Korean pro-gaming's high drama. The popularity of *StarCraft* around the world is remarkable for its longevity, but the context of ongoing South Korean play remains its most curious legacy. Jun-Sok Huhh argues that *StarCraft* "ensured Korea's position in the global gaming industry" and youth culture "abandoned popular leisure activities such as billiards, arcade games, and Korean checkers" in favor of wholesale uptake of the game.[2] The game has a degree of synonymity with Korea's growth of digital leisure, and especially with the development of *PC bangs*. The game has become a site in which a multiplicity of other dramas and narrative unfurl and unfold; a toy map for larger cultural dramas to express themselves.

As an English-speaking Australian scholar, an analysis of this situation would be powerless to interpret anything essential to Korean-ness in

StarCraft play, but I rather seek to foreground a looking-at-Korea through the game text and the depth of strategy visible in it. To do so, I will enter an interpretative theorization of *StarCraft* gameplay structure—rather than as pure text—that uses concepts of play developed by Clifford Geertz. His writing on social sports specifically described the power of balanced gameplay to draw in cultural narratives and become proxy conversations about broader culture.[3]

In the deep structures of expert gameplay, analysis is possible of all the other structures that have come to be reliant on the game. If the Boxer vs. Yell0w match is instructive of anything, it is that powerful narratives have formed and accumulated around the game; narratives that are only possible given specific locations, and given specific deep knowledge of the game's play structures To make sense of these complex structures, I will assemble a notion of what it is to play strategically, then in turn to play *StarCraft* strategically, then finally for progamers to play *StarCraft* strategically. By building these narratives, and carefully constructing all the forces that come to bear on an otherwise simple game, a sense of *StarCraft* in South Korea can be built.

LAYING DOWN OF STRATEGY

> Each side, in so far as it has managed to preserve its freedom of ma-noeuvre, is obliged to choose between operations for the undertaking of which the means available are bound to be wanting, in some respect or another, in terms of space and time.[4]

In developing a game's strategies, Guy Debord and Alice Becker-Ho produced a discourse about war that the game would feed into and reproduce through play. This choosing-between-operations foregrounds the fundamental problem of strategy; if I do this, what do I lose elsewhere? *A Game of War* is a deep variation on the fundamentals of chess; pieces in two armies move on a grid—though with complex scenarios and rules that draw out play into rounds. Lines of communication must be maintained in order to supply the troops, but they must be stretched to reach the enemy.[5]

In writing around Guy Debord's game and the essays surrounding it, theorist McKenzie Wark makes a diagnosis of the game's use of strategy, and in so doing speaks through the game's strategy to how the game "speaks" to strategy:

> In the war of position, tactics are dictated from above by strategic concerns with taking and holding one bunker after another across the landscape of state and civil society. *The Game of War* refutes this territorial conception of space and this hierarchical relation between strategy and tactics. Space is always partially unmarked; tactics can sometimes call

a strategy into being. Some space need not be occupied or contested at all; every tactic involves a risk to one's positions.[6]

If the author Stephen Zweig intimated in *The Royal Game* that chess was "a unique bond between every pair of opponents, ancient and yet eternally new,"[7] *A Game of War* refutes some of chess's openness, ironically, by complexifying the rules of combat and makes the playspace behave differently in the mind of the player. The bond is less unique, less ancient, and as Wark intimates, refutes a hierarchical relationship between strategy and tactics that makes traditional chess play so deep.

If we take chess to be a living record of strategic simulation, a mark in the sand of many beaches, we see its antecedents and precedents located not across, but deeply within cultural specificity. David H. Li argues that chess owes much of its formal properties to Xiangqi, visible in various forms in Western China since 300 BC.[8] The more conservative histories look to India where conversational games such as Chaturanga evolved into "Western" Chess by the thirteenth century along trade routes such as the Silk Road.[9]

The players of strategy games arrange matter and units in accordance with patterns of consciousness in a consistent way exploring their capacity to think forward and backward in the space optimized to represent their thought: the designated game board. The games are meditations on temporality, operating vertically through scale and horizontally through time. The rules of the game expand and contract the sociality, the competitiveness and the quality of play. It is because of the specificity of strategic play, not despite it, that local contexts become important. Not, as it may be tempting to believe, because different cultures play the same games in different ways and create variants—but because the stakes which inform play, which make the resources and units what they are—can only be local.

To make sense of what connections play has to a culture, both the strategic impulses of the game and the stakes of its play need to be examined. Most importantly, what is termed here the "temporal ecology of skill," or accumulation of significance in the history of the game in that culture, draw lines and connections that a coincidental reading of text and culture cannot undertake.

Geertz's "Deep Play: Notes on The Balinese Cockfight" is an in-depth anthropological account of the forces which come down to bear on a single play-act or game.[10] The brutal match between trained cocks and the arrangement of bets between the trainer-players creates the formal engagement, while Geertz extends the focus to the visibility of cultural impulses in the way the match is conducted. The study concerns the degree to which other forms of status and power become part of the economy of signs. Geertz arrays the utilitarian notion of deep play from Jeremy Bentham's "The Theory of Legislation," in which the risk of loss in any play or wager is too high to be considered a rational one.[11]

Geertz reconsiders risk itself in terms of an ongoing exchange of signs— the status of players, the spectacularity of the cockfight, and the effects of exterior forces on the actual fiduciary wager. For the stakes to be raised, Geertz looks to the even probability of success, the equality of the cocks set down to fight and the relationship it bears to the center bet, or "*toh ketengah*."[12] The relationship of the bet-between-the-combatants and the cultural stakes is very clear:

> . . . the centre bet is a means, a device, for creating "interesting," "deep" matches, not the reason, or at least not the main reason, why they are interesting, the source of their fascination, the substance of their depth.[13]

The closeness of the opponents works to raise the *toh ketengah* even though the risk for both parties grows as a result. The dramatic power of the bet then causes a secondary wave of betting on the outside of the ring among the spectators—"*toh kesasi*." What Geertz identifies is the very impulse of "deep play" against utility (keeping in mind the origin in Bentham's theory) that encourages the competition to be fine and equal (more likely destroying both animals), to raise the "*toh ketengah*," to make the match more spectacular in both the in-ring and narrative sense. Geertz turns his attention to the accumulation of cultural narratives on the cockfight as a result:

> What makes Balinese cockfighting deep is thus not money in itself, but what, the more of it that is involved the more so, money causes to happen: the migration of the Balinese status hierarchy into the body of the cockfight.[14]

In doing so, he identifies the equality of the combatants, the unpredictability of the outcome, and the "fine" quality of the fight—that is to say its grain and closeness—as being elements that allow the "migration of status hierarchies." This relationship, once deepened, (in this case, through the mechanism of the *toh ketengah*) preconditions a fight to be spectacular, regardless of only its outcome, but the entirety of its conduct. The migration of status onto the game means that entire new structures are readable on the surface of play long before the first claw draws blood. Families are betrayed, villages pitted against another, brother seeks to avenge brother, the old master returns. These ephemeral narratives are meaningless until the stakes are raised in the center of the ring, and status becomes the real wager.

THE SURFACE OF *STARCRAFT* PLAY

StarCraft is one of the most startling examples of such deep play. A decade into the ecology of permutation has not exhausted the enthusiasm of player communities for the game, as thousands of player-created maps, campaigns and total conversions (more aggressive reworkings of the game that include changes to the original code and resulting interface) are still produced each year. The three in-game races that players can choose from in *StarCraft*; the human Terran, magico-technological Protoss and insectile Zerg exist in an ecological balance of actions that nevertheless has points of tendency from which tactics evolve.

The "maps" on which the game takes place are fields of play with various raised terrains and accesses, bridges, open water/space and various incidental, non-interactive elements which reflect the setting. Players begin near "resource points," where mineral deposits and gas geysers are clustered. At the beginning of a round of play, each team has a base of operations that can produce worker "units" to gather the resources and bring them into the base. With those resources being gathered by the growing economy, the player will quickly begin to spend minerals and gas on several things—new buildings which can in turn build new units, non-visible upgrades which change internal values and capabilities of units, and most importantly, the fighting units themselves. Every step up the economic ladder costs minerals and/or gas, and often requires a series of purchases to access the most powerful units. The strategic focus in the first few minutes of a *StarCraft* match are in purchasing worker units and gathering minerals quickly enough to replenish defenses and furnish attacks.

In the minutes that follow, a player then turns their attention to continuing the growth of the workers and miners, but also beginning to produce attack units of varying types, and buildings to multiply their options much of the early and middle parts of gameplay are taken up with balancing economic and military expenditure.[15] Once entrenched, expansion across the remaining resources on the map becomes an issue—controlling the areas and building new bases multiplies the income and potential size of the armies. So, once the map is fully developed by the players, the comparative armies are the strategic focus—a slight imbalance in one type of attack will disadvantage a player.

With such a complex set of strategies, the pro-gamer culture of *StarCraft* has developed around efficiently moving from these early-game concerns to the later ones. Speed, therefore, is a major factor in the structure of the game. That is, the more rapid the ability of the player to go beyond the phase of mere need and become able to impress their deeper play styles, the better. Developing a strong style is not merely a metanarrative impulse that alludes to the formation of star culture, but is more importantly a way to self-teach efficiency with specific goals—for example, building a second base as soon as practicable changes the game significantly and requires a different play focus. Forming a play style also forms a style of practice, so that over thousands of hours a player may highly refine a specific sequence of moves, actions and commands. This type of deep ingrained expertise becomes both key to the player's perception of the game's flow, and an overly structured expectation that can be exploited by opponents.

The stakes for a pro-gamer match of *StarCraft* are not comparable in any sense to cockfighting in Bali—certainly not for roosters. But the mechanisms by which status hierarchies come to settle around the edge of the gaming ring are often the same. The fine grain of gameplay concentrates on the privilege of tactical consistency over and above the selection of the race. For example, pro-gamers collect nicknames that describe or encapsulate the meta-narrative of their playstyles. Hong Jin-Ho (using the name "[NC] . . . Yell0w" in games) is described on forum boards and South Korean pro-gaming television as the "Storm Zerg," referring to a playstyle that favors sudden attacks. Kang Min ("Nal_rA" in games) is referred to as "Dreaming Protoss" for developing unusual and creative methods in building up a Protoss army. Seo Ji-Hoon ("Xell0s"), the subject of a National Geographic documentary on the lead-up to the World Cyber Games of 2005, eventually gained the nickname "Perfect Terran" for having no obvious exploitable weaknesses in his offensive or defensive strategies.[16] These names operate in the community to form narratives leading in and out of championships and leagues.

Theorist Alexander Galloway approached the game in a 2007 article for the journal *Grey Room*, entitled *"StarCraft, or Balance."*[17] The article produces a close analysis of the qualities of the racial types in *StarCraft*, looking to the in-game race of the Zerg as the establishing point for a political critique of what Galloway perceives as the inevitable assimilation of any swarm-like, rhizomatic forces into the structures they face. By describing a situation in which asymmetry and symmetry face off in an ordered play area, Galloway foregrounds a broad analysis of how the relationship between ordered and open forms are represented. The Zerg are cast as the invading, antagonistic force which threaten the Terran and Protoss civilizations. Galloway produces an analysis of the Zerg race as swarm-like:

> They attack en masse, overwhelming the opponent by bombarding it on all sides. Each individual Zerg attack may be relatively weak, but the sheer size of the swarm creates a formidable strike.[18]

From his close reading of the Zerg typology as a "resounding," "resonant" force, Galloway interprets their status as resolutely and essentially multiple. In many important respects, this analysis is fruitful as it is purely generated from the material situation of the game text—the Zerg are situated fictionally as an inchoate, asynchronous force:

> . . . the very premise of the swarm is that of asymmetry, the structural incompatibility of two different modes of presence and two different modes of the expression of force. Thus the overcoming of such a structural incompatibility in the form of the game's race-based play styles (Zerg, Terran, Protoss) consummates what was thought to be an impossibility: The Zerg is a swarm, but it is in perfect ecological balance with the nonswarm.[19]

Galloway's broader analysis follows a circuit; the Zerg possess the qualities of a swarm, and find themselves in conflict with more ordered, appreciably structured forms of organization, and are consequently "recuperated" into a form of balance, which neutralizes the qualitative difference they possess.[20] This is the basis of an ongoing critique of neo-liberal attitudes to organization, which Galloway more thoroughly pursues in his 2006 book *Gaming: Essays On Algorithmic Culture*.[21]

Galloway asserts a typological similarity between *StarCraft* and the later Blizzard title, *Warcraft III*. In his formulation, RTS games propose a conflict of organizational forms that automatically predicates a market value of objects and actions, this forming the basis of racial types that situate themselves in the market in different strategies.

> Because each software cluster is apt to be quite complex, the techniques of racial balancing generally operate in a rather roundabout way, eschewing any neat and tidy trade-off between this or that trait mirrored across two or more races. Instead, balance is achieved through the delicate art of exchanging qualitatively different values; for example, shaving *time* off one racial ability and transmutating it into a *damage* boost in another race's ability.[22]

This approach is visible in close detail in *StarCraft* as the past ten years have seen the game morph and contort in reaction to player use and abuse of the systematic tendencies of the game. Patches applied to the game, distributed by executable file, alter the values of buildings, change the time needed to produce units and appreciably alter the flow of the game—games are then given software nomenclature—1.0 being the original state at release, and 1.1, 1.2, 1.3 marking differences and degrees of difference. Applying a patch updates the game files to the numerical value of the patch. (Example; applying the 1.08b patch to *StarCraft 1.0* produces *StarCraft 1.08b*.) Furthermore, the patch is not a universal fixture in the community and culture—a player without an Internet connection, or one chooses to play only among friends or against the computer may never apply a given patch. A *StarCraft* disc bought in 2008 can still install onto a computer the 1.0 variant of the game, though some packages may include later patches. There are, in every literal and figurative sense, many "*StarCrafts*"—each bearing proof of the accumulated cultural capital of the community.

In qualifying the relationship of the races in *StarCraft* as merely balanced is to describe only the matrix of economies that sets them in play, and does not perceive the temporal ecology of skill and culture, accumulated over time—most visible, perhaps, in the patch. What may be more instructive to a close analysis of *StarCraft* is the accumulation of actions that produces deep play—the shared history of the game as a sport. That history, in turn, opens up viewership, provides a sensation of accumulated value and allows for the nuances of skill to be viewed as increasingly important. Galloway's approach is keenly directed at a critique of neo-liberalism and for that purpose it is suited, but for broader work, it is only describing the cockfighting ring, and not the fight itself.

For example, in discussing the cephalopodan horrors of the Zerg as swarm-like, the tactical use of the "rush" method, intimately woven through the fabric of Zerg play, is the basis by which their multiplicity and formal essence derives. The fundament of the "Zerg rush" strategy is best explored in an example: In an otherwise equal match, a Zerg player can produce six basic ground attack units (known as Zerglings) before a Terran or Protoss player can produce an equivalent force. The Zerg player can then send these units out to harass the other player's units and buildings, diminishing their ability to gather resources in the early minutes of the game. While both of the other races have tactical methods by which to defend against an early use of this advantage, the Zerg advantage was lessened by a game patch on March 22, 2001—patch 1.08b—after which the ability for players to rush was hampered by the rising cost of the Spawning Pool, the building from which the Zerglings are produced. The patches to *StarCraft*, as well as correcting coding errors and stopping exploitative behavior, is in many senses a literal recalculation of the game's economies along the accumulated labor of deep play. To play *StarCraft* is then, in one sense, to contribute our free labor to the next corrective impulse from the game's creators.

ECOLOGIES MADE VISIBLE BY DEEP STRATEGIC PLAY

Another impulse is decipherable on the textual surface of *StarCraft* play—the historical context under which the game was made. As Geertz's model would have it, the historical context feeds into the raising of the stakes. The tradition of the Weird, most famously locatable in the work of H.P. Lovecraft, makes horror generically possible along the axes of ancient unknowable beings and the disintegrating sanity of the few humans that remain.[23] Non-Euclidian architecture, the notion of the unspeakable, and the impossibility of fractured language feature heavily. What makes the Weird a tradition of its own—high Weird—is this inference of the unknowable, which is classically located in the myths surrounding the octopus. The octopus has a historical position as an alienating (in the literal sense) sensory deviant. The folding over of the body, the limbs that are not limbs, make the octopus a limit case of palpability.[24] This tradition and its symbolic champion, Lovecraft's high Weird "Cthulhu" mythos underpins the design of the Zerg, and results in the "resounding" and "asymmetrical" qualities that Galloway's diagnosis of *StarCraft*'s surface qualities bears out.

However, *StarCraft* owes its entire design imprimatur to another gaming text—and no reading of the qualities of its play is possible or advantageous without consideration of this history. *Warhammer 40,000*, a vast overlapping system of complex board, miniature and computer games produced by the company Games Workshop takes place in a science-fiction setting which predates *StarCraft* by many years and is a clear template for the Blizzard game. In *Warhammer 40,000*, a militarized human race under imperial rule faces the insectile and swarm-like Tyranids who swarm over worlds and infest them, while the ancient unknowable Eldar mourn the decay of their once-great techno-magical society. Books written to outlay the ever-complexifying rules and outline the lore are often written in-character and in-setting to encourage textual immersion.[25] As *Warhammer 40,000* forms the template for *StarCraft*, so does the humans-orcs design of *Warcraft* take its imprimatur from the original Games Workshop setting of *Warhammer*. What is carried over in both circumstances is the imprint of dramatic form—facsimiles of both narrative and strategic impulses.

Galloway asserts that the Zerg are the simulated swarm, "a copy without an original," a phrase quoted from Baudrillard's *Simulacra and Simulation*.[26] The analysis rests on the Zerg being "acephalous and unhuman," and an "exemplar" of how essenceless, rhizomatic structures are subsumed by coming into conflict with formal structure.[27] Yet the Zerg have several points of origin—in game narrative they are led by an "Overmind" consciousness which is revealed in-game to be an experiment in controlling the Zerg by another origin point, the unseen Xel'Naga.[28] In addition, a human character (Sarah Kerrigan) is subsumed by the Zerg and quickly becomes another anthropomorphic leadership figure. The Zerg's antecedent Tyranids of *Warhammer 40,000* are cast as an ever-returning darkness made up of "Hivefleets" that consume galaxies unless met by organized resistance, a story mirrored in *StarCraft* with backstories and accumulated ephemera.[29] There are, in fact, a bonanza of origin points and control figures in the Zerg. Reference points situate the text in *Star Trek* mythology (Sarah Kerrigan references the Borg Queen), Aliens (units repeat lines from the films), and so on.

While all these origins could be easily dismissed as "inessential" surface textualities that might not interrupt the reading of swarm-to-structure, they accumulate and speak to the underlying structure of *StarCraft-the-game*—as opposed to *StarCraft-the-text*, and consequently, signal deep shifts in the way competitive strategy games are played and produced in its shadow. The Zerg are not a force in conflict, but a force in circulation. Their strategic affordances, in fact, pin them to a controlled space far more than the other two races—what appears to be a rhizome acts as boundary space. The Zerg base must be build on "creep," a purplish growth that has to be expanded and maintained. The Protoss must build within range of "pylons," which emit zones of affordance. It is, in fact, the Terrans who are the most rhizomatic, as many of their buildings can relocate and require no spatial precondition—they can build anywhere, and quickly.[30]

Pro-gamer culture reflects this, as players grow fine-grained reputations for being better at playing their usual race against the other races in specific detail. A Zerg player will have invested thousands of hours in developing strategies against other Zerg players or Protoss players, but may have not yet developed as much against Terran. Below that layer of strategy, the patches and code base of the game give leaning affordances which players complement, exploit or nullify. In an interview before the game's original release to corporate game website Gamespot, Bill Roper, a then-Director of Blizzard and oversight producer for many of the company's games, signaled a drastic shift in the design of the game away from the two-race structure which had made *Warcraft* so successful:

> I tend to think of *Warcraft* as being kind of like chess. You have similar pieces, and the strategy involves the different ways you use those pieces against the other player . . . What we may do [with *StarCraft*] is take a "rock-paper-scissors" approach, though not so drastic. Rock won't always beat scissors, but rock will have a definite advantage over scissors. But there's always paper to balance things out.[31]

The quintessence of *StarCraft*, then, is not balance between types of strategy, but imbalance writ large into manifold possibilities. The rock-paper-scissors dynamic of *StarCraft* is simply described; the Zerg tend towards quick attacks, or "rushing." The Terrans sacrifice strength and speed for the tendency towards "rapid expansion" by which they grow and consume territory. The slow and stoic Protoss are built for "turtling." The Zerg have a natural advantage against the Terrans, the Terrans against the Protoss, and the Protoss against the Zerg.[32] This foundation is made fertile by dovetailing the game's backstory and lore with these advantages. The once-great Protoss are inefficient and require a bureaucratic structure. The Zerg require "Overlord" units to maintain control but seek to overwhelm their ancient enemy, the Protoss to complete their devouring of the races. The Terrans squabble amongst themselves, but are willing to employ scorched earth strategies to succeed.

CONCLUSION: WATCHING KOREA PLAY

The high drama and deep play of professional *StarCraft* play is founded on how players leverage against this ecology of skills. Yet, this foundation has to emerge in an entirely different and complex social environment. South Korea's wildly popular culture of *PC bangs*, or network café, is the subject of two articles in a 2008 issue of the journal *Games and Culture*— "The Culture and Business of PC Bangs in Korea" by Huhh and "Age of New Media Empires: A Critical Interpretation of the Korean Online Game Industry" by Dal Yong Jin and Florence Chee.

Huhh's in-depth analysis identifies the confluence of circumstances that feed into *StarCraft*'s success; the International Monetary Fund's bailing out of the Korean economy in 1997, the regulation of the Internet access business away from monopoly, and the growth of the Hanaro corporation to compete with the ex-monopoly holder, KT.[33] *StarCraft* became, then, a metonymic battlefield by which Internet subscribers would be controlled and mined in the new economy. It was not so much that *StarCraft* was successful, but that it was leveraged to make broadband Internet itself successful in turn.[34]

At the same time, the wildly popular *PC bangs* thrived on providing a space for local *StarCraft* competition that at first provided for players who had no broadband access, or access to older (or no) computers, making the *bang* a zone particularly attractive to young students of the late 1990s traveling between the institutions of school and home.[35] The *PC bang*, too, used *StarCraft* to form a social arena and draw in young players for whom access at home was not assured, and for whom the income from work was better spent by the hour in a *bang* that saved up for expensive access and equipment.[36]

If the broadband Internet access and *PC bang* markets were the stakeholders in the wager, the fundament would be the elevation of *StarCraft* itself to more than a computer game. The stakeholders quickly shifted, as early as 1998, to promotion of the game's fine strategies—rather than the game itself—in coordinated television broadcasts, and later dedicated e-sports channels. Jin and Chee note that the broadcasting of game footage on cable television would promote a return to the *PC bang* to emulate the strategies seen against (or with) your friends, and a corporate-controlled celebrity culture had emerged out of the more local *PC bang* competitions by 2001.[37] Online gaming came to be an industry supported and driven by e-sports and the professional gaming scene, which Jin and Chee begin to cast as a class myth hiding the vast number of service-economy jobs that also emerge in games, such as RMT (real money trading) in which players purchase in-game items with real money to gain advantage. What makes these high stakes possible is similar to the aggregation, investment and eventual migration of status hierarchies identified by Geertz, as players come to represent broader concerns: class, narrative, strategy. The most visible consequence of this expansion of meaning is the elevation of strategy to that of a true spectacular:

> With drama similar to that of professional wrestling matches and live color commentary, the *StarCraft* tournament . . . ends with team members of the losing side weeping—all to be rehashed shortly after on game news websites such as Ongamenet.[38]

The stakes, the bet, the fight and the audience liquefy their roles as the importance of the match increases. Rather than diagnose symptoms of Korean gaming culture because of the importance of *StarCraft*, it follows more that the importance—the raised stakes of the tearful fans, the dozens of websites, the hushed community looking at the live broadcast—is made possible by the "fine grain" of play possible in *StarCraft* itself. The closeness of combat is commercially (and, arguably, culturally) productive. Huhh's historical contextualization and Jin and Chee's analysis of the e-sports industry destroys any notion we may form as readers (especially non-Koreans) that *StarCraft* is popular in Korea merely due to some ephemeral cultural reason, or that we can speak about Korea as a result of its popularity. The confluence of events and artificial production of culture by the e-sports, *PC bangs* and online access corporations speak more to the Korean service economy than to Korean culture.

What is interesting, what is visibly deep, is how the game is played out under these circumstances, and what stakes are raised. Meta-narratives of gameplay occur over several strata—the biography of the player, the clan they belong to, the leagues they perform well in, the history of play against others, the race they prefer, the building and attacking strategies they use against each race, their tendencies for psychological or purely strategic play, and the tendencies of pro-gaming more generally.

Because pro-gamers either earn money, or as Jin and Chee explain, merely subsist on their winnings, their personal stakes are ever-rising. Income for players comes from press and sponsorship more than the winnings of tournaments. With the stakes so high, a player's decision to finely hone a particular style of play can only resonate with ever-greater impact. The driver is not success, but more depth, more raising of the stakes. A match that makes visible as many of the above strata as possible can propel a player's visibility, gain them a nickname, entrench their style. In doing so, their narrative becomes more competitive, more visible, more deep.

Victory diminishes in importance, as does the usual conversational quality associated with strategic games, such as the "unique bond" belonging to chess. What constitutes success becomes conflated with fame, with narrative surprise and conduct—more and more with the continuance of all the strata that feed into the readable surface of the game. Remembering that Geertz identified the centre bet as the *means and device* by which deep play emerges, but not the reason, Korean pro-gaming *StarCraft* uses the conflation of strategy, fame biography as a commercial and cultural driver. The *reason* they are deep is intimately bound up with Korea's shift into a service economy, and the metonymic role the game plays in representing leisure to a new class.

With this context fully appreciated, we can return to the site of Boxer's use of the unorthodox "bunker rush" technique against Yell0w in 2004. In this Terran tactic, now common due to the match, six or five or the worker units usually used to gather minerals are deployed in a very early surprise attack alongside two attack units, before any adequate defenses will be ready. The attack properly timed, they will overwhelm an opponent in two or three minutes; usual play can often go over ninety. The tactic worked three games in a row, with no easy way to defend against them—all made more possible by Yell0w's inability to change race, reluctance to change tactics and we imagine, incredulity at the cruelty of the tactic. The narrative focus was not victory, but for avid readers of the various strata, it was the drama of Boxer using such a forceful tactic, and introducing a (largely) new method of play into mainstream *StarCraft* culture. The road less traveled, in this case, was a return to pure utility—the knockout hammer blow in the first round. At risk was reputation and style—the real resources being mined by the pro-gamer milieu and millions of amateurs alike. The elevation of an American-produced RTS game, designed with deep strategic impulses in mind, to the stage of grand national psychopomp for class and status concerns echoes the derivation of older board games from road to road, village to village, city to city. The affordances of media culture and the pressure of commercial needs perform the work that regional variation once did; the same game reads very differently in Korea than it does elsewhere by imbuing the tactical and strategic with new properties. A poem, "Sacchia Ludus" (the sweet game), by Marcus Hieronymus in 1527, long marshaled by theorists of strategy in describing their work—including Guy Debord—reads:

We play an effigy of war, and battles made like /
real ones, armies formed from boxwood, and play realms, /
As twin kings, white and black, opposed against each other, /
Struggle for praise with bi-colored weapons.[39]

Losses are not losses, but levees retained against comebacks. Wins are never wins, but the passing of young champion to old hands. The story of play trumps the story of the game in the struggle for praise.

NOTES

1. 'Marciano,' "The Road Not Taken" on *The Sense of Star*' website, 2006. Retrieved 11 September 2008 from http://senseofstar.blogspot.com/2006/06/road-not-taken.html.
2. Jun-Sok Huhh, "Culture and Business of PC Bangs in Korea," *Games and Culture*, 3(1) 2008: 26.
3. Clifford Geertz, "Deep Play: Notes On The Balinese Cockfight." In *TheInterpretation of Cultures; Selected Essays* (New York: Basic Books, 1973), 420–453.
4. Alice Becker-Ho and Guy Debord, *A Game of War* (London: Atlas, 2007), 34.
5. Becker-Ho and Guy Debord, *A Game of War*.
6. McKenzie Wark, *Fifty Years of Recuperation of the Situationist International* (New York: Temple Hoyne Buell Center for the Study of American Architecture, 2008), 23.
7. Stefan Zweig, *The Royal Game & Other Stories* (New York: Harmony Books, 1981).
8. David H. Li, The Genealogy of Chess (Bethesda, Maryland: Premier Pub. Co., 1998.)

9. H.J.R. Murray, A History of Chess (Oxford, United Kingdom: Clarandon Press, 1962).

10. Geertz, "Deep Play: Notes On The Balinese Cockfight," 432.

11. Jeremy Bentham, Étienne Dumont, Richard Hildreth, and C. K. Ogden, *The Theory of Legislation. International Library of Psychology, Philosophy and Scientific Method* (London: K. Paul, Trench, Trubner & Co. Ltd., 1931).

12. Geertz, "Deep Play: Notes On The Balinese Cockfight," 432.

13. Geertz, "Deep Play: Notes On The Balinese Cockfight," 432.

14. Geertz, "Deep Play: Notes on the Balinese Cockfight," 434.

15. Bart Farkas, *StarCraft Expansion Set: Brood War: Prima's Official Strategy Guide* (Rocklin, Calif: Prima Pub, 1998).

16. Eric Lim, *National Geographic: World Cyber Games* (Seoul, South Korea, 2005;Television Broadcast).

17. Alexander R. Galloway, "Starcraft, or, Balance," in *Grey Room* 28, 2007: 86–107.

18. Galloway, "*StarCraft*, or, Balance," 93.

19. Galloway, "*StarCraft*, or, Balance," 101.

20. Galloway, "*Starcraft*, or, Balance," 100.

21. Alexander R. Galloway, *Gaming: Essays On Algorithmic Culture* (Minneapolis: University of Minnesota Press, 2006).

22. Galloway, "*Starcraft*, or, Balance," 95.

23. China Miéville, "M.R. James and the Quantum Vampire: Weird; Hauntological: Versus and/or and and/or or?" *Collapse: Journal of Philosophical Research and Development* iv, 2008: 105–128.

24. China Miéville, "M.R. James and the Quantum Vampire: Weird; Hauntological: Versus and/or and and/or or?" 115.

25. Simon Spurrier, *Xenology: Notes From The Alien Bestiary of Biegel, and Studies of its Vile Specimens, by Those Present at its Destruction* (Nottingham: Black Library, 2006).

26. Jean Baudrillard, *Simulacra and Simulation* (Ann Arbor: University of Michigan Press, 1994).

27. Galloway, "*StarCraft*, or, Balance," 103.

28. Gabriel Mesta, *Shadow of the Xel'Naga*. StarCraft Series (New York: Pocket Books, 2001).

29. Mesta, *Shadow of the Xel'Naga*, StarCraft Series.

30. Bart Farkas, *StarCraft Expansion Set: Brood War: Prima's Official Strategy Guide* (Rocklin, Calif: Prima Pub, 1998).

31. Ron Dulin, "*Starcraft* Preview," *GameSpot*, 1996. Retrieved 18 April 2008 from http://uk.gamespot.com/pc/strategy/StarCraft/news.html?sid=2563222&mode=previews.

32. Farkas, *StarCraft Expansion Set: Brood War: Prima's Official Strategy Guide.*

33. Huhh, "Culture and Business of PC Bangs in Korea," 28.

34. Huhh, "Culture and Business of PC Bangs in Korea," 29.

35. Florence Chee, "The Games We Play Online and Offline: Making Wang-tta in Korea," *Popular Communication,* 4(3) 2006: 225–239.

36. Dal Yong Jin and Florence Chee, "Age of New Media Empires: A Critical Interpretation of the Korean Online Game Industry," *Games and Culture* 3 (1) 2008: 53.

37. Jin and Chee, "Age of New Media Empires: A Critical Interpretation of the Korean Online Game Industry," 51.

38. Jin and Chee, "Age of New Media Empires: A Critical Interpretation of the Korean Online Game Industry," 54.

39. Becker-Ho and Guy Debord, *A Game of War,* 12.

11 The Re-presentation of Country as Virtual Artifact in Australian Aboriginal Cultural Heritage Using a Game Engine

Theodor G. Wyeld, Brett Leavy and Patrick Crogan

INTRODUCTION

The single greatest artifact of Australian Aboriginal people is landscape or, as it is more affectionately known, "Country."[1] Country both belongs to, and embodies much of, the Australian Aboriginal peoples' cultural knowledge. Country is central in sustaining its people in a reciprocal survival "pact" that dates back more than forty millennia. With few material passions and no written language, Australian Aboriginal culture is held in memory and exchanged through performative storytelling. A form that defies Western notions of space, spatial understanding and ownership. It is a living culture. Ancient practices which honor Country and valorize their cultural heritage continue in everyday ceremony, ritual and storytelling. However, this continuity *is* being eroded by the apparent attractiveness of an alternative modern life style. This is especially so for the younger generations, more interested in materialist consumption and visual entertainments than actively engaging in their ancestors' cultural practices.

Paradoxically,[2] these same materialist, entertainment-oriented activities also provide a platform for the re-engagement of traditional cultural heritage knowledge practices. A group of researchers in Australia, working closely with rural and urban Indigenous Australians, have been developing the 3D game platform as a storytelling vehicle. The Digital Songlines (DSL) digital storytelling project,[3] has been developing protocols, methodologies and toolkits to facilitate the collection, education and sharing of Australian Aboriginal cultural heritage knowledge since 2004. The project explores the areas of effective and culturally sensitive, recording, content management and virtual reality delivery capabilities involving Aboriginal custodians, leaders and communities from around Australia. It investigates how players, in a serious gaming sense, can experience Australian Aboriginal cultural heritage in a high fidelity fashion with seemingly culturally appropriate digital tools.

The 3D computer game (3DCG) is a vehicle for sensitively re-presenting Australian Aboriginal knowledge practices embedded in landscape. As this paper will explore, more than this, the 3DCG—a favored pastime of many of the younger generation—simulates a virtual reality which in some ways mirrors the virtual reality that is at the foundation of Australian Aboriginal spirituality, the "Dreaming" or "Dreamtime": the basis of their creation mythology. The Dreamtime refers to a time when the Ancestral People, as mythical beings, roamed the land creating its forms, giving its features their names, and inhabiting it as a literal coalescence of spirit and matter. The virtual reality of the Dreaming corroborates and nourishes Australian Aboriginal cultural heritage through a performative storytelling practice. The game engine provides a simulational space for the enactment of much of the storytelling that constitutes and continues their cultural heritage. The game engine acts as a vehicle for simulating Country in which performative Dreamtime storytelling can occur. It is also highly portable and flexible—supporting multiple regional variations. The simulation of Country in a 3DCG assists the maintenance and sharing of Aboriginal cultural heritage. In this sense, the 3DCG is a surrogate living, extensible, contemporary museum space.

What the 3D game engine of the DSL digital storytelling project does is to support a re-presentation of the land as a vehicle for storytelling. Hence, the DSL virtual world is an immersive narrative first and a 3D environment second. In a sense, the space of DSL game engine can be described as a series of unfolding relationships where wanderers make up their own cultural maps along the way. Individual experience in the space overlaps with that intended by the world builders. In de Certeau's (1984) sense, the space is not concrete but a concept generated by one's interaction with it.[4] One is invited to participate in its narrative.

Three major indigenous cultural heritage game engine applications have been developed by the DSL team to-date. They include: *Vincent Serico's World* (the artist, Vincent Serico (1949–2008), discussing the stories behind his paintings embedded in their country of origin, Carnarvon Gorge, South West Queensland); *Irene Ryder's World* (community worker and bush tucker expert, Irene Ryder, discussing traditional bush camp practices and bush tucker walks, in Mitchell, South West Queensland); Virtual Warrane (simulation of Sydney Cove prior to White settlement with traditional hunting and fishing quests, overseen by the Cadigal people of Sydney). Of these, Serico's World is the focus of this chapter. Vincent Serico's use of contemporary and traditional iconography in his paintings along with his storytelling embedded in the specific locations they refer to in a simulation of his country provides a unique insight into past and current knowledge practices. The DSL team worked closely with Vincent Serico and other members of his community to create an authentic virtual environment for archiving and sharing of their knowledge for current and future generations. The scale of the project means that much more can be encompassed in the relatively unbounded space of the

3D virtual environments used than what is, more typically, held in a museum space. Moreover, the very nature of the environment closely parallels the disjunctive nature of Australian Aboriginal storytelling in general—the primary method for communicating cultural knowledge practices. However, this format also presents a number of dilemmas, most importantly the inclusion of sacred sites. The elders engaged in this project felt the inclusion of some sacred sites, ordinarily left out of traditional archiving media, was necessary and important in maintaining their cultural heritage. That they felt compelled to include these sites is testament to the importance of this work and this mode of representation.

ADOPTING NEW TECHNOLOGIES

Approaches to representing traditional Australian Aboriginal cultural knowledge can only be fully evaluated by an Australian Aboriginal person. For an Australian Aboriginal person, knowledge is a commodity to be earned, traded and restricted. It is the basis of the ceremonial power it imbues in ritual. Through constant negotiation the knowledge is maintained and shared. While the notion of a social network is essential to all cultural formations, the way it manifests varies. For the Aboriginal it is not simply the naming of places and events (more common to the Eurocentric view) but the interconnectedness of these places and the meanings behind the names that count. This interconnectedness takes a long time to learn and hence much capital is invested in what knowledge each individual is allowed to retain and repeat. More than this, the network is tangible[5] (it is artefactual, embedded in a changing landscape) and needs to be actively maintained through oral and ritual transmission. "Behind this is the 'working assumption' that human activities 'create' places by socializing space . . . intimately tied to human purpose and action."[6]

Non-Aboriginal people can only begin to understand the complexities of Australian Aboriginal culture by accepting that, with few material possessions and no written language, their memories have been held in a dream-like virtual spacefor millennia. They describe this space through abstract dot paintings, dance and song, imparting their subconscious ethereal landscapes by projecting them back onto the physical world through everyday ritual and performative storytelling. The role of much Aboriginal tangible culture and technology is to mobilize the connection between the virtual and the actual. Central to the unity of the virtual and the actual in traditional Aboriginal knowledge and thought is their connection to the land.

Much of what non-Aboriginal people know about Aboriginal cultural knowledge stems from exposure to the physical artifacts, anthropological studies, and images residing in museums around the world. Indeed, since the advent of anthropological studies of Indigenous cultures in the nineteenth century, there has been a shift from the three-dimensional versions of tangible indigenous knowledge representational forms—tactile, haptic, carvings, impressions in sand, elaborate weavings, assemblages, castings, masks and so on—to two-dimensional or flattened, printed, photographed, dyed-on-cloth contemporary versions more easily sold to collectors, tourists, museums, researchers and so on. This has coincided with the West's increasing reliance on two-dimensional recording media—print, film, video and so on. Hence, much of what constitutes contemporary notions of Australian Aboriginal culture has been distorted by the prism of a museum culture that has relied largely on the reproduction of artifacts and reproducibility for controlled public consumption.

Until recently, museums were largely confined to the domain of repositories of an objective factual history. They contained objects that bore testimony to a past reality. This object-centeredness was predicated on a historical object's enchantment—or what Walter Benjamin has called "aura"—defined by its physical presence and derived from ascribed social meanings, message-bearing abilities and traceability.[7] The "aura" of an object stems from notions of ritual and ceremony associated with historical objects. According to Fiona Cameron, the notion of the "real" as solid, and thus authentic, is a Western cultural construct.[8] Museum objects may transport us back to a former time, but what we experience are contemporary notions, visions and learned histories of that time. Hence, the game engine is also a contemporary vehicle for that expression.

Australian Aboriginal people have been adapting and adopting new technologies for millennia. Their sand painting (similar in purpose to the Hindu and Buddhist sand mandalas, see Figure 11.1) was transferred to

Figure 11.1   Western Desert (Papunya) sand painting ceremony.
Source: Bardon.[10]

paint on board in the 1970s in response to the need for a more permanent record. Yet, it still communicates messages about underlying cultural practices and evokes their stories. With clear organizing strategies, the impressions in sand map topological landscape features which can be loosely likened to an aerial view. As a cultural "style," these spatial narratives have survived the transition to a more permanent medium. Whether they have lost their original, ceremonial, spiritual, ritualistic, transitory, ethereal meanings remains problematic. Nevertheless, these transitions in media type suggest a rigorous cultural underpinning that responds to and adopts new technologies in furthering its own message or function. Embracing 3D computer game technology is in this view the latest iteration in a short contemporary history of such adoptions.[9]

The *iconographic* spatial communications of Australian Aboriginal peoples, predating the Western realist, perspectival, imagery that emerged from the European Renaissance, continues to talk across the aeons uninterrupted. Its messages, once decoded, are clear, concise, and complex. The encodings of their iconography—at the same time mapping space, knowledge and emotions—used in their performative storytelling is anchored in its Country of origin. The 3D game engine provides a platform for sharing this cultural knowledge by embedding it in a simulation of its Country of origin. The embedding of storytelling as a knowledge exchange medium in Country is re-presented or re-enacted by the game engine.

As a metaphor for Country, the world generated by the game engine can be understood as the mapping of one conceptual domain (virtual reality and the Dreamtime stories) in terms of another (a simulational Country).[11] There is a correspondence between the domains of the Dreamtime and Country. As performative storytelling, this reflects the concretization of thought in language in which there occurs a coalescence of Dreamtime and Country. Neither is understood in isolation. They rely on a complex web of existent syncretic understandings.

In this way, the Dreamtime transcends the present and the landscapes it inhabits. As the ancestors, in the form of animals, acquiesced with the landscape, creating its features, they gave the world its forms, identities and names. These features and the tracks connecting them and their significances link all identifiable places into a whole. These places, features and tracks are sung into and out of existence by performative storytelling. Their connectedness is referred to as a songline—both a literal, physical line (connecting two places), and an ancestral hereditary connection. The continent of Australian is criss-crossed by these "songlines." As Aboriginal knowledge is coincident with the creative activity of the Ancestral Beings that created the topography, provided the names for places along the songline paths, and linked groups of people, all interact forming a cohesive knowledge network, constituted through a spatial connectivity. Unlike the European approach which makes connections between places using abstract metric quanta, for the Australian Aboriginal, the tracks *are* the landscape.

In this sense, the Aboriginal theory of land sees the landscape as a map of itself.[12] What the DSL game engine does is to manifest Country for the virtual maintenance and sharing of these Songlines.

AUSTRALIAN ABORIGINAL STORYTELLING

Responding to nature, Aboriginal people obey and adore its forces by celebrating these in rituals of song, dance and image. Their ceremonies unify all the elements of nature in a supernature. Their Dreaming ceremonies describe particular places or events of this supernature. The Dreaming stories draw from body painting, ornaments and sand painting.[13] In sand painting, a selected area of ground is prepared by clearing away any debris and smoothing it. Colored sands, ochres, feathers, charcoal and other materials are used to depict the story. The area is completely destroyed on completion of the story-telling ceremony (as is the Buddhist mandala).

In the way one might inscribe topological features in the sand as a navigational *aide memoire*—pointing out features, places and past events—the Aboriginal sand doodlings are a kind of survival map. They demonstrate a transcendental reality of spirit and world in their markings and the unfolding of its story.

Describing events that have occurred in place, their sand doodlings recount journeys across Country. As a combinable knowledge in the form of narratives of journeys across the landscape, Australian

> Aborigines inculcate and invoke conventions . . . through conferences and agreement. They call them business meetings; anthropologists call them ceremonies and rituals. Songlines (which are accounts of journeys made by Ancestral Beings in the Dreamtime) connect myths . . . across the [land] . . . One individual will only 'know' or have responsibility for one section of the songline, but through exchange and negotiation, the travels of the Ancestors can be connected together to form a network of Dreaming tracks.[14]

Each clan is responsible for its songline that refers to the Dreaming of their ancestors. It refers to the specific series of stories, songs, dances and graphic representations about that creative epoch as well as the Country it defines. The Songlines or tracks form a network which constitutes the political and economic processes of the included societies.

In their depiction as sand painting, one is a part of the processes of the creation of the Songlines—literally and virtually walking around in the painting. This is unlike Western art where one is external to it observing or looking on. The markings themselves rarely have any particular orientation. They can be looked at from many different angles and sides depending on one's orientation to that which is depicted and their orientation to the story. Indeed, they can be seen from all sides at once and collectively gives the appearance of an x-ray image. The arbitrariness of the abstract illustration's edge[15] means its relativity to the viewer is absolute. It is this arbitrariness of framing and perspective that denies the normal certainness we associate with Western art. Unlike the Western figurative style, the Aboriginal artist enters rather than delineates the world from outside.[16]

The space within this arbitrariness is understood as an emotional ideal—a social space that is felt rather than seen. One "sees" in relation to the existing social organization. This denies the very capacity of the landscape to be formed by the eye; that form itself is arbitrary (not fixed in the conventionality of a Western mode). Instead, the forms *are* representations and embodiments of matter; and all understanding is reduced to a four-dimensional or spatiotemporal space where time is both still and ever changing.[17] This spatiotemporal arbitrariness is common in many forms of Australian Aboriginal creative expression.[18] The 3DCG can also be entered from many sides. Thus, the apparent arbitrariness of the 3DCG goes some way towards accommodating and making available the sharing of this concept in a highly regionally contextualized manner.

With the transition from sand-mosaic painting to acrylic on board, this gives the once ephemeral/transient images permanence. With it the stories can be preserved and interpreted by others not having access to the original ceremonial sand constructions. But, this also means the new form changes the way the stories can be told. In the original form, space was continually expanded upon by the infinity of the landscape to transform. Now the frame of the painting itself becomes a metaphor for the perimeter of the space beyond. On the other hand, the land that is represented in the painting has distinct form, and has an eternal life force which transcends space and time.

In the 3D game engine, the landscape is also constant, whereas the simultaneity of the eternal Dreamtime stories are free to unfold as a consequence of the user's or, more precisely, "inter-actor's" explorations. These interactive landscape elements generate a narrative adventure more like *Myst* than a First Person Shooter game. In Ryan's identification of the different kinds of interactive works the DSL interactivity can be seen as a narratalogically internal or exploratory medium.[19] The DSL interactor is immersed in the unfolding narrative of the world. This is unlike the player of a civilization game (such as *Age of Empires*) who is above everything, interacting at a literal, almost physically engaging manner. The DSL interactor, by contrast, explores, not really changing the world's nature or material development, rather becoming part of the story of encounters with forms, spaces, objects and events. In the same way one cannot change the contents of a book, but can explore alternative scenarios in one's imagination. The important distinction is that one can act out those imagined scenarios in the virtuality of the game world.

The European abstract artists Delaunay, Kandinsky and Klee understood this relativism of perception and temporality that is within one's self.

Similarly, in Australian Aboriginal culture, time becomes space differently than in the more common figurative art of Western culture. There is no sense of linear sequence in their storytelling; rather, it is simply the accretion of space or place, since space or place is part of the retelling of the story. Hence, the story is an eternal ideal with no particular reading direction.

Unlike in the European landscape painting, with its horizon separating land and sky, in Aboriginal representational culture these two are united as one. As survival or navigation maps, Australian Aboriginal representative forms—dance, song, bark painting, sand painting and so on—only appear ethereal because they do not attach the same value to recording places, events and times as common practice dictates in the West. Nevertheless, their sense of space and time *are* bound within the web of logical relations governed by a grammar and metaphor determined by their spatial consciousness invoked through that performative art.[20] In the virtual environments of DSL's 3DCG, the performative storytelling occurs in a dreamlike state. The web of logic that underlies their relations only become clear over time with the exhaustive telling and retelling experienced through sustained exploration of the world.

SIMULATIONAL SPACE AS NARRATIVIZED ARCHIVE

Modern society has become dependent on the image to articulate its view of the world. In Pierre Bourdieu's terms of cultural capital,[21] much is invested in visual reproduction as a tool of reification of cultural norms and expectations of what needs to be known or learned about the past to make sense of the present. In this era of digital technology and connectivity, much of this cultural capital is invested in the consumption of signs, electronic images and simulacra. So much so that, 3D models can be taken as the hallmark of authenticity, effectively creating a reality beyond the real. This is despite the obvious reduction of the artifact to visual simulation disrupting its connection to material evidence and thus to history.[22] This replaces the aura of the original in the sense that it creates an imagined aura. The verisimilitude used to indicate the illusion of a reality creates that reality. In interactive 3D immersive environments, this is supplemented by the myriad unfolding narratives possible adding a new dimensional reality. However, in such "virtual worlds" it is not their verisimilitude to a physical corollary, real or imagined, that one is immersed in but one's own involvement in the narrative.

3D Computer Game spatial simulation is unlike other forms of spatial simulation that are based on normative conventions of narrativised text—films, storybooks, theatre and so on. 3DCG simulation introduces interactivity with the spatial narrative not possible in other genres.[23] Spatial narratives—the interaction with, navigation of, and cognitive inhabitation in space—mean different things to different cultures. Indeed, space itself as a concept has been redefined in many different ways over time and by different cultures.[24]

The interactors in the simulational space of the DSL game engine can play out interactive narratives within the simulated spaces with apparent impunity. Unlike the more conventionally received narrative, the game space allows new narratives to evolve through interaction with the space. The DSL game engine space allows for undirected narratives to unfold over time. The elements of its narrative are experienced as an "emergent narrative"—the re-cognition of one's experiences in the simulational space after the event, on reflection, as continuous narrative—especially when communicated to others.[25] With no defined entry point or exit (other than the initial spawning of one's avatar in the gamespace) it closely resembles the lack of linearity of Australian Aboriginal performative storytelling. More than this, the various nodes or points of interest are circumstantially framed by the very Country their stories refer to. Interactors can experiment with these "places" that might normally be censored by cultural protocols from traditional media such as sacred spaces or places. That they are able to do this is a product of the underpinning technology's openness and faithful reconstruction of a universalized space, which includes sacred places as part of notions of a holistic integrity that sees all spaces as equal in the modeling process. But this presents a dilemma for the use of the 3DCG as a vehicle for Australian Aboriginal storytelling.

Modeled space invites experimentation. As such, 3DCG simulational spaces are about what can be done with the spaces modeled; experimental spaces; spaces for speculating on what ifs?[26] In the Western sense of reducing reality to potentially calculable knowns, the spaces are simulations of the real. Within the scientific reductivist paradigm, experimentation does not raise questions of the sacredness of spaces. For, Western representations are abstractions of the real—metaphorically: This as that. However, for Australian Aboriginal culture, abstraction and reality, subject and object, are merged. Hence, representation is not abstract. It is a re-presentation of the real, because the "real" is not the same as in the Western opposition of real and represented. In this sense, the simulated spaces in the DSL game engine are as sacred as their physical-world corollaries. Hence, the notion of how to protect the sacredness of places depicted in the simulational space is a recurrent theme in the DSL project.

In the simulation of Australian Aboriginal sacred spaces in the DSL game engine they are no longer only restricted to those initiated to its inner circle. In the construction of the DSL simulational space, many sacred spaces are re-presented. These sacred spaces are identified by their custodians as important parts of a larger story needing to be passed on to current and future generations. In turn, this raises questions of how this objective can be reconciled with the ability of the uninitiated or the ignorant to transgress these spaces within the simulated environments. However, the central charter for the construction of these simulational spaces is for the dissemination of cultural heritage knowledge. Hence, in order to address the issue of transgressions of sacredness by the uninitiated, the DSL project involves a different kind of conditional engagement or encounter with the artefactual material represented. It is one where the interactor is accepted as an honorary clan member for the duration of their time in the simulational space.

The DSL project uses its simulational spaces as active knowledge archives, including sacred spaces. This is different to traditional archiving (documents, photographs, video, film, audio, and so on) where reference to sacred spaces may be restricted or absent. An archive is something that preserves and stores and provides access to things that are past. Its primary function is for the heritage and benefit of the people who come after. What the use of a 3DCG engine by the DSL team to create a simulational space provides is a digital platform that is dedicated to exploration and experimentation with the spaces encountered and its correlation with the physical world. This includes the possibility to utter sacred verses or view normally forbidden vistas. But this also allows for active participation in the creation of contemporary stories contextually situated in their place of origin and access to historically sensitive stories often involving reconstructions of sacred sites. The tension between the possibility for futural experimentation and traditional archiving that this generates means the re-presentation of the knowledge recorded can often be too intrusive. However, the ability to control access and reproduction available to the traditional archive is foregone in favor of experimentation with the "spaces" of the archive because the custodians of this knowledge consider it is too important not to be included. Of course, much material can never be accessed, but many of the sacred sites included are simply considered too important to the authenticity of the stories to be left out.

Added to this notion of the importance of the inclusion of sacred knowledge and spaces is the notion that archives often become a substitution for the thing they are trying to record or represent. The DSL project presents a different version of the same problem. The "space" becomes the archive. The DSE is a database which is activated by the spatializing engine that it uses. It becomes the simulational space for encountering those things it contains in terms of a different temporal orientation. The simulational spaces become a substitute in the archival sense for the real, and they also inform the real in terms of the possibility for experimenting with what is possible within those spaces that it simulates. It means interactors can do things that they could not necessarily do in the real. However, in time, these actions can also become a substitute for the real: If most peoples' interaction with the spaces is in the virtual, what happens when they visit the physical and expect to have the same access rights as those in the virtual, and so on? For example, to climb on the sacred rocks of Carnarvon Gorge, while difficult yet possible in the 3DCG environment, may be considered offensive to the custodians of the physical rocks.[27] Thus, protocols for what can be included, excluded and accessed are vital.

ARCHIVING PROTOCOLS

The past, present and future are conflated in the DSL worlds. The archive becomes the reality. Everything that is simulated, in any kind of archive, is a representation of that space-time or spatialization of the past. In this sense, anthropological work is always an interpretation. Hence, it becomes archival, "the fact" of that period. However, each subsequent generation interprets this same archive in terms of their own contemporary understandings. The need for protocols is clear. For example, Charles Mountford is an anthropologist from the mid-twentieth century who recorded Aboriginality in his time.[28] He talks about his encounters with Aboriginal people and builds characters around them. Particular individual Aboriginal people are photographed in his books, for which there were few protocols for how this should be done at the time. Geoffrey Bardon is another non-indigenous person working in close relationship to Aboriginal groups, recording their art and craft in the 1970s.[29] He did establish some protocols, but these were more about what he was hoping to achieve than a consensual set of guides open to negotiation with the people he was trying to protect. The major books Bardon produced of the period,[30] of beautifully illustrated works, represents an archive in itself. Some of the works recorded are the most important Aboriginal artworks in Australia because of Bardon's meticulous recordings and the iconography captured in them. Many of these icons are not seen in today's paintings because they are considered too sacred (the early paintings Bardon recorded were produced in an atmosphere of naivety about who would have access to them). Mountford and Bardon's recordings are only two examples of the many anthropological works that demonstrate the evolving need to establish protocols for dealing with notions of Australian Aboriginal cultural heritage and in what forms it can or cannot be re-presented.

As an archiving project, DSL is faced with the same challenge of respecting the cultural material it records. Where DSL differs from previous Australian Aboriginal archival projects is both its emphasis on contemporary culture contextualized within its historical background and that each project is instigated by a member of the culture it purports to re-present. DSL has established a set of protocols that are open to negotiation with the Australian Aboriginal peoples involved.[31] Yet, many compromises are confronted in its attempt to marry contemporary Aboriginal culture with traditional culture. The need to overcome these is paramount, as the elders claim they are very worried that once they are gone their culture will go with them if it is not recorded. As mentioned earlier, the younger generation they are trying to reach are too interested in playing computer games and engaging in mainstream culture to learn about their own heritage. Hence, in using the computer game as a platform, the elders are hoping to reach that generation using the same vehicle.

THE DSL GAME ENGINE AS ARCHIVE

Australian Aboriginal culture is very complex. It is not so easily reduced to the determinist confines of the 3DCG. Yet the very notion of simulation is to simplify the complex; to model phenomena in a manner that makes it more easily understood for a specific, instrumental purpose.[32] As such, by its very nature, simulation is selective from the beginning, because there is only so much that it can support. In a similar manner, only so much can be retrieved from a regular search of archives, in terms of documentation, and the documents themselves are very selective. At the least, because they are interpretations of events and already large deductions of what could potentially be recorded or shown, and the very choice of inclusion in the archive is often a selection from available materials. The most expensive flight simulator in the world cannot perfectly model every facet of flight, but they can do it to a level of functional effectivity which is good enough for pilot training. Hence, the DSL project can only ever be a compromise. Whether it achieves its goals of preserving the important aspects of the cultural heritage it seeks to capture is open to interpretation in perpetuity. What makes the DSL project unique is its idiosyncratic use of the 3DCG format and game-play. Combined, these express the needs of its creators rather than the 3DCG genre *per se*. The DSL's game engine has the potential to be an authentic and meaningful platform for communicating Australian Aboriginal storytelling, and is recognized as such by the various Aboriginal communities engaged in its production. This is not to discount the ongoing dilemma of whether to include sacred sites and what this means to notions of sacredness in an open simulational space that invites experimentation.

AN IDIOSYNCRATIC ARCHIVE

What differentiates the DSL game engine from other game platforms is its idiosyncraticity. The recent emergence of idiosyncratic games, outlined by Crogan,[33] represent a counter challenge to the spread of simulational culture in general. They actively question what can be done with goals other than the mainstream commercial applications such as vehicle instrument training, various kinds of tactical and group mission drills, "serious" educative gaming, CAD and other audio-visual design and demonstration, or entertainment. The DSL project is an example of the idiosyncratic use of a game engine to archive and reinvigorate cultural knowledge and practices.

DSL's use of the 3DCG engine as an archive is different from gaming in general because it engages the user in certain functions that are not related to game play but more like search functions. Nonetheless, the background to this—the fact that it uses simulation of space—and the whole game engine genre is historically, a military development. In a military context, simulational space becomes a trajectory, a series of trajectories to be overcome or navigated. This type of space simulation is a dominant model in contemporary society.[34]

On the other hand, the DSL 3DCG's "idiosyncraticity"—its localized (spatiotemporal) subjective interpretation and innovation—announces its peculiarly Australian Aboriginal cultural format and differentiates it from the more mainstream, historically militaristic games. The legacy this represents comes from a merging of the need of the Aboriginal peoples involved and what the game platform can provide. Yet, the standard game behaviors that it implicitly involves or encourages or assumes still come from the history of computer culture in general: militarily techno-scientific developments around the 1940s onwards.

The project avoids much of the militaristic legacy of the traditional 3DCG because the fundaments of the DSL database are highly contextualized landscapes that resist reduction to "trajectile" space. Everything is built on the notion of Country as an entity. Country manifests the ancestral beings in terms of the Dreaming and their utterance into existence through the telling of stories embedded in their simulated Country. The naming of the landscape features in Country not only brings them into existence and maintains their existence, but it also allows for change over time. The game engine experience of this is not a linear excursion. It is disjunctive, in that one can wander around and find things which are both contextualized but approachable in many different ways. In this sense, the use of a game engine emerges as an appropriate medium for this disjunctive wandering and discovering.

For example, in the DSL's *Vincent Serico World*, one can stumble across one of Vincent Serico's paintings relating to that part of Country one finds themselves in. The interactor can then right click and a screen pops up with his painting taking up most of the available interface (see Figure 11.2). Sweeping the mouse cursor over the painting, the interactor notices hotspots. Clicking on one of these launches another popup with Vincent talking about that part of his painting and the stories behind it. In a sense, this non-linearity closely parallels the nature of Australian Aboriginal storytelling; a story does not start at the beginning and end at the end, it can be entered at any point, and it can be changed and so on. In this manner, Serico's simulated world reflects some of those qualities.

The addition of hotspots as an aside surprise found in *Vincent Serico's World* is also an established strategy of mainstream game construction for maintaining interest in a game. In a contemporary mainstream first person shooter game these aside interactivities are used so the player can discover

Figure 11.2 Vincent Serico painting embedded in DSL game interface and Country, near Carnarvon Gorge, South-West Queensland, Australia (Vincent Serico, *Bush Honey*, 2003, acrylic on canvas 60x103cm).

secrets which are usually superfluous to game play, if the main objective of the level is to kill all the monsters and go to the next level. While this may be the main goal, the additional asides make the game space more interesting. However, the main trajectory design of the space is still about moving through it and eliminating the targets to get to the next level. In the DSL simulated world, on the other hand, in the absence of this main role-play trajectory, it is, instead, discovery of the asides that becomes the main goal. It is this tension between moving in and out of the mainstream trajectory to an activity function inside the space, moving it from being peripheral to central, that captures the interactors' imagination. Many of the aside interactions discuss issues of deep spiritual significance. There remain many sites that are held as sacred, not discussed yet accessible within the simulational space.

ADDRESSING NOTIONS OF SACREDNESS

The simulational space of *Vincent Serico's World* contains sacred spaces (rock art, monolithic rock totem formations, waterholes and so on) (see Figure 11.3). Ordinarily, visitors are discouraged from touching, seeing, or interacting with their physical manifestation. For example, one should not touch or deface the rock art or approach it without paying particular attention to seasons and so on; one should not clamber to the top of a monolithic rock just because a "scenic view" is available from there; and, one should

Figure 11.3   Aboriginal rock art at Mt. Moffatt, in the Carnarvon Gorge National Park, Queensland Australia. Camp fires and tools dating back 19,400 years have been recorded here.

not swim in a waterhole without the appropriate permission from the local tribal elders. All of these are possible in the *Vincent Serico World*. Hence, the simulational space is both referent to the real, a re-presentation of the real, and at the same time, there is an implied and explicit permission to suspend some of the strictures of sacredness. Mentioned earlier, the Elders felt these sites were too important to the stories to be left out. Ordinarily, for interactors to gain access to these sites they should go through an initiation process that enlightens them to the secret sacred knowledge of these sites. This is not possible. Instead, some of the sites are included without explanation. An explicit conferral of clanship is bestowed upon the interactors as a condition of entering the game space by the Elders. This does not surrender the sacred sites to open exploration. Rather, in this conferral of clanship respect for these sites is implied ad must be recognized by the interactor.

Nevertheless, where simulation in serious gaming and training is normally approached with a hypothetical future orientation—what can we do with this simulation?—and typically in a very prescribed, instrumental relationship of the simulation to the real, with the DSL game engine, it is both prospective and also archival. Hence, despite the clan elders' permission to explore their Country, there still exists a tension between the simulational temporal engagements about what can be done with it and the sorts of historical preservation, hopes and ambitions are expected of it in an archival manner by the elders who instigate it.

Thus, it remains both a challenge and a crucially important project to be undertaking. The use of a 3DCG engine provides a platform to support the essential character of Australian Aboriginal cultural practice— the emphasis on Country as all-sustaining, spiritually and physically. Nonetheless, the restrictions of the 3DCG engine, when compared to the rich physical-world narratives possible, are symptomatic of the reductivist approach exemplified in the Western modeling paradigm and manifest by gaming culture in general. The supremacy of the visual over the haptic that identifies Western culture[35] stems from the same renaissance concept of placing oneself outside the space and experimenting objectively on it. This reduction of the whole to things in isolation is anathema to Australian Aboriginal cultural practices. Hence, the use of a gaming engine in the project must necessarily encounter and engage with the clash of cultural perspectives on an ongoing basis.

On the other hand, what the DSL project heralds is also a departure from this "visual monism."[36] The unfolding narratives embedded in their Country of origin see the landscape not as a backdrop but as an active, central, participant in the storytelling. In this sense, the DSL project challenges the gaming norm through its idiosyncraticity. Its subscription to the current global paradigm, what Jacques Derrida calls "globalatinization,"[37] both supports and makes it possible to be counter to this visual monism. Hence, the DSL project is not a departure from the gaming genre norm but rather a paradigm shift within the existing system. As such, it also offers a new way forward for idiosyncratic gaming in general. Here is a simulational space that negotiates a reserve of sacredness by providing limited, virtual access rights from the outset. One enters with an understanding that there are certain behaviors to be observed when engaging with the sacred spaces contained. In turn, a new respect and understanding about another culture's notions of sacredness are honored. For example, consider Serico's account of a tree containing native bees that can be harvested for its honey (see Figure 11.2). Embedded in the actual location of the tree in Country, Vincent's recounting of past journeys to the tree emphasizes the singularity of the space, transforming the tree from just one more random tree simulation supporting the "realism" of the landscape to one which concurrently holds location, story and graphical depiction. The interactor, already immersed in the simulation space, is further drawn into the slow melodic voice of Vincent's storytelling—entering a part of his story. In this way, one is also captive to the learnings of the elders—a principal goal of this project.

CONCLUSION

As a virtual museum-like archive of past and future cultural heritage, the DSL's use of a 3DCG for Australian Aboriginal storytelling embedded in Country both supports and encourages young Aboriginal and non-Aboriginal people alike to engage in this cultural heritage from within rather than outside the global paradigm. More importantly, that the Elders are better able to engage the respect sought from the younger generation targeted means the maintenance of their cultural heritage finds new impetus. In more general terms, the global paradigm that both provides the mechanism for their engagement and the tools to challenge it, is not reinforced by the technology, rather it is co-constituted by mainstream media technology in general (in McLuhan's sense).[38] This is because electronic media are increasingly the primary means by which the world is encountered. Hence, to the extent that the West's media technology dominates perceptual experience today, it is also important for any kind of project, not only projects dealing with Indigenous issues, but all kinds of artistic and other culturally important projects, to engage the mainstream technology to have their messages heard. The DSL project has done this by idiosyncratically altering the accepted norms, to temporalize their message in ways that highlight and counter what makes them different to the mainstream. This promotes a basic characteristic of Australian Aboriginal culture—the embedding of storytelling in its Country of origin—and makes this appealing to potential Aboriginal and non-Aboriginal interactors alike. It also announces an important shift in the exposition of Australian Aboriginal cultural heritage from the confines of a museum culture back to its original custodians in a dynamic and changeable yet persistent medium.

NOTES

1. Country is understood by Australian Aboriginal people as a benevolent entity that provides for and is maintained by its people.
2. Paradoxically rather than ironically, as the use of a 3-D game engine presents as many challenges to the sanctity of Australian Aboriginal knowledge as it seems a most appropriate vehicle for its re-presentation.
3. Originally funded by the Australasian Cooperative Research Centre for Interaction Design (ACID).
4. Michel De Certeau, *The Practice of Everyday Life* (Berkeley, California: University of California Press, 1984).
5. Much like texts and images are tangible manifestations of Western culture.
6. David Turnbull, *Maps are Territories: Science is an Atlas* (Geelong: Deakin University Press, 1989), 31, 61.
7. Walter Benjamin, "The Work of Art in the Age of Mechanical Reproduction," in Hannah Arendt (ed.) *Illuminations: Essays and Reflections*, trans. Harry Zohn (New York: Schocken Books, 1969). Fiona Cameron and Sarah Kenderdine, eds., *Theorizing Digital Cultural Heritage: A Critical Discourse* (Cambridge: MIT Press, 2007).
8. Fiona Cameron, "Beyond the Cult of the Replicant—Museums and Historical Digital Objects: Traditional Concerns, New Discourses," in *Theorizing Digital Cultural Heritage: A Critical Discourse*, eds. Cameron and Kenderdine (Cambridge, Massachusetts: MIT Press, 2007).
9. Laurel Evelyn Dyson, Max A. N. Hendriks and Stephen Grant, *Information Technology and Indigenous People* (Singapore: Information Science Publishing, 2007).
10. Geoffrey Bardon, *Papunya Tula: Art of the Western Desert*, (NSW, Australia: J.B. Books, 1999), 101.
11. George Lakoff and Mark Johnson *Metaphors we live by* (Chicago: University of Chicago Press, 1980).
12. Turnbull, *Maps are Territories*.
13. Their more familiar, accessible, graphical, iconographic art forms, such as acrylic on board paintings, have their origins in sand painting.

14. Turnbull, *Maps are Territories*, 27.
15. This edge-wise arbitrariness is also extended to its more conventional paint-on-board forms. As paintings in galleries, they are often hung in whatever orientation suits the viewer.
16. Bardon, *Papunya Tula*. In other words, the "right" perspective, the one that orients, is so dependent on the oral and artefactual cultural context that meaningfulness can only be attained through familiarity with that context. This is unlike Western textual and pictorial traditions whose techniques are such that the work's signifying potential can travel from context to context. For example, through alphabeticized phonetic script, and framing and representational conventions based on geometrical mathematical abstractions.
17. Bardon, *Papunya Tula*.
18. Fred Myers, *Painting Culture: the Making of an Aboriginal High Art* (Durham: Duke University Press, 2002).
19. Marie-Laure Ryan, "Will New Media Produce New Narratives?" in *Narrative Across Media: The Languages of Storytelling*, ed. Marie-Laure Ryan (London: University of Nebraska Press, 2004).
20. Turnbull, *Maps are Territories*, on Wittgenstein (1989).
21. Pierre Bourdieu, and Loïc Wacquant, "An Invitation to Reflexive Sociology," Chicago: University of Chicago Press, in *Bourdieu: A Critical Reader*, ed. Richard Shusterman (Oxford: Blackwell Publishers, 1999)
22. Bernadette Flynn, "The Morphology of Space in Virtual Heritage," in *Theorizing Digital Cultural Heritage: A Critical Discourse*, eds. Cameron and Kenderdine (Cambridge, Massachusetts: MIT Press, 2007).
23. Gonazo Frasca, Simulation 101: Simulation versus Representation, 2001. Retrieved April 1st, 2003, source: http://www.jacaranda.org/frasca/weblog/articles/sim1/simulation101d.html; Ryan, "Will New Media Produce New Narratives?"
24. Margaret Wertheim, *The pearly Gates of Cyberspace: A history of Space from Dante to the Internet* (Sydney: Doubleday, 1999).
25. Henry Jenkins, *Convergence Culture: where Old and New Media Collide* (New York: New York University Press, 2006).
26. Gonazo Frasca, "Simulation versus Narrative: Introduction to Ludology," in *The Video Game Theory Reader*, eds. Brian Perron and Mark Wolf (New York and London: Routledge, 2003).
27. Such a conundrum is not easily solved but the custodians are aware of this and see a higher priority at stake.
28. Charles Mountford, *The Aborigines and their Country* (Adelaide: Rigby, 1969).
29. Bardon, *Papunya Tula*.
30. Geoffrey Bardon, *Aboriginal Art of the Western Desert* (Adelaide: Rigby, 1979); Geoffrey Bardon and John Bardon, *Papunya: a place made after the story* (Australia: Miegunyah Press, 2004).
31. Brett Leavy, Theodor Wyeld, J. Hills, C. Barker and S. Gard, "Digital Songlines: Digitising the Arts, Culture and Heritage Landscape of Aboriginal Australia," in *New Heritage: New Media and Cultural Heritage*, eds. Yehuda Kalay, Thomas Kvan, and Janice Affleck (London/New York: Routledge, 2007).
32. Gonazo Frasca, Simulation 101: Simulation versus Representation.
33. Patrick Crogan, *Gameplay Mode: Between War, Simulation and Technoculture* (Minnesota: Minnesota University Press, 2008). See book for Crogan's expansion upon Stiegler's (1998) concept. Bernard Stiegler, *Technics and Time 1: The Fault of Epimetheus*, trans. Richard Beardsworth and George Collins (Stanford: Stanford University Press, 1998[1994]).

34. Lev Manovich, The Language of New Media (Massachusetts: MIT Press, 2001); Paul Virilio, *War and Cinema: The Logistics of Perception*, trans. Patrick Camiller (London: Verso, 1989).
35. Lev Manovich, "The Mapping of Space: Perspective, Radar, and 3-D Computer Graphics," 1993. Rertrieved May 20, 2000 from http://jupiter.ucsd.edu/~manovich/text/mapping.html.
36. Manovich, "The Mapping of Space."
37. Jacques Derrida, "'Above All, No Journalists!'" in *Religion and Media*, eds. Hent de Vries and Samuel Weber (Stanford: Stanford University Press, 2001).
38. Marshall, Eric McLuhan and Frank Zingrone, eds., *Essential McLuhan*, (London: Routledge, 1997).

12 Sticky Games and Hybrid Worlds

A Post-Phenomenology of Mobile Phones, Mobile Gaming and the iPhone

Ingrid Richardson

Mobile and handheld gaming presents a complex interplay of cultural, contextual and corporeal factors. The mobile phone and handheld game device are simultaneously—and often equally—acoustic, visual and haptic mediums. The mobile screen is now populated by data menus and files, scrolling text, web pages, word and image software, still photographs and video, animations, casual and hardcore online and offline games, virtual objects overlaying actual environments and other transformations brought about by third (3G) and fourth generation (4G) technologies and networks. Such portable media devices are becoming increasingly sophisticated, and should be examined in their own right as nascent new media forms. While the mobile phone is perhaps the most significant technology in the context of mobile converged technologies, it is part of a more general trend towards wearable, handheld and pocket communications and entertainment media.

Aside from the smartphone, mp3 player and PDA, there exist a number of handheld interactive media devices including Nintendo's GameBoy, DS (dual screen) and DSi (with camera functionality and playback capability), Sony's PlayStation Portable (PSP), and phone-game hybrids such as Nokia's N-Gage QD. More recently, it has been suggested that the introduction of Apple's 3G iPhone may potentially transform mobile game-play, with the release of the Software Development Kit (SDK) for iPhone game/application developers, combined with the handset's innovative touchscreen, real-time 3-D and accelerometer features.

In this chapter, I will investigate existing mobile game-play practices based on insights gained from two case studies[1] that took place in Perth and Melbourne, Australia, in April and July 2008, and weekly interactions with a group of 32 game students at Murdoch University, Western Australia. In particular, I will focus on the cultural and phenomenological, or *socio-somatic*, aspects of mobile gaming, seeking to provide some critical insights into the way mobile devices and smartphones impact upon our experience of embodiment in culturally specific ways. Smartphones (such as the iPhone) offer advanced capabilities such as Internet access, media software, a keyboard and open operating system. They mark a significant shift away from the "phonic" functionalities of the mobile phone, resulting in a correlative modification to the human-technology and embodiment relations specific to mobile interfaces. It is this change, in the context of mobile gaming, which is the focus of this chapter. Throughout the chapter I also offer a somewhat speculative exploration of the 3G iPhone as a "serious" mobile game console that may potentially bridge the gap between the mobile phone and more dedicated handheld game devices such as the DS and PSP.[2] In particular, I examine the potential cultural and corporeal effects of the iPhone, and some of the implications of iPhone gaming for our embodied and spatial engagement as they relate to mobile game-play.

IDIOSYNCRASIES OF THE MOBILE USER

Although there might appear to be certain commonalities in the practices of mobile gaming, we also need to attend to the cultural, corporeal and technical specificities of mobile game-play, and moreover, consider the wide-ranging idiosyncrasies in the individual take-up of mobile media and games. As Dean Chan notes, the "micronarratives" associated with new interfaces "need to be incorporated into macroperspectives on convergence culture if only to invest the latter with additional levels of nuance and complexity."[3] The participants in the April 2008 case study, for example, indicated that they rarely if ever used their mobile phones for web-browsing, chat and emailing, contrary to studies of mobile phone use in Japan which show that a majority of young people regularly access the web with their phones "either as their only access point or as complements to PC-based access."[4] Similarly, Mizuko Ito states that "[w]ith the majority of Japanese accessing the Internet through mobile phones . . . computer and TV screens are no longer privileged access points to the virtual and the networked world."[5]

In the April 2008 study, most respondents stated that they either did not know or had "never bothered" to find out how to access the web on their phone or use GPS functionality. Those who did use the web functions of their phones did so sporadically and usually did not venture beyond the services available through their provider's portal. Only two of the participants were what might be regarded as expert users, fully aware of the capabilities of their handset and able to use it proficiently and regularly as a cross-platform device. This is despite the fact that the majority of our sample purchased, or were given, their first mobile phone between the ages of 10 and 14. This disinclination to access the web via the mobile phone is partly attributable to the perception that such activity was likely to incur costs that the respondents were unable to sustain, and also because they were uniformly unfamiliar with the details of data packaging costs associated with their phone plan.

It was also the case that the physical limitations and material contours of available handsets, particularly the small size of the screen, resulted in poor ergonomic conditions for web access. Reluctance to access the mobile web has significant implications for mobile game-play, both because it prevents the practice of downloading casual games directly to the mobile phone, and prohibits engagement in online multiplayer and cross-platform location-based gaming. As I will suggest, however, the launch of the iPhone in Australia may reconfigure our mobile web practices.

As Amanda Third and I proposed in our ethnographic analysis of young people's use of the mobile phone as a technology of convergence, the proliferation of functionalities in mobile handsets is paralleled by highly idiosyncratic usage patterns,[6] findings that are also echoed in Gitte Stald's recent investigation of mobile phones and identity among Danish young people.[7] That is, tracking our sample of young users highlighted the way that mobile media practices are far from predictable and uniform; rather, the young people in our study incorporated mobile handsets into their everyday lives in ways that were intensely individualized. As Leopoldina Fortunati suggests, the mobile phone is both multiform and multifunctional, an "open work" requiring a complex range of hermeneutic skills on the part of the user, and also highly mutable because "it is held very close to the body or stays on the body surface."[8] Indeed, the descriptive trope of the mobile phone as a "body-part" is common, as evidenced in a number of studies.[9] Similarly, many of our April 2008 case study participants experienced the loss of their mobile phone as analogous to the amputation of a limb—one respondent stated "it's like having your arm cut off."

In this context, and turning towards a more phenomenological interpretation, to Chan's focus on the "micro" and the need to "cultivate contextual knowledge"[10] surrounding mobile games and mobile media use within the broader global context, I would add both *micro/macro-perceptions* and *micro/macro-mobilities* to the analysis of mobile gaming. The first couplet refers to the sensory minutiae—haptic, auditory, visual and spatial—that we individually and collectively experience through our use of mobile devices, and to the ways in which mobile gaming impacts upon our broader spatial and environmental perceptions. The second couplet, borrowed from Kenton O'Hara et al.'s analysis of videophoning, refers respectively to the small and "handy" motor movements such as those required to orient the mobile screen or use the number pad, and to the "larger" full-bodied or pedestrian actions such as walking while talking, texting or gaming.[11] In addition, as I will suggest in the context of the iPhone, the specificities of mobile platforms and interfaces must also be accounted for, including the way in which the technical aspects of mobile devices traverse and effect our everyday experiences and modes of embodiment. That is, in an environment of multiplying handsets and frequently upgraded portable game consoles it is salient to examine the perceptual specificity of our interactions with and experiences of such devices, and the ways in which particular games (casual, location-based, hybrid, online, discrete, etc) reflect different relationships between users, handsets, content, the physical and socio-cultural environment, and spatial and corporeal circumstance.

CONVERGENCE, DIVERGENCE AND THE
PHENOMENOLOGY OF MOBILE MEDIA

As I have argued elsewhere[12] considering mobile phones and media in terms of their own specific corporeal and cultural effects implicitly assumes the much-used media theory concept of medium specificity. Although some might question whether medium specificity is still a central concept at a time of digital convergence, multi- and cross-platform media, I suggest that each interface (and even experiencing different kinds of services and content within the one apparatus) can be interpreted in terms of specificity. Mobile media interfaces—or more precisely, for the purposes of this chapter, the increasing array of third generation handsets and smartphones that enable online and offline gaming—can be critically understood as complex and divergent instantiations of new media forms, each demanding a particular mode of embodied interaction. That is, when previously discrete media functionalities come together and are mobilized—in newer model mobile phones, for example, this may include the telephone, digital camera, television, Internet and casual gaming—what emerges is not a single all-purpose device but a seemingly endless iteration of handsets with varying capabilities and design features, each prioritizing a specific *techno-somatic* arrangement. Literally, I use this term to connote the irreducible relation between human bodies and technologies—what Mark Hansen[13] refers to as the "originary technicity" of the human, and Don Ihde[14] terms the human-technology relation—our fundamental ontological condition.[15] For example, as I will suggest, in its deployment of a multi-touch interface, accelerometer, GPS, real-time 3-D graphics, and 3-D positional audio, the iPhone demands a unique *corporealization* of game-play. Moreover, in enabling game and application developers to create and upload their own creations into the App Store,[16] there is potential for significant innovation and variation in terms of the technosomatic skills required by the gamer.

Yet this is not to say that the term convergence holds no validity; rather we can work towards a more nuanced or flexible understanding of the relation between convergence and medium specificity. For Henry Jenkins convergence is a term that broadly describes technological, industrial, cultural and social changes, and the complex interaction between old and new media.[17] That is, it conveys how consumers "make connections among dispersed media content"[18] such that one technology or interface is used to provide many services, or many interfaces provide access to the same content/service.[19] Thus convergence is a dynamic *process* that is fundamentally unstable, wherein divergent modes of engaging with the same or similar content (such as playing a *Crash Bandicoot* game on your laptop or desktop computer, iPhone or smartphone, Nintendo DS or game console in single or multiplayer mode) intersect in complex ways with a range of services or applications (both official and unofficial). Indeed, the remediation of older forms of media into newer and mobile devices is a process of dynamic interplay between medium specificity and convergence, complexly embedded in the usability and intuitiveness of the interface. My particular interest in this chapter is how this interplay and usability is manifested in terms of the cultural context and embodiment of users, an interpretation carried out primarily via a phenomenological and post-phenomenological approach.

Maurice Merleau-Ponty famously claimed that the body "applies itself to space like a hand to an instrument,"[20] an "application" that depends as much on the specificities of perception and bodily movement as it does on the materiality of the tool-in-use. In his well-known description of the blind man and his stick, Merleau-Ponty describes how the corporeal schema of the body dilates and retracts to accommodate tools:

> The blind man's stick has ceased to be an object for him and is no longer perceived for itself; its point has become an area of sensitivity, extending the scope and active radius of touch and providing a parallel to sight. In the exploration of things, the length of the stick does not enter expressively as a middle term: The blind man is aware of it through the position of objects rather than of the position of objects through it. The position of things is immediately given through the extent of the reach that carries him to it, which comprises, besides the arm's reach, the stick's range of action.[21]

This quote describes the actuality of what Merleau-Ponty refers to as our corporeal or body *schema*, which is not determined by the boundaries of the material body but rather reflects the way that our corporeality extends and withdraws—changing its very reach and shape—in its dynamic apprehension of tools and things in the world. Merleau-Ponty argued that this schematic is inherently open, allowing us to incorporate technologies and equipment into our own perceptual and corporeal organization. Indeed it could be argued that the corporeal schema is just another name for Hansen's "originary technicity." Or, as Martin Heidegger[22] claimed, our being is always-already situated within domains of equipment—so there is a direct and implicatory relation between the tools/technologies we use and the way we "have" a body.

There is thus a kind of anticipatory mobilization of the body in relation to any specific situation and environment, an "entering into a relationship" with the world.[23] The variable and relational ontology that is embodiment emerges through a network of extended relations between the body-subject and the equipmental environment. Subsequent theorists such as Don Ihde[24] and David Morris[25] have complexified this body-tool relation by including the nuances of personal practices and cultural specificity. Ihde's post-phenomenological approach focuses on the body-technology relations that emerge from particular cultural milieus and collective habits, and the way in which various technologies "transfer" asymmetrically across cultures. Similarly, Morris argues that the dynamics of perception "are not anchored in a fixed, objective framework, they are intrinsic to the situation of perception, and can differ across individuals, habits, and social setting."[26] This kind of analysis, which embeds cultural, historical and gender specificity into our relational ontologies, has also been the particular focus of corporeal feminists such as Gail Weiss[27] and cultural phenomenologists such as Thomas Csordas[28] and others. In these terms we can see how the cultural and technological specificity of media interfaces and apparatuses can be understood as deeply integral to our individual and collectively realized corporeal schemata. Indeed, considering the number of hours that many people spend engaging with media in contemporary life, the body-screen relation in particular may be one of our most significant human-technology relations.

Phenomenology is an apt method of analysis as it counters the notion that *dis*embodiment is a condition of using the Internet or the phone, is able to consider the ways that tele-technologies modify the body, and the kind of embodiment afforded by telepresent and mobile media. Mobile devices clearly antagonize any notion of a disembodied telepresence that is seemingly endemic to screen media, as we are frequently on-the-move, on-the-street and purposefully situated in local spaces and places when engaged in mobile phone use and mobile game-play. While recognizing the "distancings" or alterations to somatic involvement that may inhere in such practices, mobile phone "being" is nevertheless very much embodied, motile, mobile and *in*-the-world.

Within this theoretical framework, I consider both our corporeal relation to mobile phones, and how mobile game-play in both urban and domestic places evokes particular kinds of embodiment, indicative of emergent habitual and quotidian behaviors, gesturings, positionings and choreographies of the body, at times partially determined by the culture of the user, at others by the technical specificities and demands of the interface. For example, Chan cites a public survey taken in 2006 which found that for most Japanese casual mobile games are played in their bedroom or in the home, suggesting that mobile games are often engaged with in non-mobile, sometimes private and "sedentary domestic contexts."[29] Of the 21 female students surveyed in July 2008 at RMIT and Murdoch University in Australia, the 11 that played casual mobile games most often did so while waiting for friends in public places or while traveling on public transport, revealing how the mobile game becomes co-opted by the "body-in-waiting," in situations of solitary co-presence. In terms of *micro-mobilities*, three of the four Murdoch University game students who owned iPhones at the time of writing, claimed that with previous mobile phones they only occasionally played casual games on public transport or while waiting for someone, and rarely in the domestic context, but yet they often played iPhone games at home; many iPhone games, they commented, required more dedicated attention, and games that utilized the accelerometer demanded a "noticeable" or "obvious" orientation and movement of the hands, arms and upper body which was at times somewhat embarrassing in public places. Such specificities of use reveal a quite complex range of cultural deployments of, and corporeal attachments to, the mobile game device. In what follows I will provide a post-phenomenological analysis of several aspects of mobile gaming: our corporeal attachment to the mobile game screen, and our experience of the mobile game and mobile media device as, respectively, microworld and technology of "containment."

STICKY GAMES AND HAPTIC SCREENS

Mobile phone use and mobile gaming is often characterized as a mode of engagement that requires only sporadic attention up to a threshold of around five minutes (hence the popular notion that casual games are the mobile phone's predominant game genre). With this understanding, in a previous article I argued that gameplay on the mobile phone was quite unlike conventional computer, portable console or video game-play:

> [E]ven in the seemingly committed practice of game-play, mobile phone engagement is characterised by interruption, and sporadic or split attention in the midst of other activities, a behavior quite distinct even from handheld console game-play on the Nintendo DualScreen (DS) or PlayStation Portable (PSP). This is recognized by the growing mobile phone game industry and its labelling of a key market as 'casual gamers,' who play at most for five minutes at a time and at irregular intervals; it seems mobile phone gamers don't want immersion. [30]

As a way to interpret the mode of attachment particular to mobile gaming, I considered Chris Chesher's categorization of "ways of looking" specific to cinema, television and console games—characterized by the gaze, the glance and the glaze respectively[31]—and suggested that the ill fit of mobile phone conventions of viewing within this schema highlights the need to theorize a cross-modal and medium specific taxonomy of vision specific to both game and nongame use of portable micro-screens. In fact, the mobile phone device crosses over each of these ways of looking if only because we can—and do—watch movies and live TV, and play games on our phones at varying levels of immersion and distraction. Chesher suggests that console games are "sticky," holding the player to the screen via both a quasi-visceral immersion in the depth-perspective of virtual space, and a haptic attachment to the hand-controller and peripherals: "In glazespace [players] suspend their awareness of their day-to-day world to become cybernetically suspended within a virtualized sensorimotor space of the game world."[32] Casual gamers, on the other hand, must deliberately avoid this "stickiness" so that they are perpetually ready to resume their temporarily interrupted activities.

Yet in phenomenological terms, this analysis does not fit comfortably with the experience of playing iPhone games that utilize the accelerometer and touchscreen. Such game play demands a multi-sensory engagement, perhaps more akin to the stickiness of console gaming in Chris Chesher's terms, or at least comparable to DS and PSP game-play.[33] That is, traditional console and computer games (adventure, racing, first-person shooter, etc.) played on the iPhone (for example, *Mario Racing* or *Nitro-Cart*), demand a corporeal attachment that necessitates an adroit oscillation between "glaze-space" and attentiveness to one's spatial surroundings. In this way, the iPhone screen could be said to challenge the perception of mobile games as predominantly casual or *nagara* games (i.e., played while doing something else), recuperating some of the "stickiness" and immersion proper to console games played on a television or computer screen. Or, at least, we might identify a broad spectrum of attachment across a range of game-play—from casual games to console-based games—based upon levels of immersion, engagement and distraction.

As Jacob et al., observe, the immersive or sticky qualities of the iPhone and similar graphical user interfaces are enhanced by employing "physical metaphors that add the illusion of gravity, mass, rigidity, springiness, and inertia to graphical widgets."[34] Such illusory physical metaphors, deployed in a number of iPhone applications and games, are reliant on the supposition that user-interaction works most effectively and deeply when multiple sensory engagement is required. Malcolm McCullough argued in *Abstracting Craft: The Practiced Digital Hand* that our deepest engagement is through touch."[35] Such a view is prevalent in both game design and the game industry more broadly, and echoed in Nintendo's labeling of the Touch Generation, which includes anyone aged between 8 and 80 under the assumption that we are all frequent users of touchscreen interfaces, whether via Automatic Teller Machines (ATMs) or the vastly more composite mobile phone touchscreen. The iPhone is specifically created for use with the finger or fingers for multi-touch sensing, and because the screen is a "capacitive" touchscreen, it depends upon electrical conductivity that can only be provided by bare skin.[36] Moreover, the iPhone screen can track the movement of five fingers simultaneously; in a keynote speech on game development for the iPhone, Freeverse game designer Justin Ficarotta stated: "Several touches can be combined into gestures . . . Drags, swipes, flicks, pinches, with a variable number of fingers . . . It's very different from what we're used to with mainstream games".[37]

Jacob et al. coin the term "Reality-Based Interaction" to classify post-WIMP[38] interfaces such as the iPhone which rely on a corporeal schema that has several defining features: a somatic and visceral understanding naïve physics, an awareness of the proprioceptive capacities of one's own body, an understanding of the spatial arrangement of the physical environment, and a complex awareness of other people.[39] For example, naïve physics "in the form of inertia and springiness" can be found in most iPhone's applications, and provide the illusion that windows, objects and icons on the device have mass.[40] Naïve physics can also include our body-memory of hardware such as the keyboard and joystick that are simulated in the iPhone GUI. Yet despite the use of intuitive and reality-based interaction, in achieving skillful dexterity with the iPhone touchscreen we are compelled to develop a new visual and haptic literacy; the touchscreen thus adds to the complexity of the eyes-hands-screen circuit, and the incorporative (and dis-incorporative) "fit" between the mobile device and the hand/eye body. As one game student observed, playing games on the iPhone was "like learning to use a new hand controller," or discerning a new relationship between the hand, device and visual perception.

Indeed, a notable aspect of the embodiment of mobile phones and screens in general is the manner in which what is seen on the screen is tangibly and contingently dependent on the hand's movement and dexterity. In her work on the biomechanical relationship between the hand and mobile screen device (MSD), Heidi Rae Cooley describes the tactile vision demanded by mobile screens as a "material and dynamic seeing involving eyes as well as hands and MSD."[41] Thus there is a certain intimacy with the mobile phone that renders it an object of tactile and kinaesthetic familiarity, a sensory knowing-ness of the fingers that correlates with what appears on the small screen. This is nowhere better exemplified than in iPhone games that depend on reality-based interaction which enfold the player into a temporary and incomplete simulation of real-world physics. The reality-based features of the iPhone (the Multi-Touch interface, the accelerometer, GPS, real-time 3-D graphics, and 3-D positional audio) are deployed in a number of racing games where the iPhone device simulates a steering wheel, and in games such as *MonkeyBall*, which requires the player to tilt the screen on a horizontal plane to control the movement of the ball through various obstacles and gradients.

Yet in the process of appropriating touchscreens such as the iPhone as a "fresh instrument" (*pace* Merleau-Ponty), sometimes the "fit" between mobile touchscreens and our corporeal schemata is noticeably imperfect, resulting in often idiosyncratic and spur-of-the-moment adaptation to the touchscreen in an attempt to overcome the initial sensory dis-incorporation of the device. The lack of tactile feedback on the iPhone, for example, means "players can't tell when their fingers have slipped or 'how far' they are 'pushing' the joystick button."[42] In addition, the accelerometer itself lacks the acuity of the analog stick used with console game hand controllers, resulting in "lots of random data" and imprecise control of both objects within the game and the game-space itself.[43] In the case of the iPhone, then, "fit" must accommodate a range of new micro-mobilities that have to be either learned or remembered. When playing games on mobile touchscreens such as the DS and iPhone, for example, we can bring to the experience our haptic familiarity with other modes of non-mobile gaming, and as suggested in the case of the iPhone, recuperate some of the immersive and sticky qualities of both portable and domestic console games. An interesting corollary here is that the "noticeable" bodily movements associated with some iPhone games means that solitary or domestically-situated play may be preferred (as indicated by several of the game students I interviewed) until the game-player adapts to more economical motor movements and constrained micro-mobilities. Such adaptation is evident in the way Nintendo Wii game-players "learn" to replace generous movement of the body—standing up and swinging the arm in a bowling game, for example—with more somatically efficient flicks of the wrist while sitting down.

In this section, I have considered the sensory engagement particular to game-play on mobile phone screens, and the haptic literacy required for post-WIMP interfaces such as the iPhone. In the following section, I focus on another aspect of our embodiment of the mobile phone, exploring the way in which we variably perceive of the mobile phone in terms of metaphors of containment, and the way in which mobile gaming and the iPhone trouble these perceptions and corporealizations.

ENFOLDING AND CONTAINMENT: METAPHORS OF THE MOBILE

The use of the mobile phone as a portable, personal, safe and always-accessible data archive carried on the body indicates both how the mobile phone is appropriated as a pocket microworld or *container*, and the way "discrete" mobile gaming works to provide a "cocooning" effect when in public. As Michael Bull notes, the "mediated isolation"—a mode of non-communicative co-presence when one is "alone" in public—enabled by devices such as the mobile phone and mp3 player "becomes a form of control over spaces of urban culture in which we withdraw into a world small enough to control."[44] In such contexts, casual gaming and "noodling" with one's phone in public places allows us to "fill gaps or empty moments with a precise rituality."[45] The transient and non-dedicated attentiveness required by the small screen and casual game—you can "switch off" but "not totally" as one April 2008 case study respondent observed—allows the user to both remain alert to the "arrival" which marks the end of waiting, yet able to avert their gaze from others and so cooperate in the tacit social agreement of non-interaction among strangers. For some of the respondents in the July 2008 survey, this kind of engagement with the mobile screen provided a means of safe seclusion from unwelcome interaction in potentially risky situations of co-present waiting, yet allowed them to remain "open" or attentive to the proximity of that risk. One commented, for example, that mobile game play enabled her to avoid eye contact with "drunks and weirdos." As noted above, this strategic and frequent deployment of casual gaming in public places differs somewhat from findings in Japan, where casual games are more often played in sedentary domestic contexts.[46]

In pondering the social-cultural effects of the mobile phone in his aptly named paper "The Mutable Mobile," Geoff Cooper comments that the mobile phone is an indiscrete technology.[47] Indeed, no networkable or online digital device is "discrete" or containable in a communicative sense and, in phenomenological terms, no material object in-the-world is extricable from our somatic involvement. Yet the respondents in both Australian studies cited in this chapter nevertheless often referred to the spatial and ontological boundaries of both their mobile devices and their perceptual experience of mobile phone use. In particular, in the April 2008 study participants often expressed a desire to configure their mobile phones as contained in some way—whether as a personal photo and SMS archive, in terms of putting in place personal boundaries between private and public life, as a way of managing connectivity with their friends and family, or as noted above, as a way of "cocooning" oneself from strangers in public places. Thus, participants often described their phones as containing "my whole life," or as a material object that held a dynamic array of textual and image content that could not be "invaded" by others. Indeed, techno-mediated spaces such as televisual, computational and game spaces are dominated by this metaphor of containment, and our ability to enter or be *in* these spaces is predicated on a perceptual and corporeal assimilation of this metaphor. In what follows, I will first consider metaphors of technological containment more generally, and then suggest how mobile game-play complexifies, reinforces and contradicts these tropes.

In trying to establish a critical understanding of the relation between human embodiment and our experience of media interfaces, the work of Lakoff and Johnson[48] offers an insightful take on the "container" metaphor. For them our experience of the world is mediated through our bodies and the fact that we are "bounded" beings, thus experiencing ourselves as containers. They write:

> We are physical beings, bounded and set off from the rest of the world by the surface of our skins, and we experience the rest of the world as outside us. Each of us is a container, with a bounding surface and an in-out orientation. We project our own in-out orientation onto other physical objects . . . view[ing] them as containers with an inside and an outside.[49]

Our everyday experience of material things—the fact that we "bump up" against objects in the world through vision, haptic, aural and olfactory sensory involvement—means that we learn to treat objects and substances as variably contained and discrete entities, and to ascribe these qualities to seemingly abstract or uncontainable things like feelings and minds, and to digital and data spaces.

In her theorization of the material and metaphorical characteristics of "container technologies," Zoë Sofia[50] argues that containment is an important theme in our use and experience of tools and technologies. In the contemporary context, the notion of information flows that are contained by conduits, popular cultural notions of cyberspace and the matrix, and the everyday use of information technologies like computers and mobiles as housing for information, all render technology as container, particularly in terms of storage/memory, access, supply, distribution and archive. As Sofia observes:

> Books, photograph albums, telephone directories, the television, the stereo, cassettes and CDs: all these media technologies . . . [have] their container-like aspects. [E]lectronic and print media are storage technologies for other spaces and experiences: a CD or tape can open up a whole concert . . . ; a book can disclose another world.[51]

Techno-mediated spaces such as televisions, computers, game devices and mobile phones are dominated by metaphors of containment, and our ability to enter or be telepresent in these spaces is predicated on a perceptual and corporeal assimilation of such metaphors. Touchscreen phones such as the iPhone add another haptic dimension to this assimilation, as we can literally press the surface of the mobile device to manipulate, visually and acoustically, that which "presents" itself on the screen. The accelerometer feature in iPhone games such as Backgammon also allows the player to "shake" the phone to simulate a roll of the die, conveying the sense that the device itself contains moving objects that virtually replicate real-world physics.

Indeed, we are quite well attuned to the notion that mobile phones are containers. The Motorola Razr advertisement broadcast in Australia in 2005 very effectively captured our collective understanding of the mobile phone as a device of containment. The ad depicted a woman seated alone in a domestic loungeroom in which there were several state-of-the-art digital interfaces such as a laptop and flat-screen panel; the walls and furniture fold origami-like into each other, and finally they and the rest of the world collapse into an open flip-top Razr that comes to rest on the woman's hand. The woman, surrounded only by a white void, smugly snaps the phone shut, demonstrating both the safe and handy containment of her environment, and the simultaneous control she has over both actual and data worlds. Although somewhat overstated, this containment of a world within the mobile phone is a common experience of both expert and everyday users; interviewees in the April 2008 study frequently referred to their phones as microcosms of their lives, far exceeding the containment capacities of wallets and handbags. Similarly, in a more recent telecommunications advertisement broadcast in Australia in September and October 2008, a young man prepares to leave his home and on his way folds his TV, DVD player, laptop, books, CD collection, world map (and, finally, his sleeping girlfriend), into his pocket as if each item represents a smart feature of his mobile phone, securely enclosed yet dynamically and always accessible.

Yet we can look at this tendency to "contain," effected by the transference of our sense of bodily integrity to objects in-the-world, in a more nuanced way. Rather than presuming that we are uniformly attempting to turn the world into a set of discrete objects because that is what we ourselves—as bodies—are, it seems equally viable to suggest that our ability to apprehend "things" at all is due to the fact that we can somewhat paradoxically—yet unproblematically—ascribe containment or entity characteristics to things that often *don't* have (and can never have) distinct or locatable boundaries. This is the case in the material realm, for example when attempting to mark out one's "personal" space, and also in a non-material sense (which is always-already grounded in our corporeality), when we say we are "entering" game-spaces, telepresent environments or immersive virtual worlds, or attributing microworldly properties to actual devices and hardware. Here, we can know that the boundaries are approximate, arbitrary, temporary, virtual or perpetually unrealizable, yet despite (or because of) this we can suspend disbelief and reconcile our experience of a space or entity "as if" it is a container of some kind. It is thus the plastic flexibility of our conceptualization of things and boundaries—and the phenomenological experience of our corporeal schemas as extendible and mutable *qua* tools and objects—that has enabled and sustained the container trope. This knowing ignorance accounts for our experience of the mobile phone as a data-container—we know that the device does not contain things in any macro-physical sense, and that it is not a temporally or spatially coherent place, but this does not prevent us from loosely apprehending it as such.

The satisfying appeal of the Razr ad lies in this "as if" structure of perception, such that we can both understand and desire, yet know the impossibility of achieving, a neat and foldable being-in-the-world. Participants in the April 2008 case study frequently referred quite paradoxically to their phones as personal worlds or "microworlds," yet at the same time voiced concern over their uncontainability: An impulsive SMS once sent could not be retrieved or controlled; it was not always possible to protect one's phone content from a nosy friend or partner; and every participant had experienced the discomfort of their phone's ringtone noisily invading a public soundscape. Mobile phones and handheld devices, then, work as both "handy" or pocket containers of data, media content, and photos, but also as leaky communicative conduits. On the one hand, participants in the study often paid particular (though varying) attention to the on-going maintenance or house-keeping of their mobile dataspaces, routinely scrolling through and deleting SMS messages on a daily, weekly or less frequent basis, or uploading photographs and video onto their computers. Yet over half of our participants also spoke of their concern that texting was always—potentially at least—a risky practice, and were careful to neither store nor send messages that might "incriminate" them. The flexible and paradoxical experience of the mobile phone as both microworldly and uncontainable, I would argue, is made possible by a corporeal schema that is not simply experienced as container, but also concomitantly as both contained *and* extendible or uncontainable, and by an ability to hold these seemingly antagonistic experiences within the same corporeality. Indeed, this ability to embrace ambiguous spatial perceptions and modes of embodiment within one's corporeal schema, and to oscillate between, conflate and adapt to ostensibly disparate modes of being and perceiving, is precisely why telepresence, and hybrid, virtual spaces, are both somatically and ontologically tolerable.

The proliferation of mobile online activities—broadly via mobile phones, laptops, pagers, PDAs, MP3 players and other hand-helds—has also changed the way we think about being "on," "at" or "in" a simulated or computer space, and the way we think about being "on" or "off" line.[52] As Adriana de Souza e Silva argues: "Because many mobile devices are constantly connected to the Internet, as is the case of the i-mode standard in Japan (NTT DoCoMo, 2006) users do not perceive physical and digital spaces as separate entities and do not have the feeling of "entering" the Internet, or being immersed in digital spaces, as was generally the case when one needed to sit down in front of a computer screen and dial a connection."[53] Being online and networked thus becomes another function of the mobile phone, but it is importantly a *different* experience of the Internet and online connectivity: The supposedly dematerializing effects of cyberspace and telepresent interaction become enfolded inside present contexts, at best scattered moments amidst an array of other micro- and macromobilities, like the embodied and itinerant acts of walking, driving, face-to-face communication and numerous other material and somatic involvements.[54]

Although currently Australian mobile phone users utilize their mobile phone as a web-capable device less frequently than in countries such as Japan and Korea, the launch of the iPhone in Australia may significantly change these practices; that is, the experience of the mobile web, along with changing perceptions of being "online" and "offline" noted above, may well become more habitual and commonplace. As Chan notes, "packet fees" (charging by the packet, which is equivalent to 128 bytes) are an obstacle to mobile web-browsing, downloading and mobile location-based and casual gaming.[55] Significantly, in Australia the arrival of the 3G iPhone was accompanied by competitive "flat-rate" data packages, and thus may radically shift the mobile web practices of Australian users. Statistics gleaned from a survey of 10,000 iPhone users in the United States show marked differences between iPhone web-use and non-iPhone web-use, largely attributed to AT&T's unlimited data plan for iPhone users.[56]

In this shifting context, it is worth considering the domain of location-based and hybrid reality gaming that combines web and mobile functionality, and the way in which such gaming practices counter both the perception of mobile devices as discrete containers, and the correlative experience of games as enclosed microworlds. Location-based gaming (LBG) ventures such as *Mogi*[57] in Japan have had at least partial success among a tech-savvy population living in the densely populated urban setting of Tokyo, creating a pedestrian gamer who integrates their game-play with their everyday trajectories through the city as they hunt and trade virtual objects, and message one of a thousand other active users; such gaming enacts a fascinating palimpsest of macro- and micro- perceptions and mobilities. The players of *Mogi* quite often alter their passage through the city, dynamically reworking the spatial order and macro-perceptual experience of familiar and unfamiliar urban space. A frequent player of the game describes how his trips to the city became physically "randomized" or diverted as an effect of the game, such that he "got a chance to discover part of the city that I ignored, [motivated] to check out that parallel street I never took."[58] Social designer of networked environments Amy Jo Kim suggests that *Mogi* is ideally suited to the casual gamer: "It nestles in your everyday life, rather than requiring you to change your behavior . . . It amplifies your ordinary behavior—it changes going on an errand into a piece of a game."[59] Such "mixed-reality" games, rather than creating an escape from "real life" through sticky screen immersion, work to integrate play and game interaction into the patterns of everyday life and work. In speaking of his own vision for the potential of such games, LBG creator John Paul Bichard imagines a future scenario where the physical environment itself becomes a "vast game engine," and objects, places and people "part of an intertwining series of episodes."[60]

Cipher Cities presents a quite different instantiation of location-based gaming. Recently launched in Australia, *Cipher Cities*[61] is a Brisbane-based project that enables global users to build, share and play both non-located and location-based games. "Citizens" can join one of a dozen or so user-generated location-based games with designated "play areas" of varying sizes (some are by invitation only and currently all are located in the city of Brisbane), or are encouraged to build a do-it-yourself mobile adventure in their own neighborhood or familiar streetscape using a web-based authoring tool. The games of *Cipher Cities* are thus of a lesser geo-spatial and macro-perceptual scale than *Mogi*, sometimes exclusive and restricted to a select group of people, and depend largely on the individual and collaborative creativity and local knowledge of its user-participants. Both games, however, create a network or connective sensibility in which the mobile phone, web, community of participants and built environment coalesce. Location-based and next-generation mobile phone games thus potentially work to seamlessly combine the corporeal schematics of actual and virtual worlds as they are actively negotiated on-the-move, effectively creating a hybrid mode of being where the boundary between imaginary and real life collapses, and the microworldly containment attributes of both mobile media device and gameworld are effectively disassembled.

CONCLUSION

In this chapter I have offered a phenomenology of mobile phone use, focusing on the embodiment of handheld screen devices as hybridized new media and game interfaces. In particular, I have considered some of the cultural, corporeal and technical specificities of mobile phones and mobile gaming based on insights gained from research located in the Australian context, and speculated on the potential impact of the iPhone upon our individual and collective embodiment of game-play. In sum, I have suggested that the apprehension of mobile phone screens into our corporeal schemata is not uniform, and that in the perceptual and cultural literacy specific to the mobile phone, the modalities of mobile gaming—casual, immersive, post-WIMP and reality-based, online and offline—each have their own intra-mediatic demands upon our perception and embodiment. As exemplified by the practices of mobile gaming, the mobile phone requires an ever-evolving sensibility, of which our corporeal schematas, in their ontic and relational flexibility, are inherently and essentially capable.

NOTES

1. The first case study was carried out with Amanda Third (Murdoch University) as part of a larger study on 'Moblogging and Belonging' funded by the Telstra Foundation, Australia. We aimed to document and evaluate how young Australian people use their mobile phones in the contexts of their everyday lives, along with the range of attitudes they hold towards mobile phone technologies. We undertook half hour semi-structured interviews with 25 project participants aged 18–24 in which we asked each participant to talk about how, when and where they used their mobile phone and to show us examples of their usage. In particular, we were interested in establishing how the mobile phone as a material artefact is implicated in shaping young people's mobile media practices, the various forms of materiality and corporeality that emerge from mobile media use, and more broadly, the spatial, perceptual and ontological effects of mobile media forms. An in-depth analysis will be published as a book chapter "The Material Culture of Mobile Media," co-authored with Amanda Third in *Material Culture and Technology in Everyday Life: Ethnographic Approaches,* ed. Phillip Vannini, Peter Lang Publishing (forthcoming 2009). The second case study was carried out with Larissa Hjorth, RMIT University, and sought (via surveys) to understand the mobile gaming and online practices of young women living in Melbourne (Victoria, Australia) and Perth (Western Australia). Findings will be published in an article titled "The waiting game: notions of (tele)presence and distraction in casual mobile gaming," in the *Australian Journal of Communication* (forthcoming).
2. Neil Young, former head of Electronic Arts Blueprint, announced in June 2008 the formation of Ngmoco, a new iPhone-focused studio, largely due to the development opportunities brought about by Apple's release of the SDK for game developers and the App Store, which enables game and application developers to create and upload (and sell) their own iPhone games, effectively "reinventing the relationship between developers and publishers of software and the customers themselves." Young claims that with the iPhone emerges a genre of mobile phones that cross "the threshold of usability that is really changing patterns of usage. . . . [F]rom a performance standpoint, [the iPhone] is pretty close to a PSP, but unlike the PSP, it's got a touchscreen, accelerometers, a camera, it's location-aware, it's got all of your media on it,

it's awake with you, it's always on, and it's always connected to the network. So if you think about the types of games and entertainment experiences that you can build on a platform like that, it's got to get pretty exciting pretty quickly." See Christian Nutt, "Q&A: EA Vet Young Reveals iPhone Publisher Ngmoco," *Gamasutra* (June 30, 2008) http://www.gamasutra.com/php-bin/news_index.php?story=19229.

3. Dean Chan, "Convergence, Connectivity, and the Case of Japanese Mobile Gaming," *Games and Culture* v1, n1 (2008): 13.
4. William H. Dutton et al. (2004) *Transforming Enterprise: The Economic and Social Implications of Information* (MIT Press, 2004), 480–481.
5. Mizuko Ito, "Technologies of Childhood Imagination: *Yu-Gi-Oh!*, Media Mixes, and Everyday Cultural Production," in *Structures of Participation in Digital Culture*, ed. Joe Karaganis (New York: Social Science Research Council, 2007): 97.
6. Ingrid Richardson and Amanda Third, "The Material Culture of Mobile Media," in *Material Culture and Technology in Everyday Life: Ethnographic Approaches*, ed. Phillip Vannini (New York: Peter Lang Publishing forthcoming).
7. Gitte Stald, "Mobile Identity: Youth, Identity, and Mobile Communication Media," in *Youth, Identity, and Digital Media* (The John D. and Catherine T. MacArthur Foundation Series on Digital Media and Learning), ed. David Buckingham (Cambridge, MA: The MIT Press, 2008), 143–164.
8. Leopoldina Fortunati, "The Mobile Phone as Technological Artefact," in *Thumb Culture: The Meaning of Mobile Phones for Society*, ed. Peter Glotz, Stefan Bertschi and Chris Locke (Bielefeld: transcript Verlag, 2005): 152–153, 156.
9. Larissa Hjorth, "Being mobile: in between the real and the reel," *Asian Pop and Mobile Cultures Conference, Asian Cultures Forum* (Gwangju, 2006): 9; Bella Ellwood-Clayton, "All we need is love—and a mobile phone: texting in the Philippines," *International Conference on Cultural Space and Public Sphere in Asia* (Seoul, Korea, 2006): 358.
10. Dean Chan, "Convergence, Connectivity, and the Case of Japanese Mobile Gaming," *Games and Culture* v1, n1 (2008): 17–18.
11. Kenton O'Hara, Alison Black and Matthew Lipson, "Everyday Practices with Mobile Video Telephony," in *CHI 2006 Proceedings, Everyday Use of Mobiles*, (Montréal, Québec, Canada, April 22–27, 2006).
12. Ingrid Richardson, "Mobile Technosoma: some phenomenological reflections on itinerant media devices," *Fibreculture* Issue 6. Retrieved October 20, 2007 from http://journal.fibreculture.org/issue6/issue6_richardson.html
13. Mark Hansen, *Bodies in Code: interfaces with digital media* (New York: Routledge, 2006): ix.
14. Don Ihde, *Technology and the Lifeworld: From Garden to Earth* (Bloomington: Indiana UP, 1990).
15. For a detailed description of the *technosoma*, see Ingrid Richardson, "Telebodies & Televisions: Corporeality and Agency in Technoculture," doctoral dissertation (University of Western Sydney, 2003). http://library.uws.edu.au/adt.phtml.
16. http://www.apple.com/au/iphone/appstore/.
17. Henry Jenkins, *Convergence Culture: Where Old and New Media Collide* (New York: NYU Press, 2006).
18. Henry Jenkins, *Convergence Culture: Where Old and New Media Collide* (New York: NYU Press, 2006): 3.

19. Interestingly, Jenkins documents how this dynamic process of convergence was predicted by Ithiel de Sola Pool in 1983 (Jenkins, 2006: 10).
20. Maurice Merleau-Ponty, *Signs* (Illinois: Northwestern University Press, 1964): 5.
21. Maurice Merleau-Ponty, *Signs* (Illinois: Northwestern University Press, 1964): 22.
22. Martin Heidegger, *The Question Concerning Technology and Other Essays* (New York: Garland Publishing, Inc., 1977).
23. Maurice Merleau-Ponty, *Phenomenology of Perception* (London: Routledge and Kegan Paul, 1962).
24. Don Ihde, *Postphenomenology: Essays in the Postmodern Context* (Evanston, Illinois: Northwestern UP, 1993).
25. David Morris, *The Sense of Space* (New York: SUNY Press, 2004).
26. David Morris, *The Sense of Space* (New York: SUNY Press, 2004) 23.
27. Gail Weiss, *Body Images: embodiment as intercorporeality* (New York: Routledge, 1999).
28. Thomas J. Csordas, "Embodiment and Cultural Phenomenology." 143–164 in *Perspectives on Embodiment: The Intersections of Nature and Culture*, eds. G. Weiss and H. F. Haber (New York: Routledge, 1999): 143–164.
29. Dean Chan, "Convergence, Connectivity, and the Case of Japanese Mobile Gaming," *Games and Culture* v1, n1 (2008): 23.
30. Ingrid Richardson, "Pocket Technospaces: The Bodily Incorporation of Mobile New Media," *Continuum: Journal of Media & Cultural Studies*, Vol. 21, No. 2 (June 2007), 205–215: 210.
31. Chris Chesher, "Neither gaze nor glance, but glaze: relating to console game screens," *SCAN: Journal of Media Arts Culture*, vol 1, no 1 (2004), http://scan.net.au/scan/journal/display.php?journal_id=19.
32. Chris Chesher, "Neither gaze nor glance, but glaze: relating to console game screens," *SCAN: Journal of Media Arts Culture*, vol 1, no 1 (2004), http://scan.net.au/scan/journal/display.php?journal_id=19.
33. Indeed, the iPhone has been touted as the Wii of mobile gaming, and as a device that competes with the Nintendo DS and PSP. See Steven Johnson, "Games and the iPhone," *stevenberlinjohnson.com* (6 March 2008) http://www.stevenberlinjohnson.com/2008/03/games-an-the-i.html.
34. Robert J.K. Jacob, Audrey Girouard, Leanne M. Hirshfield, Michael S. Horn, Orit Shaer, Erin Treacy Solovey and Jamie Zigelbaum, "Reality-Based Interaction: A Framework for Post-WIMP Interfaces," in *CHI 2008 Proceedings · Post-WIMP* (Florence, Italy: April 5–10, 2008): 202.
35. Malcolm McCullough, *Abstracting Craft: The Practiced Digital Hand* (Cambridge, Mass.: MIT Press, 1996).
36. http://en.wikipedia.org/wiki/iPhone.
37. Jill Duffy, "iPhone Game Development Tips," *Game Career Guide* (10 September 2008) http://www.gamecareerguide.com/features/624/iphone_game_development_tips.php.
38. Robert J.K. Jacob, Audrey Girouard, Leanne M. Hirshfield, Michael S. Horn, Orit Shaer, Erin Treacy Solovey and Jamie Zigelbaum, "Reality-Based Interaction: A Framework for Post-WIMP Interfaces," in *CHI 2008 Proceedings · Post-WIMP* (Florence, Italy: April 5–10, 2008).
39. WIMP stands for Window, Icon, Menu, Pointing Device, the standard tools for navigation and control of the interface. Robert J.K. Jacob et al., "Reality-Based Interaction: A Framework for Post-WIMP Interfaces," in *CHI 2008 Proceedings · Post-WIMP* (Florence, Italy: April 5–10, 2008): 201.
40. Robert J.K. Jacob et al., "Reality-Based Interaction: A Framework for Post-WIMP Interfaces", in *CHI 2008 Proceedings · Post-WIMP* (Florence, Italy:

April 5–10, 2008): 207. They suggest that these "real-world themes" are more-or-less "universal" (i.e., a-cultural), and that bodily awareness can be understood independent of the environment, problematic claim for post-phenomenology as it does not account for the specificities of embodiment and socio-cultural context. That is, each "theme" is always-already embedded within a wide array of human-technology relations.

41. Heidi-Rae Cooley, "It's All About the *Fit*: The Hand, the Mobile Screenic Device and Tactile Vision," *Journal of Visual Culture*, Vol 3, No 2 (2004): 137. It is worth noting here that from a phenomenological perspective, *all* vision is tactile vision; as Merleau-Ponty would remind us, there is no *essential* or ontic difference between vision and television, between touching and seeing; looking, tasting, smelling and hearing are all variants of "handling" the world. Indeed, palpating with the eyes *a prehension, a prise*—literally translates as *holding* (Merleau-Ponty, 1964: 133).

42. Jill Duffy, "iPhone Game Development Tips," *Game Career Guide* (10 September 2008) http://www.gamecareerguide.com/features/624/iphone_game_development_tips.php.

43. Jason Chen, "The iPhone is More Powerful Than the DS, But Sucks As a Controller," *Gizmodo* (16 July 2008) http://gizmodo.com/5025931/the-iphone-is-more-powerful-than-the-ds-but-sucks-as-a-controller.

44. Michael Bull, "The intimate sounds of urban experience: An auditory epistemology of everyday mobility," in *The Global and the Local in Mobile Communication*, Proceedings of the Third International Workshop on Mobile Music Technology (Brighton, UK: March 2–3, 2005), 169–178.

45. Leopoldina Fortunati, "The Mobile Phone as Technological Artefact," in *Thumb Culture: The Meaning of Mobile Phones for Society*, eds. Peter Glotz, Stefan Bertschi and Chris Locke (Bielefeld: transcript Verlag, 2005): 157.

46. Dean Chan, "Convergence, Connectivity, and the Case of Japanese Mobile Gaming," *Games and Culture* v1, n1 (2008): 13–25.

47. Geoff Cooper, "The Mutable Mobile: Social Theory in the Wireless World," in *Wireless World: Social and Interactive Aspects of the Mobile Age*, eds. B. Brown, N. Green & R. Harper (UK: Springer-Verlag, 2001): 25.

48. George Lakoff and Mark Johnson, *Metaphors We Live By* (Chicago and London: Chicago UP, 1980).

49. George Lakoff and Mark Johnson, *Metaphors We Live By* (Chicago and London: Chicago UP, 1980): 29. Jean-Pierre Warnier similarly discusses the "container" of the human body and the way it "supplements itself with innumerable surfaces and containers." Jean-Pierre Warnier, "Inside and Outside: Surfaces and Containers," in *Handbook of Material Culture*, eds. Christopher Tilly, Webb Keane, Susanne Kuechler-Fogden, Mike Rowlands and Patricia Spyer (UK: Sage Publications, 2006): 186.

50. Zöe Sofia, "Container Technologies," *Hypatia*, 15 (12) (2000) : 181–201.

51. Zöe Sofia, "Container Technologies," *Hypatia*, 15 (12) (2000): 189–190.

52. Lantz, Frank. "Big Games and the porous border between the real and the mediated," *receiver* #16 (2006). Retrieved October 5 2007 from http://www.receiver.vodafone.com/.

53. Adriana de Souza e Silva, "From Cyber to Hybrid: Mobile Technologies as Interfaces of Hybrid Spaces," *space and culture* vol 9, no 3 (August 2006): 263.

54. Though it is not possible to expand on the following point here, the "corporeal turn" in cultural and post-semiotic theory, which has incorporated the work of Merleau-Ponty and other phenomenologists, has been used effectively as a counter-argument against those who claim that online interaction is "disembodied." In this context, the oppositional relation between virtual

and locative spaces would be moot, since both dedicated Internet use and use of context-aware mobile devices would be considered different ways of being embodied, each educing distinctive corporeal schematics.

55. Dean Chan, "Convergence, Connectivity, and the Case of Japanese Mobile Gaming," *Games and Culture* v1, n1 (2008): 13–25.

56. Brad Stone, "iPhone Users Love That Mobile Web," *The New York Times* (October 22, 2008). Retrieved December 20, 2008 from http://bits.blogs .nytimes.com/2008/03/18/iphone-users-are-mobile-web-junkies/.

57. http://www.mogimogi.com/.

58. Justin Hall, "Mogi: Second Generation Location-Based Gaming," *The Feature* (1 April 2004). Retrieved December 20, 2008 from http://www. thefeaturearchives.com/topic/Gaming/Mobi_Second_Generation   _Loca- tion-Based_Gaming.html.

59. Justin Hall, "Mogi: Second Generation Location-Based Gaming," *The Feature* (1 April 2004). Retrieved December 20, 2008 from http://www .thefeaturearchives.com/topic/Gaming/Mobi_Second_Generation_ Location-Based_Gaming.html.

60. Cited in Mark Frauenfelder, "Are We There Yet?" *The Feature* (2 March 2005). Retrieved December 20, 2008 from http://www.thefeaturearchives. com/topic/Gaming/Are_We_There_Yet.html.

61. http://ciphercities.com/.

Part IV

Players, Playing and Virtual Communities

INTRODUCTION

In this concluding section we turn to the players themselves and virtual communities, one of the areas that—in age of participatory, crossplatforming and collaborative media such as Web 2.0—is changing dramatically. However, one must be cautious of overdetermined user-empowerment rhetoric. As the Internet confluences into the creative social networking potentialities of Web 2.0 localities, the fact of technosocial inequalities and the role of power collectively problematizes a "bottom-up" egalitarian model that participatory online popular culture claims. In this section, we are provided with different case studies that complicate simplistic sociocultural binaries surrounding Web 2.0 agency.

As a region renowned for its highly advanced, turbo-capitalist technocultures (such as Tokyo and Seoul) that boast sophisticated technonationalist policies and infrastructure, it is not by accident that the Asia-Pacific has recently gained much interest in terms of its demonstration of multiple "Internets" constituted by dynamic virtual communities. Behind images of the Internet as affording new forms of democracy, e-participation, digital storytelling, trans-media and netizen e-politics, the so-called social networked revolution has far from eroded vertical impositional models of power. Despite the increasingly mainstream preoccupation with games as part of popular culture, it is not by accident that gendered connotations of technology still prevail. In Web 2.0 multiple Internet localities—that are trans-media, trans-cultural, trans-disciplinary and trans-community—we are provided with various models for new forms of engagement, agency and empowerment as well as residual modes of exploitation and misuse. This is no more apparent than in the dynamics of game players playing within virtual communities.

As noted earlier in Chapter 1, with Web 2.0 we see new forms of community, authorship, agency and engagement, creativity and community being ushered in. This is apparent in the localized self-organized and self-regulated massively multiplayer online role-playing game (MMORPG) guilds as discussed by Lin and Sun in Chapter 13. In their study on a *Lineage* guild in Taiwan, Lin and Sun reflect upon the different processes at play within the online community. Here we consider some of the positive and negative ("risks") surrounding players and online community, which, in turn, offer us new ways for conceptualizing new regional-specific forms of media literacy, creativity, intimacy and labor that, in turn, can provide new insights into our region in the twenty-first century. As a changing and increasingly localized phenomenon, the agency, engagement and immersion afforded to players in online game worlds reflect offline forms of community and sociality.

Lin and Sun's analysis demonstrates that guild formation does not operate on the premise that the virtual is completely substituted for the actual; rather the gamer's prerogative is on reflexively negotiating the virtual as a site for expanding upon and supplementing actual relationships. The gamers interviewed by Lin and Sun asserted that offline "real contacts" are much more reliable in terms of potential guild membership. Real world identification thereby becomes a vital criterion for extending online trust in persistent game worlds and a reflexive measure to minimize potentially "risky" game play with complete strangers. Lin and Sun argue that the maintenance of face-to-face social capital and the "online replication of offline networks" are strategically deployed as a tactical "risk-reduction mechanism."

The changing boundaries between online and offline communities, as well as between once finite categories such as fans, players and creative producers are blurring in an age of participatory, conversational media[1] as highlighted by the appropriation of Alvin Toffler's "prosumers"[2] (consumer as part of the production process) into what Axel Bruns calls "produser."[3] The "participatory" nature of contemporary online media is affording some types of players and produsers new forms of expression, agency and visibility. In Chapter 15, Hjorth explores the phenomenon of young female cosplaying games students to understand how that these types of Japanese "gender performativity"[4] afford them avenues for entering into the still male-dominated area of the games industry. *Vis-à-vis* cosplaying and the particular types of gender performativity offered by Japanese tropes of femininity that Laura Miller calls "kogals,"[5] Hjorth contextualizes how the "consumption of Japan" can offer young females new types of gaming role models and agency.

Cosplay (short for "costume play"), as Hjorth notes, has become a key part of the expanding media cultures and discourses surrounding gaming, as well as playing a central role in the rites of passage for many young females to enter the conventionally male-centered gaming worlds. Through the phenomenon and practice of cosplay, we vividly witness how technological customization becomes branded with specific types of gendered performativity. Hjorth argues that cosplay affords a significant avenue for young women to re-imagine and renegotiate their place and role in gaming cultures as they move from consumer to active fan to games designer or producer—from player to produser to producer.

The role of gender—specifically young women and gaming—is also the topic of Chapter 14, in which Hjorth, Na and Huhh paint a different, gendered picture of the successful South Korean games industry. Behind the triumphal images of the MMOs phenomenon synonymous with the main socializing space for Korean youth, the *PC bang* (PC room), and with the rise in ancillary discourses such as e-sports, the reality for young women—as both players and designers—is still far from equal. As Hjorth et al. note, game playing is still positioned as a relatively male-oriented activity and for many female players, their only entrance and legitimation into the gaming world was via either playing with brothers or boyfriends. Here we can see how gaming cultures reflect broader inflections of locality, especially, in this case, tropes of gendered performativity around the consumption, production and identification games.

NOTES

1. Henry Jenkins, *Fans, Bloggers, and Gamers: Essays on Participatory Culture* (New York: New York University Press, 2006).
2. Alvin Toffler, *The Third Wave* (William Morrow and Company, Inc.: New York. 1980).
3. Axel Bruns and Jason Jacobs, eds., *Uses of Blogs* (New York: Peter Lang, 2006).
4. Judith Butler, *Gender Trouble* (London: Routledge, 1991).
5. Laura Miller, *Beauty Up* (Berkley: University of California, 2006).

13 Managing Risks in Online Game Worlds

Networking Strategies Among Taiwanese Adolescent Players

Holin Lin and Chuen-Tsai Sun

INTRODUCTION

Online computer gaming is an enormously popular pastime for Asian teenagers and young adults, with multiple-player online games winning the hearts of players but not the trust of parents or the general public. In addition to usual rhetoric around the addictive qualities of computer games, online gaming also entails personal interactions and resource exchanges among strangers, which can be viewed as creating a public image of virtual worlds replete with risks and uncertainties. From the perspective of game companies, the community-oriented nature of multiple-player online games (MMOs) is increasingly viewed as the foundation for commercial success.[1] MMOs highlight the social and cultural dimensions of game play as well as demonstrating the active role players take in the creation, recreation and dynamics of the game space. This has made MMOs a plentiful site for considering the relationship between online and offline gaming communities.

Players of Massively Multiplayer Online Role-Playing Games (MMORPGs) regularly form social networks to carry out game missions, hunt down monsters, share treasure, and fight other groups. Depending on the game in question, these groups are variously known as clans, squads, or (as we will refer to them throughout this paper) guilds. Guilds serve as (a) functional units in which players complete game tasks that are difficult to accomplish by individuals, or (b) social units in which characters interact while increasing their skill levels. However, while guilds often operate efficiently for the performance of collective actions that require coordinated mobilization, guild membership rarely exerts true binding power on individual behaviors, and many members remain nearly complete strangers to each other. Considering that most guilds rely on oral commitments from their participants, it is surprising that so many maintain such high levels of stability and loyalty.

Our goal in this chapter is to analyze social network construction and cooperation in self-emerging, self-organizing communities that now stand at the center of two of the world's most popular MMORPGs—*Lineage* and *Ragnarok Online* (*RO*). Specifically, we will look at the social dynamics of online gaming guilds and their offline associations from a risk management perspective. After examining motivations for forming guilds (especially in light of a complex mix of membership costs, risks, duties and obligations), we will investigate the nature of cooperation and networking among anonymous individuals in gaming situations that profess to emphasize independence. Last, we will look at reasons why and how offline connections are introduced for coping with risks associated with online gaming. Our goal is to shed light on structural factors that shape those risks, and to add to our understanding of how gamers develop strategies to minimize risk and manage frequently encountered uncertainties.

LITERATURE REVIEW

Nicholas Ducheneaut, Nick Yee, Eric Nickell and Robert Moore are among the researchers who have observed that online gamers tend to initially play as individuals or in small groups, and that even experienced players are prone to "playing alone together."[2] This raises questions concerning why players form guilds that nurture unique MMORPG cultures. In the early days of online gaming, player guilds used to be viewed as informal and unplanned organizations, and scholars tended to profile the social lives of gamers in contexts of shared-interest subcultures.[3] During that period, researchers also focused on the issues of identity formation/transformation[4] and gender interaction[5] in ongoing game worlds.

Current game designs encourage MMORPG players to compete against each other in task-oriented scenarios, with competition and collective action stimulating social interactions and group behaviors in ways that are not observed in other virtual communities. As competition levels grow in tandem with gaming community size, collective action becomes increasingly necessary for MMORPG success—and in some cases, for simple survival. It is now clear that keeping players "hooked" online and establishing and maintaining active gaming communities are central to game company success, leading to the preponderance of design features and game mechanisms aimed at increasing player interaction. Examples include avatar/experience upgrading and limitations on average level and number of avatars allowed to participate in group missions. Recently released online games are even incorporating guild formation into their structure, adding mechanisms for establishing guilds and designing goals and missions that require coordinated actions by members of well organized teams.[6]

There are additional and perhaps more sociological ways of studying online game guilds and the ways they shape (and are shaped by) complex social network processes. Network diffusion is often cited as a motivating factor for creating online gaming communities. When succinctly explaining the *Lineage* frenzy in South Korea,[7] an educational psychologist said, "If everyone you know plays *Lineage*, you have to play it."[8] The simplicity of this statement is attractive, but perhaps at the expense of neglecting the mechanisms through which such processes evolve. A closer look at how guilds recruit members may reveal that "natural diffusion" is insufficient for analyzing offline networks.

On the other hand, players may be motivated to join organizations in order to cope with what they view as excessively sophisticated in-game worlds. This might be explained (at least in part), by the growing presence of grief players. "Griefers" behave in disruptive or distressful ways and negatively affect other players' gaming experiences, apparently for the sheer enjoyment they derive from such behavior. By doing so, they give regular players a strong reason for joining in-game organizations so as to avoid them or to make some attempt at resisting them.[9]

Dealing with risky environments or situations is a complex process for real-world organizations and online gaming guilds alike. Ellick Wong notes that the degree of commitment required of group members to deal with such scenarios is tied to risk propensity, risk perception and outcome expectancy.[10] Howard Kunreuther and Paul Slovic conceptualize risk as a game in which dynamic rule processing must be socially negotiated within specific problem contexts.[11] Anonymity presents another dimension of risk in virtual worlds: Finch observes that online transactions between unknown buyers and sellers carry significant risks that are not present in traditional exchange interactions.[12]

Business e-teams can be analyzed as a type of guild, with researchers listing required factors behind healthy dynamics as group cohesion, trust among members, appropriate norms and the shared understanding of tasks and goals—all demanding time, commitment and frequent interactions.[13] However, while businesses act according to professionally created models and regulations, online gaming guilds are for the most part created and managed by teenagers who have little (if any) interpersonal and organizational experience. Since children, adolescents and young adults constitute the large majority of online gamers,[14] game culture generally reflects youthful ideas on friendship, competition and community. The marginal status of adolescents and children in mainstream society also colors how the general public views online gaming culture. Isolated incidents of violence[15] and addiction[16] are seized by gaming detractors and presented as indicators of deeper problems in gaming communities and proof that adolescents are passive and uncritical consumers of computer games and game messages.[17] In the next section we will discuss how adolescent gamers create online social enclaves and how they establish rules and disciplinary actions to make such cooperative activities possible. Our analysis will be guided by four research questions: (a) how are guilds formed? (b) what incentives do players have to join guilds? (c) what are the inclusive and exclusive principles of guild membership? (d) what are the mechanisms that support cooperation among guild members?

LOCAL CONTEXTS[18]

Taiwan has long been one of Asia's most important markets for online games, especially since it enjoyed an early start compared to other countries in terms of Internet infrastructure development. By 2007, 79.4% of all Taiwanese households owned at least one PC; in the capital city of Taipei the 2007 ownership rate was 89.5%. Household Internet connection rates have also increased rapidly, from 45.9% in 1992 to 74.9% in 2007. Nevertheless, many young people still choose to play online games at Internet cafes, perhaps due to the large percentage of parents who view the activity as nothing more than a distraction that interferes with schoolwork.

Unlike Internet cafes in the some Western countries (primarily places for net surfing or checking email), Taiwan's Internet cafes are similar to video arcades, filled with game posters, merchandise and computers with the newest graphic cards and large varieties of games to choose from. In 2001 alone there were more than 7,000 registered Internet cafes; although this number has decreased due to competition and the growth of household broadband connections, these cafes are still very popular among young people as places to enjoy video gaming with friends.

LINEAGE AND *RO*

Lineage is a "Dragons-and-Dungeons" type of fantasy game. Players take on the personas of knights, wizards, elves and members of royal families as they move through worlds filled with adventure, treasure and monsters and other challenges that must be overcome in order to increase skill levels and earn virtual rewards. To gain control of castles that dot their virtual worlds, *Lineage* players fight each other as members of teams or guilds headed by guild masters. Victors levy taxes upon the virtual villages they control, and charge fellow gamers a percentage of every online weapons sale they make. In Asian countries, a *Lineage* frenzy has resulted in a booming black market of products that blur the line between virtual and real worlds. Players exchange real money for virtual treasures or game currency.[19]

RO players start off as novices with no special powers. As they approach the highest novice level they are given a choice of six occupations: swordsman, thief, acolyte, magician, archer or merchant. Each occupation has its own game settings, but character goals are essentially the same: To buy and sell items and use available money and equipment to defeat monsters in order to earn experience. At the end of August 2003, an estimated 1 million Taiwan residents (out of a total population of 23 million) had active *Lineage* accounts; the record for players online at the same time is approximately 180,000.[20] The estimated number of Taiwanese *RO* subscribers was 1.8 million at the end of July 2003.

GUILDS

In online gaming worlds, guilds represent self-emerging player organizations, with *Lineage* guilds known as "blood pledges" and their *RO*
counterparts simply called "guilds." According to the official Taiwanese websites for the two games, there were 450,000 *Lineage* guilds and
7,610 *RO* guilds[21] in 2003. Guild sizes range from three to hundreds of
members.[22] Complex actions such as castle sieges require as many support
players as can be recruited, therefore short-term alliances are often made
among guilds of various sizes. Some guilds have gone so far as to orga-
nize last-minute recruitment programs or to hire mercenaries to increase
their numbers. Guilds are also used as staging areas for organizing temporary subgroups to complete less challenging tasks such as defeating certain classes of monsters. Outsiders are occasionally invited to participate
in these task-oriented, short-term projects, but it appears that most guilds
prefer using established members when creating sub-units.

Guild masters have complete power to accept or reject new members.
Lineage and *RO* players have the power to activate four and three characters each, respectively, but individual characters can only belong to one
guild at a time. After joining a guild, most players choose nicknames that
are shown above their avatars, and use exclusive chat lines to communicate
with fellow guild members. Members are also given access to guild-owned
warehouses for storage. More sophisticated guilds have their own virtual
accommodations for socializing, resting and working on fighting skills.[23]

According to our observations, the percentage of online game players
who are not attached to at least one guild is very low, since most online
gaming activities are now somehow related to or controlled by intra- and
cross-guild interactions. We therefore chose guilds as our locus for observing adolescent online networking and for collecting data on four issues:

1. When making a decision on which guild to join, what are the most
   common motivations and factors to consider?
2. What functions are served by guilds—for instance, leisure, economic
   or social?
3. Do guild circles and player offline social networks overlap?
4. What adolescent leisure characteristics are revealed by their participation in online gaming communities?

RESEARCH METHODS

To collect data on adolescent social networks in virtual gaming spaces
we conducted interviews, used online questionnaires, adopted participatory observation techniques and analyzed secondary data on online game
development in Taiwan (i.e., media coverage, video gaming magazines,

video gaming programs on television and game exhibitions). In addition to observing game play, we entered game worlds as players and interacted with fellow guild members. Throughout our research on game culture we have continuously monitored exchanges that take place on online gaming forums. Since online gaming culture emphasizes the sharing of experiences and feelings, and since real names and identities are not required, forum members usually have no reservations about expressing their opinions and emotions. We compared these first-hand and real-time descriptions with data collected via interviews and questionnaires to establish a comprehensive picture of online gaming culture.

We used a snowball sampling procedure to find 14 *Lineage* and *RO* gamers who were willing to be interviewed. Eight of the interviewees were experienced *Lineage* gamers, five were experienced *RO* players, and one claimed to be an experienced player of both games. Only two of the interviewees were female, reflecting the general under-representation of female players in online gaming. To ensure the heterogeneity of our sample and to build a greater understanding of guild culture, we made an effort to find interviewees from guilds representing a range of orientations, sizes and member compositions. During our initial contact, we allowed potential informants to choose their preferred interview situation or location. Seven respondents chose MSN or Yahoo instant messaging systems or e-mail, while the other seven respondents chose to be interviewed in person.

Regarding our online questionnaire, we made announcements on game websites and bulletin boards for players to voluntarily respond to questions posted on our research website. Other potential respondents were contacted via the inter-personal networks of the researchers and interviewees. Over an eight-day period we collected data from 518 *Lineage* players, of whom 427 were between the ages of 13 and 23.[24]

RESULTS AND DISCUSSION

The vast majority of online gamers belong to at least one guild at some time during their playing careers. According to our survey of *Lineage* gamers, only 5.4% claimed to have never joined a guild. The two most commonly cited reasons for joining a guild were finding game-related assistance (39.3%) and the emotional need to participate in an interpersonal network (35.4%).[25] According to our interviewees, most gamers feel a need to join a guild to take advantage of the support it offers. Several described a "law-of-the-jungle" attitude in game worlds and the interdependent structure of game design as motivations for guild membership, and the majority used such terms as "dark world" and "a world that makes you lose faith in humanity" when describing gaming environments. We heard arguments that solo game play can be unpleasant or even "dangerous," especially for newbies. The most frequently cited example in support of this position is treasure being stolen by onlookers after a character single-handedly defeats a monster. Inexperienced players are also frequent victims of fraud or bullying. Being victimized is bad enough in any game, but such situations are made worse when virtual goods take on real cash value. Inexperienced players are therefore happy to find virtual comrades and mentors to show them the ropes and to back them up against bullies.

Playing solo can be frustrating in other ways, since access to more interesting adventures is restricted to characters at certain levels. Without the required capital and equipment, a character may find it very hard to move to the next level of play. One interviewee told us, "In *Lineage*, monsters are hard to beat and money is hard to earn." New characters need guidance and gifts from experienced gamers, who in turn need support to achieve certain MMORPG goals—for instance, defeating more challenging monsters. When asked to describe what kinds of help they received from their guilds, interviewees most often mentioned: (a) asking guild members to team up and accumulate points, (b) borrowing money and treasures from other members, and (c) borrowing fighting equipment from others. Even when players have other means for organizing teams, they show a clear preference for selecting fellow guild members. Just under two-thirds (63.9%) of the players who completed our online survey said that they gave guild members first priority when forming teams to complete specific tasks.

In an effort to recruit more players, game companies are purposefully designing scenarios that require group action. For example, *RO* characters have different attributes and special abilities: Swordsmen are slow yet effective fighters, archers fast but vulnerable, and acolytes weak physically but with healing powers. In *Lineage*, royal family members are weaker than all other characters in every specialty, but they are the only characters with the power to establish and lead guilds. Differences in role specialties make solo survival very difficult, since most game tasks now require cooperation among participants who play various roles. Castle sieges are typical in this regard: Capturing or defending a castle requires cooperation by a combination of perhaps hundreds of different role characters—a powerful motivation for guild formation and membership.

RISKS OF COOPERATION

Joining a guild and cooperating with fellow guild members cannot be considered risk-free. Members have obligations, and helping or simply chatting with other members can be time-consuming. When asked, "What would you do if one of your members were being bullied?", more than half of our interviewees stated that they would help their guilds get revenge. In some cases, that means doing battle with other guilds and exposing one's avatar to injury.[26] Some *Lineage* gamers went so far as to describe castle sieges (often referred to as "ultimate guild goals") as dubious enterprises in terms of costs and benefits. In addition to requiring extensive planning and huge resource investments, participants are at high risk of getting hurt in battle. The cost of hiring 200 mercenaries willing to participate in a siege can be as high as four million *Lineage* dollars; basic water and blood supplies for siege supporters can cost as much as 10 million.[27] Still, the odds of success for an inexperienced guild are small, and some players are unwilling to wait for their guilds to gain the necessary experience. One interviewee told us that 10 members of her guild left rather than take part in a questionable siege.

Offering assistance to fellow guild members can backfire. We have heard many stories of thefts and scams involving money and coveted virtual weapons. Our interviewees shared many stories about cheating, betrayal and espionage. Lending valuable equipment to fellow members is a difficult decision for many, since recipients sometimes hold on to borrowed equipment beyond the agreed-upon time period, or in some instances, refuse to return it. Some guild members who lose items that they borrow neither apologize nor provide compensation to the original owners.

The most common guild disputes are about dividing treasure, collectively owned equipment or collectively obtained resources and rewards. Since participating characters differ in terms of experience and contributions, entitlement and share size issues can become very complex. In interviews and in chat rooms we have noted hundreds of complaints about members who reaped profits without doing anything to earn them, about greedy players who refused to share captured items and about cowards who abandoned difficult missions. Stealing treasure accumulated by others via the completion of arduous tasks is perhaps the greatest source of online gaming discontent.

An important difference between *Lineage* and *RO* should be noted here. When a *Lineage* monster is slayed by means of a collective effort, the resulting treasure is immediately and automatically transferred to each participating gamer. In *RO* the treasure simply falls to the ground—meaning that anyone can pick it up, including outsiders who did not participate in the slaying. In *Lineage*, no one knows exactly how much each participant gets, unless they decide (and convince others) to openly discuss the issue. This design feature underscores the importance of trust among *Lineage* gamers.

REDUCING RISK

Due to social norms and economic rationality, reciprocal supportive relationships are expected among guild members. Loaning equipment that is not in use can help a guild become stronger in the long term, eventually benefiting all members when larger rewards are earned and distributed. However, the risks of lending can become excessive if a guild suffers from too many "free-riders," creating a sense of unfairness that can damage healthy interactions and basic operations. For this reason, most guilds feel compelled to develop mechanisms for securing trust and reducing risk.

The most important mechanism in this regard may be the creation of online networks based on existing offline social relationships among core members. In Taiwan, the vast majority of these social networks revolve around the players' schools, with core guild members mostly consisting of classmates, friends from the same school and siblings and neighbors. For the most part, online guild members with no offline connections to other members hold marginal positions. Guilds centered around offline social networks more often than not refuse to accept new online members; however, exceptions are made for special campaigns or when a large number of members have schedule conflicts. Most of our interviewees argued that offline "real contacts" are much more reliable in terms of potential guild membership, and that online strangers should not be trusted. While this may seem obvious on the surface, the online replication of offline networks holds considerable meaning. According to the rationality principle underlying network crossovers, offline relationships are more likely to guarantee mechanisms for tracking down perpetrators of fraud, theft, and other online infractions, thereby reducing risk and minimizing potential damage. The point of such mechanisms is not just reducing risk by having reliable friends as fellow partners, but also minimizing potential damage by making it easy to locate individuals for compensation. As a Chinese aphorism puts it: "A monk can run, but not the temple he belongs to."

Distinctions between online and offline relationships raise many questions regarding trust. Several interviewees emphasized the risk of not being able to retrieve loaned items. One in particular made it very clear that he would only make loans to online friends who were willing to share their verifiable real-world addresses. This sense of real-world identification is increasingly becoming the standard for extending online trust in game worlds. We observed that a guild with a strong orientation toward engaging monsters in combat had enacted a ban on equipment loans so as to prevent all potential conflicts. The ban guidelines were very clear in stating that any violators risked expulsion. In summary, offline connections are welcomed because they make it easy to locate anyone who breaks guild rules; online friends must be willing to give up the anonymity that is such an important feature of online gaming.

Alex (a pseudonym), a guild master we interviewed, provided a detailed description of how the trust-securing system works. All 76 members of his guild have offline connections with the guild core—absolutely no strangers or online friends allowed. During our interview, Alex described his guild's membership qualifications:

> Our rule on personal connections is this: Either I have to know the person directly, or there can only be one person between the would-be member and me, just to be sure that we can find the person directly through a member. This way is convenient and not too complex.

Why do you have this rule?

If connections are too remote, an individual may simply disappear after doing something bad, and we won't be able to find him . . . Since everybody knows each other, if anything happens the one who introduced the member to the guild is responsible for finding him.

Alex's description is one of a ripple-like pattern of resource allocation and job assignments, in which smaller numbers mean a higher percentage of direct connections to a guild master or core founders. He also told us, "The first 30 members are fine because they take care of each other." In other words, those 30 members get the largest shares of any resources or rewards that need to be distributed. During collective missions, core members are the only ones entrusted with critical game character roles (for example, magicians). By placing more resources and obligations into trusted hands, virtual risks attached to cooperation are reduced.

RULES, DISCIPLINE AND PUNISHMENT

The second risk reduction mechanism most often cited by the study participants is the combination of discipline and punishment. The threat of discipline from social contacts has a preventative effect, and rules and punishments—all the way to expulsion—allow guilds to control both the actions of their members and potential negative effects of dealing with strangers. According to our survey, approximately one-fifth (21%) of all cases in which a member was banished from a guild were tied to stealing accounts, treasure or currency from other members; another 9.2% were due to members not sharing currency or treasure in an equitable manner.

For the largest guilds, discipline and punishment mechanisms are considered essential, but there are certain guild types that rarely use them. One interviewee said that his large guild did not exclude outsiders, but its members seldom conducted large-scale, high-risk and potentially profitable operations, thereby reducing the need for major time commitments from core groups of trustworthy comrades. Instead, the primary activities in this guild were chatting with other members and defending a castle in return for pay from the guild master. This type of guild resembles a large bureaucratic system. In contrast, another interviewee's guild (oriented toward clashes with monsters) had a very strict set of rules, including bans on lending or borrowing equipment so as to prevent conflicts. Anyone violating the rule was automatically expelled. Based on our observations, guilds that are open to having strangers as members either suffer no problems related to trust, or rely on strict discipline and punishment rules.

EXCHANGE RELATIONS AND BEYOND

Social interactions in online gaming communities reflect mixes of economically rational exchange patterns and adolescent culture. Exchange relationships among gamers are generally balanced, with guild member obligations corresponding to their entitlement status. Unless two parties have a particularly strong relationship, gift exchanges are mostly limited to small items of marginal value. Also, the more powerful a guild, the less likely it is to accept members who lack immediately useful skills; conversely, skillful characters tend to avoid joining weak guilds.

Still, it would be incorrect to summarize resource exchanges and social dynamics in online gaming worlds as calculated behaviors in response to economic incentives, since the influences of social role expectations on character behavior are also evident. The role of guild master is an interesting example of social expectations. In *Lineage*,[28] living up to the social expectations of a guild master and/or member of royalty requires the frame of mind of "taking care of one's people," which extends beyond purely economic calculations. According to our observations, some guild masters take so much pleasure in the responsibilities of good leadership that they are willing to invest a great deal of time and wealth in support of their followers. Such popular works as *Lord of the Rings* provide virtual role models and game culture scripts for interactions between guild masters and their supporters—with both positive and negative results. When asked why he obeyed the orders of a weak, unreasonable guild master, one interviewee replied, "Because he is the King, and this is the culture of the story!" Clearly, it is important to play one's hierarchical role properly, even in a virtual society. This explains why, among reasons cited for member expulsion from a guild, the most common (25.1%) is "behavior outside game norms."

We observed a number of similarities between adolescent and online gaming guild cultures, including exclusivity in social interactions and a tendency toward inter-guild fighting. According to our survey, only 6.7% of the guilds that our respondents belong to had never gotten involved in an inter-guild fight. In addition to stories of unprovoked killings of outsiders by guild members, we heard claims of members running into fights and immediately joining in without asking questions. Heroic behavior in such situations is considered admirable, and running away cowardly. Group awareness and an emphasis on solidarity are also remindful of adolescent culture, although without the same degree of criminality.

These social and cultural factors have profound impacts on and implications for shaping online gaming guild networks. We found that online/offline crossover extends beyond mere play among acquaintances to serve as a risk-reduction mechanism. Adolescent players benefit not only from rational game calculations, but also from extensions of gaming stages to the physical world, which allows acquaintances to share and acknowledge gaming achievements.

Alex (described above as being devoted to good leadership) enjoyed both online and offline fame, even from students in the same grade but in other classes—an unusual scenario in Taiwanese high schools.

CONCLUSION

We gathered data on *Lineage* and *RO* guilds in Taiwan to investigate their compositions, operations, social dynamics and interactive cultures, and found that character survival and game success (as opposed to social interactions) are the primary reasons for guild formation. Local MMORPG design features are making collaboration a necessity for slaying monsters, capturing castles or performing other large-scale game tasks. Game managers and player cultures have also contributed to the creation of a "law-of-the-jungle" atmosphere in the online gaming world, in which single characters are bound to consistently confront dangerous and frustrating situations. In their position as committed groups dedicated to providing mutual support for successful gaming, guilds may be best analyzed as an adaptive survival strategy.

Exchanging favors and resources has its own set of risks, especially when the same resources have value in the physical world. To reduce potential risk and damage, online guilds in Taiwan are generally rooted in offline social networks; however, overlapping online and offline networks should not be considered simple extensions of existing offline communities, since considerable rational calculation is involved. Many online organizations restrict outside membership to the friends of core members (in some cases introducing acquaintances to what is for them a new game or pastime) in order to avoid the risk of filling a guild with online strangers. Limiting online membership to acquaintances once removed from a guild master also ensures that online rule violations can be effectively addressed offline, resulting in effective damage control.

Finally, the mainstream cultural narrative concerning video games views them as sources of addictive behavior leading to negative consequences. We found that teenage online gamers have developed various mechanisms to cope with complex interpersonal interactions, among both game characters and the individuals who control them. They carefully evaluate risks and benefits to avoid being cheated, and lower their expectations of strangers in a manner that we consider very practical. This finding resists the portrait of teenage gamers as being restless, careless and vulnerable. We view such images as false stereotypes.

NOTES

1. J.C. Herz, "Gaming the system: Multi-player worlds online," in *Game On, the History and Culture of Videogames*, ed. L. King(London: Laurence King Publishing, 2002), 86–97.
2. Nicholas Ducheneaut, Nick Yee, Eric Nickell and Robert J. Moore, "Alone together? Exploring the social dynamics of massively multiplayer games,"

Presented at the *Conference on Human Factors in Computing Systems* (Montreal, Quebec, Canada, 2006).

3. Catherine Beavis, "Computer games: Youth culture, resistant readers and consuming passions." Paper presented at *Australian Association for Research in Education annual conference* (Adelaide, Australia, 1998). Retrieved July 14, 2004, from: http://www.aare.edu.au/98pap/bea98139.htm; Jo Bryce and Jason Rutter, "Killing like a girl: Gendered gaming and girl gamers' visibility," Paper presented at *Computer Games and Digital Cultures (CHDC) Conference* (Tampere, Finland, 2002); Herz, "Gaming the system: Multi-player worlds online."

4. Pavel Curtis, "Mudding: Social phenomena in text-based virtual realities," in *Culture of the Internet*, ed. S. Kiesler (Mahwah, New Jersey: Lawrence Erlbaum Associates, 1997), 121–142; Sherry Turkle, *Life on the Screen: Identity in the Age of the Internet* (New York: Touchstone, Simon & Schuster, 1995).

5. Brenda Danet, "Text as mask: gender, play and performance on the Internet," in *Cybersociety 2.0: Computer-mediated Communication and Community Revisited*, ed. S. Jones (Thousand Oaks, CA: Sage, 1998), 129–158; Nancy R. Deuel, "Our passionate response to virtual reality," in *Computer-Mediated Communication*, ed. S. C. Herring (Amsterdam, Philadelphia: John Benjamins, 1996), 129–46; Jonathan Kandell, "Internet addiction on college campuses: The vulnerability of college Students," *CyberPsychology & Behavior*, 1 (1) 1998. Retrieved July 14, 2004, from: http://www.behavioraledu.com/sampler/ia_resources.html.

6. Chien-Hsun Chen, Chuen-Tsai Sun and Jilung Hsieh, "Player Guild Dynamics and Evolution in Massively Multiplayer Online Games," *CyberPsychology & Behavior*, 11 (3) 2008: 293–301.

7. Taiwan shares many similarities with Korea. In 1999, the original release year for *Lineage*, membership immediately ballooned to 2.2 million users, with the number of players online at any single moment regularly reaching 180,000, second only to Korea. Until very recently, Taiwan and Korea were the only two countries in the world where *Lineage* was more popular than *Lineage II*, which is described as having better 3-D graphics and game play features. Another similarity with Korea is the popularity of Internet cafes for online gaming, similar to *PC bang* centers in which young Koreans gather to play, relax and socialize with their friends.

8. Michelle Levander, "Where Does Fantasy End?" *Time magazine*, 157 (22) June 4, 2001.

9. Holin Lin and Chuen-Tsai Sun "The "White-Eyed" Player Culture: Grief Play and Construction of Deviance in MMORPGs," in *Changing Views: Worlds in Play—Selected papers of the 2005 Digital Games Research Association's Second International Conference*, eds. S. de Castell and J. Jenson (Vancouver: Digital Games Research Association, 2005).

10. Ellick KFE Wong, "The role of risk in making decisions under escalation situations," *Applied Psychology—An International Review—Psychologie Appliquee-RevueE Internationale* 54 (4) 2005: 584–607.

11. Howard Kunreuther and Paul Slovic, "Science, values, and risk," *Annals of the American Academy of Political and Social Science*, 545, 2006: 116–125.

12. Byron J. Finch, "Customer expectations in online auction environments: An exploratory study of customer feedback and risk," *Journal of Operations Management* 25 (5) 2007: 985–997.

13. Stephen J. Zaccaro and Paige Bader, "E-Leadership and the challenges of leading E-Teams: Minimizing the bad and maximizing the good," *Organizational Dynamics*, 31 (4) 2003: 377–387.

14. Johannes Fromme, "Computer games as a part of children's culture," *Game Studies* [Online], 3 (1) 2003. Available: http://www.gamestudies.org/0301/fromme/; Sonia Livingstone, Leen d'Haenens and Uwe Hasebrink, "Childhood

in Europe: contexts for comparison," in *Children and Ther Changing Media Environment. A European Comparative Study*, eds. S. Livingstone and M. Bovill(Mahwah, NJ: Lawrence Erlbaum Associates, 2001): 3–30.

15. Craig A. Anderson and Brad J. Bushman, "Effects of violent video games on aggressive behavior, aggressive cognition, aggressive affect, physiological arousal, and prosocial behavior: A meta-analytic review of the scientific literature," *Psychological Science*, 12 (5) 2001: 353–359; Michele J. Fleming and Debra J. RickWood, "Effects of violent versus nonviolent video games on children's arousal, aggressive mood, and positive mood," *Journal of Applied Social Psychology*, 31 (10) 2001: 2047–2071; Jeffrey H. Goldstein, "Immortal Kombat: War Toys and Violent Video Games," in *Why We Watch: The Attractions of Violent Entertainment*, ed. J.H. Goldstein (New York: Oxford University Press, 1998): 53–68; J.C. Herz, "Moral kombat," in *Joystick Nation*, ed. C. Herz (Boston: Little, Brown, and Co, 1997): 83–195; Russell B. Williams and Caryl A. Clippinger, "Aggression, competition and computer games: Computer and human opponents," *Computers in Human Behavior*, 18, 2002:495–506.

16. John P. Charlton (2002). "A factor-analytic investigation of computer 'addiction' and engagement," *British Journal of Psychology*, 93, 2002: 329; Mark Griffiths, "Internet addiction: does it really exist?" in *Psychology and the Internet*, ed. J. Gackenbach (San Diego: Academic Press, 1998): 61–75; Jonathan Kandell, "Internet addiction on college campuses: The vulnerability of college students," *CyberPsychology & Behavior*, 1 (1) 1998. Retrieved July 14, 2004, from:http://www.behavioraledu.com/sampler/ia_resources .html.

17. Beavis, "Computer games: Youth culture, resistant readers and consuming passions."

18. By 2003, *Lineage* had been on the Taiwan market for almost three years. When the first draft of this paper was written in 2003, it held the number one position in the local online gaming market. *RO* has given *Lineage* strong competition ever since its release in August 2002. In 2003, the Taiwan distributor for *RO* claimed that the game's market share had surpassed that of *Lineage*, but the claim was never verified.

19. In September of 2003, the exchange rate for New Taiwan Dollars to *Lineage* Dollars experienced a sharp increase, from 1:1,000 to 1:1,500. In *Taipei Times*, July 25, 2002.

20. Y. C. Lee, Lineage II is About To Be Released, *China Times Express*, August 25, 2003.

21. However, the number of *RO* guilds is underestimated, since they are not required to register with the official website.

22. In *Lineage*, the upper limit of guild members was only 40 until April 30, 2003, when *Lineage* administrators started giving permission for gamers to form much larger guilds. At that time they began helping gamers document their various affiliations.

23. Players can recover their competitive power more quickly in a guild house than "in the wild."

24. We conducted the online survey only on *Lineage* players because they had a longer history of guild development at that time.

25. One could select more than one reason in response to this question.

26. Fighting can cause virtual health and economic damage to individual characters. Wounded players must buy magic potions or use the value of their experience to recover. They also run the risk of losing equipment.

27. As of 2003, approximately USD $290.

28. In *Lineage*, guild master positions are exclusively reserved for members of the royal class.

14 Games of Gender
A Case Study on Females Who Play Games in Seoul, South Korea

Larissa Hjorth, Bora Na, and Jun-Sok Huhh

INTRODUCTION

As a country lauded with the highest broadband rates[1] and with the best IT policies[2] in the world, South Korea (henceforth Korea) provides a fascinating picture of twenty-first century postmodernity. Central to this vignette is the image of turbo-capitalism[3] in which new media—such as mobile and Web 2.0[4] technologies—has been deployed within Korea's own version of technoculture. Boasting one of the oldest Social Networking Systems (SNS), Cyworld mini-hompy, that is accessed by over one-third (18 million out of 48 million) of the population daily, an active blogosphere[5] and netizen media such as *OnMyNews*, Korea provides a pivotal model for twenty-first century technoculture. Indeed one of Korea's most famous industries is online gaming and its attendant industries such as e-sports that have enamoured the global gaming industry as a possible future model.

However, within this often-utopian image of gaming's successful integration into mainstream public preoccupation, the issue of gender is overlooked. Why are most pro-league players male and fans female? Are these images of gender stereotypes changing as the industry matures? Are we witnessing new modes of what Judith Butler calls "gender performativity"[6]—as a regulated set of actions—in game play and game spaces? Is the growing body of female players transforming the industry and gendered types of game play, or is it merely reinforcing gender stereotypes?

In this chapter, we explore one of the dominant locations for massively multiplayer online games (MMOGs), Korea, and the way in which female gamers are configured in this phenomenon. In Korea's booming gaming cultures, can females move beyond the role of "fans" and "casual" players into what Axel Bruns calls Web 2.0 rise of user created content (UCC) in the form of "produsers"[7]? Can female players move into the realms of professional players (pro-leagues in e-sport) and occupy creative and managerial forms of employment in the industry? Or does Korea, despite its successful model of games as part of mainstream culture, continue to deploy traditional gendered dichotomies around technologies? Regardless of the fact that just as many females are now inhabiting the social spaces of *PC bangs* (PC rooms) as their male counterpart and that the *PC bang* of the 1990s—described by Jun-Sok Huhh in Chapter 6—has been transformed into various niche type spaces (including *PC bangs* just for couples or females), clichés around gendered types of gaming prevail. Drawing from a case study of young female gaming in the "third" space[8] of *PC bangs,* this chapter considers the way in which notions of masculinity and femininity are configured through gaming practices for female players.

We aim to explore some of the "anomalies" surrounding girl gamers in Korea and how this, in turn, reflects gender stereotypes ingrained within techno-nationalist normalizations. In order to do so, this chapter will firstly outline both the games and technologies industries in Korea, and then discuss the rise of female gaming as an emerging culture (and its relationship to the industry), before moving onto a sample study we conducted with 30 young female gamers, followed up with five in-depth interviews. This study marks important preliminary fieldwork into this "invisible" phenomenon in order to expose gender stereotypes that are normalized around socio-technologies.

THE GAME OF TECHNO-NATIONALISM: LOCATING SOUTH KOREA IN THE TWENTY-FIRST CENTURY

In Korea, Internet and mobile telephonic spaces are helping to progress Korean forms of democracy.[9] For Korean sociologists Shin Dong Kim[10] and feminist anthropologist Hae-joang Cho,[11] the rise of a specific type of democracy in Korea has been supported in part by new technologies such as mobile phones. In particular, in Seoul one can find two types of youth sociality predicated around two convergent technological spaces: firstly that of the *haendupon*; and secondly that of the Internet through virtual communities (such as Cyworld's mini-hompys), and online multiplayer games and their attendant social spaces (i.e., *PC bang*). This usage of technological spaces is *not* about substituting the virtual for the actual but rather about supplementing actual relationships.[12] The relevance of the technology is intrinsically linked to maintaining face-to-face social capital. As Kyongwon Yoon observes, the rise of *haendupon* technology in Korea after 1997 was linked to the rise of youth cultures and their often-subversive use that saw them labelled "Confucian cyberkids."[13] Parallels can be made between the "youth problems" associated with the rise of mobile technologies in both Korea[14] and Japan,[15] and the reorientation by government and industry to rectify the negative press.

As a broadband "center" with the world's highest penetration rates and fastest speeds, Korea represents a prime example of innovative and emerging convergent mobile technologies. Now, Korean companies such as PandoraTV and afreeca allow users to have their own broadcast channel that they and others can view on their mobile and PC. This growth in UCC content and distribution systems also marks a period in which Korean users are shifting from being defined by activities of "scooping" or *per-na-ru-gi* (i.e., copying or transferring of other people's content) to new patterns of actively creating their own content.[16] The coordination between mobile and PC usage of the Internet to access and update virtual community sites has seen the emergence of new forms of UCC in Korea.[17]

Gracing the second floor of most commercial buildings in the bustling city of Seoul is a *PC bang*. These rooms are not the equivalent of "Internet cafés"—why would you need one in a city dubbed the most broadbanded country in the world[18]? Rather, *PC bangs* fuse game cultures with social spaces, functioning as a "third space" in between work/school and home.[19] As Huhh notes in Chapter 6, the "culture and industry" of *PC bangs* has been an integral in the nurturing and growth of Korea's most famous gaming genre, MMOGs. In the socio-technological fabric of Korea, games function as a vital industry for the Korean youth of today. And yet, like much of the global games industry, it is still dominated by men—as players, as makers, as professionals.

As a burgeoning center for innovative technologies and with a conspicuous usage of technologies in the everyday, Korea's capital Seoul could be viewed as a showcase of techno-nationalism as discussed eloquently by Dal Yong Jin and Florence Chee in Chapter 2. The projection of "dynamic Korea" (the tourism slogan used from 2005–2007) is one that has infused notions of technological innovation with the rise of power associated with Korea as a nation. In September 2006, approximately 6.4 million *PC bang* operated on the dominant Korean Internet portal, Daum. Almost 80% of Koreans use these *PC bang* as a social space, participating both online and offline for an average of over six hours per week.[20] With over 20,000 *PC bang* in Seoul alone, and with over one-third of Korea's population spending hours per day online playing MMOGs or the virtual community of Cyworld mini-hompy, the relationship between online and offline appears seamless in comparison to other locations. Although Koreans do, in general, place relative trust in technological spaces such as the Internet as a site for reliable information and democratic communication, the online is still no substitute for offline sociality.

In Chee's persuasive ethnography on *PC bang* and the politics of online multiplayer games, she argues that these spaces are *social spaces* that are viewed as "third spaces" between home and work.[21] For Korean youth, most of whom still live at home before (and even after) getting married, these *third spaces* operate as private spaces to connect with other people. As Huhh observes in Chapter 6, *PC bang* ensured the success of online games in Korea by nurturing both the culture and the business side of the industry; thus the online game is seen as synonymous with the *PC bang*.

In *PC bang*, female participants make almost half of the demographic. However, unlike male users who visibly and actively take part in MMOGs, female users appear to graze between mini-hompys, nate email and casual games. Females who do play games seem embarrassed to be defined as "gamers" and would reject such a "masculine" title. Even a cursory look at the games industry reveals that stereotypes about gendered forms of employment are omnipresent and all-pervasive. We will now turn to provide a snapshot history of the role of female fans and players within the Korean games industry and how this now manifests in the employment sector. Can female game players begin to challenge gendered norms around new media and the creative industries in Korea? Why are feminists visible within new media and creative media industries[22] and yet continuing to be invisible within the games industry?

RE-GENDERING OF THE *BANG*: THE RISE
OF FEMALE GAMERS IN KOREA

Technology is never neutral, and in the games industry gender and generational distinctions come to the forefront. Technological brands such as Samsung have become synonymous with Korea's postmodernity projected globally; but behind this story of technological innovation and sophistication lies another agenda, the role of gendered technologies[23] and performativity.[24] Indeed, the symbolic element of technology and its relationship to gender is not just an issue exclusive to Korea, rather a global phenomenon.[25] The gendering of technologies is most apparent in the sphere of the gaming industry, an industry that is quickly being transformed. In these changes, the role of women and games is undoubtedly a key issue.[26]

The symbolic dimensions at the level of the national are also reflected through the gender performativity in which both males and females utilize technologies to represent their femininity and masculinity.[27] It is important to conceptualize the rise of the Korean games industry with Korea's general embrace of turbo-capitalism, particularly within the framework of twenty-first century postmodernity in which Information and Communication Technologies (ICTs) and such media as Web 2.0 have become the new center for global financial and cultural capital investment. In the context of Korea's turbo-capitalism, key figures such as Cho have been swift to highlight the gendered naturalization operating such socio-technologies.[28]

So how does gender performativity operate within the games industry in Korea? How do "rites of passage" spaces such as *PC bangs*—in which games are an integral part of the socializing rituals—function in informing gender stereotyping as well as providing new avenues for gendered performativity? According to Gyongran Jeon in "A Study of Women in Digital Games and Their Gaming," the history of the male-dominated games industry has continued to see "women and girls who play digital games are, if visible, typically seen as oddballs and anomalies."[29] As Jeon conjectures,

In gaming activities female gamers are not only seeking parity with male counterparts, but are adopting and enacting oppositional stances to categorizations of gender appropriateness, access to leisure activities and consumption. Female gamers, however, are seen as intruders rather than inhabitants of gaming culture.[30]

Like many locations globally, Korean female gamers did not figure prominently in the old age of dark, smoke-filled arcades. As console gaming was not popularized in Korea, there were few other avenues for women to enter into the world of gaming. Whilst a handful of females visited arcades on a regular basis, this was mainly in the company of their brothers. For these females, most of their gaming experiences were episodical and sporadic. In short, Korean female gaming "culture" did not exist prior to online games.

Two interrelated factors saw the introduction of female gamers in Korea. First was the birth of the game that defined the Korean gaming industry, *StarCraft*. With the momentum of *StarCraft*, the popularity lead to many women becoming interested in the games as both professional players (e-sports) and as consumers of e-sports. Although women were not the main or most well known contenders in Korean *StarCraft* tournaments, their symbolic importance cannot be overstated.[31] According to one survey by Korea Game Industry Agency (KOGIA) 76% of e-sport fans are women. In Korea, top *StarCraft* pro-gamers are like rock idols—always been surrounded by female groupies. This image only operates to further indoctrinate the role of females as consumers and fans rather than players and even professionals in the creative sectors of the games industry. Much of the screen imaginary on the three TV stations devoted to e-sports has done little to challenge the gendered roles within the games industry and cultural production.

Another key factor was the explosion in Korean online gaming after the economic crisis of 1997, in which the International Monetary Fund (IMF) rescued Korea. Emerging from this crisis, online games absorbed new players who had not been familiar with computer gaming culture, with MMOGs in particular becoming synonymous with mainstream gaming. This was fed by the instrumental role played by the *PC bang*. As Huhh notes in Chapter 6, the rise of online gaming cannot be separated from the pivotal role played by the *PC bang*. Originally, the *PC bang* was typically a male-oriented place.[32] However, the advent of online games, nurtured within the social space of *PC bangs*, brought with it the emergence of hard-core women gamers for the first time in Korean gaming history. As there were much fewer obstacles that prevented women from engaging in online gaming, some female players began to spend as much time as their male counterparts. Nowadays, according to data by GameReport.co.kr (an online game consultancy), popular MMOGs have over 10% women subscribers.

As online games grew in Korea industry and competition got intense, new breeds of games targeting more diverse and broader audiences emerged. Even though some female players gathered around MMOG, the genre was foreign for many potential female players. Some game developers addressed this gap in the market by converging online gaming within the ever-burgeoning "casual" games genre. The intriguing strategy of many casual games is the concoction of simple logic found in classic games combined with the persistent and social nature of online games. The social aspect of online gaming also connected with many female players and their friends. Another wave of female gamers was ushered through with the early hit of the clone *Worms* game, *Fortress*. The popularity of *Fortress* resulted in the industry and popular culture in Korea becoming more aware of female gamers. As a result, many online game developers turned their attention from typical MMOGs to casual games in the hope of attracting female players.

As the developer of *B&B* and *Kart Rider*, Nexon is a leader in casual gaming. Drawing from a game style and logic akin to *Mario Kart*, *Kart Rider* was a phenomenon success with subscriptions surpassing the formidable *StarCraft*.[33] Nexon deployed a new business model of micro-transaction that worked very well with their casual player base. Whilst many female players might tend to hesitate in paying monthly fees for a game they might only play "occasionally," the company instead made its money from customized content—making in-game items purchasable. The element of customization was central in the success of *Kart Rider* and *B&B* where female players could become produsers in configuring their environment and characters.[34] This success draws from the pivotal role customization has played in the key Korean SNS—Cyworld mini-hompy—since it begun in 1998.

More recently, the burgeoning of casual games has afforded women more opportunities to become gamers. As demonstrated in Table 14.1, many of the popular games after 2004 have females as their key player

Table 14.1   The Percentage of Mainstream Games Played by Females

Title	% of Female Players	Genre	Publisher
Audition	55–60%	Casual (Dancing)	Yedang Online
Kart Rider	40%	Casual (Racing)	Nexon
Sudden Attack	35%	FPS	CJ Internet
Special Force	29.7%	FPS	NeoWiz
Maple Story	45%	MMORPG/Casual	Nexon
LoveBeat	60%	Casual (Dancing)	NCsoft

Source: Game Infinity.

base. With this rise in female gamers, it is interesting to consider how these gender shifts translate, if at all, into gender equality within the industry, especially regarding women occupying higher levels of management and responsibility rather than the typical administrative or designer role. Comparing 2005 to 2006 statistics from KOGIA (see Table 14.2), women's presence in roles such as game producer, graphic designer, system engineer, or games manager has increased slightly—concurrently their visibility has decreased in areas such as game planner, computer programmer, H/W development, PR/Marketing and office workers. While women employees have increased slightly from 20.3% (2005) to 21.0% (2006), the overall proportion of women in the industry is palpably small. Unsurprisingly, men have continued to dominate areas such as game producer (96.5%), computer programmer (93.8%), sound creator (94.0%) and hardware development (95%). The gendered stereotypes continue with women predominantly found in jobs such as office workers, graphic designer, GM and PR/Marketing.

While such a snapshot of the industry shows the perpetuation of gender stereotypes about gaming, it is in the everyday space of *PC bangs* in which young women are starting to explore new realms of gender performativity

Table 14.2   Game Industry Employment Statistics in 2007

Jobs	Number of Employees	% of Females
Game producer	1,379	4.2
Game planner	3,521	10.8
Graphic designer	8,554	26.1
Computer programmer	7,809	23.9
Scenario writer	204	0.6
Sound creator	267	0.8
H/W development	689	2.1
Sound engineer	1,331	4.1
GM	2,100	6.4
PR/Marketing	2,672	8.2
Office worker	4,188	12.8
Total	32,714	100.0%

Source: KOGIA[35]

that, in turn, could suggest future demographies and directions of the Korean games industry. Unquestionably, in Korea's twenty-first century turbo-capitalism gaming, broadband and mobile technologies have become embedded within the country's rise as one of the global leaders. But how is gender configured within these post-industrial narratives? Perhaps these *PC bang*—as places of play and performance—can give us insight into the politics (both personal and collective) of being a young woman in Korea today. Let us now turn to a sample study of female respondents who play games in *PC bangs* and how they, individually, reflect upon the notion of gendered play, being a female and playing games.

Figure 14.1 a and b　Some examples of *PC bangs* in Shinchon area. This *PC bang* is a smoke-free zone (once an anomaly for *PC bangs*) in which the computers are "naturalized" by plants.

Figure 14.2 a and b The new phenomenon of PC "love" *bangs* in which couples date further legitimates the role of PC *bang* as a social space for heterosexual romance.

THE GAME OF A GIRL: A SAMPLE STUDY OF YOUNG FEMALE GAMERS IN SHINCHON

In the winter month of December 2007 we visited various *PC bangs* at different times in the Shinchon area. The area of Shinchon is marked as a university area and thus highly populated with a sundry of "youth" attending the various universities such as Yonsei and Ewha. During the day and night, the streets are bustling with students looking for fun and adventure to chill out from studies. The plethora of PC and DVD *bangs* is all-pervasive. Girlfriends go to the *PC bang* to relax and socialize after dinner. Dating couples go to the *PC bang* to mix romance and game play (see Figure 14.2a and b);

so much so that one can find *PC bangs* just dedicated as dating spaces for couples. Once a site consisting of smoke-infested dark rooms in which male players appear like mushrooms growing by the electronic glow of the computer, *PC bangs* have transformed into customized spaces with ambience catered to specific clientele. Almost as many girls occupy most trendy *PC bangs* as their male counterpart, suggesting a shift in the gendered nature of gaming in the popular consciousness of twenty-first century Seoul. However, some stereotypes persist, particularly around the association with "feminine" casual game play versus "masculine" hardcore game play. The notion of a "girl gamer" was often disavowed for its unrelenting negative connotation as a type of awry gender performativity.

We surveyed over 30 females between the age of 15 and 34 years old, many (almost two-thirds) were students, while other occupations included fashion designer and office worker. Over 80% of respondents preferred to play games in *PC bangs* (80–100% of playing was conducted in the *bang*) than at home or on the mobile phone. Many chose the *PC bangs* because it offered access to a greater selection of online games and also the connection rates were higher and faster thus making more fluid game play. If they played at home they tended towards more casual games and simple puzzles. Despite these observed differences, many noted that they did not view a discernible disparity between these spaces and the types of games played. Over two-thirds of the respondents were in the *PC bang* with their boyfriend (in some cases their boyfriends were also guild members), with the other one third attending with class mates or club (of the games community) mates; in many cases these were the respondents' regular playing partners.

When asked whether they played games with many male or female players and why, many noted that it was predominantly men as a matter of convenience—male players seemed more interested and committed to game play. One respondent, playing with her boyfriend, noted that she preferred "male games" because men played "better" than most females; alternatively, another respondent played "mostly with guys since (there) were no women who liked games around." This sentiment was echoed by many respondents as "online games tend to have more male users," especially "since RPG have more male players." One respondent summed up the situation when she noted that she had to play with males "since females rarely play games, which is odd." In the survey, those who felt the gender imbalance as odd was outweighed by many who just accepted the stereotype of male players being more "dominant" and "better." For another respondent, she preferred playing games with other females "since (she) can feel more companionship"; another played consistently with a female friend "since I was introduced (to the) game by her." Here the social role of games for this female respondent is central—thus highlighting the relationship between intimacy and gaming.

When asked if they noted a difference between playing with females or males, over 80% argued that there was no difference. One respondent stated "the bad women player" is a myth. It's up to the individual." This was juxtaposed to another respondent who said, "women usually don't play games and good female game players are very rare." Those that noted a discrepancy stated that "men are more persistent and stubborn" or "men are better players in most cases" and, for another respondent, she tended to get "more nervous when playing with men since they tend to be better." Alternatively, one respondent who plays with her boyfriend said it is "more fun and playful when playing with my boyfriend." For one respondent, she had never played with a female player whilst another concurred that it was "hard to find female game players." One respondent stated, "I don't know whether the other person is a woman or a man."

The role of genres and game play was then discussed. We inquired about what types of games they played with most respondents noting a diversity of genres from RPG (role playing games), RTS (real time strategy), FPS (first person shooters), online games (such as *StarCraft*, *World of Warcraft* [henceforth *WoW*] and *Lineage)*, casual games (such as *Kart Rider* and *Tetris)* and sports/action/dancing games. Of all the games RPG dominated as the most played, challenging stereotypes about RPG being male games and female gamers preferring casual games.

When asked when they began to play games, many began in high school (middle and elementary). When asked who introduced them to game play many stated friends, with a few noting that their parents bought them a console, and a couple of other introduced by boyfriends or older brothers. Half of the respondents predominantly played MMOGs with the other half preferring FPS and then RPG. Asked why they continued to play the same games, many noted that it was "fun" playing together and that they felt a sense of achievement. Other responses included,

"Addicted to feeling achievement through role-player in virtual reality."
"It's repeats and I like that my skills are improving."
"It ends fast and kinda of thrilling; also I like earning game money."
"I might have been bored if I played alone but I'm a member of a club and it's fun"
"Because it's fun and easy, also everyone can play together in MMOGs"
"Personal satisfaction—games begin under equal conditions."
"I'm a better player in the game world than in real world."

Over half the respondents played about two hours per days, with the other half playing twice a week, mainly on weekends. When asked about their relationship to avatars, over half noted that they had positive relationships with their avatars. When asked about how female characters were depicted in game spaces and whether they thought that was problematic, over half of the respondents stated yes. Some of the responses included,

"Female characters tend to be passive. When there is the case of stronger female characters, they are sexually depicted."

"In my guild, male gamers asked why the sub-master was a woman and
I thought something was wrong."

"In *Sudden Attack*, male characters are free, female characters are not
free and wear sexy outfits."

"Unrealistic appearance of female characters . . ."

"Male characters are too strong . . ."

"Women are always pretty and slender, while males are strong and mus-
cular (lack of diversity)."

"Female characters are too sexual."

"Men who play female characters are similar to perverts."

"Many people get confused between reality and games and character is
everything to them."

Over one-third of the respondents noted the overly sexualized nature of
women and how unrealistic it was. The issue of female representation—
both within the games and the actual game spaces of *PC bangs*—was
an issue for most of the respondents. From the comments we can see
that many females played with male gamers through necessity rather
than desire and many noted that the representation of women in games
was less than adequate. It was interesting to note that some respondents
discussed the importance of equality—gender or otherwise. Many of the
respondents transcend gender stereotypes about women being casual
players and often they enjoyed frequently playing games deemed as masculine such as FPS and RPG. We could argue that this is only the beginning of a new market and phenomenon of "visible" female gamers after
years of "non-existence."

Perhaps what was more telling about individual females experience and
identification with (and against) gaming was in the in-depth interviews.
Unlike the sample surveys that were conducted in *PC bangs* and which
surveyed respondents who both did and didn't identify with, or as, female
game players, the interviews gleaned a more in-depth understanding of
females who were happy to elaborate upon their experiences of games
as part of their maturation. In a series of five interviews with five female
respondents aged between 20 and 30 years old, we could gain a sense of
how females entered the world of games, often outside the normal rites of
passage for men (i.e., via the *PC bang*). What became apparent was the role
played by older and younger siblings in contextualizing and introducing
girls to games. Thus gaming for these respondents was linked initially to
a familial form of intimacy, and then later, to friends and future familial
relations (i.e., boyfriends).

For one graduate student aged 27, her first experience of games was via
her older brother. For this respondent, her experiences of gaming also provided a way in which she could bond with her older brother and share
"secrets" from the parents. As she noted,

My first experience of gaming was a hand-held game console that I played with my older brother. I remember playing some kind of Quiz games with him. Most of the gaming was done at home, but once in a while I visited arcade with my brother. I rarely visited arcade by myself. We visited arcade when we came back from private evening lessons. As our parents did not like us going to the arcade, it was our little secret. Entering middle school, there is no chance to visit arcade. The school was for females only, so interests in gaming were hard to find.

She noted that during this time in middle and high school, with little shared time with her brother, her games began to differentiate from that of her brother. While her brother played *Ages of Discovery* (by Koei) on the computer, she played easily available games like *Blues Brothers* and *Doleman*. With school friends she rarely played computer games and they never visited an arcade. Here we see the way in which gendered divisions played out in schooling operate to create and reflect larger gendered performativities for young people as they grow into teenagers and young adults. Clearly the respondent is highlighting the way in which the female school intervened into her experiences of games as a site for bonding and sociality with her brother so that she may become conditioned into certain types of performativity and associated types of "casual" game play. Unquestionably, she infers that she would have preferred to try other game genres but she was only socially allowed to play the "casual" cute games. When asked what games she played at home she noted *Kart Rider* (although she played this mostly at a *PC bang*) and NDS games such as *Nintendogs*, *Super Mario*, *Let's learn English*. When asked how she compared the gendered spaces of the arcade and its predecessor, the *PC bang*, she notes,

> In case of the *PC bang*, as it was not so manly as the arcade. I prefer cleaner places so I avoid old and manly *PC bang*s. I visited in *PC bang* first when I was university student. At that time, most of people were men and it was a very smoky place. Men looked at me strangely as if to say, "why is a girl at here?" Now, this is not so . . .

When the same respondent asked whether gaming is for men, she demurred,

> When I meet girlfriends, going café is more expensive than going *PC bang*. It is a natural choice to go *PC bang*. When I meet gamer friends, it is more fun to play games in a *PC bang*. I think that *PC bang* is not so much masculine space as gaming place. I found that there were a lot of women gamers in *Kart Rider*.

For this respondent, the first time she visited a *PC bang*, she was a freshman. She "went there with male seniors, not with female friends or seniors.

Most of visits were done to learn how to play *StarCraft*." For this respondent it allowed her to have face-to-face contact with the opposite sex and made the game play much more "fun." As she noted, "playing games at *PC bang* is one of favorite activities when I meet friends."

For another graduate student aged 29, her initiation into gaming was vis-à-vis her induction of her younger brother. She describes her introduction.

> In the mid 1980s when some game consoles came out, I played them first at my relative's house. I teased my parents to buy one. At first, I played with my father, later with my younger brother. Game cartridges were circulated among friends. I rented some of games at local game shop. Information about new games was obtained via friends; I was not active in pursuing this. These friends were younger male relatives (who guided me to video-gaming) and friends of the same church. Some of my relatives lived in my neighborhood, so we played together a lot. I played with my own age group as elders were much more proficient in gaming. I remember some names—*Mad Max*, *Super Mario*, *Wonder Boy*. I very occasionally visited the arcade with my relatives but not so much time. My parents told me that going arcade would ruin my schoolwork and that the arcade was full of bad scum who loot money from children. I remember that playing at arcade was more fun when playing for money as it made me concentrated more on the game than when I played at home with game console.

Like the first respondent, this respondent played games less when she entered an all-girl middle and high school. However, this was less to do with the male connotation of gaming but that it seemed childish. Gaming appeared as opposite to studying, something that interrupted education and learning, rather than providing other forms of knowledge. Once again, the notion of gaming as a interfering with studying was enforced by parental disapproval. She notes,

> I rarely played games when I was in middle school and high school. Videogames looked childish. Also, it seems to me that studying was more important than playing. My parents scolded me when I was playing games. At that time, as I attended women middle school and high school, there were few opportunities to have contact with new games. If I had attended co-ed school, I would have been interested in gaming. My favorite leisure activity is meeting friends. When I became a university student, I rarely played game, either. Although on sleepless nights I played *Puyo Puyo* or *solitaire*.

When asked to reflect upon the differences between the arcade and *PC bang* she noted,

In early days, the *PC bang* had a similar bad image to early arcade. In late 90s, when the *PC bang* first appeared, many inappropriate off-line incidents involving selling sex were conducted at the *PC bang*. I think this made me associate the *PC bang* with something bad. I also went to *PC bang* to play games and also for printing. Later, I visited the *PC bang* for chatting. My friends played *StarCraft*, but I did just chatting. Nowadays, the *PC bang* seems to be very clean and nice place. Overall services are exceptional when compared to the old days.

For this respondent, she often attends the *PC bang* with her boyfriend who loves playing games. Together they play *Kart Rider* as a way to chat and play together. For this respondent, like the first respondent, her re-induction into gaming was via *StarCraft*. As she reflected,

> *StarCraft* made me interested in games again. I didn't do well in the game, but it lighted my fire again. As I study film, I was attracted by the gorgeous images in games and the thrilling elements. *Kart Rider* is my favorite. It is very simple and fun. In 2004–2005 when I had not a regular job, I played the game a lot. I played *YulHeolGangho* (a Korean online game). My boyfriend told me that the game earned me money by real-money trading. I didn't earn, but he did. I played online games primarily at the *PC bang*. The games tended to be played by a group, so I played it at the *PC bang* with off-line contacts. My gaming friends consisted of friends from the same church. I was the only woman at this circle.

For respondent three, a 25-year-old graduate student, like respondent one, it was her older brother that initiated her into the world of family at age six with Game Boy and Gamix (the modified PC game console). During her middle and high school years, she observed that few girls played games. Thus respondent three was quite motivated playing both with her older brother and by herself. She even purchased games magazines. As she noted,

> . . . during my middle and high school years, I went to arcade with some of my women friends. We talked and played arcade games like *Bubble Bubble*, *Tetris*, and *1945*. Then I played games on the console. On my computer, I played RPG and strategy like *Romance of Three Kingdom*. Throughout my university years, I played in many games in a *PC bang*. I met many gaming friends playing online games mostly.

The *PC bang*, for this respondent, was not an appropriate place for high school students. She noted that the used to perceived as "kind of ghetto for the game addicted." It was a place where girls did not belong, similar to the dark image of the old arcade in Korea. But now she views the *PC bang* as a "casual place for young people." During her freshmen year at university she began to visit the *PC bangs* with fellow students, most of whom were male. As she liked many of the games, playing games at night in *PC bangs* became a ritual. She started playing *StarCraft* in 2000, and while she confessed that she was not good at the game, she found online games fun, especially because it involved playing together with others.

For this respondent, her favorite games were the simple puzzle games such as *Fortress* and *Worms*. She also noted that all of her male friends enjoyed games, especially her boyfriend who liked to go the Game *bang* for PlayStation (called *PS bang* in Korea). At the *PS bang*, they played *Smackdown*, *Tennis*, and *Golf*—the choice of game was always hers. Sometimes the boyfriend carried the game console to her home. In contrast, she viewed the *PC bang* as a place where she played with her friends, not her boyfriend. When asked about the gender stereotypes around gaming, she replied,

> After university, I played *StarCraft*. Some told me girls are not well-suited to gaming. I disagreed, showing them that girls can play games also. Now, there are many female players although the number of male gamers is still much larger than that of female. I do not play or talk about games only with women. However, boys can go to *PC bang* or PlayStation *bang* to play, but girls do not.

She noted that male players often assume a player is a girl if they play badly. She said that when boys tell her that she is proficient player this is in comparison to other girls. She said that while she likes games very much, she is "not good at game considering my time investment. When other players knew that I'm a girl, I have not experienced any insults or harassing. I think other players recognize me as girl when I'm playing badly." When asked to elaborate how gendered play manifests within genres and modes of game play, she observes,

> There are few female players in fighting games. Characters of games reveal their targeting audience. In online games, styles of chatting can provide many clues about gender of players. Cute words and many emoticons are girl's style. Girls use emoticons at their playing ID. I talk in straight way for I hate such an attitude of the girl gamer. When other players speak badly, I presume that they consider me as a male. I do not treat others differently by their gender. My playing friends do not want to treat me differently because of my gender.

Respondent three clearly identifies gendered gaming stereotypes that she perpetually undermines in her online gaming practices. By not deploying emotional cuteness and by not partaking in games such as *Kart Rider* she is an example of how young women are challenging some of the conventions around gendered gaming. For the fourth respondent (aged 28, unemployed), similar to the second respondent, her entrance into gaming was via a bonding with her younger brother. As she noted,

> When I was young, I liked to play games. I acquired game console after my brother and I that begged our parents to buy. I liked to play outside with boys. Information about games was shared from male friends. I play mostly with males, occasionally with a female. I became a game player easily and thus had many male friends.

Unlike the first two respondents where attending all female middle and high school interrupted their gaming, respondent four still managed to maintain her interest and participation. As she observed,

> I liked games during my middle and high school years. Even though I attended female only schools I still liked to play games. But I did play less time than elementary school years for I began to develop other interests. I visited arcades at that time to play *Tetris* and *Bubble Bubble*. During my university years, I became addicted to games again. The *PC bang* was at its peak and I played *StarCraft* every night.

As one of the most openly embracing respondents in identifying as a girl gamer, respondent four did note that being interested in gaming as a female did have a stigma. As she reflected, "When I was young, people did not look fondly onto girls that went to arcade or *PC bang*. I didn't care, however; my desire to play was so overwhelming and all encompassing. I went the arcade with my friends, and sometimes I went alone." For respondent four, the *PC bang* is the place in which to spend time with her boyfriend. As she noted, her and her boyfriend have been playing games in a *PC bang* since their first date. It is their "meeting place"—it "is cheap, and when one is late, it is good place to wait." She sees playing games with her boyfriend as good for developing their interpersonal skills and shared experiences. They play *StarCraft*, *Lineage* and *Kart Rider*. When asked about whether she still sees gendered issues about gaming she noted,

> People told me that girls are not viewed well if they play games. In particular, people have pity for women who play game at the later age. Strangely, it is women who look at girls gaming more negatively than men. When *StarCraft* was popular, there were no couple gamers at the *PC bang*. *Kart Rider* changed this situation a little bit, but gaming is hobby of boys. In case of *Lineage*, there are some female waitress players, and some girls who sell sex for items which has created a negative image for women. I think that there are more female players than those that would openly admit.

As respondent four insightfully identifies, much of the assumptions and stereotypes seem to be predicated via other women another than men. Indeed, as the rites of passage from childhood to teenage years and then early adulthood suggest, it is the invention of going to a same sex school that stops girls playing games. In the case of respondent four, she had to defiantly continue to play games despite being aware of how others were judging her.

For the fifth respondent aged 26 (unemployed), unlike the other four, it was her older sister that initiated her into the world of gaming. As a child, she remembers having a Game Boy at home, and while she had a PC with games, she didn't install them herself. During her high school years *Dance, Dance Revolution* and *PUMP* (locally developed variant of DDR) were her favorite games. Attending a co-ed school, she played a few games with boys, noting that talking about games was a way to talk to boys. But, it wasn't until at university that her "real gaming" began. During her high school years was when she first visited a *PC bang*, which she noted, concurring with the other respondents, that it was very much like the old arcades.

Since then she observed that the interior and atmosphere of the *PC bang* has changed dramatically, rendering it as a space in which females can feel comfortable. She now attends a *PC bang* regularly with her gaming friends. While she began with *Kart Rider* and *Pangya* she then moved onto WoW. Having played *WoW* for six months, she's now at highest level. She plays with both males and females and never plays alone (she has no games installed at home). Like the other respondents, she plays with her boyfriend. She introduced him to play both *WoW* and *Kart Rider*. The "*PC bang* was casual dating place for us" she stated. However, she noted that he often got irritated by people who couldn't play well—resulting in them quarreling. The respondent noted that games can provide an appropriate setting to take a date online, stating, "My friend took a date to a place in the game where the game scenery was very beautiful. She told me that it created the perfect mood for a date." She continued, "the advantage of *PC bang* date is playing a game with partner. When I'm not playing at *PC bang*, I feel disconnected."

CONCLUSION: BEYOND *THE FAN*

As Korea turns a new chapter in its turbo capitalism and its games industry continues to grow unabated, it seems appropriate to not only rethink the way in which "games" have been institutionalized in the selling and consuming of Korea but how they relate to the politics of gendered play more generally. As noted in the surveys, many females in *PC bangs* refute the title of "girl gamers"—this is partly to do with the fact that often they will do many things in a *PC bang* such as homework, mini-hompy, nate emailing along with playing casual games. Games are not seen as a separate to the other activities—rather, games are part of the technoculture that keeps them returning to *PC bangs* daily. This also has to do with the ongoing stigma of games as a "boy" or male-orientated activity. This stereotype is hard to shift, both inside and outside Korea.

As the industry diversifies and continues to make hybrid games that converge the socializing of online gaming with cute casual gaming, will this lead to females more proudly announcing a "girl gamer" title? Or will the "casual" adage continue to devalue and illegitimate such game play as mere "girl games?" Why, if games are so mainstream, does the divide between fans and players, fans and makers, continue to be determined by gender? Is this but a mirror onto society?

In this sample survey and interviews we have attempted to engage with young women who both identify and announce labels such as "girl gamers" within the site for much of this activities, the *PC bang*. As we can see in the few young female voices, gaming and *PC bangs* are very much part of becoming an adult in contemporary Seoul. Far from the stereotypes of gendered gaming, we are seeing new modes of transgression and play that contest these notions. As identified by the interviewees, the entrance into gaming is through shared sibling experiences that distinguish them from their parents' generation. Games and *PC bangs* not only provide a space in which young people share experiences and emotions between males and females.

Beyond providing a vehicle for heteronormality and match-making, *PC bangs* are also providing a space in which women can explore and perform various forms—both conventional and transgressive—of gendered performativity. As respondent four noted, she openly challenged the association of female players with bad and also made an active choice to partake in non-feminine modes of game play. Indeed, this study identifies that as the *PC bang* has replaced the café as the everyday space to socialize, more studies on how gender is being played in these "third spaces" needs to be explored. Just as the *PC bang* no longer resembles the "dark image" of the arcade of the past, so too, are emerging new forms of gendered play that transgress online and offline spaces. This study is not meant to be conclusive, rather we are trying to engage with the complex game and reality of what it is to be a young female growing up in Korea and what role gaming spaces and *PC bangs* provide and facilitate, both materially and symbolically, in this formation.

NOTES

1. Organization for Economic Co-operation and Development (OECD), *OECD broadband statistics, 2006*. Retrieved 20 December 2006 from *http://www. oecd.org/sti/ict/broadband*
2. Darrell M. West, *Global e-government, 2006* (Providence, Rhode Island: Center for Public Policy, Brown University, 2006).
3. This is a new form of late twentieth century capitalism that deploys technology, free trade, deregulation and privatization. See Edward Luttwak,

Turbo-Capitalism: Winners and Losers in the Global Economy (London: HarperCollins Publishers, 1999).

4. Tim O'Reilly 2004.
5. Han Woo Park and Randolph Kluver, "Affiliation in Political Blogs in South Korea: Comparing Online and Offline Social Networks," in *Internationalizing Internet Studies*, eds. G. Goggin and M. McLelland (London: Routledge, 2009), 252–264.
6. Judith Butler, *Gender Trouble* (London: Routledge, 1991).
7. Axel Bruns and Jason Jacobs, eds., *Uses of Blogs* (New York: Peter Lang, 2006).
8. Florence Chee, "Understanding Korean Experiences of Online Game Hype, Identity, and the Menace of the 'Wang-tta,'" presented at *DIGRA 2005 Conference: Changing Views—Worlds in Play*, Canada, 2005.
9. Shin Dong Kim, "The Shaping of New Politics in the Era of Mobile and Cyber Communication," in *Mobile Democracy,* ed. K. Nyíri (Vienna: Passagen Verlag, 2003), 317–326 (325).
10. Kim, "The Shaping of New Politics in the Era of Mobile and Cyber Communication,"
11. Hae-Joang Cho, "Youth, Internet, and Alternative Public Space," presented at the *Urban Imaginaries: An Asia-Pacific Research Symposium*, Lingnan University, Hong Kong, 2004. Hae-Joang Cho, "Reading the 'Korean Wave' as a Global Shift," *Korea Journal*, Winter 2005: 147–182.
12. Larissa Hjorth and Heewon Kim, "Being there and being here: gendered customising of mobile 3G practices through a case study in Seoul," *Convergence* 11 (2005): 49–55.
13. Kyongwon Yoon "The Making of Neo-Confucian Cyberkids: Representations of Young Mobile Phone Users in South Korea," *New Media and Society*, 8 (5) 2006: 753–771
14. Yoon "The Making of Neo-Confucian Cyberkids: Representations of Young Mobile Phone Users in South Korea." Also see Kyongwon Yoon, "Retraditionalizing the Mobile: Young People's Sociality and Mobile Phone Use in Seoul, South Korea," *European Journal of Cultural Studies* 6, 2003: 327–43.
15. Misa Matsuda, "Discourses of *Keitai* in Japan," in *Personal, Portable, Pedestrian: Mobile Phones in Japanese Life,* eds. M. Ito, Okabe, D. and M. Matsuda (Cambridge, MA: MIT Press, 2005), 19–40.
16. Yoon cited in Seung-hyun Yoo, "Internet, Internet Culture, and Internet Communities of Korea: Overview and Research Directions," in *Internationalising Internet Studies,* eds. G. Goggin and M. McLelland (London: Routledge, 2009), 217–236. Also see Larissa Hjorth "Gifts of Presence: A Case Study of a South Korean Virtual Community, Cyworld's Mini-Hompy" in *Internationalising Internet Studies,* eds. G. Goggin and M. McLelland (London: Routledge, 2009), 237–251.
17. S.Y. Park and S.H Yoo, "The effect of the sense of on-line community on website loyalty and purchase intention," 경영학 연구, 32(6) 2003: 1695–1713.
18. OECD, *OECD broadband statistics.*
19. Chee, "Understanding Korean Experiences of Online Game Hype, Identity, and the Menace of the 'Wang-tta.'"
20. National Internet Development Agency of Korea (NIDA), *Netizen Internet usage: Press release* (2006). Retrieved September 30, 2006 from *http://www.nida.go.kr/doc/issue_sum_report.pdf.*
21. Chee, "Understanding Korean Experiences of Online Game Hype, Identity, and the Menace of the 'Wang-tta.'"
22. Cho, "Youth, Internet, and Alternative Public Space."

23. Misa Na, "The Cultural Construction of the Computer as a Masculine Technology: An Analysis of Computer Advertisements in Korea," *Asian Journal of Women Studies* 7 (3) 2001: 93–114.

24. Underlying this socio-technological success story of Korea *vis-à-vis* companies such as Samsung is the deployment of the "discursive strategies" of the *Hyoja* (meaning a son devoted to filial duties/industry) as the symbol of the mobile phone industry. For Jung-eun Hong, the *Hyoja is the* "normalizative idealization" of Samsung Anycall that is seen as the national mobile phone. Moreover, the *Hyoja Samsung Anycall conflation is also indicative* of what Hong sees as the "neo-liberal deregulation of mobile phone industry" (Hong 2007: n.p). See Jong-Eun Hong, "Mobile Phone Machine and Its Discourses Analysis," paper presented at *Mobile Media Seminar,* Yonsei University, December, 2007.

25. Leopoldina Fortunati, "Gender and the mobile phone" in *Mobile technologies: From Telecommunications to Media,* eds. G. Goggin and L. Hjorth (London/New York: Routledge, 2009), 23–34. Judy Wajcman, Michael Bittman and Jude Brown "Intimate Connections: The Impact of the Mobile phone on Work/Life Boundaries," in *Mobile technologies: From Telecommunications to Media,* eds. G. Goggin and L. Hjorth (London/New York: Routledge, 2009), 9–22.

26. See Henry Jenkins and Justine Cassells, *From Barbie to Mortal Kombat: Gender and Computer Games* (Mass: MIT Press, 1998). Pam Royse, Joon Lee, Baasanjav Undrahbuyan, Mark Hopson and Mia Consalvo, "Women and games: technologies of the gendered self," *New Media & Society* 9 (4), 2007: 555–576. Elisabeth Hayes, "Gendered Identities at Play: Case Studies of Two Women Playing Morrowind," *Games and Culture* 2 (1) 2007: 23–48. Kristen Lucas and John L. Sherry, "Sex Differences in Video Game Play: A Communication-Based Explanation," *Communication Research* 31 (5) 2004: 499–523. Helen W. Kennedy, "Lara Croft: Feminist Icon or Cyberbimbo? On the Limits of Textual Analysis," *Game Studies* 2 (2) 2002. Retrieved 20 January 2006 from *http://www.gamestudies. org/0202/kennedy/.*

27. Na, "The Cultural Construction of the Computer as a Masculine Technology: An Analysis of Computer Advertisements in Korea."

28. As Cho notes in 'You are entrapped in an imaginary well,' Korea in 1990s experienced a period of pivotal "high-growth economic development" that saw an "economic miracle." Korea's example of successful turbo-capitalism was viewed as a type of "Confucian capitalism" that contested the west's "Protestant capitalism." However, the 1997 financial crisis—which resulted in the IMF financial rescue—transformed the tune of optimism into a state of national disgrace. The backdrop to the new turbo-capitalist consumerism—in which Korean youth were beckoned by conservative gender stereotypes around labor—was, for Cho, undoubtedly highlighted the conflation between the notion of "*kukmim*" (a member of the nation) and "*kajok*" (family). See Hae-Joang Cho, "'You are entrapped in an imaginary well': the formation of subjectivity within compressed development—A feminist critique of modernity and Korean culture," *Inter-Asia Cultural Studies* 1(1) 2000: 49–69.

29. Gyongran Jeon, "A Study of Women in Digital Games and Their Gaming," 사이버커뮤니케이션학보, Vol. 22, 2007: 83–117 (116).

30. Jeon, "A Study of Women in Digital Games and Their Gaming," 116-7.

31. It is not unusual for coaches to be female—one female pro-gamer, Kim Ga-Eul, is the head coach of a pro-gamers team, Khan (sponsored by Samsung electronics).

32. The earlier versions of *PC bangs* were dark and filled with smoke, a far cry from the types of feminine environments where women would feel welcomed. This has changed dramatically with the emergence of various types of *PC bangs* such as smoke-fee spaces or dating places.
33. Larissa Hjorth, "*Playing at being mobile*: Gaming, cute culture and mobile devices in South Korea," *Fibreculture journal* 8, 2006. Retrieved 10 January 2007 from *http://journal.fibreculture.org/*.
34. Nexon's focus upon women gamers is unique. The company even regularly hosts professional *Kart Rider* gaming competitions for women only.
35. KOGIA, "Guide to Korean Game Industry and Culture 2007" (April 2007). Retrieved 20 February 2008 from *http://www.gameinfinity.or.kr/game/gb_main.jsp*.

15 Playing the Gender Game
The Performance of Japan, Gender and Gaming via Melbourne Female Cosplayers

Larissa Hjorth

INTRODUCTION

Last September I went to the Tokyo Game Show. Of all the games expos, the Tokyo Game Show is the Holy Grail for those working in the games industry. All the major companies promote their new showcase game there—it's a "make or break" for the games industry. If you make a splash in the sea of games at the Show, the success of your game is ensured. For game players and games enthusiasts, the Show is not just the "Mecca" of all that is new and classic in the games industry and a chance to play pre-released block-busters. Rather, one of the dominant drawcards can be found just *outside* the showrooms . . . No, I am not talking about industry networking but one of the key drawcards to the Tokyo Game Show, *the cosplayers*.

Cosplay is short for "costume play" and cosplayers take their inspiration from games, *manga* (comics), *anime* (animation), and movies. As a sub-cultural movement, various forms of cosplayers can be found both within Japan and globally. Cosplaying provides new avenues for fans to express their interest in Japanese popular culture; they rewrite the role of fandom in the scripting of media discourses as well as being examples of twenty-first century transmedia storytelling.[1] Re-scripting relations between gam-ing and other media such as *anime* and *manga*, cosplayer also create new forms of fandom/player agency in both online spaces and offline at conven-tions. Cosplayers have become a key part of the expanding media cultures surrounding gaming, as well playing a central role in a rites of passage for young females to enter the traditionally male-centered gaming worlds.

Arguably, dressing up as game characters affords new types of gender performativity such as what Laura Miller calls "kogals"[2]—a hybrid of vari-ous forms of Japanese female types such as *shôjo* (young female), female high-school (*gyaru*), (trendy female in her twenties) *kôgyaru*. For Miller, *kôgyaru* are "kogals" and they represent "a new girl subculture . . . a vehicle for mainstream outrage at the economic and cultural power of youth, espe-cially the subcultural compositions of young women."[3] In particular, the kogal and their various subgroups such as *ganguro* and *yamamba* partake in a "new aesthetic of the non-cute, or cute infused with an ironic twist."[4]

These kogals—through their creative and empowered deployment of new media technologies epitomized by mobile novels (*keitai shôsetsu*)—de-center the male role of the *otaku* as prime game consumer. Cosplayers provide new avenues for expression and subjectivity, operating in an ambiguous space in which females are both objects and subjects. Transformation and subversion are all part of the game as cosplayers perform online and offline fantasies and fictions, bringing the politics of "techno-cuteness"[5] into the corporeal world.

Cosplayers are a key example of the fan as a co-producer in interpreting and adapting game characters into a haptic offline world. The art of cosplay is that it highlights that the boundaries between fans, players and creative producers are blurring and transforming mainstream culture. Once fans were believed to break down boundaries between text and reader,[6] now the roles of player and co-producer—or what Axel Bruns calls "produser"[7]—has been transformed. Pointing to the rise of Web 2.0[8] and its emphasis upon "participatory culture," Henry Jenkins argues that fans are increasingly impacting mainstream culture, policy and intellectual property.[9] Characterized by a focus upon "conversational media" and user created content (UCC) and communities, Web 2.0 has afforded new ways for fans to creatively connect as well as providing new avenues for distribution. Through vehicles such as Web 2.0, new forms of media such as cosplaying can spread across the region, demonstrating the increased presence of females in a world once dominated by males (in the form of the *otaku*), gaming.

The emergence of cosplayers has highlighted the growing interest and agency of female game players. Emerging from Japanese game and *anime* cultures, the phenomenon has spread across the Asia-Pacific, providing a platform for female fans and gamers to participate actively in the process of gaming cultures, and, specifically, Japan's role as "gaming center." As gaming becomes increasingly mainstream it is ancillary cultures—such as cosplaying—that are demonstrating new forms of gendered performativity and, in turn, how Japan is configured in the role of interactive entertainment in the twenty-first century.

The circulation of images of cosplayers operates curiously across transnational borders, complicating the role of "consuming Japan"[10] globally. Increasingly, as more women enter the games industry as both players and producers/designers, so too has the phenomenon—or fan-omenon might be more apt—of cosplay grown. Cosplaying enables young women to shift from player to the hybrid of the produser and then onto, in some cases, producers. By exploring the role of cosplayers in the region, we can gain insight into how female gamers are both consumers and active participants in the imagining and re-imaging of "Japan." Moreover, given the gendered performativity proffered by cosplay and Japanese-specific gender types such as kogal, how does this help young females to conceptualize themselves in the still very male-dominated area?

In this chapter, I explore the role of consuming Japanese gaming cultures—as part of broader media scapes and digital literacies of the twenty-first century—and how young female gamers and future game makers deploy the mechanism of cosplay to rethink gendered performativity in the future of gaming. This chapter explores the shift from player to produser to producer and the way cosplay provides an avenue for young women to re-imagine their role in the games industry as they move from consumer to active fan to games designer/producer. In order to do, I have surveyed a group of 15 young female cosplayers in Melbourne.

Drawing on a diverse range of cultural backgrounds, these cosplayers show how the imagining of "Japan," and gendered performativity, is part of the "magic circle"[11] of game play while also being outside that suspension of belief (or disbelief). They show that game play highlights the "ambiguities of play"[12] that are subject to various forms of age, class, and ethnicity in the localisation process. These young females range from 16 to 26 years old and have divergent interests in cosplaying as a dualistic portal into gaming and Japan. I chose to focus upon respondents that were studying to become game designers and artists as this seemed to be a relatively new phenomenon that needed unpacking. I was particularly interested in this avenue as an emerging "rites of passage" for young females entering the games industry—from player to produser to producer. For many, cosplaying is synonymous with both Japan and gaming, and thus to partake in cosplaying is to enter into a world in which interpretations of gaming and Japan are continuously put into question.

This chapter marks a preliminary study into the region's female gamers and the important role the consumption of Japan plays in locating themselves in the relatively male-dominated industry. This study highlights the need for longitudinal studies into young women's deployment of cosplaying as a vehicle for entering the games industry. One can't help but wonder whether cosplaying is about them being "fans" and game players, and that once they finish tertiary education and move into employment, whether they continue to be cosplayers once they move from player to produser to producer.

However, before moving onto the sample study of cosplayers in Melbourne (some of whom are currently studying in games degrees), I will firstly contextualize cosplaying within the gendered technocultures of Japan—particularly kogal *kawaii* (cute) cultures. Part of this understanding is the way in which technological customization is branded with specific types of gendered performativity—epitomized by Brian McVeigh's notion of "techno-cute"[13]—that is, the warming up of cold technologies by cute customization. Through the role of *kawaii* culture, we can see many types of gendered performativities that afford different possibilities to female and male consumers. These modes also provide pathways to transgress models of engagement and agency from *player-produser-producer*.

LET THE GAMES BEGIN: LOCATING JAPAN AND
EMERGING GENDERED PERFORMATIVITIES

Japan's key role in producing technologies and, more specifically, domestic technologies for global markets since 1970 is renowned to the point of cliché. Behind the global images of techno-savvy youth adorned with the latest technological gadgets in "electric cities" such as Akihabara, Japan's role in producing and consuming new technologies—from the Sony Walkman, Atari games console, PlayStation and *'keitai* (mobile phone) IT revolution'—has been pivotal. For Mizuko Ito et al., the market success of these technologies can be best explained by characteristics of the new media that they call the three P's—pedestrian, personal and portable.[14]

The significance of these three P's is that they transform technological gadgets into socio-cultural artefacts by relocating them into the dynamic space of cultural production. Tokyo, in the games world, is arguably the originator of gaming. This has also resulted in further enhancing Japan's soft capital, or what Douglas McGray called "Gross National Cool,"[15] in which technology has been a key node in Japanese twenty-first century nationalism.[16] As a center for gaming and media technologies deploying innovative "electronic individualism,"[17] Japan has often provided a "default sci-fi"[18] backdrop for Western imaginings of the future. For many a player and maker of games the consumption of Japan as the "center" is the standard rites of passage.

However, Tokyo is also the center for ancillary subcultures in which media cultures of gaming, *manga* and *anime* merge. The phenomenal role of gaming in Tokyo undoubtedly has its lineage (no pun on the game intended) in Japan's key role in developing innovative domestic technologies globally. The symbol of the *otaku*, once denigrated as a social misfit, has, like the gentrification of Akihabara post *Densha Otoko*, been reconfigured as a positive icon of Japanese culture—both locally and globally. As the story goes, an *otaku* saved a young lady (Hermés) on a train while she was being harassed. The *otaku* then wrote about the incident and his love for her on the biggest BBS forum 2ch and before long it was the longest and most talked about posting. It became a series of *manga*, feature film and, most importantly, part of the urban mythology. The phenomenon of *Densha Otoko* marked a pivotal shift in which Japan reinvented the once denigrated male icon, the *otaku*, to become a twenty-first century male icon. As media technologies became increasingly prevalent in the publicness of intimacy within twenty-first century global lifestyles, a revision of the *otaku* as symbolic of "geek chic," provided an avenue for re-centering Japan's reign on contemporary global popular media technologies.

Concurrent to this re-scripting of the *otaku* was the rise of the female *kôgyaru* in which new technologies such as the *keitai* were deployed as part of her diet of restructured femininity. In the latter part of the twentieth century, Japan's national icon, the *oyaji (salaryman)*, had been displaced by the *kôgyaru* (trendy female in her twenties) and her often-subversive deployment of the *keitai*.[19] In her disavowal of traditional notions of femininity as passive, she demonstrated through vicarious consumption that she did not need a man (except perhaps an *oyaji* to subsidize her materialistic desires). It was the phenomenon of subsidized dating that undoubtedly gave her a further negative connation. As Misa Matsuda[20] notes, government and industry worked hard to realign *keitai* culture away from these negative associations of female empowerment (often at the price of men); the *otaku* offering a perfect decoy. However, while *Densha Otoko* grabbed the popular imagination of Japan in 2005 and 2006, the rise of *keitai* creative industries—and the dominance of female creators and fans in such areas as *keitai shôsetsu*—has highlighted that emerging female-orientated cultures cannot be ignored.

The visibility of empowered—or at least "independent" in the case of *kôgyaru*—images of young females in Japan are almost inseparable from the rise of *keitai* cultures in Japan. However, in the case of gaming, the male figure of *otaku* continues to dominant. However, one could argue that such produser practices as cosplay complicates the gender division, remixing *kawaii* cultures,[21] echoing the rise of what Miller calls the "kogal" and her new media practices in Japan. One might interpret a snapshot of the rise of the *keitai* in Japan as synonymous with the highly visible group of users, *shôjo*.[22]

As John Whittier Treat perspicuously notes, the *shôjo* signified a sexually neutral, consumption-focused female, quite distinct from the *kôgyaru*.[23] According to Miller, the *shôjo* and the *kôgyaru* represented two very different forms of femininity.[24] Although both deployed *kawaii* and *keitai* cultures in conspicuous ways, the *shôjo* and the *kôgyaru* demonstrated the multiple possibilities for femininity, hyperfeminization and mobile gender performativity. For Miller, the kogal transforms the role of *kawaii* and femininity,[25] adapting it into the realm of irony and playful postmodernism.[26]

I would argue that the emergence of these new types of gender performativity can be linked to the transformation of *kawaii* cultures into new media spaces such as the *keitai*, Web 2.0 and gaming. These performativities are related to subcultures and new media literacies in which media consumption has shifted from consumer/player to produser. Thus, rather than deploying the notion proposed by Ito et al. that Japanese technocultures are defined by the three P's: Pedestrian, Portable and Personable,[27] I would argue that in the case of women, gaming and cosplaying, the more appropriate three P's would be: Player, Produser and Producer. The question remains as to how these different modes of engagement are explored.

As a prominent example of the rise of subversive female subcultural languages in the 1970s, *kawaii* culture in the form of kitten writing has been linked to female and feminine cultures in Japan,[28] particularly in light of its role in customizing domestic technologies in the form of the "techno-cute."[29] The various possibilities for women as players and makers is undoubtedly catered and addressed by the *kawaii* within games cultures. As Ito notes in the case of American girls' deployment of Japanese games, "from the perspective of style, Japanese media mix content is also distinctive because of the centrality of '*kawaii*' (cute) culture. Hello Kitty and Pikachu are the face of *kawaii* culture overseas."[30]

Kawaii culture can be viewed as part of the growth in the personalisation of new media spaces, a phenomenon discussed by Hirofumi Katsuno and Christine Yano in their study on the rise of the *kaomoji* from early Internet usage, to pagers, and then to *keitai*.[31] Face marks are most commonly known in the form of "smileys"; however it is interesting to note that while, in English, the smileys are vertical (i.e., :)) in Japanese they are horizontal (i.e., ^_^). With the proliferation of personalizing modes of signification through mobile e-mail, photo e-mail and SNS, the growth of what Sharon Kinsella described as kitten writing are becoming a leading form of techno-cute customization of technological spaces.

Katsuno and Yano argue that the *kaomoji* is not a form of post-humanism but rather neo-humanism; it domesticates and customizes the technological spaces, reminding us that technologies are shaped by cultural and social processes. One of the enduring features of Japanese customization is its role in creating emotion and affect as a type of warmness in the coolness of technological spaces. For Tomoyuki Okada this is characterized by the importance of *yasashisa* ("kindness")[32]; for Anne Allison it is *yasashii* ("gentle") that makes Japanese character culture so easily consumed both within and outside Japan.[33]

In "Portable monsters and commodity cuteness; *Pokémon* as Japan's new global power," Allison eloquently outlines the phenomenon of *Pokémon* both in Japan and the United States. In doing so, she not only helps reinterpret the role of cuteness as a Japanese form of global commodity, but also explains how this allows us to see Japan's changing role on the global economy. For Allison, cuteness isn't necessarily linked to the cliché of girlishness and the "feminine." Cuteness is—as she finds in interviews with both Japanese and US youth consumers of Japanese commodities such as *Pokémon*—deeply embedded in the idea of *yasashii* or gentleness.[34]

Kawaii culture is also, according to Allison, "postmodern" in nature—"it is this polymorphous, open-ended, everyday nature of *Pokémon* that many of its Japanese producers or commentators refer to under the umbrella of 'cuteness.'"[35] Just as *kawaii* cultures have given rise to various forms of gender parody and irony[36] that reflect new forms of femininity in Japan, this is even more amplified with gaming and *anime* contexts. The deployment of *kawaii* for both male and female game characters in such key games as *Final Fantasy* have afforded many female players new "flexible" modes of gender performativity. It is the opening up of cuteness as a site for new female subjectivities and agencies that is recognized and adorned by young female gamers outside of Japan.

Phenomenon such as cosplay reasserts Japan's central role in the imaginings of digital popular culture circuits in the region. For many, the rites of passage into gaming in locations such as Australia and Taiwan involves a disavowal of US "mainstream" games for the "subcultural" and "cool" Japanese games. Generally speaking, while US games such as *GTA (Grand Theft Auto)* demonstrate explicit forms of violence and gender stereotyping, Japanese games such as *Final Fantasy* focus upon characterizations that reconfigure gender performativity. So begins the alternative entrance into global gaming, uniting players across transnational borders, while reorienting Japan as the alternative center for popular culture. But, it is not a mere mirroring of Japanization with Americanization, rather, it is about emerging forms of localization as gaming shifts from periphery to center of twenty-first century media cultures. As Craig Norris has discussed, through *anime* and *manga*, Australian fans can explore gendered and racial identities that produce different forms of cultural capital and identity.[37]

Games both provide a space for popular imagination and performativity as well as a site for localization. As Benjamin Wai-ming Ng notes in his eloquent analysis of consuming Japanese games in Hong Kong in Chapter 5, "consuming Japanese games in Hong Kong is not a form of cultural imperialism, because we have witnessed the making of a dialectical nexus between global (Japan) and local (Hong Kong) in terms of ongoing cultural hybridization."[38] This is complicated further by the active fan cultures of cosplayers in which Japanese gendered performativity can be preformed by both Japanese and non-Japanese but also the roleplay of gender types can be explored. Male cosplayers can become female characters, female cosplayers become male, extending and re-orientating Judith Butler's poststructural notion of performativity as a series of actions and regulations.[39] Gender performativity becomes infused with processes of localization. And, in the case of young women (of various ethnicities) studying to be game producers and designers, cosplaying is a complex and complicated cocktail of localization, cultural hybridization, gender and ethnic performativity *vis-à-vis* a particular avenue of consuming and imagining.

GAME ON: A SAMPLE STUDY OF COSPLAYERS IN MELBOURNE.

Although Japanese gaming has not been considered central to the girls gaming movement, the role of Japanese gaming genres in bringing girls into electronic gaming should not be overlooked. Much as the *Sims* has provided a relatively gender-neutral avenue into gaming for women, *Pokemon* broke new ground for girls who subsequently adopted the Game Boy platform and trading card games.[40]

Away from Tokyo, the presence and re-imagining of Japan via Japanese commodities and images has remained unabated in the games industry. As aforementioned, much research has explored the identification of "Japan" through global consumption of Japanese products, particularly the iconic role of *kawaii* cultures. In Melbourne, with a strong and vibrant independent games scene, the presence and re-imaging of Japan can be found in various forms. In University games programs, most—if not all—applicants submit a folio full of *manga* inspired drawings; the 101 in games design. For many, gaming is synonymous with Japan.

At the Melbourne games expo, incomparable to the Mecca of all games shows, the Tokyo Game Show, the presence of Japan is omnipresent—both implicitly and explicitly. With the games industry still a very male-dominated arena (males still dominate in positions of programming and CEOs, with females relegated to design, art or administration) the presence of women is often in the form of images. However, at the Melbourne games expo, women did feature—and not just as sales assistants or Lara Croft hyperbolic. In particular, they featured through the gender performativity of cosplay.

While there is a growing body of scholarly research on cosplayers in locations such as Japan, Hong Kong, Taiwan and South Korea, in Australia there has been comparatively little research despite the fact of conventions such as Animania[41] dedicated to the "key" event, the cosplay competition. As Patricia Maunder notes in "Dress up and play cool," cosplay provides a space where "games meet reality . . . In Australia, cosplay took root early this century—several years after blossoming in Japan—when games were more accessible than anime."[42] One of the obvious differences in the politics of cosplaying in Australia as opposed to Taiwan or Hong Kong is the issue of multiculturalism. Young people from various ethnic backgrounds can take the guise of a cosplayer, performing a different ethnicity and gender.

For Melbourne cosplayers Anna Nguyen and Jeni McCaskill, "they are not limited to female personas, as many male characters in Japanese pop culture are what Nguyen describes as 'pretty'".[43] In Australia the consumption of Japanese popular culture provides an alternative avenue for imagining localization and globalization, it re-orients Australia away from its colonial past and into its geo-ideological proximity. It re-imagines Australia as part of the "Asia-Pacific." Events such as Manifest provide cosplayers with official occasions to perform, however, for many, much of the time of being a cosplayer is as much about not being one and preparing or adapting everyday clothing to incorporate elements of cosplay. Indeed for many cosplayers, this is a full-time passion that runs through their various activities that extends beyond periods when in costumes. Cosplayers are always looking for inspiration to make their costume better, often reflecting upon potential choices and decisions.

For many of these young women, their entrance into the still-male dominated games industry is via their positions as game players and cosplayers; by becoming cosplayers they are able to locate themselves in the games industry through the consumption of Japan as a historical and contemporary "center" for the global games industry. Cosplay allows them to transgress boundaries between player, produser and producer; in turn highlighting one of the defining debates in game studies—the ludology versus the narratology. Cosplay redefines boundaries and distinctions between play and games that are often conflated under the concept of "game play."

Indeed, game play is one of the dominant ongoing conflations that has continued to haunt games studies since the ludology versus narratology debate in 1990s that attempted to differentiate *paidea* (play) from *ludus* (game). It is this fusion that can provide us with insight into emerging forms of localization within twenty-first century globalization. While narratology (predominantly American scholars) argued that narrative is the defining feature of all media—games, film, literature, etc.—ludology (mostly Scandinavian researchers) claimed that factors such as interactivity and simulation were more important than the narrative elements in games.[44] As Brian Sutton-Smith identifies, game spaces are social spaces; through games we can both reflect and escape our everyday.[45] Play not only reflects the local, it is inflected by gender. In this light, cosplay can be seen to highlight new modes of play that contest traditional gendered models of game play in the industry.

Given Melbourne's relative multiculturalism, the issue of ethnicity further complicates the gendered performativity and re-imagining of Japan evoked by cosplaying. Cosplay provides a space for cross-cultural and inter-cultural imagining for many of these players. Cultural, ethnic and gendered performative diversity is celebrated rather than undermined. It is this ethnic diversity in constructing types of femininity around imagining Japan *vis-à-vis* cosplaying, along with the role of cosplaying in affording young women entrance into the games industry, that is the focus of this chapter. I want to explore, though a preliminary, limited case study, the consumption of Japan—and specifically Japanese femininity and female role models—as the respondents reconfiguring themselves both in the games industry and within general social scenarios in Melbourne. For example, how does a Hong Kong born respondent, studying in a games program in Melbourne, reconfigure her identity *vis-à-vis* a Melbournian context for consuming Japan?

Moreover, many of the cosplayers I interviewed are indeed studying in games programs and hoping to gain long-term employment in the industry. A subsequent longitudinal study needs to be conducted to see some of the changes that occur in terms of cosplaying as a student and whether that continues, and for how long, when the student becomes employed in the industry. Can future female games makers and producers be taken seriously as cosplayers? Or is the practice of cosplay an integral part in informing new types of strong female role models?

For the respondents, almost all entered the world of cosplay via both *anime* and Japanese games, however for two of the respondents—the only two that have a grasp of survival Japanese language skills—it was the studying of the language at primary school that subsequently made them interested in Japanese culture, and thus cosplay. Each respondent had their own ways of continuously evoking and imagining Japan through the regular activities of listening to music (especially visual *kei* groups), watching *anime* and reading *manga*, attending "cosplay friendly" events, looking and dressing in Japanese fashion (*gyaru*, lolita, EGL etc) as well as partaking in frequent consumption of Japanese food most days. As one 18-year-old student said,

> I love Japanese foods such as Pocky, aloe vera or nata de coco drinks, lychee drinks (yum!), and the cute eclectic dress sense. Usually I'll go to an Asian supermarket and buy the aforementioned foods once a week.

For another art student aged 21 years old, she even did a martial art. As she said,

> (I do) cosplaying several times a year, keeping up with niche Japanese fashions (gothic lolita) along with practising martial arts (aikido) weekly. I'm also interested in Japanese homewares and cooking (*bento* and *amigurumi*) as well as owning several BJDS (ball jointed dolls).

When asked whether their network of friends mirrored their tastes and interests in Japan, only half said they had friends "interested in Japan." The only respondent who seemed to have an active group of liked-minded friends noted,

> Kind-a, most my friends are into *anime* and *manga* and only a handful that cosplay, and then there are those who don't really have an interest but still eat the food.

Of the respondents, the only two who could not speak Japanese language were keen to learn. Many spoke survival Japanese with one 22-year-old student having eight years of studying. When asked how they first heard of cosplay, some of the responses included,

> R3: I guess, growing up I already knew of "Cosplay" (since cosplay is really no different from dressing up).
> R4: Around year 7 at high school (2004), through my older brother who showed me pictured of some cosplayers he had found on the Internet.
> R5: In 2002 at my first Manifest.
> R6: I heard about cosplayers when I was first getting into anime, so when I was approximately 14 . . . I knew of people doing it at game conventions but I hadn't heard of it for anime until that time.
> R7: At my first convention in 2000—some people turned up in costume, and I wanted to do the same for the next year.

When asked what interested them in "crossing over" and becoming a cosplayer, some of the responses included,

R4: It looked fun! I was always interested in sewing clothes and crafty stuff and cosplay seemed to incorporate all these interests (like, molding stuff from clay for accessories, sewing for the clothing, woodwork for some people) into one larger interest. I also liked the chance to dress up as someone different and see the outcome of the hard work.

R5: It looked fun to dress up.

R6: Well the idea of dressing up as a character and "being them" (to a degree) for a day appealed to me because it's a chance to do some acting, try out a different personality (for example, a shy person cosplaying as an extroverted character has to be extroverted for the day) and dress cutely without people thinking you're a total freak!

R7: Use of creative skill and general "coolness" of being that character.

The respondents were then asked how the practice of being a cosplayer has changed their definition and understanding of cosplayers. I asked them to consider how cosplaying functions as a mode of identity and self-expression. Here we see cosplaying can help elevate situations in which the female feels shy, much like *kawaii* culture "softens" the hardness of communication. Two respondents replied,

R4: Hasn't changed much really, I started cosplaying because I wanted to give a new dimension to my pre-existing hobby and bring to life characters whom I liked in *anime/manga*, and I still get the feeling that the majority of people still cosplay for those reasons. MAYBE cosplaying serves as a way for people to escape to a different persona and identity, but I don't think so because most of the time the cosplayers still seem to act like themselves . . . their personality stays the same even though they are in costume, so I don't believe they are trying to find a different identity for a day. Self-expression works, in the sense that I want to express my interests (sewing, etc.) in a different form and cosplaying allows me to do that.

R5: I find that once you've cosplayed, it's really addictive. I think cosplay has helped me be a little less shy in crowds, especially after my first Manifest cosplay. I'm not much of an attention-seeker (no, really!), but I liked the attention I receive when I cosplay. I also found in the past that it can help boost some people's self-esteem and help people make new friends (happens often, it's great). What's also helpful is the information and knowledge that comes from researching, for example, different fabric types, costume-making techniques, [fake] weapon-crafting, etc. This sort of knowledge can be useful in future (especially considering I am a design student and could use this knowledge).

I then asked them to reflect upon the role of the "fan" and how they view traditional definitions of fans changing and becoming more active co-producers in the meanings. The responses varied greatly as to the degrees of agency that came with "fandom," especially pertaining to cosplaying. The two contrasting views were,

> R4: Well if you put it that way, fans have always been "co-producers" with examples like fanart, fan fiction. I don't think the roles have changed too much, just the level of dedication and time seems to have increased. Instead of just, say, drawing something for a few hours, we dress up and go to conventions to show off our work and mingle with other people who have the same interests . . . For me, to be a fan of something, you just have to like it. You don't need to fawn over it, cosplay, draw it, talk about it, as long as you know that you enjoy that particular activity, you can call yourself a fan. Someone who spends more money on a particular hobby doesn't necessarily show they are more of a fan; if you enjoy it, you are a fan.

> R7: I don't see cosplayers as "co-producers," since this implies that they have an active role to play in the production of the original series/ game/source material. While some developers and artists may take cosplayers into account when designing character concepts and outfits, I don't think they would have as much interest or input, as say, live-action actors . . . I would say that to be a fan, you must express an interest in the source material and/or characters. The depth of this expression is how "much" of a fan you are. However, simply being a cosplayer does not necessarily mean you are a fan—there are many cosplayers who make a costume for the technical challenge, or just because that character is popular. Personally, however, I believe cosplayers have the most fun, and produce the best results if they are also fans of that series and/or character.

COS-PLAY: PLAYER TO PRODUSER TO PRODUCER— NEW GENDER GAMES FOR TWENTY-FIRST CENTURY

For many of the respondents, cosplay provides them with a space to play and explore forms of self-expression as well as articulating and deepening their interest in Japanese culture. Cosplay provided them with a way to overcome shyness and meet new friends as well as providing them with a space for self-expression and performativity. The role of the *kawaii* featured prominently, so much so that it often seemed self-explanatory. For many of the respondents, they had dressed as both male and female characters, enjoying the flexibility of gender provided within *kawaii* culture. For games students, it helps further solidify their commitment to games without necessarily surrendering their femininity or succumbing to gender-stereotypical roles. In games programs in Australian Universities, where a commitment to Japanese culture is almost standard rites of passage, we can see how the deployment of cosplay enables young females students in particular to graduate from players and produsers to producers/designers/programmers.

For one young Eurasian female student studying a games degree, being a cosplaying and a gamer provides her with a "better connections with people. Although those connections are more based on the fact that we enjoy the Japanese culture and watch *anime.* Talking about cosplay is just another sub topic of something much larger." The fact that cosplayers often dress up outside their everyday environments means that often it is hard to spot a cosplayer unless one sees them at cosplay conventions. As the student continued,

> The thing with cosplay is, when outside a convention or a photo shoot or stuff like that, it's hard to tell who is a cosplayer or not. Sometimes you can tell who is a cosplayer outside of these events, a cosplayer's casual clothing sometimes stand out more then the "everyday" person's (Let's face it, cosplayers can be attention whores) . . . but at the same time, you can't really tell them apart from people who like to dress differently.

When I inquired as to whether she imagined still partaking in cosplay once she graduates and gains employment in the industry, she stated,

> I think I'll keep cosplaying till the day where my kids get embarrassed by it and tell me to stop . . . but then again I don't think I'd listen to what my kids have to say, um, but really, I think I'll still be cosplaying when I'm working in the industry, the only real different will be unlike high school and Uni, I just won't cosplay to work . . . unless they pay me for it. Cosplay is a hobby; at some point it can become a way of life and it can also be a phase, there is no real age limit to cosplay, because there will always be a character you can relate to and dress up as and act like you really are that person and so forth . . . Seeing that I have like one and a half years till I leave Uni and find a (poorly paid) QA (quality assurance) job to start my climb to the top, I'm pretty sure I'll be still cosplaying.

I then concluded by asking her how cosplay helps her negotiate the gender politics in a games degree whereby male students still dominate (typically 65% males, 35% females) and she replied,

> I'm very lucky, there are no currently no gender politics among the gamer within this degree, there are height politics but no gender. If there was, I think being a cosplay would be useless in a gender battle. Unless you use it as a bribe, "I'll cosplay a bunny girl for you if you be nice to me!" "Deal!" gugh . . . I guess it could be helpful in the fact that

cosplayers are normally females. There are few males who cosplay. So if there was a gender issue you could also try and outnumber the males with your cosplay buddies at a convention, but that won't really help . . . it would become like a gang war or something . . . In fact I think it would make it worse.

With cosplaying, the "magic circle" associated with game play takes new dimensions. For some of the female students enrolled in games degree, it can be a way to not only connect to others who enjoy consuming "Japan" but also provide avenues for gendered performativity and empowerment. As the young female student notes above, the fact that most cosplayers are female affords her with a space in order to build strong female relationships in an industry still attempting to address its inequalities. Rather than deploying the three P's—Pedestrian, Portable and Personable—as identified by Ito et al.[46] as central to Japanese technoculture, perhaps, in the case of young women entering the games via Japan, there are grounds to argue in favor of an alternative three P's—Players, Produsers and Producers. In the case of these young women's entrance into the games industry, the gender performativity of cosplay provides a bridge between players, produsers and producer agencies. Game on?

NOTES

1. Henry Jenkins, *Convergence Culture: Where Old and New Media Collide: Where Old and New Media Collide* (New York: New York University Press, 2006).
2. Laura Miller, *Beauty Up* (Berkley: University of California, 2006).
3. Miller, *Beauty Up*, 30.
4. Miller, *Beauty Up*, 31.
5. Brian McVeigh, "How Hello Kitty Commodifies the Cute, Cool and Camp: 'Consumutopia' versus 'Control' in Japan," *Journal of Material Culture*, 5 (2) 2000: 291–312.
6. Henry Jenkins, *Textual Poachers: Television Fans and Participatory Culture* (New York: Routledge, 1992).
7. Axel Bruns and Jason Jacobs, eds., *Uses of Blogs* (New York: Peter Lang, 2006).
8. Tim O'Reilly 2004.
9. Henry Jenkins, *Fans, Bloggers, and Gamers: Essays on Participatory Culture* (New York: New York University Press, 2006).
10. Koichi Iwabuchi, *Recentring Globalization: Popular Culture and Japanese Transnationalism* (Durham, NC: Duke University Press, 2003).
11. Johan Huizinga, *Homo Luden* (Boston: Beacon Press, 1938).
12. Brian Sutton-Smith, *The Ambiguity of Play* (London: Routledge, 1997).
13. McVeigh, "How Hello Kitty Commodifies the Cute, Cool and Camp: 'Consumutopia' versus 'Control' in Japan."
14. Mizuko Ito, "Introduction: Personal, Portable, Pedestrian," in *Personal, Portable, Pedestrian: Mobile Phones in Japanese Life*, eds. M. Ito, D. Okabe and M. Matsuda (Cambridge, Mass.: MIT Press, 2005), 1–16.

15. Douglas McGray, "Japan's Gross National Cool," *Foreign Policy*, May/June 2002: 44–54.
16. Misa Matsuda, "Discourses of *Keitai* in Japan." In *Personal, Portable, Pedestrian: Mobile Phones in Japanese Life* eds M. Ito, D. Okabe and M. Matsuda (Cambridge, MA: MIT Press, 2005), 19–40. Brian McVeigh, *Nationalisms of Japan: managing and mystifying identity* (Oxford, New York: Rowman and Littlefield, 2004).
17. Tetsuo Kogawa, "Beyond Electronic Individualism," *Canadian Journal of Political and Social Theory/Revue Canadienne de Thetorie Politique et Sociale*, 8 (3), Fall 1984. Retrieved 20th July 2007 from http://anarchy.translocal.jp/non-japanese/electro.html.
18. Lisa Nakamura, *Cybertypes: Race, Ethnicity, and Identity on the Internet* (New York: Routledge, 2002).
19. Matsuda, "Discourses of *Keitai* in Japan."
20. Matsuda, "Discourses of *Keitai* in Japan."
21. Mizuko Ito, "The Gender Dynamics of the Japanese Media Mix," paper for the *Girls 'n' Games Workshop and Conference*, May 8–9, University of California, Los Angeles, 2006.
22. John Whittier Treat, "Introduction," in *Contemporary Japanese Popular Culture*, ed. J. Whittier Treat (Honolulu: University of Hawaii Press, 1996), 1–16. However, it was the *kôgyaru* who gained notoriety in the late 1990s through her often sexually subversive use of the PHS (Phone Hand System)—and later the *keitai*—to extract capital from the traditionally dominant group, the *oyaji*. Commonly depicted as wearing platformed boots, bleached hair and darkened skin, the *kôgyaru* actively undermined notions of the Japanese female as passive and subjugated by Japanese men. Overtly contrasting any notion that of femininity as passive, the *kôgyaru* openly challenged definitions of femininity from their dress to their "unfeminine" and aggressive language and gestures.
23. However, as *kawaii* culture married *keitai* scapes and was forged into virtual spaces, the *kawaii* gender-without-sexual identity took on new characteristics (Hjorth 2003a). Most notably, the *kôgyaru* deployed ironic appropriations of *kawaii* to infuse the gendered commodity with sexual connotations, thus transforming the *kawaii* into a gender *with* sexuality. This was predominantly enacted through *kawaii* customization whereby the cute was no longer deployed in an a-sexual manner. See Larissa Hjorth, ""Pop" and "Ma": the landscape of Japanese commodity characters and subjectivity," in *Mobile Cultures: New Media in Queer Asia*, eds. F. Martin, A. Yue and C. Berry (Durham, NC: Duke University Press, 2003), 158–179.
24. In their open disavowal of Japanese femininity and traditionalism, along with their conspicuous deployment of mobile technologies, that made the *kôgyaru* not just subversive but a perceived threat to the status quo. It was the way in which the *kôgyaru* usage of the *keitai* reflected her general undermining of Japanese traditional culture—and particularly the role of the female—that signaled a sharp departure from the *keitai shôjo* symbolising the female high-school pagers revolution. Here the use of the distinctive deployment of the uniform by the *shôjo* and *kôgyaru* marked two different roads towards performing femininity—and particularly through mobile technologies—in Japan. One reproduced traditional forms of femininity (*shôjo*), the other (*kôgyaru*) openly rejected Japanese traditional culture by assertively appropriating non-Japanese forms of fashion (uniform), gestures and language.
25. Miller, *Beauty Up*.

26. Anne Allison, "Portable monsters and commodity cuteness; *Pokémon* as Japan's new global power," *Postcolonial Studies* 6 (3) 2003: 381–398.
27. Ito, "Introduction: Personal, Portable, Pedestrian."
28. Sharon Kinsella, "Cuties in Japan," in *Women, Media and Consumption in Japan*, eds. L. Skov and B.Moeran (Surrey UK, Curzon Press, 1995), 220–254.
29. According to Kinsella's seminal research, *kawaii* culture arose as a youth subculture in the 1970s as a means of self-expression and re-articulation, and as a reaction to the overarching traditions that were perceived as oppressive. Young adults preferred to stay childlike rather than join the ranks of the corrupt adults. This phenomenon highlighted the way in which "childhood" as a construct is conceived and practiced in locations such as Japan, with its premature adulthood, in contrast to the west (Ariés 1962; White 1993). Practices such as "kitten writing" are examples of youths subverting Japanese concepts by intentionally misspelling words in acts of political neologism. Kitten writing can be seen as earlier examples of *emoji* before it was institutionalized by industry as part of built-in *keitai* customization. The *kawaii*, while stereotyped as a young female's preoccupation, and thus associated as female, was seen as traditionally asexual—that is, a gender without sex. Like the typical consumer, the *shôjo*, the *kawaii* was a female without sexual agency in a society where the *oyaji w*as the national symbol post World War II. See Philip Ariés, *Centuries of Childhood: a Social History of Family Life*, trans. R. Baldick (New York: Knopf, 1962) and Mary White, *The Material Child: Coming of Age in Japan and America* (New York: Free Press, 1993).
30. Ito, "The Gender Dynamics of the Japanese Media Mix," n.p.
31. Hirofumi Katsuno and Christine Yano, "Face to face: on-line subjectivity in contemporary Japan," *Asian Studies Review*, 26 (2) 2002: 205–231.
32. Tomoyuki Okada, "Youth Culture and the Shaping of Japanese Mobile Media: Personalization and the *Keitai* Internet as Multimedia," in *Personal, Portable, Pedestrian: Mobile Phones in Japanese Life*, eds. M. Ito, D. Okabe and M. Matsuda (Cambridge, Mass.: MIT Press, 2005), 41–60.
33. Allison, "Portable monsters and commodity cuteness; *Pokémon* as Japan's new global power."
34. Allison, "Portable monsters and commodity cuteness; *Pokémon* as Japan's new global power," 385.
35. Allison, "Portable monsters and commodity cuteness; *Pokémon* as Japan's new global power," 384.
36. Miller, *Beauty Up*.
37. Craig Norris, "Cyborg girls and shape-shifters: The discovery of difference by Anime and Manga Fans in Australia," *Refractory*, October 2005. Retrieved 2 September 2008 from http://blogs.arts.unimelb.edu.au/refractory/2005/10/14/cyborg-girls-and-shape-shifters-the-discovery-of-difference-by-anime-and-manga-fans-in-australia-craig-norris/.
38. See this collection.
39. Butler, *Gender Trouble*.
40. Ito, "The Gender Dynamics of the Japanese Media Mix.".
41. (www.animania.net.au)
42. Patricia Maunder, "Dress up and play cool," *The Age Green Guide*, Thursday April 17th 2008: 23.
43. Maunder, "Dress up and play cool," 23.
44. Gonzalo Frasca, "Ludologists love stories too." Retrieved 10 July 2008 from http://www.ludology.org/articles/Frasca_LevelUp2003.pdf.
45. Sutton-Smith, *The Ambiguity of Play*.
46. Ito, "Introduction: Personal, Portable, Pedestrian."

Contributors

Dean Chan teaches at the School of Communications and Arts, Edith Cowan University, Australia. His research focuses on diasporic Asian cultural production (especially visual arts, comics and graphic novels), East Asian digital gaming and Asian transnationalism. He has published on Asian gaming cultures in journals including *Games and Culture*, *International Review of Information Ethics*, *Fibreculture Journal* and *EnterText*.

Florence Chee is a Ph.D. Candidate in the School of Communication and Researcher at the Centre for Policy Research on Science and Technology (CPROST) and the Applied Communication and Technology (ACT) Lab at Simon Fraser University in Vancouver, Canada. Her long-term goal is to make technology relevant to the specifics of local cultures on a global level. Research interests focus on the ethnographic investigation of how users define themselves socially amidst their technologies and lived realities. She is currently conducting her Doctoral fieldwork in Korea, which is supported by a Korean Government Research Scholarship from the National Institute for International Education (NIIED) and an SFU Graduate International Scholarship.

Peichi Chung teaches in the Communications and New Media Programme at the National University of Singapore. Her research interests include new media culture, global entertainment media industries and film studies. She has published articles in *Journal of Inter-Asia Cultural Studies*, *Media International Australia and Journal of Science, Technology and Society*. Her current research project compares the influence of globalization in the online gaming industries of South Korea, Singapore and China.

Patrick Crogan is a critic on film studies and games and has published widely in these fields. His work on computer games is from the perspective of theories of contemporary technoculture. His is an Executive Board Member of the international Digital Games Research Organization, and on the editorial board of *Convergence, Scan, Games and Culture*, and the *Australian Journal of Emerging Technologies*. He currently lectures in Game Theory at The University of the West of England.

Sam Hinton is a lecturer in media arts and production at the University of Canberra, Australia where he teaches classes in narrative structure, motion graphics and 3D animation. In a previous incarnation, Sam dabbled in game programming, writing game code for a mod based on id Software's *Quake 3* Arena. Since then Sam has focused his creative energy on studying the structure and political economy of the games industry in Australia and the global market more generally, but he still finds time to hack bad code when he gets a free moment.

Larissa Hjorth is researcher, artist, and Senior Lecturer in the Games and Digital Art Programs at RMIT University. Since 2000, Hjorth has been researching and publishing on gendered customizing of mobile communication, gaming and virtual communities in the Asia-Pacific which is outlined in her book, *Mobile Media in the Asia-Pacific* (London, Routledge, 2009). Hjorth has published widely on the topic in journals such as *Convergence journal, Journal of Intercultural Studies, Continuum, ACCESS, Fibreculture* and *Southern Review*. In 2009, Hjorth will be an ARC APD fellow (with Michael Arnold) conducting a three-year cross-cultural case study of online communities in six locations (Manila, Singapore, Shanghai, Seoul, Tokyo and Melbourne) in the region. www.larissahjorth.net.

Jun-Sok Huhh is doctoral candidate of Seoul National University of Korea, the leader of a Korean game research group, Gamestudy.org. Huhh's research focuses on online games and their cultural and economic impacts on society. His specific interests are effects of RMT on online gaming service, the company, and gamers, economic dynamics of gaming industries. Currently Huhh consulting for several game companies.

Dal Yong Jin is Assistant Professor at Simon Fraser University, Canada. He finished his Ph.D. degree from the Institute of Communications Research at the University of Illinois at Urbana Champaign in 2004. His major research and teaching interests are globalization and media, new media and game studies, transnational cultural studies, telecommunications policy and the political economy of culture. He is the author of a forthcoming book entitled *Hands On/Hands Off: The Korean State and the Market Liberalization of the Communication Industry*, and his recent work has appeared in several scholarly journals, including *Media, Culture and Society, Games and Culture, Telecommunications Policy, Television and New Media* and *Javnost-the Public*.

Brett Leavy is the Managing Director of CyberDreaming Australia, established in 1998, and was the creative director of the now completed Digital

Songlines (DSL) project for the Australasian CRC for Interaction Design (ACID) between 2004 and 2007. In 2006 he was invited as the Australasian Representative for ICT on the World Indigenous Association, NGO, United Nations in Tunis. He is a person of Aboriginal descent.

Holin Lin is a professor of the Department of Sociology at National Taiwan University. Her major research interests include computer-mediated communication, information technology and society and gender studies. She has written articles on the social dynamics of in-game communities, game tips sharing behaviors, cash trades of in-game assets, norms and deviance negotiation in MMORPGs and gendered gaming experience in different physical spaces. Currently, she serves on the editorial board of *Games & Culture.*

Christian McCrea is a Lecturer in Games and Interactivity at Swinburne University of Technology, Australia. His work concentrates on philosophies of play, especially concerning physicality, nostalgia, horror and explosive body aesthetics. Recent essays have examined the extraordinary apotheosis of animated violence, the sacred and profane in film philosophy, apparatuses of capture in horror games, and the poetics of contemporary game art.

Bora Na is a Ph.D. Candidate at Yonsei graduate school of Communication & Arts, majoring in Visual communication and member of Research Group of Gaming culture in Korea @ www.gamestudy.org. Na's master's thesis explored the limitations of theoretical approaches towards gameplay. Since then, she has worked on game/gameplay as a phenomenon and looked into the mechanism of gameplay experience. Currently she is working on the gaming culture of Korea for her Ph.D. thesis.

Benjamin Wai-ming Ng is a professor in the Japanese Studies Department at the Chinese University of Hong Kong. His research and teaching areas include Japanese intellectual history, Japanese popular culture and Sino-Japanese relations. He is working on a research project on the interaction between Japan and Hong Kong in animation, comic and game. The chapter is substantially modified and expanded from an article he published in *Game Studies*, 6:1 (October 2006). This study was supported by a grant from the Research Grant Council of Hong Kong (Project No: CUHK4680/05H). His e-mail: waimingng@cuhk.edu.hk.

Ingrid Richardson is a Senior Lecturer at Murdoch University, Western Australia, teaching in the fields of Multimedia and Cultural Studies. Her research interests include philosophy of technology, phenomenology, new and interactive media theory and embodied interaction. Ingrid has published journal articles and book chapters on the cultural and embodied effects of mobile media, virtual reality, biomedical imaging, technologies for sustainability, TV and public screens. Her more recent research focuses on the way mobile media have impacted upon screen cultures, the proliferation of "small media" (user-generated content) and the emergence of the mobile web.

Chuen-Tsai Sun is a Professor of Computer Science, National Chiao Tung University, Taiwan. He has been working in the fields of artificial intelligence modeling, digital games, digital learning and social simulation-based modeling. He has published digital-game-related articles on players' altruistic behavior, negotiation of social norms, dynamics of player guilds and free-game models, among others.

David Surman is Senior Lecturer in Computer Games Design at the University of Wales Newport. His research focuses on the relationship between history and aesthetics in fields of videogame design, animation and graphic arts. He is co-editor (with Suzanne Buchan and Paul Ward) of *Animated Worlds* (2007) and is author of *The Videogames Handbook* (2009). Recent essays have examined the relationship between videogames and contemporary art, and the relationships between play and pleasure in fast-paced fighting games.

Melanie Swalwell is Senior Lecturer in Screen and Media at Flinders University, Adelaide. Melanie's research centers on newer media with particular attention to media arts and digital games, as well as the intersections of these. Her work has been published in journals such as *Convergence, Reconstruction, Vectors and Journal of Visual Culture*. Together with Jason Wilson, she edited *The Pleasures of Computer Gaming: Essays on Cultural History, Theory and Aesthetics* (McFarland, 2008).

Theodor G. Wyeld has a background in architecture and planning and games development and is widely published in these fields. He has given keynote lectures on the topic of digital media and its relation to creative practices. He currently lectures in Interaction Evaluation at the Swinburne University of Technology, Melbourne, Australia.

Index